JANE DUNN has been described [as one of Britain's] best biographers', and her writ[ing about relation]ships, and sisters in particular, ha[s ... Her books] include a biography of the sister[s ...] and the bestseller *Elizabeth & Mary*, which looks at the lives of the cousin queens Elizabeth I and Mary, Queen of Scots. She is a Fellow of the Royal Society of Literature and lives in Bath with her husband, the writer and linguist Nicholas Ostler.

Praise for *Daphne du Maurier and Her Sisters*:

'Jane Dunn specialises in female relationships, and she has found three splendid women for her new book ... Dunn writes with haunting delicacy ... and she evokes a long-lost England in which women felt deep passions and survived emotional hurricanes with amazing outward restraint' RICHARD DAVENPORT-HINES, *Mail on Sunday*

'Perceptive and exuberant ... a saga that is sparklingly re-told'
VALERIE GROVE, *The Times*

'Meticulous, perceptive ... it is a sign of Jane Dunn's generous professionalism that she accords the du Maurier girls the same respect that she gave Bloomsbury's high priestesses in her acclaimed study of Woolf and her sister Vanessa Bell'

PETER J. CONRADI, *Financial Times*

'Compelling ... sensitive and sympathetic ... loneliness is the thudding heart of Dunn's book, about three pampered sisters who never quite overcame the handicap of not being boys'

NICHOLAS SHAKESPEARE, *Daily Telegraph*

'The fascination for readers is the different character and destiny of each sister, plus their relationships with one another and with the dynamics of the family romance – and few family romances have been more potent than that of the du Mauriers'

VICTORIA GLENDINNING, *Spectator*

'An original, well-researched and very readable book full of well-chosen details and perceptive observations. In the subject of rivalry between literary sisters Jane Dunn has found a little goldmine'

JESSICA MANN, Literary Review

'Engaging ... this book's strength lies in its account of a trio of lives developing during a period of class and gender upheaval, and the sisters' response to social change'   HELEN TAYLOR, Independent

'Dunn is excellent on the lesbian 1920s and 30s in London, with delicious detail'   SIMON CALLOW, Guardian

'As she has proved before – with her joint biography of Virginia Woolf and Vanessa Bell – Jane Dunn is particularly good at looking at siblings and how their relationships affected their work'

JOHN PRESTON, Daily Mail

'[An] intriguing and revelatory biography ... [of] complex and contradictory lives'   LESLEY MCDOWELL, Scotsman

---

By the Same Author

Moon in Eclipse: A Life of Mary Shelley
Virginia Woolf and Vanessa Bell: A Very Close Conspiracy
Antonia White: A Life
Elizabeth and Mary: Cousins, Rivals, Queens
Read My Heart: Dorothy Osborne & Sir William Temple,
a Love Story in the Age of Revolution

DAPHNE DU MAURIER AND HER SISTERS

JANE DUNN

WILLIAM COLLINS

William Collins
An imprint of HarperCollins*Publishers*
77–85 Fulham Palace Road
London W6 8JB
WilliamCollinsBooks.com

Paperback edition published by William Collins in 2014
First published in Great Britain by HarperPress in 2013

2

A catalogue record for this book is
available from the British Library

ISBN 978-0-00-734709-4

Typeset in Minion with Avenir display by
G&M Designs Limited, Raunds, Northamptonshire
Printed and bound in Great Britain by
Clays Ltd, St Ives plc

MIX
Paper from
responsible sources
FSC
www.fsc.org   FSC® C007454

In celebration of all sisters,
and particularly mine:
Kari, Izzy, B, Trish and Sue
(and our outnumbered brothers Marko and Andy)

CONTENTS

DU MAURIER FAMILY TREE

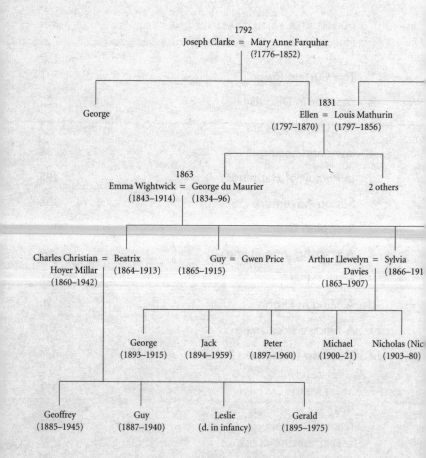

1792
Joseph Clarke = Mary Anne Farquhar
(?1776–1852)

George

1831
Ellen = Louis Mathurin
(1797–1870) | (1797–1856)

1863
Emma Wightwick = George du Maurier
(1843–1914) | (1834–96)

2 others

Charles Christian = Beatrix
Hoyer Millar | (1864–1913)
(1860–1942)

Guy = Gwen Price
(1865–1915)

Arthur Llewelyn = Sylvia
Davies | (1866–191
(1863–1907)

George
(1893–1915)

Jack
(1894–1959)

Peter
(1897–1960)

Michael
(1900–21)

Nicholas (Nic
(1903–80)

Geoffrey
(1885–1945)

Guy
(1887–1940)

Leslie
(d. in infancy)

Gerald
(1895–1975)

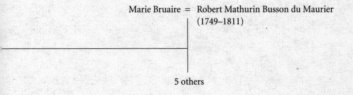

Marie Bruaire = Robert Mathurin Busson du Maurier
(1749–1811)

5 others

Emily Bidwell = Harry Beaumont
(1850–1933)

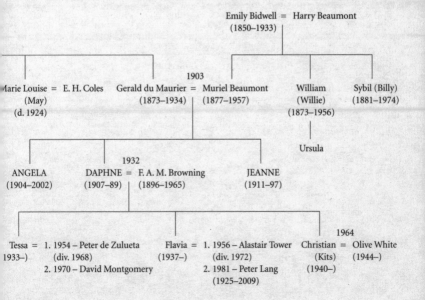

Marie Louise = E. H. Coles   Gerald du Maurier = Muriel Beaumont   William   Sybil (Billy)
(May)   1903   (Willie)   (1881–1974)
(d. 1924)   (1873–1934)   (1877–1957)   (1873–1956)

Ursula

ANGELA   DAPHNE = F. A. M. Browning   JEANNE
(1904–2002)   (1907–89)   (1896–1965)   (1911–97)
             1932

Tessa = 1. 1954 – Peter de Zulueta   Flavia = 1. 1956 – Alastair Tower   Christian = Olive White
(1933–)   (div. 1968)   (1937–)   (div. 1972)   (Kits)   (1944–)
       2. 1970 – David Montgomery   2. 1981 – Peter Lang   (1940–)
                                               (1925–2009)   1964

PREFACE

But it is very foolish to ask questions about any young ladies – about any three sisters just grown up; for one knows, without being told, exactly what they are – all very accomplished and pleasing, and one very pretty. There is a beauty in every family. It is a regular thing. Two play on the piano-forte, and one on the harp – and all sing – Or would sing if they were taught – or sing all the better for not being taught – or something like it.

JANE AUSTEN, *Mansfield Park*

JANE AUSTEN UNDERSTOOD about sisters. *Mansfield Park* and *Persuasion* seethe with them. *Pride and Prejudice* is as much about the affection, rivalry and vexation of sisters as it is about the complicated progress of true love for Jane and Elizabeth with Bingley and Darcy. Jane Austen shared a bedroom with her elder sister Cassandra all her life and they relied entirely on each other's love and support. There is something infinitely touching about their relationship, and tragic too, for Cassandra lived on alone for twenty-eight years after her younger sister died.

In biography, families are the soil out of which character grows, and one of the richest composts is the relationship of sisters. They are ever fascinating, cast from the same mould yet struggling for difference, brought up in the same family yet each with a childhood unique to herself. For good and ill, the sibling bond lasts a lifetime, longer than any other relationship with parents, partners or children, and it is sisters who weave the most complex webs of love and loyalty, resentment and hurt. Adults can turn sisters against each other by cruel comparisons and overt favouritism, as happened in the lifelong feud, continuing into their nineties, between the star of the film of Daphne du Maurier's *Rebecca*, Joan Fontaine, and her elder sister Olivia de Havilland, who landed the starring role in Daphne's other great blockbuster, *My Cousin Rachel*. When sisters' affections turn sour it can be deadly, for each knows the family's secrets. More often, however, sisters are a foil and support to each other, a source of inspiration and close conspiracy; the safety net encouraging flight and breaking a fall.

Daphne du Maurier was fascinated by the Brontë siblings and identified with them all, but she jokingly hoped she and her sisters might emulate Charlotte, Emily and Anne one day, if only she could get her artist sister to write too. A bevy of sisters is more than the sum of its parts and it is to this protean relationship that I, as a biographer, like to turn. The first pair I explored was Virginia Woolf and her artist sister Vanessa Bell. This was an archetypal relationship of passionate dependence and rivalry, ultimately transfigured into self-sacrificing love, remarkably well delineated in the sisters' own letters, Virginia's novels and Vanessa's portraits. I followed *Virginia & Vanessa* with other biographies that featured prominently sisters, daughters and female cousins. Then, with this book, another set of sisters drew my attention.

For most of my life I had been unaware that Daphne du Maurier, author of so many stories that had gripped my young self, had any sisters at all. To find that she had two, her elder sister Angela a writer like herself, and her younger, Jeanne, a painter, piqued my interest. To have a sister's fame so eclipse the others was psychologically interesting. Even more intriguing, however, was to find how different were the characters and lives of all three du Maurier sisters, yet how strongly imprinted with family values, bonded to each other in their desire to live in close proximity in Cornwall – with Jeanne eventually settling over the border in Dartmoor.

In writing the story of Vanessa Bell and Virginia Woolf I had set out to try and convey, as far as possible, their lives and thoughts in their own words. I hoped to do the same with the du Maurier sisters and was gratified to find how many of Daphne's letters existed, and how candid and full of interest they were. She had also written a memoir of herself when young, based on the early diaries that she subsequently embargoed. Daphne's letters are so rich, expressive and funny that they rival Nancy Mitford's for wit and brio. All three du Maurier sisters wrote excellent letters: conversational, lively with news and comment and a great deal of humour, but Angela's and Jeanne's have been largely destroyed or withheld.

Angela was a prolific writer of letters all her long life. She had many friends and acquaintances, but when she was old it seems that she wrote to her closest friends and asked them to destroy her letters. She had already burnt all her love letters, she explained to one of her past lovers, whose letters she had decided to keep. She also could not bring herself to burn her love poems to various important women in her life. For Angela, her deepest feelings and what made her happy in life, were in conflict with her desire to keep up appearances. She learnt early to dissemble to her parents. This conflict became more marked as she grew older, living within a close community in Fowey in Cornwall, where she was held in respect as 'Miss Angela', and attached to an Anglo-Catholic Church unsympathetic to any nonconformity in faith or life.

Despite this attempt to obscure her true self, two extrovert autobiographies, if read carefully, are full of hints of a larger life, a more independent and courageous attitude to love, than one might ever suspect from the conventional face she chose to present to the world. She did not want to be known for her guise as maiden aunt who had missed out on love. There had been much more to her than her Pekinese dogs and the roles of dutiful daughter, dependable friend and stalwart of Church and community. I hope this exploration of her life is in keeping with at least one aspect of her family's ethos, for the sisters were much influenced by their own father's view that a biography is only worth doing if it attempts to tell the truth without evasion or pretence. Daphne boldly followed this precept with her own memoir of her father, soon after his death, shocking some of his old friends with her temerity.

Whereas following Angela's clues have led me on an intriguing journey of dead-ends and surprising revelations, the search for Jeanne has been blocked from the beginning of my researches. Her lifelong partner, the intellectual and prize-winning poet Noël Welch, still lives in their exquisite house on Dartmoor with the best collection of Jeanne's paintings, all her papers and her memories. Now in her nineties, she has been adamantly set against any biography of the sisters, despite writing her own insightful piece on them for *The Cornish Review* nearly forty years ago. There are vivid glimpses of Jeanne in other people's letters and memoirs. In the few letters that have surfaced, an expressive, amusing, highly creative voice rings out through the years as freshly as when they were written.

The du Maurier girls could not have been more closely brought up. They were consciously sheltered from the contamination of school; for them there was no escape where, freed from controlling adults, they might speak of taboo subjects like sex and God and money. Largely lacking outside friends, the sisters were thrown on each other's company and their own imaginations in a way that seems peculiarly intense compared to modern childhoods, with the ready distractions of the wider world. Moreover, they never quite managed to cast off the bonds of their family: the tentacles of the past spread into every part of their adult lives. Their influence on each other as children was potent and undiluted and it both held them back and spurred them on. For this reason I have dwelt at some length on their shared early life at Cannon Hall in London's Hampstead.

In this, the last generation to be named du Maurier, as daughter after daughter was born, it was hoped that at least one of them would have been a son, to ensure the continuation of the family genius and name. As mere girls, however, they would have to do as best they could. It was good indeed, but could it ever be good enough? The superlatives that surrounded their parents and forebears entered the romance of their family inheritance. 'These things added to our arrogance as children,' was how Daphne described the effect in her scintillating recreation of a theatrical childhood in her novel *The Parasites*: 'as babies we heard the thunder of applause. We went about, from country to country, like little pages in the train of royalty; flattery hummed about us in the air, before us and within us was the continual excitement of success.'[1] Edwardian parental influence and du

Maurier expectation was paramount. But given the distinctiveness of their upbringing, the sisters relied on each other for education and entertainment, with little change of view contributed by outside friends or adults who were not in the theatre. This hot house amplified their importance in each other's lives; family dynamics are seldom more complex and long-lived than in the love and rivalry of sisters.

'You have the children, the fame by rights belongs to me,'[2] Virginia Woolf famously wrote to her elder sister, the painter Vanessa Bell, expressing an age-old sense of natural sisterly justice. But this fragile balancing act was overthrown in the du Maurier family. For as it transpired, Daphne, the middle sister, not only had the fame but also the children, the beauty, the money, the dashing war-hero husband; she won all life's prizes, her fame so bright that it eclipsed, in the eyes of the world, her two sisters and their creative efforts as writer and painter. However, Daphne did not value these prizes. Nothing mattered as much to her as the flight of her extraordinary imagination that animated some of the most haunting stories of the twentieth century.

Her elder sister Angela, more extrovert and expressive, had the emotional energy for children and wrote of her longing to have been a mother. Certainly fame too promised to bring her more pleasure than it ever did to Daphne, who recoiled from publicity and the importuning of fans. Angela, eclipsed as she was, nevertheless came so close to claiming a share of the limelight; when she turned to singing she did not even get to first base as an opera singer, although her love of opera was to last a lifetime and she tried yet failed to join her parents' profession and become an actor. Insecure and easily discouraged, she quickly abandoned her youthful dreams of a life of performance as enjoyed by her parents. Instead, her emotional nature found an outlet in fiction, a highly regarded aspect of the family business thanks to the success of their grandfather the artist George du Maurier, whose late career as a novelist brought him transatlantic fame.

Soon after the publication in 1928 of Radclyffe Hall's notorious novel, *The Well of Loneliness*, a plea for understanding 'sexual inversion' in women, Angela began writing her own first novel, *The Little Less*. Given the damning prejudices of the time, together with her father's powerful influence and horror of homosexuality, Angela showed surprising courage – even revolutionary zeal – in exploring the bold theme of a woman's love for another. Like *The Well of Loneliness*, Angela's novel was not a great literary work, but it was a brave one and would have brought her a great deal of notice and some riches. Publication and attention would have established her as a novelist to watch and encouraged her to continue, and grow. Instead, she was met by rejection from publishers scared of another scandal. Her tentative flame of independence was snuffed out and she was left demoralised, perhaps even ashamed, for she had thrown light on a taboo subject and been silenced. She put the manuscript away, returned to the distraction of a busy social life and did not write again for almost a decade.

Meanwhile, Daphne had been writing a few startling short stories since she was a girl and then, sometime later in 1929, had begun her first novel. *The Loving Spirit*, a rather more conventional adventure story, was spiced with what was to become the characteristic du Maurier sense of menace. This too was not a particularly good book but it was a much safer subject and easily found a publisher in 1931. Daphne was launched as a writer on a spectacular career that powered her through four books in five years to the darkly atmospheric *Jamaica Inn* and then, two years later in 1938, her creative prodigy *Rebecca* stormed to bestseller status. The momentum was now entirely with her. Daphne's writing career, financial security and reputation were all made by the phenomenal success of *Rebecca*, and the haunting Hitchcock film that followed. The eclipse of her sisters was complete.

Jeanne, seven years younger than Angela, had also made a bold move that went against the powerful family ethos. She had tried her hand at music and was a fine pianist all her life, but her real love was painting. Hers was a family brought up to decry anything modern in the arts. The French Impressionists, the English Post-Impressionists, whose exhibition in London in 1910 had caused uproar among polite society, all horrified their father Gerald du Maurier. He was vocal in his derision of any art after the mid-nineteenth century and his opinions were held in Mosaic regard by his adoring family. 'Daddy loathed practically everything that was modern. He hated modern music, modern painting, modern architecture and the modern way of living … Gauguin horrified him I do remember,' Angela wrote, adding, 'I'm not at all sure it's a good thing to be as impressed by one's parents' ideas and opinions as I was by Daddy's.'[3]

Angela was not alone. All the sisters were in awe of their father's opinion on most things and Angela and Daphne never came to appreciate twentieth-century art. This made it all the more remarkable, but also painful for her, that Jeanne made her career as a painter, not of conventional, narrative, realistic pictures that her family might have appreciated, but of quiet, contemplative, modernist works. Her family did not value her art enough to hang it with pleasure on their walls, although her paintings were considered good enough by the art establishment to be bought by at least one public gallery. Jeanne seemed not to long for children, neither did she court fame, but her painting was the mainspring of her life and her immediate family's lack of appreciation of her work was a kind of denial too.

The intriguing threads of inheritance, character, family mythology and circumstance combine with early experience to create the pattern of a life. It is in childhood that these elements make their deepest impression. Here can be found possible reasons for Angela's lack of perseverance that became a lasting regret: 'I have always been an easily discouraged person … I had not the "guts" to start again writing'.[4] Inheritance and familial experiences gave Daphne the contrary commitment; imagination and writing were the things most worthwhile in life. It helped that her talent was encouraged by her doting Daddy who saw so much in his favourite tomboy daughter to remind him of his own father. '[He] told me how he had always hoped that one day I should write, not poems, necessarily, but novels … "You remind me so of Papa," he said. "Always have done. Same forehead, same eyes. If only you had known him."'[5]

In childhood Jeanne found the seeds of her later independence. Her mother's favourite and perhaps the most honest and down-to-earth of them all, she was the youngest sister who chose a discredited style of painting as her life's work and managed to live openly until her death with a woman poet as her partner, despite the oft-expressed antipathy of her father towards people like her.

The sense the family had of being glamorous, exceptional and blessed with French blood was reinforced by the private language they shared. This was a highly visual and entertaining creation that bound them together as a tribe and kept out pretenders. Daphne's fascination with the Brontës and Gondal, their imaginary world, brought the verb 'to Gondal' into the sisters' lexicon, meaning to make-believe or elaborate upon. Nicknames too were a du Maurier habit. Angela became various forms of 'Puff', 'Piff' and 'Piffy'; Daphne was 'Tray', 'Track' or 'Bing'; and Jeanne was 'Queenie' or 'Bird'.

Exploring Daphne's character and work in the context of her sisters, means she appears in a quite different light from the one that shines on her as the solitary subject of a life. She was shyly awkward and intransigent, a girl who escaped into her own imaginary world, where she was supreme. Intent on wresting control over her destiny she thereby influenced the lives of others, not least her sisters'.

In introducing her two much less famous sisters, I hope this book draws them from the shadows. I like to think that Angela, who longed for more notice during her lifetime and dreamed of having a film made from at least one of her stories (Daphne had ten – the unforgettable *Rebecca*, *The Birds* and *Don't Look Now* among them), would have been delighted to be rediscovered, her books read, possibly even inspiring a belated dramatisation. Where Daphne controlled her universe, Angela, at the mercy of her emotions, seemed to be buffeted by hers. Unfocused when young, and wilting under pressure, her youth was marked by humiliations and missed opportunities, while she was intent on the pursuit of love. Later she discovered a remarkable courage to tackle in her novels and her life injustice in matters of the heart, and to live as unconventionally as she pleased. As she aged, however, the constraining bonds of her Edwardian upbringing tightened around her once more.

A little light shed on Jeanne might also lead to a wider audience for her art, with paintings taken out of storage in small galleries and hung on the walls, for new generations to appreciate. The largest public collection is at the Royal West of England Academy in Bristol, where the quiet atmospheric beauty of her works rewards the eye with a spare, unsentimental vision. She was perhaps the most solid and least flighty of them all. Jeanne was always the honest, boy-like sister and did not apparently struggle with questions of identity or her role in life. When she decided what she wanted to do, all her energy was committed to it, unlikely to be deflected by emotion or propriety.

Much has been written on every aspect of Daphne du Maurier's work and life. Margaret Forster's impressive biography published nearly twenty years ago remains the authority on her life, but there are other essential contributions from Judith Cook's *Daphne: A Portrait of Daphne du Maurier* and Oriel Malet's *Letters from Menabilly*. Her daughter Flavia Leng's poignant memoir adds another layer of understanding. Daphne's writing attracted penetrating analysis in Avril Horner and Sue Zlosnik's *Daphne du Maurier: Writing, Identity and the Gothic Imagination*, and in Nina Auerbach's personal take on the themes of Daphne's fiction in *Daphne du Maurier, Haunted Heiress*. The rewarding mix of *The Daphne du Maurier Companion*, edited by Helen Taylor, and Ella Westland's *Reading Daphne*, add their own layers of meaning. There is also a highly successful yearly literary festival at Fowey, established to honour Daphne's close connection and imaginative contribution to that part of south-east Cornwall.

In this book I do not set out to write a full biography of each sister; nor have I the space to analyse their individual works in any depth, although I have discussed them when they offer extra biographical or psychological insights to the story. I have considered the du Maurier sisters side by side, as they lived in life. This adds a new perspective to the characters of each, as they evolve through the tensions and connections of ideas and feelings that flow within any close relationship. Most marked is how much the opinions and experiences of one sister find their way into the work of another. In their fiction particularly, Angela and Daphne each used aspects of their sisters' lives to animate her own work. But all the du Maurier sisters drew on their unique childhood, a past that was always present, bringing light and dark to their lives and work.

1

The Curtain Rises

Coats off, the music stops, the lights lower, there is a hush. Then
up goes the curtain; the play has begun. That is why I'm going to
begin this story 'Once upon a time …'

ANGELA DU MAURIER, *First Nights*

To be born a du Maurier was to be born with a silver tongue and to
become part of a family of storytellers. To be born the last of the du
Mauriers, as the three sisters would be, was to be born in a theatre
with the sound of applause, the smell of greasepaint, and the heart
attuned to drama, tension and a quickening of the pulse. The du
Mauriers were in thrall to myths of their ancestors. Even the romantic
name that meant so much to them was an embellishment on something more mundane. As soon as they were old enough to understand, Angela, Daphne and Jeanne du Maurier realised they were
special and had inherited a precious thread of creative genius that
connected them to their celebrated forebears.

Although Daphne did marry, all three sisters evaded the conventional roles of wife and mother and rose instead to the challenge of
living up to their name, a name they never relinquished. Two sisters
expressed themselves through writing and the third through paint.
The du Maurier character was volatile and charming, inflated with
fantasy and pretence; characteristically they hung their lives on a
dream and found little solace in real life once the romance had gone.

These three girls inherited a name famous on both sides of the Atlantic: their grandfather George du Maurier was a celebrated illustrator, *Punch* cartoonist and bestselling novelist. His most famous creation was *Trilby* and this sensational novel enhanced his fame and made him rich: it gave the world the 'trilby' hat and made his anti-hero, the mesmerist Svengali, part of the English language as a byword for a sinister, controlling presence. It was his first novel, *Peter Ibbetson*, however, that impressed his granddaughters most, insinuating into their own lives and imagination its haunting theme that by 'dreaming true' one could realise the thing one most desired. The sisters attempted in their different ways to practise this art in life and incorporate the idea in aspects of their work.

George's grandfather, Robert, had expressed his love for fantasy by inventing aristocratic connections for his descendants and adding 'du Maurier' to the humble family name of Busson. His own mother Ellen, great-grandmother to the sisters, was filled also with the sense she was not a duckling but a swan. As the daughter of the sharp-witted adventuress Mary Anne Clarke, she was brought up with the tantalising thought that her father might not be the undistinguished Mr Clarke, but the Duke of York, the fat spoiled son of George III. Such stories, lovingly polished through generations, contributed to the family's sense of pride and place. Only Ellen's great-granddaughter Daphne, with her cold detached eye, was not seduced. She recognised the destructive power of this pretension: 'She will wander through life believing she has royal blood in her veins, and it will poison her existence. The germ will linger until the third or fourth generation. Pride is the besetting sin of mankind!'[1] Yet the du Maurier story ensnared her too.

The family myths centred on these three tellers of tall tales: Mary Anne, Robert and the sisters' grandfather George du Maurier. If imagination and creativity ran like a silver thread through the du Mauriers, so did emotional volatility and lurking depression. In some this darkened into madness, with George's uncle confined to an asylum and his father so subject to bi-polar delusions (he believed he could build a machine to take his family to the moon) that he lived a life of impossible ambition and frustrated dreams. Some of these soaring flights of fancy would find alternative modes of expression in subsequent generations.

George's elder son, Guy, like George himself with *Trilby*, was overtaken in 1909 by an extraordinary flaring fame with *An Englishman's Home*, a patriotic play he casually wrote before going to serve as a soldier in Africa. This was five years before the start of the Great War and he satirised his country's unpreparedness. Sudden international celebrity was followed too soon by Guy's heroic death in the world war he had foretold. George's youngest child, Gerald, became an actor whose naturalistic lightness of touch changed the face of acting, where life and art seemed to combine in an effortless brilliance. Gerald made memorable the character of Raffles, the gentleman thief, and was the first actor to play J. M. Barrie's Mr Darling and Captain Hook in *Peter Pan*. His portrayal of this unpredictable cavalier pirate set the template for that character's appearance and behaviour in subsequent productions. This was the father of the du Maurier sisters, Angela, Daphne and Jeanne.

As with all sisters, the du Mauriers' relationship with each other was an indissoluble link to their childhood: for them that meant above all a link with their father and with *Peter Pan*. The play's creator, J. M. Barrie – Uncle Jim to the girls – was a prolific and successful Scottish author and playwright who, nearly a generation older than their father, had been influential in Gerald's early career and become a friend. Ever since they could first walk, the girls were taken on the annual pilgrimage to see the play performed at their father's theatre, Wyndham's. There, as the pampered children of the proprietor, they sat dressed in Edwardian satin and lace in their special box, saluted by the theatre staff and stars. They were celebrity children.

Throughout their childhood the sisters would re-enact the play in their nursery, the words and ideas becoming engraved deep into their psyches. Daphne was always Peter; Angela was more than happy to play Wendy, while Jeanne filled in with whatever part Daphne assigned her. *Peter Pan* excited their imaginations and intruded on every aspect of their lives. Their father was closely identified with the double personae of Mr Darling and Captain Hook, and Peter himself, brought to life the same year Angela was born, remained the seductive ageless boy. While the du Maurier sisters reluctantly accepted that they had to grow up, Peter Pan lived on in an unchanging loop of militant childishness, mockingly reminding them of what they had lost. The excitement and wonder of the theatre, however, was something they never lost. It informed their lives, finding expression in their work, in the dramatic character of their houses and their attraction to those with a touch of stardust in their blood.

Angela claimed *Peter Pan* as the biggest influence in her childhood: she saw it first performed when she was two and then finally played the role of Wendy in the theatre when she was nineteen. Her steadfast belief in fairies and prolonged childhood was encouraged by the play's compelling messages. But the influence on Daphne was profound, for her own imagination and longings so nearly matched the ethos of the story: the thrill of fantasy worlds without parents; the recoil from growing into adulthood and the fear of loss of the imaginative power of the child. The tragic spirit of the Eternal Boy plucked at the du Mauriers, just as he did the Darling children who left him to enter the real world stripped of magic. The place between waking and dreaming would be very real to Daphne all her life and her phenomenally fertile imagination propelled her into her own Neverland, whose inhabitants were completely under her control.

Neverland was never far away. Daphne still referred to *Peter Pan* as a metaphor when she was old, considering her children's empty beds and imagining the Darling children having flown to adventures that she could not share. Her powerful identification with this world of make-believe fuelled her spectacular fame and riches and an intense life of the mind, but held her back in her growth to full maturity as a woman. Her sisters, excited by the same theatricality in their childhoods, responded very differently. Angela, never quite taking flight, was shadowed by her sense of earthbound failure, yet she had the courage to grow up and risk her heart in surprising ways. Jeanne largely cast it off to go her independent way and turned to the down-to-earth pleasures of gardening, and the sensuous realities of paint. These evocative childhood experiences brought the sisters not only the comfort of familiarity – 'routes' in du Maurier code – but nostalgia too for the past they had so variously shared. Just a word could transport them back to the thrill of the darkened theatre of their youth, full of anticipation of the big adventure about to begin. 'On these magic shores [of Neverland] children at play are for ever beaching their coracles. We too have been there; we can still hear the sound of the surf, though we shall land no more.'[2]

These du Maurier girls were born as Edwardians in the brilliant shaft of light between the death in 1901 of the old Queen Victoria and the beginning of the First World War. It was a time when new ways of being seemed possible: pent-up feelings erupted into exuberant hope in the dawn of the twentieth century. Under a new and jovial king, the longing for pleasure and freedom replaced Victorian propriety and constraint, and this energy infected the nation. Such optimism extended to a young theatrical couple who married in 1903. Gerald du Maurier, as an actor and then theatrical manager, was already on a trajectory that would bring him fame, riches and a knighthood. His wife was the young actress Muriel Beaumont, cast with him in a comic play, *The Admirable Crichton*, a great hit in the West End. She was very young when responsibility and care for him was passed ceremonially to her from his mother (for whom he would remain always her precious pet 'ewe lamb') together with a list of his likes and dislikes. Muriel was a pretty actress who eventually gave up her career to be the wife of a great man and the mother of his children. Her two elder children would recall her impatience and irritability when they were young, her lack of humour, and her beauty, always her beauty.

On cue, just over a year after their marriage, on 1 March 1904 a plump baby girl was born in No. 5 Chester Place, a terraced Regency house close to London's Regent's Park. While Muriel laboured in childbirth with their first child, Gerald managed to upstage her. Suffering a serious bout of diphtheria, a potentially fatal respiratory disease, for which the cat was blamed, he lay in isolation on the floor above and, it seemed, at death's door.

When Gerald had recovered and could at last see his firstborn he was delighted to have a daughter. Girls were a rarity in this generation of du Mauriers. His sister Trixie had three boys, Sylvia five, and his brother Guy and wife Gwen were childless. Most importantly, his adored father George du Maurier had longed for at least one grand-daughter. 'That endless tale of boys was a great disappointment. If only he was here to see Angela.'[3] For Angela is what this jolly baby was called.

In the du Maurier family it was not enough to be a girl, however rare. Aside from ancestor worship, this was a family who adored beauty, demanded beauty, particularly in its women. This aesthetic sensibility was very marked in George whose drawings of gorgeous Victorian wasp-waisted females graced his witty cartoons. Despite his father's good looks, Gerald's attractiveness owed more to his charm and animation than the rather ungainly proportions of his face. He may have thought himself lacking in romantic good looks, but he was lightly built and elegantly made and expected grace and beauty in others, especially his womenfolk.

Gerald's wife Muriel was exceptionally attractive and stylish all her life, but their first daughter, by her own admission, was not: 'I was a plain little girl, and I got plainer. Luckily, when I was small I was, apparently, amusing, but no one could deny I was plain.'[4]

Muriel was still pursuing her acting career and baby Angela was handed over to 'Nanny' when she was eight months old, heralding Angela's first great love affair in a life in which there would be many. This kind, inventive, affectionate young woman was the central loving presence in Angela's universe and when she was dismissed, as surplus to requirements eight years later, the little girl's bewilderment, grief and loneliness seemed to her 'like a child's first meeting with Death'.[5]

Angela's earliest memories, before her sisters joined her in the nursery, were fragments of life. Between the ages of two and three she could remember her canary dying and being replaced, seamlessly, by another. This sleight of hand was enacted a few times more during her childhood. She remembered dancing as her mother played on the piano the hymn, *Do No Sinful Action*, and being sharply reprimanded for this serious but inexplicable sin. But her very first memory was of wetting her pants in Regent's Park when dressed in her Sunday best of bright pink overcoat with matching poke bonnet, trimmed with beaver fur. To complete the vision of prosperous Edwardian childhood, white suede boots clothed small feet that were not expected to stamp in puddles or run in wet grass. This memory of her immaculate outward appearance, contrasting with the shameful evidence under her coat, remained with her for life.

When Angela was three the family moved to 24 Cumberland Terrace, a larger house in a grander terrace a few hundred yards away, just as close to Regent's Park. Muriel was expecting another baby and this time it was hoped she would produce the son and heir. Gerald's obsession with his father made him long for a boy who might embody some of the lost qualities of artistry, imagination and charm that so distinguished George du Maurier: he wanted continuance of the du Maurier name and his father's genius somehow reincarnated in a son.

The baby was born late in the afternoon of 13 May 1907. After a week of heat the weather had finally broken and rain pelted down from a thunderous sky, and into the world came not the expected son but another daughter, although this time she was pretty, which was some consolation. Angela did not remember her sister's arrival but she recalled her mother insisting 'she was the loveliest tiny baby she has ever seen'.[6] Gerald was playing that night to packed houses in a light comedy called *Brewster's Millions*. The eponymous hero, who had to run through a million-dollar legacy before he could inherit another seven million, mirrored something of Gerald's own cavalier attitude to money: his characteristic off-hand style and sense of fun endeared him to the audience. He returned from the theatre to find Nanny in charge of this second daughter.

Gerald decided to call her Daphne, after the mesmerising actress Ethel Barrymore, who had much preferred the name Daphne to her own, and had jilted him before he had met Muriel. One wonders if Muriel knew after whom her second daughter was named – perhaps thinking the impetus was the nymph Daphne who ran from Apollo and his erotic intentions (as a last resort transforming herself into a laurel tree), rather than the American beauty from a great acting dynasty who ran from Gerald and his ravenous need for uncritical adoration.

Daphne fitted into a nursery routine long practised by Nanny and Angela. Angela was almost four and for nearly all that time had been the focus of Nanny's love. She may not have remembered her sister's birth but recalled she had to relinquish sole command of the nursery and share her beloved with a demanding interloper. Apart from a couple of terms, Angela did not go to school and was not able to establish a new kingdom for herself outside the confines of the nursery. Life continued in its soothing routines but now everything had fundamentally changed.

The highlight of the day was the walk to the park with the enormous coach-built pram, enamelled white to match their front door. There Nanny met other nannies and their charges were allowed some sedate play while the women chatted. The sisters were always impeccably dressed, and dressed alike, something that frustrated them as they grew older and struggled for their own identities. Their days were spent away from their parents, everything done for them by Nanny who never, it seemed to Angela, had a day off. In her eight years' employment with the family there were only two holidays, but looking back this was such an unjust state of affairs that Angela wondered if she had misremembered it.

The children were brought to their parents at the end of the day, washed, brushed and on their best behaviour. Good manners and above all quietness were instilled into them from an early age; Gerald was extremely sensitive to sound: even the singing of a blackbird could be too plangent for his peace of mind. As he and Muriel slept late and had a rest in the afternoon when they were working, Angela and Daphne, whose nursery was on the floor above their room, learnt to creep around and talk in whispers. When he was available to them, however, he was unusually interested in their young selves, endlessly inventive, funny and full of jokes and games. He was iconoclastic and mocking of others behind their backs and drew his daughters into the joke, though insisting at all times they maintain high standards of politeness and deference to adults, to their faces.

Muriel finally gave up the stage when she was pregnant with her third baby – surely this time a boy. Angela had been praying for years for a baby brother, perhaps giving voice to the whole family's hopes. She was just seven years old when Gerald and the doctor came into the nursery at lunchtime to tell them that they had a new baby sister.

Angela, ever one to enjoy the dramatic in life and art, got down from the table (she had been eating cold beef and beetroot) and walked to an armchair where she knelt and gave thanks. Jeanne was born on 27 March 1911, the day after Gerald's thirty-eighth birthday. Perhaps by now he was resigned to the lack of a son, for Muriel, at thirty, seemed unwilling, or unable, to add to their family.

Luckily, Jeanne too was a pretty baby who managed to keep her crowd-pleasing charms; according to Angela, between the ages of two and six, Jeanne was the loveliest child she had ever seen. This verdict was not just a big sister's pride, for the infant won a baby beauty contest. Having given up work during her pregnancy, it was not perhaps surprising that with more energy and time for her children Muriel's youngest became her favourite. Gerald's energies too had shifted. His career had been given greater propulsion when in 1910 he became an actor-manager by joining with partner Frank Curzon to manage Wyndham's Theatre, in London's West End. Although the current play there, *Mr Jarvis*, was a flop he was to have many more successes than failures and the family's income and consequent standard of living rose dramatically.

The girls' childhoods were lastingly vivid to them, revisited often in memory and in the atmospheric energy of Angela's and Daphne's fiction. Their experiences, however, were very different. Angela was romantic and theatrical and easily gulled. Daphne was critical, detached and distrustful, even from young, of some of the stories told by the adults who cared for them. Angela was convinced that Father Christmas was real and, overcome with excitement, had swept the lowest curtsey possible when, aged seven, she came across an actor friend of her father's in full fig of snowy beard, buckled red tunic and a throaty *Yo ho ho*. She was twelve when a friend's insistence that the philanthropic old gent did not exist sent her to her mother in panic, certain she would be reassured: 'When poor Mummie apologised and said, "I'm sorry darling, I'm afraid there *isn't*," [it] knocked the bottom out of childhood. With that bit of news went a bit of one's trust.' It was remarkable that she had maintained her belief almost into adolescence, testament to their isolation from other children, but also to Angela's resolute romanticism and childlike sense of wonder.

The maintaining of childish innocence, even ignorance, was positively encouraged by their father who loved having his family around him and dreaded his children growing up. Through his profession he conjured the theatrical template for Captain Hook, but in life he was a true Peter Pan, ever youthful, full of tricks; 'gay, innocent and heartless'[7] as the boy who was afraid to grow up. Nowhere was this enforced innocence more pernicious in its effects than in the area of sex. Angela was told some fantastical story of where babies come from involving angels descending from the sky bearing fluffy bundles; a common enough deception at the time, but one that the highly emotional Angela would take to heart. When she was enlightened with the real truth in graphic detail by a 'Miss Know All', she was disgusted. 'My father would never do such a thing,' Angela declared in alarm. But worse than the crude explanation was the realisation that she had been lied to by the people she trusted most.

The twelve-year-old worked out that the reason for these lies was 'because the truth was so HORRIBLE that they couldn't bear to tell it to me'. Inevitably, the parents got to hear of the schoolgirl chatter and Angela, somehow singled out as the source of this taboo revelation, and overcome with fear and shame, faced her appalled mother. Muriel 'harangued [her] like the devil for having learned the truth',[8] and histrionically declared she could never trust her daughter again. Angela's anger and dismay were still alive three and a half decades later when she wrote in her memoir how it was inevitable that she concluded, '"all that" [sexual intercourse] was horrible, unnatural, repulsive, disgusting and ugly'.[9] It came close to blighting her emotional future, she explained; her youth, her whole life even, 'came near to ruin',[10] through this particular piece of evasion and the shame-filled aftermath.

Daphne was never so blindly trusting of those closest to her. Nor was she ever as naïve. When she was six, and Angela nine, she saw through Nanny's pretence that there were fairies on the lawn who made the fairy-ring of flowers and wrote little notes addressed to both girls by name in tiny fairy writing:

Angela, eyes wide open in wonder, smiled delightedly. I stared at the circle. I must pretend to be pleased too, but the trouble was I did not believe in them … 'They [the adults] wrote it themselves,' I said after we got back.

'They wouldn't! Of course it was real.' Angela was indignant.

I shook my head. 'It's the sort of thing grown-ups do.'[11]

All three du Maurier sisters were taken to the theatre from babyhood, to proper adult plays in which their father starred. They were treated by the cast and the theatre staff as special mascots: the glamour of the performance and the excitement when the lights went down deeply impressed these little girls and the memory stayed with them for life. Only once did Angela go as a small child to a pantomime, but she was so horrified by the harlequinade at the end – 'something about a sausage shocked me at four'[12] – that she would not subject herself to another until she was nearly grown up.

The girls regularly saw their father and mother dress up, put on make-up and become other people. It was the most natural thing to do. They visited Gerald in his dressing room after performances to find him high with adrenaline, charismatic, laughing and talking animatedly to the hordes of friends and acquaintances that always surrounded him, wiping the greasepaint off his face to return in stages to a heightened version of himself. It was thrilling and confusing and somehow conspiratorial, this almost magical transformation. Most of the family friends were also actors and actresses and they too practised this occult art. They seemed to live more intensely, their lives shiny with colour and light but speeded up, and soon over. The excitement fuelled childish imaginations and the glamour and theatricality of their existence blurred the boundaries between truth and fantasy. But if childhood certainties were proved no longer safe, what other truths would disappear as the lights went up?

For Daphne, the fantasy world she inhabited was created by her own imagination, a refuge from a world in which she felt alien and adrift. She remembered that at only five years old, after being bullied in nearby Park Square Gardens by a seven-year-old called John Poynton, she came to the cheerless realisation that everyone was ultimately alone. From very young, feelings of powerlessness and being misunderstood made her long to be a boy and therefore stronger, braver, and more important – not this outer, more vulnerable, female self. She discovered that she, like her parents, could dress up and pretend to be someone else, but for her it was a private thing, a protection from a real world in which she was a stranger. Assuming the persona of another made it less painful when surrounded by unknown adults and their expectations. It 'stopped the feeling of panic when visitors came'.[13]

Although Angela recalled her first eight years as being blissfully happy in the secure love and care of Nanny, '*all* my very happy early childhood can be laid at [her] door',[14] this was brought to a traumatic halt when, completely without warning or explanation, Angela saw this precious mother figure leave the house never to return. 'I can see Nanny now,' she wrote at nearly fifty, 'going down the top flight of stairs and carefully shutting the gate behind her, tears pouring down her face, and only then myself being told she was going for ever.' Eight-year-old Angela's cheerful spirits were replaced with 'a horrible sense of loneliness'.[15] Daphne remembered this unhappy incident too but with much greater detachment: she was puzzled to see Nanny in tears because surely grown-ups don't cry. Already, at five, she was aware that adults should never lose their dignity and she herself would very rarely cry, even as a child.

Sadly grown-ups did cry. Tragedies befell the du Maurier family during the earliest years of the girls' childhoods and it shadowed their father's careless gaiety. First, Uncle Arthur Llewelyn Davies, married to their beautiful and gentle Aunt Sylvia, died after a long battle with a painful and disfiguring cancer of the jaw. He was only forty-four and his death in 1907, the year Daphne was born, left his wife with five young sons to bring up and educate.

The Llewelyn Davies boys had been the inspiration for *Peter Pan* and J. M. Barrie, this lonely, childless man who shrank from the harsher elements of adult life, now stepped in to help Sylvia financially and practically with the education of her boys. However, the family's ills were not over and Sylvia herself had not long to live. Not even the needs of her young family could anchor her to life and three years later she slipped away, aged forty-four, the same age as her dear Arthur. She was Gerald's favourite sister and he and his family were broken-hearted for she was much loved by all who knew her.

Yet this was not the end of their suffering for only three years later their eldest aunt, Trixie, died unexpectedly aged fifty leaving three mostly grown-up children of her own. She was the most energetic and forthright of them all. It seemed unbelievable that her vibrant spirit had been snuffed out so easily. Only their Aunt May, their father Gerald and the hero-uncle Guy remained of George's five distinctive children. The Great War was further to devastate this diminishing band of du Mauriers.

In 1914, Lieutenant Colonel Guy du Maurier was waved off by his family at Waterloo Station and headed to war. His mother, Big Granny to the three sisters, was overcome with emotion and collapsed in a dead faint on the platform. Angela and Daphne watched transfixed by the sight of their formal grandmother stretched out, her long black dress decorously pulled round her ankles and her white hair escaping from her bonnet. Within months she too had fallen ill, with heart failure, endured an operation urged on her by her children, and never recovered. According to Daphne, she died in the arms of both her sons. Her death undid the family, and Gerald, her spoiled youngest, particularly felt the loss of her devotion. She had been such a central controlling presence. Her children had deferred to her, written every day while away, sought to please her and been offered all-encompassing love in return.

Only nine weeks later, while everyone was still rapt with grief, Uncle Guy, loved by his troops and his family alike and rumoured to be due promotion to brigadier general the following day, was killed as he evacuated his battalion from the front line. He was not quite fifty. Both Angela and Daphne were possessive of his love and attention for, although he was Angela's godfather, Daphne shared his birthday. Unhappiness overwhelmed the family once more. Angela was mortified that she had not written to him while he was at the front, despite being his godchild. She was put out that Daphne had sent him letters and felt that somehow this made their hero-uncle, *her* god-father, belong more to her sister than to her.

The most anguished though was Gerald. He had received the tele-gram while he was in the middle of his evening performance of the play *Raffles* and had to go the moment the curtain fell to tell Guy's widow, Gwen, the awful news. Guy had been the epitome of the heroic elder son. Attractive to everyone for his breezy good humour, he had engaged in the manly things that mattered, and given his life for King and Country. He had also created *An Englishman's Home*, the play that seemed to grasp the spirit of the age and for an extraordinary moment take by storm the theatre-going world on both sides of the Atlantic. His success as a writer had somehow proved to Gerald that their father's genius had not died with him but lived on in Guy, until extinguished tragically too soon.

Guy had added his own robust heroism to his father's creative flame. All Gerald had done so far was pretend to be other people and provide a few hours' distraction while momentous events happened elsewhere. He was overcome with regret at having taken his big brother for granted, for not writing often enough; he despaired at the apparent futility of his own life. The devoted family who had loved Gerald as their baby, protected and spoilt him, had been lost to him within a period of only five years. 'Poor darling D[addy],' Daphne wrote, 'had none of his family left but Aunt May.'[16] Gerald and May, whose health had never been good, had been considered the weak-lings and now they were all who remained from the close-knit and glamorous du Maurier clan.

The next tragedy, just a few days later, was made no less painful by the knowledge that personal catastrophe had become commonplace: young men with all their promise before them were dying in their thousands in filthy trenches in a foreign land. The sisters' cousin, George Llewelyn Davies, one of the orphaned boys, had excelled at Eton and just gone up to Trinity College Cambridge when he joined the Army on the outbreak of war. Less than a week after his Uncle Guy's death, George, a second lieutenant with the Rifle Brigade, was killed at the front, aged just twenty-one. Everywhere were families overborne by grief.

The sisters could not turn to the comforts of religion and the belief that the beloved dead would be reunited at last, for Gerald had no faith and was an emphatic atheist. Although their mother Muriel and her family were conventionally religious, Gerald's lack of belief set the tone for the du Maurier children: 'the Church was a World Apart to us'.[17] Angela, however, remembered the occasional treat of attending a very high Anglican Mass with her Aunt Billy (her mother's sister Sybil) where, she admitted, the scent of incense and the ritual ringing of little bells appealed to her emotionalism and theatricality. The rituals of the Anglo-Catholic Church would become a solace to last a lifetime, long after the appeal of *Peter Pan* had faded.

As for most children, however, the full impact of these family tragedies did not strike as hard, for the routines of daily life continued, offering comfort and entertaining distractions. London was milling with soldiers and their songs penetrated the genteel portals of Cumberland Terrace. Angela, Daphne and Jeanne marched and sang, as the troops did, memorable ditties like *Who-Who-Who's Your Lady Friend?* Angela had overheard someone tell their nurse that in wartime everyone made eyes at the soldiers. She interpreted this to mean that it was a patriotic duty and so the girls would practise 'making eyes'. Daphne thought that the soldiers in Regent's Park, rewarded with an encouraging smirk and sidelong squint, luckily did not notice.

Their father Gerald, however, was not as emotionally resilient as his children. His mercurial character had found easy expression in his early years through acting. His capricious and light-hearted delivery had pioneered a new informal, conversational style, refreshing after the more self-conscious theatricality of the older generation of actors like Henry Irving and Sir Herbert Tree. Easily bored, Gerald needed constant diversion and had already been tiring of his stage work. However, even the greater challenges in becoming an increasingly successful actor-manager, sharing the responsibilities of selecting plays and cast, directing the acting and reaping the not inconsiderable rewards when a show was a hit, did not banish entirely the sense of ennui that sometimes overcame him.

With the approach of middle age and the harsh realities of death all around, Gerald's facile emotions as readily flipped into existential gloom. This volatile seesaw of elation and depression ran in the family; his father had sought comfort in his wife and children and a wide circle of artistic friends, and Gerald did the same. To evade the abyss he filled his leisure hours with an endless round of social activity, handled with aplomb by Muriel, whose only desire apparently was to make him happy. Family holidays often involved a small party of friends and hangers-on, largely funded by Gerald whose capacity to earn money increased dramatically along with his readiness to spend it.

He was a demanding and devoted father and, given his emotional nature and love of fun and practical jokes, became the shining sun in his young daughters' universe. He was a regular in their nursery, ready to play games with them, read stories and preside over mock trials when squabbles broke out between his daughters. More than once he brought J. M. Barrie up to the nursery where the du Maurier girls, without any self-consciousness, acted out for him the whole of *Peter Pan*: Daphne as Peter, Angela as Wendy and Mrs Darling, and when necessary a pirate or two, while Jeanne was Michael and any other part as necessary. Gerald slipped into his old blood-curdling role of Hook. The girls would slither as mermaids on the floor and fly from chair to chair, thrillingly immersed in their own fantasy of Neverland. In fact for years Angela liked to believe that the lights in Regent's Park were fairy lights, 'like those in the last scene of *Peter Pan*'.[18]

All three sisters pretended to be characters other than themselves throughout their childhood. It seemed that everyone they knew did the same. Histrionics were a way of life. It was not just Angela who screamed she was being murdered if the nurse got soap in her eyes when washing her hair. With Gerald, emotions were magnified; from the anchoritic groans of a man in despair he could become the clown in the nursery or a capriciously domineering Hook. Amongst the children, Daphne was already in thrall to her imagination and became the main mover in the sisters' dramatic reconstructions of history (executions and torture were popular) or action scenes from books of adventure and derring-do.

Daphne insisted on playing the hero, only deigning to be a girl if the character was warlike and heroic, like Joan of Arc. Angela was happy enough for a while to play the female roles, even though they often ended in tears or death. She remembered the lure of *The Three Musketeers*, with herself as the responsible, elder Athos. Daphne of course was the upstart outsider d'Artagnan, their natural leader, and 'poor Jeanne becoming Aramis'.[19] The older girls didn't rate the amorous, ambitious Aramis so left him to their little sister who would not complain. No one wanted to be Porthos, whose good-natured gullibility made him too dull to be heroic.

Although Angela recalled being blissfully happy up to the age of eight, in Daphne's memory her childhood lacked even a few years of uncontaminated happiness. From early on she stood out in the family as the beauty but also as the difficult one. Angela was gregarious and outgoing and in her own estimation was a highly nervous child, but never shy. Manners were everything. The correct appearance of things mattered to the family, and shyness was considered by their parents to be extremely bad manners. Angela could converse with the adults and sweep impressive curtseys when required, but Daphne was not sociable and charming in the way that privileged Edwardian children were expected to be. Already brave and individual, in society Daphne was introverted and shy. When introduced to grown-ups, she was more likely to scowl than simper, and escape to the nursery and her own private world as soon as she could.

Being singled out in the family by her father as his favourite was a perilous honour Daphne was ill-equipped to receive. It was perhaps a major reason for the lack of sympathy between herself and her mother, 'someone who looked at me with a sort of disapproving irritation, a queer unexplained hostility'. Daphne insisted that from the age of two, when memories began, she had never once been held by her mother or sat on her lap and that this sense of thwarted longing and alienation turned her inwards. 'I became tongue-tied with shyness, and absolutely shut in myself, a dreamer of dreams.'[20] It changed the way she viewed the world. She grew watchful and wary, aware always of an uneasy exile. 'You could never be quite sure of any of them, even relations.'[21]

She recognised Gerald behind his many dramatic personae, but she was disconcerted by Muriel, fearful that her role as mother was just a façade and that she was really the Snow Queen in disguise. If those closest to you appear unpredictable and powerful, as beings possessed of knives, where as a child can you feel safe? This sense of domestic menace fuelled her extraordinarily fertile imagination, expressed all her life in macabre stories and dreams. Where Angela was wide-eyed and believed anything, Daphne took nothing on trust. Extreme wariness and diffidence followed her into adult life, perhaps magnified by her sensitive apprehension as a child that beneath her mother's lovely exterior existed something deadly to her emerging self. Even in middle age, when she was no longer afraid of a mother who had grown frail and grateful, Daphne's anxieties found outlet in cinematic nightmares about her, 'in which my anger against her is so fearful that I nearly kill her!'[22]

There was a cool steely quality behind Muriel's delicate beauty and this contrast was confusing. She seemed so compliant with Gerald's extravagances, so ready to act the perfect wife and mother, but even Angela, her responsible eldest and ever eager to please, did not elicit much sympathy from an impatient Muriel who took it upon herself to teach her eldest to read when small and reduced her to tears every time. Despite the apparent self-sacrifice of herself and her career, Muriel was considered by some of her daughters' friends to be charming, but selfish. Like many of her generation born towards the end of Queen Victoria's reign she was a snob and very keen that her daughters mixed in the right circles. The girls understood the code of the du Mauriers, as Angela recalled:

> blatantly the upper classes and lower classes were alluded to, but the middle class, to which lots of us belonged and we belong, was never mentioned by us! We probably kidded ourselves that we were of the first category, and I squirm when I remember how my darling mother would talk with a sniff about 'that class' when speaking of some servant or other.[23]

The highlight of the year for the young du Maurier sisters was the summer retreat to the country. Every May they were dispatched to a rented house with maids and a nurse and there they stayed until

August, often without their parents who remained for some of the time in London, acting or dealing with the business of the theatre. Although their behaviour was still constrained by adults' demands, their country surroundings offered a whole range of new experiences and freedoms denied them in town, where routines and lack of space stifled the spirit of childish adventure and freedom. One significant freedom was to be able to make a noise, to walk and talk without constraint, instead of creeping in silence around their London house in the mornings while their parents slept. Everything became slightly looser. The servants seemed more cheerful, the sisters squabbled less and Mummy did not wear a hat at lunch.

In the summer of 1913, when Angela was nine, Daphne six and Jeanne still only a toddler, the girls arrived at Slyfield Manor in Great Bookham in Surrey. Rented by their parents for the summer, this house impressed the elder sisters with its ancient mystery and the beauty of its surroundings. It was dark and creaky inside, a manor dating back to the Domesday Book, but the current building was largely Elizabethan: the great Queen was meant to have stayed a night here. Perhaps they learnt too of stories of the ghostly blue donkey that leapt the high gates at the bottom of the stairs (installed in an earlier age to keep fierce guard dogs at bay) to disappear into the gloom. Daphne was scared of walking these dark-panelled stairs alone, but the atmosphere of the place and the conjured presence of Elizabeth I stirred her imagination: 'Where had they all gone, the people who lived at Slyfield once? And where was I then? Who was I now?'[24]

To Angela it was much less complicated. Slyfield was 'the loveliest house I have ever lived in'.[25] It was there that this city girl discovered the beauty of bluebells and the intoxicating smell of lilac from a bush beneath her bedroom window. Her happiness that summer was made complete by her infatuation with a farmhand called Arthur who sat her on his great horse. For the first time Daphne felt she 'had come off second-best', for Angela 'smiled down at me, proud as a queen'.[26] Daphne preferred the farm animals, the great shire horses and the luscious countryside with the River Mole flowing through the manor's grounds. But mostly the country meant the precious freedom to go off on one's own, on some adventure, only to return to the adults' dominion with reluctance and impatience at their intrusion into her world.

Already very unalike in character, both girls seemed to inhabit parallel universes, Angela's emotional, connected to others and Daphne's bounded only by her imagination and peopled with her own creations. With a macabre detachment she could dispassionately watch the gardener at Slyfield nail a live adder to a tree, declaring it would take all day to die, and return at intervals to watch it writhing in its desperate attempts to break free. Aunt Billy had given Daphne two doves in a cage and she found it tiresome to have to feed and care for them when she would rather be out doing interesting things. She was struck how Angela loved administering to her pair of canaries and sang while she cleared out their droppings and sprinkled fresh sand on the base of their cage. Daphne's solution was to set her doves free and accept without complaint the scolding that would be forthcoming, for this was the price of her freedom from care. Jeanne, so much younger, amenably slipped into whatever game or role her elder sisters required. She was pretty and jolly and loved by her mother and nurse, and her life had not yet deepened into its later complexities.

While the children spent the summer at Slyfield, Gerald enjoyed one of his great theatrical successes up in town. He had produced *Diplomacy*, a melodrama by the nineteenth-century French dramatist Victorien Sardou who was known for the complex constructions of his plots and the shallowness of his characterisation. This play sprang the young actress Gladys Cooper to fame, playing Dora the beautiful spy at the centre of the action. All her life, Gladys was to remain a close friend of the whole family, loved and admired by the du Maurier daughters as much as by Gerald. Angela and Daphne were both taken to see the play in which their father, as producer, had given himself a minor role that he played with characteristic nonchalance. Angela never forgot the dramatic impact at the end of Act Two as the exquisite Dora banged the door hysterically crying, 'Julian, Julian, Julian!' When Sardou was asked what tips he would give an aspiring playwright he famously advised: 'Torture the women!' It certainly made the play memorable for an impressionable girl of eight and in their nursery productions, Angela would reprise with gusto Dora's tortured door-banging and weeping. This dramatic scene and the part of Wendy from *Peter Pan* were her two favourite acting roles, repeated many times with her sisters.

Angela also never forgot her first meeting with Gladys, not just for her luminous beauty at barely twenty-two, but for one of her father's characteristic roles as the unpredictable joker. On a summer Sunday morning in 1911, when Angela was seven, she and Gerald drew up in the family car at Rickmansworth station to meet the London train. Angela was sent off alone to pick up 'the prettiest lady' she could find amongst the throng on the platform. Luckily, Gladys stood out with her fine fair hair and dazzling blue eyes and this small child in her sun bonnet emerged from the crowd and solemnly took the prettiest lady by the hand and without a word led her back to the car where Gerald waited, highly amused. 'How like my father, Gerald du Maurier!' recalled Angela decades later, with a mixture of exasperation and affectionate pride.

The year after this great success, Britain was at war. The assassination on 28 June 1914 of the Archduke of Austria in a little known part of the Balkans was the start of what became known as the Great War. Initially, however, there was no great concern at home as eager boys were waved off as part of an expeditionary force; most people thought they would all be home by Christmas. And although everything had changed, in some respects life for the du Maurier children went on in much the same routine. They still spent the summer months in the country, each year gaining greater freedoms. In 1915 they were in Chorley Wood in Surrey and Angela, by now eleven years old, had lessons every day with a family across the common. Daphne was left on her own with their first family dog, Jock, a much-loved bottle-brush of a West Highland Terrier that became her loyal companion on solitary adventures in the gardens and countryside beyond. Jeanne was growing up and at four had become more use to Daphne in her dramatic recreations of adventure stories. This year it was *Treasure Island* that captivated her: Angela was roped in to playing the supporting parts, and Jeanne filled in as Blind Pew to Daphne's Jim Hawkins or Long John Silver.

Harrison Ainsworth, a prolific and highly successful historical nineteenth-century novelist, became for a while Angela and Daphne's favourite author, his stories providing Daphne with plenty of dramatic incident to re-enact with her sisters. *The Tower of London* provided ample opportunity for torture and death. Angela was happy enough to play Bloody Mary (for whom she admitted some affection) but was proving less tractable to joining in with Daphne's imaginative games, keener on pursuing her own more grown-up interests. Jeanne, however, was happy to be Daphne's sidekick and was beheaded many times by her elder sister without complaint. 'Jeanne, strutting past, certainly made a moving figure, her curls pinned on the top of her head, while I, the axeman, waited …'[27] Unsurprisingly, Daphne could not recall in these childhood games ever being felled herself by the executioner's axe, although she would submit occasionally to the torturer's rack or to energetic writhing in simulating a victim of a rat attack. Catholics and Huguenots provided another thrilling enactment with all kinds of grisly tortures and deaths, but on her terms.

More memorable and exciting even than Slyfield Manor was the family's visit in 1917 to Milton, a stately colonnaded country mansion near Peterborough, owned by a friend of their mother's, Lady Fitzwilliam. Daphne recalled with some puzzlement that her usual shyness and diffidence as a child, when confronted with new people and experiences, was here swept aside as she stood in the grandeur of the great hall. Instead she was overwhelmed by an instantaneous feeling of happiness, recognition, even love. This sense of familiarity and affection for the house never left her and much later became conflated with her mysterious Cornish mansion, Menabilly, to create her most famous fictional house, *Rebecca*'s Manderley.

The girls were only at Milton for ten days, Angela and Daphne sharing one spacious bedroom and their mother and Jeanne another. The sisters entertained and played cards with the convalescing soldiers who were nursed by the Red Cross in the centre of the great house, but there was so much laughter and good humour among the men that the terrors of war did not impinge on the young girls' thoughts at all. There was too much fun to be had, hiding and seeking in the unused wing, visiting the pack of Fitzwilliam hounds, rabbiting with the soldiers, hanging over the huge jigsaw puzzle that Lady Fitzwilliam worked on most of the time. She nicknamed the du Maurier girls Wendy, Peter and Jim, much to their delight, particularly Daphne's for she was awarded Peter, that most promising of boy personas.

Despite the war, plays continued to be performed in the West End and Gerald's successes added to his reputation and his growing fortune. He was becoming more interested in producing than acting but nevertheless, in *The Ware Case* by George Bancroft, his triumphant production in 1915, took the lead in what his daughter Angela considered one of the finest parts of his career. He played a financier who murdered his brother-in-law, found dead in his garden pond. After a tense trial he was declared not guilty. The trial scene itself was a dramatic novelty for the time and all the more nerve-racking for that. Daphne was gripped by it and recognised Gerald's acting skills in making the audience believe in Hubert Ware's innocence, despite so much evidence to the contrary. Angela found it impossible to forget the final scene and the look on her father's face 'of hopeless hatred and bitterness' as he cried: 'You bloody fools, I did it!' before taking poison and dramatically collapsing to the stage. She insisted, perhaps a bit defensively, that there was nothing hammy in this at all.

Daphne herself appeared in a charity production at Wyndham's of a musical version of a play by J. M. Barrie, *The Origin of Harlequin*, performed in August 1917. The star of the show was a boy, the Honourable Stephen Tennant, at eleven only one year older than Daphne herself, who was struck by how grown up he looked and how well he danced. Stephen was a pretty, clever child who was to grow into an exquisite and talented young man whose life and body became his greatest work of art. The dancing boy had also noticed the young Daphne, but then it was hard to miss her as she was dressed as a Red Indian. Reminded of this fact fifty-five years later, Daphne recalled that the costume was probably a birthday present and she had refused to appear in the show, 'unless I could be disguised, self-protection I suppose'.[28]

It was inevitable that highly imaginative children, living with this everyday theatricality, would wonder what life was really about. Murderers and fairies crowded the stage, but did the dream end when one awoke? When the lights went up and the crowds left the foyer streaming into the bright night, what was real of whatever remained? Young men were dying in a bloody war just a few hundred miles away; their young cousin, their uncle, were already dead in the slaughter. Confusingly, at home the show went on, with actors pretending to die and children executing each other with imaginary axes, and Daphne dancing on stage as a fully-feathered Indian brave.

Two years earlier Gerald had viewed a Georgian mansion for sale in the leafy village of Hampstead. Cannon Hall had once been a courthouse and it stood in proud command of its demesne of large gardens and various outhouses including a lock-up – much to the sisters' pleasure – a real jail at last. Gerald was immediately struck by the Hall's theatrical staircase and decided then and there that he would have it. To return in some style to the area of London where his father had lived and he had grown up seemed to add a nice symmetry to his restless life and would perhaps help to recapture some of the happiness and contentment that had gone. As Gerald attempted to reconnect with his past, he was unconsciously setting a new scene for his daughters' future.

2

Lessons in Disguise

Sisters? They should have been brothers. They would have made splendid boys.

NOËL WELCH, *The Cornish Review*

CANNON HALL WAS the du Mauriers' last London home. The family moved there in 1917 in the darkest days of the war, and life for the girls aged thirteen, ten and six changed for ever. The house was much larger than their town house at Cumberland Terrace, and Hampstead Heath was a vast wild territory on the borders of urban civilisation, so much more alive with possibility than genteel Regent's Park. The Hall's gardens were enormous and beckoned the sisters into a private world of make-believe and adventure, a place where they did not have to wear coats and hats when they went out, while the wider horizons of the heath were just a hop and a skip away. Gerald was earning a great deal of money from his continued successes at Wyndham's and, proud of his elegant new house, he imported furniture and *objets d'art* to match its early-Georgian splendour. The historical paintings he bought to grace the theatrical staircase impressed Daphne most: a mournful portrait of Charles II, a vast battle scene, food for many re-enactments, and a portrait of Elizabeth I, majestic on the stairs, made every trip to bed full of fascination and not a little menace.

The most dramatic change for the du Maurier sisters was school. For the first time in their lives, Angela and Daphne were to mix with a group of children and adults who did not belong to the glamorous circle of their parents' acquaintances. It was an alien experience that ten-year-old Daphne, self-sufficient and already armoured against the world, thoroughly enjoyed and Angela, three years older, nervous, conscientious and over-emotional, loathed. The school was a small private establishment in a large house in Oak Hill Park, a road in the leafy suburbs of Hampstead. It was owned and run by an elderly, strict Scot called Miss Tulloch. Elizabeth Tulloch, like many school-mistresses at the time, was an unmarried woman whose energies and talents had few outlets apart from teaching. She had established her school in 1884 and at sixty-seven was at the end of her career when the two, largely unschooled, du Maurier girls turned up on her doorstep.

Angela and Daphne walked to school every day with satchels on their backs to enter very different worlds. Daphne had a sympathetic teacher who thought her stories were the best in the class, but her spelling and handwriting were atrocious. Daphne was not particularly troubled by this criticism, although she was miffed that another girl won the short story competition with an inferior tale but better presentation. She quickly became leader of a gang of girls who intimidated any classmate who displeased them by threatening to burn her at the stake. The punishment was straight out of Daphne's historical re-enactments. She enjoyed being able to exercise her imagination and power on a bigger stage, and with a larger cast than just two sisters.

Angela admitted that she was terrified of the teachers from the start and was unprepared for the classwork, particularly arithmetic – an arcane mystery she would never fathom. Unfortunately her teacher was a fearsome Miss Webb who attacked her fumbled sums with a forbidding blue pencil and little sympathy. Maths homework was a torture and so many tears were shed that Gerald, unable to make sense of any of it himself, would ring up his business partner for help. What appeared to upset Angela as much was the chaos and noise of nearly two hundred girls going about their school day, banging desks, their feet thumping carelessly on wooden boards, their voices raised; she had been brought up to creep noiselessly from room to room while parents slept, not to chatter and laugh in corridors and stairwells. Her only companions previously had been her well-behaved younger sisters and polite adults. The cacophony of girls en masse alarmed her, until she discovered a few nice quiet girls like herself. But it was these quiet girls who revealed the real truth of how babies are made and thereby destroyed, by Angela's own admission, her trust in her parents and stunted her social development in adolescence and young womanhood.

The school got to know of these clandestine conversations and Muriel was summoned. The shame of her mother's wrath and her own horror at the grotesqueness of sexual intercourse meant Angela's reaction to the next incursion of her safe world was even more extreme. Every day on their way to and from school, the sisters would walk along a lane so secluded it seemed almost to be deep country. Just another morning turned into a day that Angela would not be able to recall without shuddering. She noticed a wounded soldier in the lane. The sisters had been taught to think of all soldiers as heroes. Their soldier-uncle Guy had died defending his country, and their young cousins were still fighting the Germans, one already killed before he had grown to be a man. This young soldier before her was not only wounded, and therefore even more heroic in Angela's naïve imagination, but was wearing a uniform of the most beautiful celestial blue. The colour so attracted her that she gazed at the man full of sympathetic feeling.

Then, this embodiment of courage and virtue, exposed himself to the schoolgirls. Angela was shocked and bewildered at the betrayal of his noble appearance and the sight of this terrible dark hidden thing. She was naturally highly strung and quite ignorant of the naked male body and had certainly never seen a man's genitals before. The shock was compounded many times by the fact she had already been sworn to silence over the previous schoolgirl debacle. She had been forbidden by her mother to mention anything about sex to Daphne, who was walking beside her and, lost in her own thoughts, completely oblivious to the situation. Angela could not turn to her, in fact felt a sense of responsibility for her – slightly misplaced in this case as Daphne, more intellectually curious and emotionally detached, would not have been so disturbed by the situation. In fact, Daphne was to be shielded from the facts of life until she was eighteen when, enlightened by a school friend, was astounded: 'What an extraordinary thing for people to want to do!'[1] But twelve-year-old Angela, more confused and distressed, could not even confide in the girls at school as, after the earlier showdown with her mother and Miss Tulloch, the small group of sexual know-alls there had been dispersed and warned not to talk of such things again.

So Angela's shock of discovery combined with disgust and fear was internalised. Years later she insisted there was no exaggeration in her description of the devastating effect these two incidents of sexual revelation and the accompanying secrecy, silence and shame had on her development. She became self-conscious, she said, felt an uneasy burden of taint and alienation, her mind straying to ghastly imaginings when confronted by any recently married woman. Hers was an elephant's memory, she declared, and her scared younger self lived on within her well into adulthood. 'Not for many years did I tell anyone, and for what it's worth not for more years than anyone would believe possible could I bear to think about a man, much less look at one.'[2] Instead, she retreated to the safer alternative of idolising her male cousin Gerald Millar, nine years her senior and already fighting in the Great War (in which he would be awarded the Military Cross). A girl given to serial crushes and longing for affection, Angela inevitably fell in love with the head girl at school but gained emotional satisfaction by imagining marrying her off to Gerald, with nothing more than a chaste kiss between them: 'Love to me meant romantic young soldiers in khaki, Keeping the Home Fires Burning, the Prince of Wales, Handsome Actors, Beautiful Actresses, and falling in love, and no sex in any of it.'[3]

Not surprisingly perhaps, Angela and Daphne's schooling at Miss Tulloch's was soon over. They attended for four terms, punctuated by most of the childhood diseases they had so far evaded. Angela thought they were withdrawn from school once a uniform of neat blue gym tunics was mooted; their parents would rather their girls gave up their education than their pretty print dresses. But a more serious reason occurred to Angela in middle age: their parents, particularly Gerald, were militant about maintaining their daughters' innocence when it came to sex and they feared what the girls might learn 'in giggled whispers from our contemporaries' about 'the wicked World'.[4]

Silence and ignorance were not bliss, as Angela painfully discovered when she and Daphne returned to the routines of nursery life to continue to learn what they could with a nursery maid as teacher. The du Maurier parents did not value academic education for their girls. The maid was already engaged in trying to teach six-year-old Jeanne to read, but luckily both older girls were already keen readers and they absorbed much about history, writing style and romance from the adventures of Alexandre Dumas and Harrison Ainsworth. Angela and Daphne became well informed on the most arcane and melodramatic elements of Louis XIII's France, Guy Fawkes, witches, London's Great Fire and Great Plague, and executions through the ages, but they were not learning much about life in their own rapidly changing century. German Zeppelins overhead occasionally broke the Hampstead calm, sending the family and their servants running for the cellar, shattering Angela's already over-sensitive nerves, but no one really discussed the drama that engulfed them all.

Beyond the graceful façade of Cannon Hall, beyond the garden parties and glittering first nights at Wyndham's with Daddy and Mummy, their supporters and friends, the world of 1917 was convulsed by total war. In England, the movement for female equality and emancipation was gaining support, with women from all walks of life campaigning with ingenuity, determination, violence and occasional hilarity. For the du Maurier girls, growing up surrounded by beautiful actresses and make-believe, it was hard to comprehend that women would rebel against the status quo. More distant still was the thought that women's work could be dirty, gruelling and dangerous – and essential to the nation's efforts, not just in the factories but also at the front line as nurses and ambulance drivers. Mrs Pankhurst had even suggested that women could be trained up as a fighting force, as they were in Russia. She saw women taking their full part in all aspects of war as strengthening her call for women's vote.

Most privileged middle-class girls of the time were shielded from the worst horrors of the war, but for the du Maurier sisters their retreat from school not only limited their contact with the wider world, it also meant their narrow view of what it was to be a woman remained unchallenged. Beauty, fine manners and charm were prerequisites, as demanded by their father and embodied in their mother, regardless of what darkness or mutiny went on beneath the surface. The lack of an independent school life with friends and exposure to different perspectives meant the overwhelming influence on the sisters' thinking and opinions came from their reading, their imaginations and their parents – and the du Maurier parents were more influential and odder than most.

As an Edwardian father, Gerald set the family's ethos and was opinionated and melodramatic in the expression of his views. Fascinating and contradictory, he was terrified of boredom yet easily bored, seeking distraction in other people and gossip. Extravagant in most things and a natural show-off, he was ever fearful of stillness and introspection. He was a physically elegant man, not tall, but slightly built with a large head and raw-boned features in a highly expressive face. Witty, light-hearted and terrific company, Gerald so often played the joker in the pack. Roger Eckersley, the genial Director of Programmes at the BBC, was struck by his subversive energy: 'I have seldom met anyone more bubbling over with the absurdist nonsense than [him].'[5] But Gerald would as easily swing into depression and self-pity when nothing seemed to be right, and he could be as petulant as a spoilt child.

Greatly fond and easy-going with his children, Gerald alternated between laxity and ridiculous strictness. Angela thought him 'a strange father because in a lot of ways he was much more like a brother, but he could be very difficult'.[6] What she found problematic was how, on occasions, he became an emotional bully: possessive and intrusive in their lives, unaware of the pernicious effects of his blundering comments and flippant ridicule. She recalled a story of how her father had often had flaming rows round the dining table with one of his sisters, probably Aunt May, and on one occasion, when she burst into tears, he had shouted after her as she left the room 'that she was "a barren bitch"'.[7] He appeared to get away with this kind of cruelty. Aunt May had indeed wanted children but not managed to have them. Their father George had only gently remonstrated with Gerald over his comment, and then rewarded him with a wink. Evidently, Gerald was still the indulged youngest child. The kindly husband of his humiliated sister could only manage a startled clearing of the throat.

His daughters liked to remember their father more as a Peter Pan than a Captain Hook. He entered their games with gusto, playing cricket on the lawn and teaching Daphne and Jeanne to box by tapping each other on the nose. As an atheist he gave his daughters no formal religious education, but he was however sentimental and superstitious. He did not rate modern art or music, even though Millais and Whistler had been some of his father's closest friends. He hated and feared homosexuality, despite many in his profession and among his friends being quite clearly sexually unconventional.

All these strongly held opinions were absorbed by the sisters. One of the contradictions most difficult for them to integrate into their own social behaviour was exhibited daily by Gerald. He was courteous and charming to a fault to everyone he met, from strangers to his closest associates, but mocked and mimicked them when their backs were turned. One of the most important lessons inculcated into the sisters was the necessity of social grace and politeness at all times. The contradiction of being expected by their father to curtsey sweetly to his friends was hard to reconcile with the encouragement to ridicule them once they had gone. Such double standards were confusing. It was hard for a child to fathom what was real in love and friendship if it all appeared to be a sham.

The mockery was often fond, aimed at his closest friends, and bonded him with his audience of admiring daughters. But it also encouraged a sense of superiority, setting them apart from the mocked, making it difficult to empathise or be intimate with someone reduced to a caricature. The du Maurier family language, wonderfully visual and effective with distinctive words and phrases practised by Gerald and expanded by his children, entertained and strengthened the sense of tribal feeling. It also excluded outsiders and reinforced the family's separateness. The writer Oriel Malet, who became a great friend of Daphne's in her middle age and then of Daphne's daughter Flavia, recalled how the coded language, colourful and intriguing as it was, could make one feel a foreigner among friends.

Daphne in her 1949 novel, *The Parasites*, evoked brilliantly the theatricality of the sisters' childhood that set them apart, describing how disconcerting the fictional Delaney (and du Maurier) children could be:

> [Maria] had the uncanny knack of exaggerating some little fault or idiosyncrasy ... and her unfortunate victim would be aware of this, aware of Maria's large blue eyes that looked so innocent, so full of dreams, and which were in reality pondering diabolical mischief ... [Niall]'s silence was full of meaning. The grown-up individual meeting him for the first time would feel summed-up and judged, and definitely discarded. Glances would pass between Niall and Maria to show that this was so, and later, not even out of earshot, would come the sounds of ridicule and laughter.[8]

Unusual for his generation, Gerald enjoyed his daughters' company and this intimacy meant his influence on their growing minds was all the more powerful and potentially malign. Unusually for any generation, Gerald confided his romantic entanglements with young actresses to Angela and Daphne and made an entertainment of it, inviting them to scoff at the young women's naivety and misplaced hopes, and compromising the sisters' natural loyalty to their mother, who was not included in these confidences. These young actresses were nicknamed 'the stable' by his daughters, who were encouraged to think of them as fillies in a race for the prize of their father's attentions. His daughters 'would jeer, "And what's the form this week? I'm not going to back [Miss X] much longer",[9] and they laughed as their father brilliantly mimicked the voices and mannerisms of the poor deluded girls.

These conversations made them feel uneasy though. Their father was positively Victorian in his attitudes to his own daughters' morals: he was pathologically suspicious of any male with whom they socialised, implying that something dreadful lurked behind the friendly wave or kiss on the cheek, and did not want them to grow up. Angela found his intrusiveness hard to bear. As a young woman returning from a party, she would see him peering from the landing window: '"Who brought you home?" he would say, if the chauffeur had not collected us. "Did he kiss you?" he would ask. Absolutely frightful. He was easily shocked.'[10] He darkly threatened that they would 'lose their bloom', which suggested to them that a young man's kiss somehow tarnished their looks, that the rot would set in, making their corruption visible to all. Angela concluded her father would have been happiest if his daughters had been nuns, with Cannon Hall as the nunnery.

Yet Gerald's own behaviour belonged more to the Restoration age where self-indulgence and the desperate desire for distraction cast constraint to the winds. Angela was confused and scared by her father's sexual hypocrisy. Daphne, wary of adults and suspicious of their motives, perhaps grew even less inclined to look to conventional love and marriage as the path to happiness, with the example of her own adored father before her. In her teenage diary she wrote, 'I suddenly thought how awful just being married would be. I should be so afraid, so terribly afraid, but of what? I don't know.'[11]

Jeanne was still young and protected by her mother's love and less susceptible to her father's charm. She spent much more time with Muriel and was a sweet-natured child who was musical and good at drawing and looked most like her mother. But all the sisters, such close companions in their games and make-believe yet temperamentally so unalike, were bound with family pride and affection. They shared too a taboo on discussing with adults the things that really mattered.

Their father had been spoilt and adored by women all his life, first his mother and elder sisters, now his wife and daughters, and the actresses who depended on him for their careers. A young John Gielgud was struck by Gerald's gift for getting what he needed from others: 'He was a very great director, particularly of women. He was a great fancier of pretty women, and he taught them brilliantly, but very often they were never heard of again.'[12] Taken up and dropped, these young women never ruffled the surface calm of his wife who had become, in effect, a second mother to him. Even Muriel's unmarried sister Billy devoted herself to Gerald in the role of personal secretary and made her life's work his every ease and comfort. Nobody challenged him or called his bluff. He was the grand panjandrum of his universe, but fundamentally weak and dependent on a constant flow of feminine admiration and solicitude. In order to maintain this life-giving stream, he had become adept at making himself as irresistibly charming and seductive as he could. And his daughters were as much ensnared as anyone.

If their mother Muriel had been more of a presence in the older daughters' lives, she might have added a creative counterbalance to Gerald's powerful influence. Strikingly attractive all her life, with fine manners and surface charm, her absorption in Gerald's life and career meant her true character was somehow effaced, leaving just a sense of chilly detachment and inner steel. Only Jeanne received the unconditional love that was left after Gerald's needs and demands had been answered. 'He was her whole life,' Daphne recalled, 'and next to D[addy] came Jeanne, petted and adored though never spoilt, while Angela and I … came off second-best.'[13]

In fact, Angela came off worst of all, as, after Nanny left, she was special to nobody and was hungry for approval and affection. Very early she recognised that in her family she was considered plain and had therefore failed the most important test of womanhood. Her need for notice and love found expression in hero-worshipping men and women alike, so much so that her father teased her mercilessly for her swooning expression. 'Puffin with her swollen look,' he would say in a not entirely affectionate way. It was partly his manner, his need to be funny and make people laugh, but there was also an element in that phrase of exasperation that his eldest daughter was slightly plump, too earnest to be cute, and not the refined beauty she ought to have been.

Daphne was clear-eyed about Gerald's lack of sensitivity to his family, describing how at the theatre he was careful not to hurt anyone's feelings but was 'constantly tactless and continually thoughtless in private life'.[14] From this jest about Angela's looks, reiterated many times, came the family nickname that would accompany her through life, Puffin, Puff, Piffy. She tried to be a good sport and see her father's comment as a trifle, something amusing, but years later was moved to write: 'DON'T always tease your children when they fall in love, it can be dangerous'. Eventually Angela grew resigned to her family's insensitivity, admitting bleakly that by the age of sixteen she knew, 'if one couldn't be the beauty one might as well be the butt'.[15]

For good and ill, Daphne was the daughter most affected by Gerald's peculiarly narcissistic character. She had been chosen as his favourite at a young age perhaps because she was the most beautiful, perhaps the one most closely resembling his longed-for son, perhaps because she reminded him of his father. She alone saw through his charming gay exterior to the uncertain, dark and flawed human being within, and yet still loved him; that might have been the most compelling reason of all. The historian A. L. Rowse, who became a good friend in Daphne's middle age, suspected that her relationship with her father haunted her adult emotional life.[16] What was problematic was not Daphne's love for Gerald so much as his cloying yet controlling need of her.

Her remarkable third novel, *The Progress of Julius*, written when she was only twenty-four, explores a pathological obsession of a father for his daughter. Julius has some of the overbearing yet mercurial qualities that made Gerald irresistible to his daughter. His intensity and high emotionalism (she feared he was always acting and so could never be sure what he really felt) made her own inchoate emotions oscillate between ecstasy and despair. In an extraordinary passage in the novel she conjures up something of this oppressive power that borders on psychological abuse:

[She was] aware of Papa who watched her, Papa who smiled at her, Papa who played her on a thousand strings, she danced to his tune like a doll on wires – Papa who harped at her and would not let her be. He was cruel, he was relentless, he was like some oppressive, suffocating power that stifled her and could not be warded off ... she was like a child stuffed with sweets cloying and rich; they were rammed down her throat and into her belly, filling her, exhausting her, making her a drum of excitement and anguish and emotion that was gripping in its savage intensity. It was too much for her, too strong.[17]

Gerald's adult neediness extended to her was far too weighty for her childlike, uncomprehending heart.

Overarching it all was his manipulative favouritism that tainted all other relationships within the family. The close emotional connection that grew between them disturbed Daphne and inevitably unsettled her mother. Musing on why there was such a mutual wariness between her and Muriel, Daphne wondered, 'could it be that, totally unconscious of the fact, she resented the ever-growing bond and affection between D and myself?'[18] Again in *Julius*, she explores this tragic transference to melodramatic effect. Not only did the intense Electral bond between Daphne and her father distress her mother, it inevitably unbalanced the family dynamic between the sisters.

It was Angela who felt most acutely the lack of admiration: the spotlight that might have fallen on her for a while, as the eldest, always seemed to swerve off towards Daphne. It was not her younger sister's fault, Daphne did not seek it and in fact the limelight made her uneasy, but her beauty and detachment seemed to draw people's attention in a way that Angela's expressive eagerness to please did not.

The huge painting of the three sisters, executed in 1918 by the society artist Frederic Whiting, and exhibited to acclaim, epitomised the shift in power between the sisters. Angela was fourteen and feeling her way tentatively towards a sense of herself in the world. Much as she had feared growing up, she was beginning to see there were some advantages. This painting captured her on the cusp of womanhood but reduced to a rather big child. She hated the pose she was expected to hold, unflatteringly dressed in baggy clothes, sitting uncomfortably with her rump to the viewer and all her weight on one hand. She resented how she was encumbered for all time with a shiny red nose, quite possibly the result of the crying fit when she had been told that she would have to spend the whole Sunday posing in Whiting's studio. The unfairness of this representation of her she felt was made more stark by the way Daphne was portrayed. Placed apart from the undistinguished bundle of Jeanne and Angela and Brutus the dog, she stood as straight and noble as an arrow with a visionary spark in her eyes. Every time she saw the painting Angela was reminded of this memorial to her eclipse. 'I realised I should be handed down to posterity with a flaming shining nose, and Daphne looking rather like a flaming shining Jeanne d'Arc.'[19]

At about the time this group portrait was painted, Angela was 'suicidally inclined for Love' and her gaze fell on a young soldier who put up with her devotion, mailing her a box of chocolates from Paris that filled her with excitement. To Angela's overactive imagination he was, 'Apollo, Mars, God, Romance, IT'. On the one occasion she got to accompany him, Muriel insisted Daphne should go too. Their destination was the Military Tournament at Olympia in West London. In a fever of anticipation Angela carefully chose something grown-up to wear, a pretty pink dress with a lowish neckline, but her mother immediately ordered her upstairs to change into a frock that matched the one Daphne was wearing. Her sister was still as slim as a sapling, and Angela felt humiliated, stuffed into the childish mauve dress that did not suit her, the linen too tight across the bust. Tears of frustration and disappointment welled in her eyes. 'Daphne looked a dream as always, and by the time my swain had called to take us to Olympia I was red-nosed with heat, discomfort, mortification and a fit of the sulks.'[20]

This god-like being was a young cadet who was training alongside her father. In what appeared to be an odd caprice, with more than an element of despair to it, Gerald had decided in the last year of the Great War to enlist in the Irish Guards. His restlessness and growing sense of futility, together with the long shadow of his hero-brother Guy, made him long to prove he was more than just the ephemeral entertainer. He was forty-five and had lived the last two decades of his life as a successful, pampered thespian, chauffeured around, clad in the most luxurious clothes and fed on the best foods and wine. Daphne understood his despair. 'He was nothing but a mummer, a trickster, playing antics in some disguise before a crowd. All he had won was a cheap popularity, and what good was that to him or the world?'[21] He had just pulled off one of his greatest theatrical successes, a new production of J. M. Barrie's play *Dear Brutus*, where night after night he received the audience's ovations. The play's conceit – whether, if we could return to something deeply regretted in our past and choose a different path, it would change anything – suffused his thinking, for he always lived his character for the duration of a play. Would life have been more satisfactory if he had taken the more difficult road?

There was a kind of bathetic heroism in Gerald's turning his back on his glittering London life to go to training barracks in Bushey, where even the officers bawling at him were young enough to be his sons. Never the most physically or mentally robust of men, he had to submit to the gruelling training and spartan conditions alongside boys who were straight out of school. Removed from home comforts and denied the reassuring balm of his wife's and friends' concern, he had only the rough camaraderie of men to sustain him. Muriel moved the whole household to Bushey to be close to him. Angela explained her mother's blinkered focus on Gerald:

> My mother, for whom wars only meant parting *her* from her family
> (me at my school in Wimbledon, and now my father) one day met the
> famous actress and beauty Lily Elsie in Piccadilly and burst into tears
> with the remark, 'Poor Gerald has gone to Bushey.' Elsie's husband was
> in the thick of the fighting but she was sympathetically full of horror
> for poor Gerald's plight.[22]

Although Muriel had done her best to remain close to him, Gerald could only escape infrequently to eat big teas surrounded once again by his womenfolk. Angela remembered how his face had 'an abject *hungry* misery'.[23] It was a nightmare from which he was luckily awoken by the Armistice. He could return home having not encountered any of the fighting, but perhaps feeling some kind of personal honour had been satisfied. The play he had left behind centred on two unhappy people, mired in misery, being given a second chance of a life different from the one each had chosen, but realising it was better to just get on and live. Perhaps Gerald returned to his life in the theatre relieved at the choices he had made, and ready for the next project.

1918 was also the year when the girls' patchy education was taken in hand by a dynamic new force. Miss Maud Waddell came into their lives to tutor them in every subject, although history was the universal favourite. Miss Waddell was quickly nicknamed Tod, as a partial rhyme on her surname, or a nod to Beatrix Potter's Mr Tod, a wily, tweed-jacketed fox. Born in 1887, she was ten years younger than their mother and a completely different kind of woman. Miss Waddell was well educated, adventurous and independent minded, with a wealth of exotic stories of her past to tell. Before she ended up in Hampstead she had already tutored the grandson of Belgium's Minister for Finance. She had enjoyed living with the family in the beautiful Château de la Fraineuse at Spa, inspired by Marie Antoinette's Petit Trianon at Versailles. The Kaiser then had appropriated it and had a bedroom for himself redecorated in pink silk.

Tod became important to all the du Maurier girls, but particularly to eleven-year-old Daphne. She quickly recognised her as someone in whom she could trust and confide, a woman who filled part of the vacuum left by her mother's emotional absence, but also a woman who responded to her intellectual curiosity and creative mind. Daphne liked to think of Tod as one of her heroines, Queen Elizabeth I. In an early letter she wrote to her:

> Divine Gloriana,
>   Why look so coldly on your slave who adores you? Have you no commpasion on the billets written with the blood of my heart (jolly good).[24]

Tod responded to this clever, imaginative child (so ill-schooled that her spelling and wayward punctuation kept Tod awake at night) and understood the yearning in Daphne for something beyond the ordinary: 'That something that is somewhere, you know; you feel it and you miss it, and it beckons to you and you cant reach it. It is'nt Love I'm sure … I don't think anyone can find it on this earth.' This longing for the unattainable owed something perhaps to Barrie's Neverland that entranced the sisters' childhoods. Daphne told Tod she was the only person to whom she could express her confused feelings, having been silenced on the things that mattered most to her by her family's mockery and lack of understanding. Although Angela, and occasionally Jeanne, wrote to Tod also, the only letters the governess kept were those written by Daphne, in what became a lifelong correspondence full of frankness and humour. Tod later told a reporter on the Australian *Argus* that Daphne was 'the most beautiful human being I have ever seen'.[25] An intelligent, feeling woman who never married, Tod was to love her all her life.

Angela had endured one last experiment with formal schooling that had failed dismally. Gerald had accompanied his nephew Michael Llewelyn Davies to visit a friend of his, Eiluned Lewis, at Levana School in Wimbledon. Eiluned was a clever girl, four years older than Angela, who became a successful journalist, novelist and poet. Whether Gerald was impressed by her or the school, he determined to send Angela to the school as a boarder. Angela was fourteen and although she made some friends she was so desperately homesick she only lasted half a term, and was soon back at Cannon Hall. Tod then became responsible for educating all three girls.

Although she would remain committed to the du Mauriers, Miss Waddell for a while had other adventures to pursue. Soon after her stint tutoring the sisters she headed off in 1923 to Constantinople to teach the Sultan's son English. This was a fascinating time for an Englishwoman in Turkey, just after the last of the Allied troops had left Constantinople, having been in occupation since the end of the First World War. Tod lived in the magnificent Dolmabahçe Palace in great splendour but did not think much of the Turks themselves. 'What an unprogressive, aggravating people they are,' she told the same Australian reporter. She thought them a nation lost in passive contemplation and her no-nonsense Cumbrian self wanted to pinch them awake from their reveries.[26] Maud Waddell then sailed for Australia in 1926, where her brilliant mathematician sister Winnie had emigrated, eventually rewarded with an MBE for her pioneering work establishing wild flower sanctuaries. For a while Maud thought she might stay, teaching in the Outback, but finding it 'too rough and windy'[27] returned to England. There, after more, but less exciting, adventures, she eventually ended up tutoring Daphne's children in Cornwall at Menabilly.

The du Maurier family's move to Hampstead had been an emotional return for Gerald to the place of his childhood where he had been happiest. Restless and increasingly dissatisfied with his working life, and missing the close bond with parents and sisters, for all except May were now dead, he began to revisit the past, recalling his youth with fond nostalgia. He had always idealised his father George and the bohemian life he lived with family and artist friends, but now that he had returned to his father's old stamping grounds the obsession with him grew. He shared his romantic reminiscences with his daughters, taking them to gaze at the old family home, New Grove House, where he had hoped to live with his own family but had had to settle for Cannon Hall instead. He would point out the studio window at which his father had once worked and then walk them up to Hampstead Heath to a twisted branch where he sat as a boy, imagining it was his armchair. The girls would climb in too, and think of their father as a boy. Then up the hill to Whitestone Pond where George du Maurier, weak-sighted and kind-hearted, had noticed a dog splashing about and plunged in, intent on rescue. But the dog was swimming not drowning. The girls then learnt how the great man, dripping wet and slightly foolish, was tipped by the dog's owner for his trouble.

As Gerald walked them through his romance of boyhood, his daughters grew more interested in the grandfather they had never known and who, in dying before Angela was born, had been ignorant even of their existence. They had seen the leather-bound copies of *Punch*, with George's elegant witty drawings, and had not thought much about the artist who had made them; but through their father's memories they began to discover a man who was important in their own stories, whose life belonged with theirs. His novels exerted the greatest imaginative pull, most importantly *Peter Ibbetson*, with its compelling central theme that people can exist in a world they had purposefully dreamed. They could meet others there, possessed also of the gift for 'dreaming true' that joined them in this extra dimension, brought into being through will and emotion. The love story between Peter and his childhood sweetheart, the Duchess of Towers, conducted in this dreamscape, freed from conventional restraints of time and space, fuelled the imaginations of his two elder granddaughters. It was a powerful idea that offered whatever the dreamer most desired: escape and adventure for Daphne; love and romance for Angela.

At about the age of thirteen Daphne's desire for escape from impending womanhood, and all the attendant embarrassments and constraints, caused her to dream up a boyish alter ego: Eric Avon. In real life she had been taken aside by Muriel and warned of the advent of menstruation, a rubicon that would unite her to her mother and the female half of experience and separate her, it seemed, from everything she valued and held dear. Nothing was explained to the horrified and bemused girl, only that she would bleed, and with it came confusing intimations of illness, incapacity, secrecy and shame. Just as Angela had been forbidden to mention the facts of life to her friends or younger sisters, so Daphne too was told not to discuss with anyone this looming threat to her freedom and integrity.

Eric Avon sprang to her aid. He was the imaginary personification of the boy she should have been, the embodiment of uncomplicated male energy, the son for whom her father had longed. He was sporty and brave, captain of cricket at Rugby School, and his day of glory came each year at the imaginary cricket match between Rugby and Marlborough School, played out in the garden at Cannon Hall. Jeanne and her friend Nan were drawn into this fantasy. Renamed David and Dick, the Dampier brothers, they bowled and batted for Marlborough, the opposing team, and invariably lost to the one-man sporting hero, Daphne in her role as Eric Avon. Angela and Tod were roped in as spectators to clap politely from the sidelines.

Daphne inhabited the persona of Eric Avon for more than two years. Only once she had turned fifteen (and Eric turned eighteen) did she have him play his last triumphant cricket match, for he would have to leave Rugby for Cambridge University the following autumn. Daphne walked into the lower part of the garden at Cannon Hall, scene of so many of Eric's triumphs. 'He wept. The moment of sadness was intolerable. Then someone from the house called "Daphne!" and it was all over. Eric Avon had left Rugby School for ever.'[28] This had so much of the emotional force of *Peter Pan*, where Peter angrily repels any suggestion he might grow up and become human, the whole play suffused with sadness at what is lost when childhood is left behind.

Years later, Daphne recognised that Eric Avon became submerged in her subconscious and never really left her, emerging in various guises as her inadequate male protagonists in *I'll Never Be Young Again*, *My Cousin Rachel*, *The Scapegoat*, *The Flight of the Falcon*, and *The House on the Strand*. Although they were weak while Eric, like Daphne herself and many of her fictional heroines, were resolute and self-sufficient, these men relied on strong male mentors, perhaps echoing something of her father's relationship with Tom Vaughan, his supremely capable and efficient business partner, or with his competent and heroic elder brother. Tom Vaughan was a remarkably successful man and central to the functioning of the du Maurier household. He managed Wyndham's Theatre with great creative and professional acumen, and fixed all the family's financial and practical problems too. Angela appreciated how crucial he was to everything. 'That the du Mauriers could get on without Tom Vaughan seemed an impossibility. Alas, when he died it became all too evident that life without him was a sadly complicated affair.'[29]

The intolerable sadness felt by Daphne/Eric in the garden the day of the last cricket match was the realisation that she could not remain this boyish child for ever. At fifteen she was aware of Angela on the verge of 'coming out' and having to enter the dreaded social whirl. The expectations of family and society would hedge Daphne in too. Perhaps the prospect of her growing up caused her father unease as well for, about the time that puberty and Eric Avon arrived in her life, he wrote Daphne a remarkable poem, celebrating her as the Eternal Girl, yet recognising her own, and his, disappointment that she was not that longed-for boy:

> My very slender one
> So brave of heart, but delicate of will,
> So careful not to wound, never kill,
> My tender one –
> Who seems to live in Kingdoms all her own
> In realms of joy
> Where heroes young and old

In climates hot and cold
Do deeds of daring and much fame
And she knows she could do the same
If only she'd been born a boy.
And sometimes in the silence of the night
I wake and think perhaps my darling's right
And that she should have been,
And, if I'd had my way,
She would have been, a boy.

My very slender one
So feminine and fair, so fresh and sweet,
So full of fun and womanly deceit.
My tender one
Who seems to dream her life away alone.
A dainty girl
But always well attired
And loves to be admired
Where ever she may be, and wants
To be the being who enchants
Because she has been born a girl.
And sometimes in the turmoil of the day
I pause, and think my darling may
Be one of those who will
For good or ill
Remain a girl for ever and be still
A Girl.

This was a poem full of complex meaning when written by an adored and influential father for his favourite daughter. Daphne stood on the threshold of adulthood, confused by her identity and struggling to find a sense of herself in the world. Gerald's elegiac words could only compound that confusion. He regretted the son that might have been, and celebrated the lovely daughter whose gender made her second best. But she was lovely only as long as she remained a girl and managed somehow not to grow to womanhood. Becoming a woman meant losing so much of value: joy in action, beauty of form, simplicity, freedom, integrity of the self.

At a time when women had been risking their lives in wars abroad, and at home taken on the Establishment and won the first concessions in their battle for the vote, Gerald's view of the roles of men and women was old-fashioned and stultifying. In the poem Daphne as a boy is full of action, a hero figure, 'brave of heart' and spurred to 'deeds of daring and much fame'. On the other hand, her place in the world as a girl is passive, her looks and the effects she has on others paramount – 'so fresh and sweet', prone to 'womanly deceit', 'dainty' and 'well attired'. Muriel was the role model for this kind of woman, and Daphne did not want to be like her at all.

Daphne and Jeanne were happiest in boy's shorts, thick socks and stout shoes. They did not care about their hair or the grime on their faces. Daphne hated her white knees after a winter of being covered up and would rub dirt into them each spring to reclaim her tomboy self. Their prettiness belied the masculine characters that swaggered in their imaginations and peopled their games. The stereotypical sporting hero Eric Avon was not based on the kind of men who loomed largest in their lives like their father and the romanticised view of their grandfather. These immensely successful men were artists and darlings of the drawing room, not men made on the sports field or battleground. In fact, George in later life had lost much of his sight and was in thrall to his womenfolk, and Gerald's love of gossip about friends' private lives, tireless practical joking, and enjoyment of the company of women made him an exceptional entertainer with an effete and dandified air, rather than an all-conquering hero. His propensity to go to pieces if separated for too long from Muriel also disqualified him from the square-jawed masculine ideal. In the du Maurier household, where the women were capable and robust and the men were pampered and indulged, sexual stereotypes were not the norm.

Unlike her sisters, Angela did not want to be a boy. She was happy enough to be a girl even though she bitterly regretted she was not beautiful and therefore felt handicapped in the great marriage game that her family considered a woman's natural destiny. She too was afraid of growing up, but it was her emotionalism that bothered her, the embarrassment of her crushes and the torrent of feeling that they unleashed. The young Angela was sensitive and serious and hated being teased, the default position in her family. She was also ignorant and afraid of the sexual male, that scary other that had grown sinister in her imagination as a result of early shocks and her inadequate education:

> The business of growing older, into 'double figures', I disliked. I was unhappy when I was told I was too old to wear my nice white socks in the summertime, and made to wear horrible brown stockings … one was a fish out of water, too young to listen to sophisticated conversation, at the same time not wishing to play cricket on the lawn with younger sisters and their friends … pulled both ways, misunderstood at times by young and old alike, and not always understanding oneself.[30]

Angela's literalness of mind and the inadvertent hurt caused by adults who did not understand was illustrated by an unhappy infatuation she never forgot. At weekends, Cannon Hall was filled with various stage people: one Sunday, even Rudolph Valentino came to lunch, to general excitement, as too did Gary Cooper, the embodiment of Hollywood star power. There were the long-established acting friends like Gladys Cooper, Viola Tree and John Barrymore, and any number of glamorous others who passed through their lives. But in 1919, when Angela was fifteen, she was taken by her parents to see a magnificent production of Rostand's *Cyrano de Bergerac*. Robert Loraine – 'Bobby' to them all – was playing the title role. From then on Angela was smitten. Only three years younger than Gerald du Maurier, he was an actor-manager like him and the theatre he successfully managed was the Criterion. A fine actor, he was usually cast as the romantic lead, and even went on to tackle Shakespeare. But he was much more than this, a true heroic figure. A pioneering aviator, he had only just survived as a flying ace in the Great War and been decorated for his bravery with an MC and DSO. Angela had a photograph of him in his Royal Flying Corps uniform and she kissed it every night, along with her picture of the Prince of Wales.

Bobby had a mellifluous voice and it amused him to spout the most rousing bits of Shakespeare under Angela's bedroom window at night. Inevitably, Angela, by now sixteen, began to dream of marrying him. The age gap seemed no barrier: perhaps the fact that he was her father's generation was a reassurance to her. Then with the thoughtlessness of adulthood, Bobby hijacked her fantasy by casually saying to Gerald at one of their family Sunday lunches at Cannon Hall, 'the day will come I expect when I shall ask you for Angela's hand'. Given her youth, innocence and supercharged romantic nature, it was not unreasonable of her to imagine the deed was done and she would be the next Mrs Robert Loraine, with accompanying beautiful house, enchanting children, dogs, the whole caboodle. (She admitted she daydreamed about weddings and babies' names, without sex coming into any of this at all.) But Angela had misunderstood Bobby's manly banter with her father, and he had misunderstood how serious she was and how tender her heart. 'The day never came, and he suddenly appeared with an exquisite wife very little older than me (which made one's frustrated misery more acute).'[31] It may have been on this occasion that Angela, in the depths of despair and with pure melodrama running in her veins, had jumped up onto a wall running along the Embankment, declaring she would cast herself into the Thames. Luckily she was with the imperturbable Tod who replied, 'Not now, dear, it's teatime.'[32]

The sisters, unable to confide in their parents, turned to each other. Daphne, struggling with deeper existential questions, turned to Tod. Their exasperated mother would complain that she could never get one sister to side with her against another as they always stood up for each other. Angela was incapable of keeping her tumultuous emotions to herself and so Daphne, already a confidante, was party to all her upset and disappointment. Daphne at thirteen had just sought refuge from the adult world in the creation of her boy-self Eric; no wonder that she retreated further when she observed the incomprehensible behaviour towards women of even the nicest men. Her body may have betrayed her by beginning to turn her into a woman, but her diary for that year was still childlike, full of cricket matches and the birthday party she gave for her teddy bear. Jeanne at nine, the favoured companion of their mother, was very much the baby and sheltered from even this incursion of the adult world.

The following summer Angela would see her longing for love thwarted at every turn while her younger sister, without seeking it, once again became effortlessly the centre of admiration and, this time, of male desire. In the middle of the family seaside holiday, fourteen-year-old Daphne glanced up from paddling and shrimping to find her much older cousin, Geoffrey, looking at her with a strange smile. Something about the smile caught the girl's attention and made her heart beat faster. She had never felt this way before. She smiled back. She knew nothing of the facts of life and was completely uninterested in the mechanics of sex and would remain so, she recalled, until she was eighteen. But in that one moment, Daphne's innocent world of cricket and reading and making up stories was intruded on by a grown-up male old enough to be her father.

It was 1921 and the du Mauriers had rented a house in Thurlestone in south Devon, and as usual other guests had been asked to join them. Cousin Geoffrey, the elder brother of Gerald Millar, who had so appealed to Angela when she was younger, was divorced from his first wife. This had caused a scandal amongst the aunts and uncles who considered divorce something that should never happen in a family like theirs; 'one might have thought a national calamity was about to occur'.[33] This raffishly good-looking thirty-six-year-old actor had subsequently remarried and had brought his second wife with him on this visit to his cousins. But his roving eye had been caught by the attractive sight of his young cousin paddling in the sea, still so obviously just a pretty child but on the threshold of sexual awakening, and he smiled.

Daphne never forgot the peculiar excitement caused by that secret smile. She could not understand it but liked the physical sensation and the sense that she was special and there was a precious understanding between them. When all the children were sunbathing on the lawn, with rugs over their knees, Geoffrey came and lay beside her and under the blanket reached for her hand. The effect on her was electrifying and unsettling; something dormant was awoken in her. 'No kisses. No hint of the sexual impulse he undoubtedly felt and indeed admitted … but instead, on my part at least, a reaching out for a relationship that was curiously akin to what I felt for D[addy].' Daphne found this frisson with Geoffrey even more exciting because it was wrong and especially because it was secret, hidden from her pathologically possessive and suspicious father and right under the nose of Geoffrey's unsuspecting wife. 'Nothing, in a life of seventy years, has ever surpassed that first awakening of an instinct within myself. The touch of that hand on mine. And the instinctive knowledge that nobody must know.'[34]

Geoffrey's behaviour could be seen as a subtle seduction by a much older, worldly-wise man of a vulnerable cousin, still a child who should have been safe in his company. In a classic ploy of the seducer, he told her he had already grown disenchanted with his new wife and now, because of his feelings for Daphne, no longer wished to go on tour to America at the end of the year. There was little doubt that the whole flirtation that summer was a deliberate manipulation of a young girl's emotions to gratify his egotistical needs. The loading of responsibility for his dubious behaviour on her child's shoulders was cowardly, and distorted her sense of power and integrity. The intrusion of a confusing adult world into her child's one, lived largely in the imagination, certainly unsettled Daphne and absorbed much of her thoughts for the rest of the year, uniting her to him in an indissoluble bond of rebellious conspiracy that was to last a lifetime. Daphne loved to think of herself as daring and she also enjoyed a growing sense of the power she had over others. Neither was she averse to causing her father anxiety and jealousy – it all reinforced her central importance in his life.

Her recognition of the similarity of the feelings she felt for Geoffrey and those for her own father informs one of the enduring themes of her fiction: that of incest and taboo. But for Daphne, always living more vividly in the mind than the body, the idea of incest would come to exert an intellectual fascination that grew, she explained, from her realisation that we are attracted to people who are familiar to us, that family provide the real romance of life.

Years after the encounter in south Devon, when she was twenty-one and her obsession with Geoffrey had cooled to an amused flirtatious affection – although he remained as smitten with her as ever – she had fun teasing him by meeting him in the drawing room at Cannon Hall to say goodnight, dressed only in her pyjamas. With her parents in bed on the floor above, she allowed him passionately to kiss her for the first – and last – time. Having not been kissed by a man before, apart from her father, she found it 'nice and pleasant', but, with a startling lack of understanding of human sexuality and empathy for the feelings of another, wished Geoffrey could be more light-hearted. He had finally managed some intimacy after years of secretive smiling, furtive knee-stroking and hand-holding, with the object of his forbidden desire prancing about in her pyjamas, at night, and she complained he was rather overexcited.

'Men are so odd,' she wrote in her diary, 'it would be awful if he got properly keyed-up.'[35] Daphne added another peculiarly detached statement: 'He is very sweet and lovable. The strange thing is [kissing Geoffrey] is so like kissing D[addy],' and went on to surmise that perhaps their family was like the incestuous Borgias, with her as the fatally attractive Lucretia. But then this was a girl who liked to shock and given how underwhelmed she was by Geoffrey's kisses, likening them to Daddy's did not suggest unbridled fatherly or daughterly passion. Any incestuous impulse between father and daughter was more likely to reside in his overbearing emotional demands on her and her answering fascination with him, united with resentment and excitement at how important she was to him. The growing realisation of her power over others through her attractiveness and detachment was thrilling.

While Daphne, only just into her teens, was quickening their cousin's pulse simply by being there, Angela recalled yet another example of her own lack of beauty and physical presence. She was seventeen when she accompanied her ten-year-old sister Jeanne to a children's party in a grand house in London. Dressed in a sober blue coat and skirt, and feeling rather overweight and shy, she was mistaken by the butler for a children's nurse and shepherded in with the other visiting servants. But 'the nurses were far too high and mighty to bother with me',[36] and, although short and appearing younger than her age, Angela was not about to become one of the children for the afternoon, so she sat in lonely exile for hours until the party was over and she could escort Jeanne home. She made a joke of it, but these humiliations and unflattering comparisons undermined the self-esteem of a young woman who already felt inadequate and in some fundamental way unworthy of love.

The summer of 1921 was clouded for the family by another tragedy that befell their ill-fated Llewelyn Davies cousins. The eldest of them, George, taken into the care of Uncle Jim Barrie after he was orphaned, had been killed in the war. Michael, the fourth brother, and the main inspiration for Barrie's *Peter Pan*, was now twenty-one and a sensitive poetic young man, a troubled undergraduate at Oxford University. On a perfectly fine and warm afternoon in May, he and his best friend Rupert Buxton drowned together in a still bathing pool in the countryside just outside Oxford. They appeared to have died in each other's arms, in what may have been a double suicide, but no one could be sure. Saving the families' feelings was paramount, and the coroner declared a verdict of accidental death. But this did not soften the blow of two immensely promising young men dying in mysterious and harrowing circumstances. There is no mention as to how the du Maurier sisters took the news except for Daphne who recorded it in her diary ('how dreadful') along with the information that their youngest Llewelyn Davies cousin Nico came to stay before the funeral.

Contrary to some suggestions that J. M. Barrie not only ruined the boys' lives but also had some malign hold over Daphne's, it was noticeable that in her early diaries, when his influence was meant to have been intense, his name did not once appear. In fact the du Maurier sisters seem not to have seen very much of him or the Llewelyn Davies cousins either, once the boys' mother had died. When Peter, the third eldest brother, came to lunch at Cannon Hall in 1925, Daphne wrote in her diary that she had not seen him for years. Barrie's creation, Peter Pan, however, continued to hold a magnetic attraction for them all.

* * *

Holidays apart, life continued at Cannon Hall with lessons during the week, wild games for Daphne and Jeanne in the garden, and paper-chases on the heath – with Daphne as the paper-scattering hare. The glamorous friends of their parents filled the house at weekends, when the du Maurier girls were expected to practise their social skills and be attendant maidens and entertainers. Both Angela and Jeanne were musical, a gift that could be traced back to the du Maurier ancestors where grandfather George and his father were known for their beautiful tenor voices which would bring an audience to tears. All three girls learned to play the piano – as well-brought-up girls did – but only Angela and Jeanne persevered into adulthood. Jeanne was particularly talented and continued to play all her life. In the du Maurier household, playing the piano was not allowed to be a private pleasure. Muriel insisted the girls play for her friends after lunch, and she refused to let them use sheet music, it all had to be from memory. This became a misery particularly for Angela who had to stumble through some standby like the *Moonlight Sonata* in front of a long-suffering audience, accompanied by her mother's audible intakes of breath at every wrong note, of which there were many.

She much preferred practising with their enthusiastic music mistress, who would come to the house and inspire Angela and Jeanne to play exciting duets, the *Ride of the Valkyries* being one memorable favourite. In fact her visits sparked both girls' love of music. Angela's love of opera and of Wagner began with these lessons.

At sixteen, Angela had a good singing voice and dreamed of being an operatic diva. She had no ambitions to be an actress but longed to sing, and as nothing but the most romantic roles attracted her, she wanted to be a soprano. This proved to be difficult as she was naturally a good contralto, but Daddy was paying, so a succession of well-regarded singing teachers attempted to turn her into a less good mezzo-soprano and finally into a reedy excuse for a soprano. 'My future at Covent Garden was soon doomed to a still-birth.'[37] This frustration of a musical career was a lasting regret to her but her love of music was to last a lifetime. Ballet too was a lasting pleasure, introduced to her when she was fifteen by one of the most beautiful women in England, Lady Diana Cooper, or Lady Diana Manners as she was then, who whisked her off to the Diaghilev season at the Alhambra, a spectacular Moorish-inspired theatre dominating the east side of Leicester Square. 'I was her slave for life,'[38] was Angela's characteristically effusive reaction to this thrilling experience.

By 1921, Jeanne was becoming more than just her mother's pet and Daphne's willing sidekick in her make-believe worlds. She was not only developing into a talented artist and pianist, she was also growing surprisingly good at tennis, and would soon be entering tournaments. Photographs showed this pretty girl growing into a sturdy, strong-limbed youngster whom Daphne nicknamed 'The Madam'. She wrote to Tod that Jeanne had grown upwards and outwards: 'her legs resemble what a stout Glaxo baby may eventually grow into, and she will probably be ten feet each way! Her taste in literature takes after Angela, she has just finished "The Great Husband Hunt"!* which she gloated over.'[39] Jeanne retained for many years the alternative identity of David Dampier, schoolboy sports star, given to her by Daphne. Many years later her partner in life, Noël Welch, who knew all three grown-up sisters very well, commented that Jeanne, 'the youngest, would have made the best boy … She has never got over not being able to lower a telescope from her eye with a suitably dramatic or casual remark, her feet apart, her square shoulders, so elegant on a horse, braced against the wind.'[40]

In another letter, Daphne wished she could be as placid and happy as her youngest sister and was disconcerted that she felt bored with life before it had even begun. She was already writing a book about a boy called Maurice who suffered from her own sense of dislocation from humanity and who identifies with the freedom of the natural world, for trees and water and sky. The whole story is imbued with a Peter Pan-like longing for something unattainable. Even the father figure whom Maurice finds to console his widowed mother is an amalgamation of her own father and Barrie, a man who had never grown up.

---

* A popular novel written by Mabel Barnes-Grundy, published in 1922.

After four years of tutoring the du Maurier sisters, Tod had left for Constantinople at the end of 1922. In her reluctant progress to adulthood, Daphne especially missed her sympathetic and practical approach to life. Miss Vigo had replaced her and although she lacked Tod's personality she was a good teacher, encouraging Angela and Daphne's writing efforts and Jeanne's drawing. Ever inventive, Daphne, as a Christmas present for Angela, created a magazine where all the stories, news, gossip, poems and articles were as if written by 'Dogs of Our Acquaintance'. Angela remembered it all her life as a brilliant piece of work that anyone who loved dogs, and was prone to give them individual characters and voices, would appreciate. The girls were not educated in science and barely any mathematics, but their French was passable. They were keen readers, could play the piano, and knew how to behave in polite society; like well-bred girls of their time and class they were being schooled to become good wives to well-bred men who were wealthy enough to keep them in style. Their lives would be determined and their horizons described by the men whom they married. But little did their parents know that an inchoate rebellion was already stirring in their breasts for there was not much about a woman's life in the first decades of the twentieth century to commend itself to them. Each sister would take her destiny in her own hands: none would become the exemplary wife that their mother had so gracefully embodied.

3

The Dancing Years

I suppose we all led pretty empty lives of enjoyment, with snatches
of good works to salve our consciences … I was amazed and fascinated by the days I'd led, hardly even a meal at home or an evening
in, parties, parties, parties – always falling in love with this or that
Tom, Dick and Harry.

ANGELA DU MAURIER, *Old Maids Remember*

THE DU MAURIER sisters grew up with the century. They were in
their teens and early twenties during the 1920s when much of the
nation entered a delayed adolescence. It was an era that became
known as the Jazz Age, when this new music provided the soundtrack,
its syncopated beat the tempo that sped the young from party to party
on a febrile flight to nowhere in particular. Dancing became all the
rage; dancefloors were rapidly laid in smart restaurants – the du
Maurier family's favourite, the Savoy, being the first to lead the way.
The waltz and the foxtrot were replaced by the highly energetic
Charleston and Black Bottom, an import from African-American
culture and based on an earlier pimp's dance, all of which brought to
its English adherents a sense of their own exotic naughtiness.

All this was a stark reaction to the general mood of the country.
Having emerged from the Great War, Britain was stunned by grief,
exhausted, broken-hearted and spiritually crushed by the scale and
brutality of the slaughter of its young. More than three quarters of a

million men, many straight from working the fields or not long out of school, had died. The sense of loss seemed almost insurmountable. Even the inspired idea of honouring all these dead by interring, with the greatest ceremony, the body of an unknown warrior in Westminster Abbey in November 1920, could not staunch the mourning for what became known as the Lost Generation. The ramifications were far-reaching: emotional, economic, political and personal. In the 1921 census it was revealed that there were nearly two million more women than men. Few families escaped unscathed.

Society was changed for ever, most notably perhaps the place of women, now that married women over thirty (and those on the Local Government Register) had gained the vote at the end of the war and Nancy Astor took her seat in Parliament in 1919 as the first woman MP. As the nation slowly began to rebuild, the wartime Prime Minister Lloyd George famously declared in a postwar electioneering speech that he wanted a land fit for heroes: some kind of hope for a new future began to bubble through the daily drabness. A group of well-off, aristocratic or otherwise well-connected young people reacted against the general mood of deprivation and worthy social responsibility and decided to throw a non-stop party.

It was largely a privileged and metropolitan phenomenon. Young men and women came together for extravagant fancy dress balls, 'stunt parties', elaborate practical jokes and outrageous treasure hunts with flashy cars driven at breakneck speed through the midnight streets of London, their exquisite occupants seeking nonsensical clues and odd objects of desire. Everything was screamingly funny or pointlessly naughty. The heroes of the hour were not Lloyd George's magnificent young servicemen, who had given their lives for their country's freedoms, but epicene youths, posing as maharajas or fairies, drawling their witticisms to a beautifully dressed crowd of braying young. Closely shingled girls in diaphanous, jewelled dresses joined in the fun, pursuing policemen's helmets or some other trophy, before speeding away to breakfast on quails' eggs and caviar, champagne and cake.

This was a highly visible group that intersected with the du Mauriers' theatrical milieu, with Angela on the verge of being carefully launched on a world that seemed half-crazy. One of the revellers, and barely a year older than Angela, was Evelyn Waugh. He famously satirised this period of relentless futility and emotional dead-ends in his novel *Vile Bodies*:

> Masked parties, Savage parties, Victorian parties, Greek parties, Wild West parties, Russian parties, Circus parties, parties where one had to dress as somebody else, almost naked parties in St John's Wood, parties in flats and studios and houses and ships and hotels and night clubs, in windmills and swimming-baths, tea parties at school where one ate muffins and meringues and tinned crab, parties at Oxford where one drank brown sherry and smoked Turkish cigarettes, dull dances in London and comic dances in Scotland and disgusting dances in Paris – all that succession and repetition of massed humanity ... Those vile bodies ...[1]

The popular press was also hungry for distraction and avidly followed the antics of this gilded youth, reporting in middle-class papers such as the *Daily Mail* and *Evening Standard* activities that made Bertie Wooster and the Drones look positively intellectual and patrician. Journalists coined a term for this group of gorgeous wastrels: they were the Bright Young Things, and by breathlessly recording every move in their newspapers, from the scandalous to the banal, they initiated modern celebrity culture. The Bright Young Things were delighted with this newfound fame based on nothing more than being fabulous. They courted the publicity, dashing for the papers each morning and counting how many photographs or news flashes they could find in the accommodating press.

Among this group exaggeratedly camp behaviour became the norm, and male homosexuality, at the time illegal and socially suicidal, was accepted, its mores copied and celebrated. Eddie Gathorne-Hardy, Stephen Tennant, Brian Howard and Beverley Nichols were amongst the more flamboyant and it was only their influential connections that protected them from the dangers of prosecution and ostracism by mainstream society. Lesbians too were suddenly fashionable and famous comedy revue acts like Gwen Farrar and Norah Blaney were extremely popular and welcomed into the boisterous parties thrown by these giddy young. Norah played the piano and sang in a sweet girlish voice while Gwen, with circular horn-rimmed glasses and a cello between her knees, played the fool with her comedy basso profundo voice. The bisexual American actress/phenomenon Tallulah Bankhead and Radclyffe Hall, known as John, were part of these artistic social sets. Severely cropped hair, masculine attire, male nicknames and a swaggering culture of smoking, drinking and drug-taking became daringly chic.

The blurring of gender and flaunting of an exaggeratedly theatrical style caused great unease as social norms appeared to break down. A popular song of the 1920s sung by, amongst others, Gwen Farrar, was called *Masculine Women, Feminine Men*:

> Hey, Hey women are going mad today
> Hey, Hey fellers are just as bad I'll say,
> Masculine Women, Feminine Men
> Which is the rooster, which is the hen,
> It's hard to tell 'em apart today? And SAY
> Auntie is smoking, rolling her own
> Uncle is always buying cologne …
> You go and give your girl a kiss in the hall
> But instead you find you're kissing her brother, Paul

And so it continued, with the suggestive frisson of what was still considered by the law, and society at large, to be aberrant behaviour.

The richer or more famous you were the easier it was to express such freedoms. Amongst this social group, largely centred on London, the 1920s became notorious for its subversive energy and flair, for freedom from the social constraints of the previous generations and for a feverish pursuit of pleasure that loosened rigid hierarchies of class and behaviour. The anarchic spirit of Peter Pan presided over the age in the irrepressible energy and rejection of responsibility, unlike the elder brothers who had marched so tragically to war. The newspapers built a picture of celebrity idlers dancing their lives away, when not otherwise engaged in various amoral pursuits.

The gossip of drug-taking and heterosexual promiscuity, however, was much exaggerated. Given that many of these young men were only just out of all-male public schools and universities with drinking clubs like the Oxford Hypocrites Club that lived by the unwritten law that 'gentlemen may prance but not dance', and that young women were mindful of their marriage prospects, it was not surprising that both were still sexually shy in each other's company. Nevertheless, the gossip appalled the mothers of well-brought-up girls – and none more than the du Maurier parents who watched as their two elder daughters entered the dubious social fray.

Before Angela was let loose, but in a very controlled way, she had to 'finish' her education in Paris. When she was nearly eighteen she and Betty Hicks, the daughter of the actor Seymour Hicks and his actress wife Ellaline Terriss, were sent to the smartest and most famous finishing school, situated close to the Eiffel Tower and run by the three unmarried Ozanne sisters, daughters of a Protestant minister. Angela had known Betty since she was fourteen and would come to consider her 'my extra sister';[2] they would remain close friends for life. They shared similar upbringings: both were daughters of actress mothers, celebrated for their beauty, and ambitious actor-manager fathers, and both girls were made to feel they were plain and failed to live up to their parents' high aesthetic expectations.

After a bout of flu, Angela arrived a little late in January 1922 full of excitement at the idea of being in Paris, but once again poleaxed by homesickness. Betty had been a boarder at Roedean School and was used to being away and consequently found the regime free and easy in comparison. Angela, horrified by the rules and regulations, thought it more like a prison. A wide range of rich and glamorous young women passed through the doors of what was a strictly run establishment more concerned with culture than education. Angela and Bet were slightly disconcerted to overhear themselves described in hushed tones by one of the Mesdemoiselles Ozanne as *filles d'artistes* and rather patronisingly commended for being surprisingly well brought up. Angela felt she learned little; in fact her French, which under Tod's tuition had progressed quite well, actually deteriorated.

Nancy Cunard, who had attended the Ozanne school a few years before, bitterly complained that the lessons were almost infantile and she loathed the dull, heavily chaperoned outings to churches and museums. But her visits to the Opéra and the discovery of César Franck's music saved her sanity. Angela's love of music was nurtured by the richness of Parisian culture but her singing and piano teachers crushed the life out of her dreams of performance. Her voice training was put in the fiercely competent hands of Gabrielle Ritter-Ciampi, a famous lyric soprano who, in her mid-thirties, was still in her prime with many performances before her. She declared herself initially quite impressed with Angela's voice but her rigorous demands and tempestuous response to any slackness or stumble – she once flung across the room a small bunch of violets Angela had brought her – destroyed her pupil's fragile confidence.

The eldest du Maurier daughter was not a fighter. Her sheltered and genteel education had not taught her resilience. 'I have to be encouraged; whether over a short story, a song, a love affair or the receipt of a bunch of flowers.' If Angela's voice wobbled over the middle C, Madame 'behaved as though the Huns were at the gates of Paris, and oneself just the most imbecile of an entirely imbecile race'.[3] This was too much for a student who had offered her heart in her singing and now quivering, tearfully excused herself from any further training.

Her natural exuberance and pleasure in playing the piano was similarly extinguished by an unimaginative and over-ambitious piano teacher, who declared that her knuckles were out of joint, her hands lacked the right tension and poise, and she was forced to spend the next term doing remedial finger exercises on the lid of a closed piano. She felt both these teachers in their heavy-handed ways had silenced her natural expression and joy through music. 'I would liken it to a stoppage of all private enterprise of the soul.'[4]

Angela's sentimental nature found outlet, however, in crushes on other girls. The highly attractive Ozanne sisters, vivacious and beautifully dressed, and with the added frisson of authority, were also a natural focus for girls seeking favour, attention and love. This experience of attraction between girls and the need for affection from charismatic women may well have set her thinking about the radical theme of the first novel she was to write. After rereading her diaries from this time, she went to great trouble in a memoir to defend the dawning erotic feelings of young women in institutions:

> it's such an entirely natural thing, this 'falling' for older girls and mistresses, that I cannot think why there is always such a song and dance made when novels deal with the subject. Victorian adults put their heads together and mutter 'Unhealthy'; what is there unhealthy in putting someone on a pedestal and giving them violets? Or hoping – in a burst of homesickness – to be kissed goodnight?[5]

Although Angela would always appreciate the beauty and fascination of Paris, her unhappiness during two terms at school there clouded her feelings for the city. She never recaptured the rapture that Daphne, for instance, never lost. But then Daphne enjoyed a seminal experience and successfully established herself as the centre of attention when it came to her 'finishing', three years later. Angela's confused emotions and homesickness were slightly relieved, however, by the arrival in March 1922 of her family, who whisked her off on holiday with them to Algiers, and then on to the South of France.

Daphne was almost fifteen and fell for Paris in a big way. She wrote to Tod, 'I adored [all the sights] and loved Paris. You don't know how I long to have a good talk with you and pour out everything. I never tell anyone anything and there is no one to turn to.'[6] Gerald had been knighted in the New Year's Honours and this was their first holiday as Sir Gerald and Lady du Maurier. They travelled in style, or as Angela remarked, '*en prince*'. They were due to be away from England for seven weeks and in their party was not just the family of five but Aunt Billy, Gerald's secretary, as well as two of his theatrical pals, the actor Ronald Squire and playwright E. V. Esmond, invited as the entertainment.

They travelled by rail and Billy had booked a fleet of cabins for their use. All Gerald's needs were accommodated, his clothes and brushes and potions all set in place, every eventuality catered for. When it came to holidays he was difficult to please as he complained he would rather be at Cannon Hall or in his favourite club, the Garrick, where he would always find his friends offering admiration and bonhomie. If anything did not meet his approval he would cast a stricken look at Billy, 'and soon some wretched manager bowed to the knees with grief would emerge and some Rajah would be turned from comfort and ourselves installed, and – "Send the chap a case of cigars, Billy darling," Daddy would remark.'[7] His mercurial emotions and lurking dissatisfaction made everyone rather tense and edgy, and keen to keep him happy if they wanted the holiday to continue, as he seemed to be always on the verge of flight.

Algiers was the most exotic place yet for a du Maurier family holiday. Settled into the Hotel Mustapha St George, the girls were excited by this assault on the senses. Daphne wrote to Tod, displaying her cavalier approach to spelling, 'lovely hotel, beautiful gardens. Full of luxerious flowers and orange trees.'[8] She was fascinated by the Arab quarter, the Moorish buildings, the carpet stalls and the noisy bartering over every transaction. Jeanne, not yet eleven, was still in her tomboy stage but perhaps her painterly eye was stimulated by the patterns of crimson madder, yellow ochre and soft turquoise that made the street and its inhabitants so vivid. Angela was more in the mood for love. She had just read *The Garden of Allah*, an atmospheric and intense romance by Robert Smythe Hichens where an unconventional Englishwoman (Domini) and an inscrutable stranger (Boris) meet and fall in love at an oasis in the desert. Angela thought it the greatest book ever written. Desert erotica was becoming all the rage since Valentino's smouldering portrayal of The Sheik in the silent movie sensation of the previous year, and young women were full of romance about the Orient. Angela described herself at the time as, 'eighteen, rather plump, hair just up (and in consequence always falling down), desperately serious and very much under the influence of [the novel]. I was ready to find a Boris under any palm tree.'[9] Soon after their arrival their paths crossed with the talented Mr Pertwee.

Roland Pertwee was a thirty-six-year-old actor, artist, playwright and producer. He had booked into the hotel seeking distraction from the shock of being dumped by his wife, and mother of their two young sons, for a wild Russo-French soldier, whom he had befriended and was half in love with himself. His pain had been slightly mollified by the payment of a remarkable £2,000 for his first serial to be published by *The Saturday Evening Post*, America's most widely circulated weekly, famous for its Norman Rockwell covers.

Angela immediately recognised her Boris. He, however, was not inhabiting the same novel and failed to recognise the femme fatale she hoped to be. 'Very different [the sisters] were from each other,' Roland noted in his memoir. 'Angela was admittedly romantic. Daphne practical, observant and a shade cynical. Jeanne was sturdy, and behaved like the boy she was supposed to have been … Angela spent most of her time writing infatuated letters in reply to infatuated letters from girlfriends from her finishing school.'[10] Roland was amused to find that she was not just in love with these nameless girls but her infatuation extended to him too. In a mad moment he wished she was 'not so dreadfully young, for no one was ever sweeter. Her grave, thoughtful eyes, fixed on me were very disturbing.'[11]

Looking back at her diaries in middle age, Angela was highly embarrassed by her behaviour. She thought Roland deserved a knighthood for gallantry for not taking advantage of her naïve eighteen-year-old self: 'If anyone threw themselves – unconsciously – at someone's head, I did.'[12] In Roland's memoir of these two weeks of intimacy with the du Mauriers, he teasingly reproduced part of a letter Angela had shown him from one of her Parisian school friends:

> I never actually saw what [Angela] wrote of me, but I saw a letter replying to one of hers, in which was the phrase: 'If he is all you say he is, how could his wife ever have left him.' There was another passage that struck a warning note. 'Darling, do be careful!!!!! I know, but you have yet to learn, how deceiving men can be!!!!! I would not have your heart broken for all the world.'

Roland found her admiration and affection rather gratifying. She wrote in her diary how she had smoked her first cigarette and rather liked it and, in another attempt at grown-up cool, had her hair washed and waved, much to her parents' dismay: 'Looked topping, row over it, however, but Roland liked it.'[13] He then had apparently kissed her hand. Such bliss!

Her father, however, ruined it all for his eldest daughter with his desire to amuse, even at the expense of another, however vulnerable. 'Gerald, who never missed a trick, used to call me "Puffin's latest crush",' Roland wrote, 'then Angela would go a kind of black red, for whatever her feelings may have been, nobody was supposed to know anything about them.'[14]

Gerald amused himself with his men friends, talking shop, fooling around, changing subjects as rapidly as shadows passing over water and Roland thought there could be no one in the world who was a better companion, investing ordinary events with a spirit of gay adventure. Meanwhile, his daughters went about their very different interests. Angela's emotionalism affected everyone; Daphne found her crushes oppressive and told Tod her sister was quite hopeless. Daphne was filled with an irritable ennui, perhaps affected by her father's innate restlessness but also isolated and alarmed by Angela's obsessional mooning over one love object after another. Is this what it was to grow up? To Tod, she confided:

I must be an awful rotter as we have a ripping time always and no kids could be more indulged and made more fuss of, yet I long for something so terribly and I don't know what it is … Everyone thinks I'm moody and tiresome and I suppose I am; and I really don't know why I feel like this. People say I'm acid and bitter, perhaps I am on the outside but I'm not really.[15]

Daphne wished she could be as placid and happy as Jeanne. She was grieving for the childhood she was being forced to leave behind, while her sister, four years her junior, was still in that uncomplicated place, sturdy and boy-like, safe in the pretence that she was one of the Dampier brothers. Only a couple of days after Roland Pertwee first met Jeanne, he was disconcerted by her arrival in his bedroom where she wordlessly folded his trousers and underwear before putting a strip of Kolynos toothpaste on his toothbrush. 'When I asked her what it was all about she replied: "I'm Dampier, your fag. Shout if you want anything else",[16] and gravely left the room.

Before the end of their time in Algeria, an expedition into the desert and the Atlas Mountains was planned by the men, and the sisters and Muriel were driven to meet them at Bou-saada, a small trading town surrounded by date palms in a true oasis on the edge of the Sahara. Having had all kinds of desert adventures, the men eventually met up with the women for dinner. Afterwards, Roland linked arms with Daphne and Angela and walked them into the night to watch the moon rise over the desert. To Angela it must have seemed as if *The Garden of Allah* had come to life. But before they had got very far, the romantic and mysterious atmosphere was suddenly riven with a ghastly cackling laugh, dwindling to a moan. The girls clutched his arm. The shrieking laugh came again. Roland enquired of a passing young Arab who was it laughing so devilishly. 'A hyena in the cemetery,' he replied. 'He is eating the dead.'[17] Then when a shot rang out in the still air, and the young man explained it was the armed guard in the gardens firing at desert robbers, Angela and Daphne decided they had had enough of moonlight and romance and would rather go home.

Cannes and Monte Carlo were their next destinations. Gerald liked to live life with a flourish: he carried gold sovereigns, using them to tip extravagantly and after paying for a purchase with gold would not bother with the change. Occasionally he was a spectacularly lucky gambler on the horses, no doubt encouraged by his partner at Wyndham's, Frank Curzon, who became as famous and successful as a racehorse breeder as he was a theatrical manager. Gerald chose horses purely on their names reminding him of something significant in his life: he naturally backed Frank Curzon's horse Call Boy, which went on to win the 1927 Derby. Then he bagged the 1928 Derby winner Felstead (the name was an amalgamation of Hampstead and his sister's house Felden) a 40–1 outsider on which he won the considerable sum of £500. He probably made an even bigger return on the 1929 Grand National when his pick Elton, at even more remarkable odds of 100–1, romped home. During the good times, when Frank was running the show, the money kept on rolling in and Gerald was extremely generous and adept at spending it, with little thought of the morrow.

During the euphoric 1920s, the Casino in Monte Carlo was filled with rich and well-connected Englishmen and women intent on diversion. Daphne found it energising: 'It had a great atmosphere of a sort of suppressed excitement all the time.'[18] Here was another natural stage for Gerald's flamboyant insouciance. His friends and daughters observed him in his familiar role:

> There was something about a casino which inspired Gerald to put on an act. He was conscious of the interest he excited, and moved briskly through admiring crowds – alert and on his toes. He had a dashing air as he roved among the tables, saying, '*Banco*'; greeting a friend: 'Hello Portarlington!'; picking up cards and tossing them down: '*Neuf*! Too bad!'; ignoring the money he had won, and having to be reminded of it. A casino offered the opportunity to display his casual, throw-away methods.[19]

Not only was he a great showman, Gerald also relished confounding people's expectations. On their escapade to the Atlas Mountains, the four men had stopped at the oasis at Laghouat, having drunk a good deal of Cointreau. Here they were entertained by the famously beautiful belly-dancing prostitutes of the Ouled Nail. These Englishmen, however worldly wise, were nevertheless born Victorians and hardly immune to the earthy sensuality of the girls, dancing in magnificent costumes and then naked, except for their elaborate jewellery and headdresses, their exotic looks made more dramatic with make-up and kohl-rimmed eyes.

Gerald took one young beauty aside and began to tell her the plot of his forthcoming production of *The Dancers* and determined, against his friends' advice, to act out every scene. Ronnie Squire lost his temper and told him to pay the poor girl some money and let her go, but Gerald took offence. 'This intelligent girl is highly interested,' he said in clipped actorly tones, and insisted on keeping her into the night while she sat perplexed, uncertain what was required of her and whether her traditional services might be called upon, and if so, when.

Significantly, perhaps, Gerald was not as keen on practical jokes if he was the victim. One of the actresses who sprang to fame in Gerald's successful production of *The Dancers* – alongside Tallulah Bankhead – was Audrey Carten. She became a great friend of the family, a romantic interest of Gerald's, and was as much a practical joker as was he. She went too far one night, however, when she filled the fountain outside the eminently respectable Cannon Hall with empty champagne bottles, suggesting some great Bacchanalian orgy had taken place behind its genteel walls. Gerald was not amused.

After Monte Carlo, Roland Pertwee and Ronnie Squire were deputed to take Angela with them to Paris where she was to return to finishing school. The train was packed and they could not get any sleeping berths, so huddled together and eventually slept, Angela's head on Roland's knee. When she awoke she was green with motion-sickness and dashed for the lavatory. Roland noticed as they approached the school that Angela shed her newly acquired veil of sophistication – 'she had the smiling gravity of a small Mona Lisa'[20] – and became a schoolgirl again as they deposited her at the Ozannes' front door. Angela's diary recorded her feeling like a dog being left at the vet's.

While Jeanne perfected her tennis and took up golf, Daphne's mind turned questioningly to religion. She was confirmed at St Paul's Cathedral by the Bishop of London in the early summer of 1922, in spite of Gerald's atheism – as this was just the done thing – but within the year lost any zest she may have felt for organised religion when the priest she liked became interested in spiritualism. In a letter to Tod she attempted to work out what she believed:

I suppose some people would say that I'm an atheist, but I'm not exactly that. I sincerely believe that the world is in a state of evolution, and so is everybody in it. Also I think the idea of re-incarnation has a lot in it. As for Heaven & Hell & all that rot, its absurd. Everyone, sooner or later, gets punished for their sins, in their own lives, but not by the way priests tell one.[21]

Daphne compared herself with Angela, who was much less critical and tough-minded. She was ill at ease with the extremes of emotion that characterised her elder sister and was proud of her own rational self-sufficiency:

> I know she secretly wants to become [a Roman Catholic]. Of course some people do need an emotional sort of religion like that! You know how emotional and rather sentimental she is. It wouldn't do for you & me I'm afraid! Not that I'm matter-of-fact but I do hate sloppiness, & I think R.C. is rather bent that way.

This thoughtful, mistrustful adolescent was painted by Harrington Mann during this time. His portrait captured Daphne's wariness, her shoulders hunched, her body in an S-shaped slouch, her world-weary eyes slipping away from the gaze of the spectator. She was persevering with her short stories, exploring with a thoroughly unsentimental eye relationships and ideas that concerned her. She showed some to her father who found them quite good, and this encouragement spurred her on. Years later she explained the creative spring of her fiction:

> the child destined to be a writer is vulnerable to every wind that blows … the essence of his nature is to escape the atmosphere about him … But escape can be delusion, and what he is running from is not the enclosing world and its inhabitants, but his own inadequate self that fears to meet the demands which life makes upon it.[22]

The fact Daphne was becoming rather an accomplished writer of stories had come to the attention of a young dandy photographer out to make his name, Cecil Beaton. The elder du Maurier sisters had become friendly with him, possibly at the Peter Pan party where he had taken many photographs of famous people, including the du Mauriers, and sold them to the papers. He had begun to get his strikingly posed portraits accepted by *Tatler* and the daily newspapers. 'We'd worked & plotted for our success & we'd got out in every paper except the *Mirror* and the *Evening Standard*!'[23] Beaton declared in triumph at the beginning of the new year of 1923. It was during this time, when Beaton was making a name for himself in society, that Angela began to meet him at parties and dances.

When Angela returned to Cannon Hall she was officially 'out'. A ball was given for her at Claridge's and she became part of the generation of Bright Young Things who went to each other's parties, not always in the company of parents. This important event in Angela's young life caused great anxiety and grief to her, and a temporary rift in the family. Angela was so afraid of being upstaged by her prettier younger sisters that she declared she did not want either Jeanne or Daphne at her coming-out party. Muriel gave her an ultimatum: your sisters or your dance, and Angela gave in. She nevertheless could not but think that they inadvertently stole her show:

> They wore pale blue velvet frocks and both looked dreams, dancing every dance; I was at my fattest and wore a white satin frock that stuck out like a crinoline and must have made me look even fatter. I wore my hair in a low knot or bun at the back of my neck, and I would imagine a tear-stained face.[24]

During the celebration that should have been one of the more triumphant moments of her entry into adulthood, she was given an unkind letter from her latest crush telling her he did not want to have the all-important supper dance with her.

Despite the advent of the Jazz Age and the general casting off of stays, the social life for young women of the du Mauriers' social class was still very formal. Anyone going to the theatre and sitting in a box or the stalls or first rows of the dress circle was expected to wear full evening dress. No woman or girl would dream of lunching out without an immaculate frock, and a hat on her head. If you were a well-brought-up young woman you could not be seen in nightclubs, although it was considered safe for Angela and her friends to flock to the Embassy Club or Ciro's, the glamorous dance club and restaurant that had been favourite family venues and where birthday parties were often held after an evening at the theatre.

In January 1923, Seymour Hicks and Ellaline Terriss gave a party for their daughter Betty's coming out. Like Angela's, it was at

Claridge's. About one hundred people were invited to dinner with dancing afterwards. One of the guests was their new friend Cecil Beaton, whose remarkably detailed diaries recorded the merry social scene. This party he considered terrific good fun, with 'such a riot of interesting people', whom he then proceeded to criticise. 'The du Mauriers were all there,' he wrote, 'they are charming except Sir Gerald whom I simply loathe. He is so conceited and so ridiculously affected. He gets completely on my nerves.' This from an equally self-conscious dandy.

Beaton seemed to be amused by Angela's grave and innocent demeanour and enjoyed dancing with her and teasing her mercilessly: 'I ragged [her] as looking [rather] Shaftesbury Avenue in a dress from Idare [the famous theatrical costumier]. It was dreadfully chorus girly & when she swished around the skirt swished up revealing knickers to match.'[25] But his attention must have helped restore some of Angela's fragile confidence. Beaton himself did not so obviously lack self-confidence, but nevertheless was immensely gratified when Seymour Hicks sought him out to tell him he had a reputation as the wittiest young man in London. He was even happier to find himself seated at dinner in a more favourable place than the precocious novelist and journalist Beverley Nichols. They were natural rivals as talented, exquisite young men on the make.

The family's annual summer escape from London took the sisters to Frinton on the Essex coast and then to Dieppe in August, where Jeanne's sporting prowess continued to grow. She was entered for tennis tournaments but Daphne's diaries do not mention how well she did. Angela sought out another crush, this time a girl named Phil, and Daphne joked to Tod that her sister's emotional nature would lead her into 'more and more compromising [situations] and I fear she is on the road to ruin!'[26] The elder sisters went to stuffy afternoon dances and complained about the body odour hanging in the air. Daphne pretended to fancy a handsome French officer purely to irritate her father, who of course rose to the bait and raged that the man looked 'an awful bounder'.[27] Their glamorous life continued with the whole family, including their Aunt Billy, spending Christmas in Monte Carlo, again visiting the Casino regularly, and Daphne and Jeanne playing tennis and golf with each other and their father.

Female fashion had changed radically and young women at parties abandoned their restrictive undergarments and appeared in slim columns of beaded and sequinned silk. Angela, still dressed by her parents' favourite theatrical costumier, remained in the waisted dirndls of her youth. While she was dancing in old-fashioned flouncy dresses, laughing at the inoffensive jokes of effete young men, Jeanne was focusing on her art and sport. Daphne, always more introspective and intellectual than her sisters, meanwhile wrote disconsolate letters to Tod about the impossibility of conventional happiness and her fear of growing up: 'It seems a morbid and stupid thought but I *can't* see myself living very long,' wrote Daphne, 'but the future is always such a complete blank. There is nothing ahead that lures me terribly, marriage doesn't thrill me – nothing – nothing remains. If only I was a man! That is the one slogan to me ... I like women much better than men.' She then described how dance music made her long to dance with someone she had a crush on, but these barely understood emotions disturbed her: 'It annoys me though to feel like that! I should love to be free from all that sort of thing.'[28] Full of anxiety and dread of the future, this was the girl who had once bitten her nails so savagely that her parents had sought medical help; theatrically she recalled what she considered a symbolic act – that of being offered bitter aloes as a cure rather than an attempt at understanding and the unconditional love she craved.

Another great theatrical family who were very much part of the sisters' youth was the Trees. Viola, the eldest daughter of the legendary Edwardian actor-manager Sir Herbert Beerbohm Tree, was larger than life and greatly loved. To call her an actress hardly did justice to her many talents; she was co-writer with Gerald on *The Dancers*, had an eccentric newspaper column in the *Daily Dispatch* and was a natural and unselfconscious comedienne. Viola was also blessed with a wonderful singing voice and would touch the heart, or the funny bone, with anything from German lieder to the rudest vaudeville ditty. Angela remembered her as 'the most brilliant, most witty, most amusing – and at times most maddening – woman it has been my pleasure to have known'.[29]

Viola was married to the drama critic Alan Parsons, and their daughter Virginia was a contemporary of Jeanne's. Jeanne was being tutored at home with her friend Nan Greenwood but at fourteen she went to school in Hampstead and made closer acquaintance with Virginia. Unsurprisingly, this younger Tree was much shyer than her mother but had her own generous helping of the family's therapeutic charm. She was beautiful and lacking in cynicism or side. She loved most humans and all animals but, most importantly for Jeanne perhaps, she was highly artistic. Her enlightened parents allowed her to have private lessons with the Bloomsbury Post-Impressionist Duncan Grant, and then with the realist painter William Coldstream. When Virginia was only sixteen she became a student at the Slade School of Fine Art, the prestigious college that Coldstream would eventually direct as Professor of Fine Art.

This was liberated, even libertine, company for a young woman of the privileged yet sheltered classes. There was no evidence as to whether Jeanne was included in her friend's art tutoring. Considering Gerald's antipathy to anything modern in art or in the education of daughters, it seems unlikely, but as Virginia's contemporary, and given the closeness of the du Maurier and Tree families, there was little doubt that Jeanne was influenced by the fact that a young woman's artistic talents could be taken so seriously. Virginia Parsons did not go on to make painting her life, but she did end up as the wife of the 6th Marquess of Bath and chatelaine to the glorious Elizabethan confection of Longleat (and its lions) in Wiltshire. Here she started Pets Corner and exercised her concern for all living creatures, charming friends, animals and visitors alike.

Angela's debutante days of gadding-about from social lunches to shopping, to attending every new film and play, all punctuated by gay conversations with other debutantes, were followed by nights of wittily themed parties, treasure hunts and extravagant balls, before the dash home by chauffeured car. They were privileged times indeed. The du Maurier girls took it for granted that Hollywood royalty like

Rudolph Valentino (so incredibly handsome and charming, they thought), Gary Cooper and Jack Barrymore (ditto) would dine with them at home at Cannon Hall. It was unremarkable that Arthur Rubinstein and Ivor Novello, also incredibly handsome and charming – and bagged by Daphne as a future husband, despite Angela's first claim on him – would play the piano to entertain them and their guests in the drawing room. It did not seem remarkable that actors of the calibre of Gladys Cooper and Jill Esmond and Laurence Olivier should be family friends, and that exotic acquaintances like Nelly Melba, Tallulah Bankhead, Cecil Beaton and Lady Diana Cooper would enliven the show. Unremarkable too, that the Savoy Hotel was the du Mauriers' home from home, the place to which they decamped when cook was ill or the maids had flu. This grand hotel was their regular haunt for Christmas Day lunch with friends, their own table specially kept for them by the vast windows overlooking the river.

Enforced sexual ignorance and unwelcome parental control took their toll on these apparently carefree days. When Angela was eighteen she spent a happy September week in a country house in Gloucestershire under the aegis of Lady Cynthia Asquith. Staying in the house was a collection of young people, among them her cousin Nico Llewelyn Davies and the rest of the Eton cricket XI, which included Lord Dunglass – the future Conservative Prime Minister, Sir Alec Douglas-Home. After a great deal of innocent games and dancing into the night, Angela allowed one of these young gods chastely to kiss her in her bedroom. When she felt vaguely sick the next morning (probably from too much gaiety the night before) she was panic-stricken by the thought that the kiss, so riskily proffered in such a taboo place as a bedroom, might somehow have made her pregnant. She could not confide in Daphne, who was even more ignorant in the facts of life than she was. She could never confess such a thing to her mother, and her father's reaction was too terrible even to imagine. So she wrote to her Aunt Billy, who luckily kept her secret and reassured her with a sanitised version of the truth.

Angela never let on whether the young god with the prepotent kiss was the nineteen-year-old Lord Dunglass. She suggested in a later memoir that it was. This young aristocrat was already a boy hero, captain of the Eton cricket team, Keeper of the Field (captain of football, in the college's own form of the game) and President of the Prefects' Society, called Pop. He was a gallant, golden, effortlessly accomplished youth who may well have attracted the over-romantic girl. Certainly Lord Dunglass trumped Daphne's creation, Eric Avon. Eric merely went to Harrow (Gerald's school): Milord went to Eton. Eric excelled at sports and acts of simple bravery; Alec did all this and was also rather good at the intellectual and social stuff too. To the eldest daughter of a family enamoured of its own breeding, Lord Dunglass held the ace, the inheritance of the earldom of Home. This dated from the beginning of James I's reign and included several thousand acres of the Scottish borderlands. Angela, whose memoirs are full of veiled clues (at least for those of a forensic mind), rather gave the game away in her second volume, where she was musing on education and recalling her ecstatic teenage self: 'I'm eighteen and last week I met an absolutely *wonderful* boy who's just left Eton. Actually he's a viscount – I wonder …'[30] Her readers, perhaps, did not need to wonder.

This young viscount who caught Angela's eye and was to become an earl and then renounce his title in order to sit in the House of Commons as an MP was described by his contemporary at Eton, Cyril Connolly, with remarkable prescience as, 'a votary of the esoteric Eton religion, the kind of graceful, tolerant, sleepy boy who is showered with all the laurels, who is liked by the masters and admired by the boys without any apparent exertion on his part'. Connolly thought had Douglas-Home lived in the eighteenth century, to which he so obviously belonged, this kind of effortless brilliance would have made him Prime Minister before he was thirty (he managed it by sixty). As it was, 'he appeared honourably ineligible for the struggle of life'.[31]

Sundays at Cannon Hall provided another stage for fun, flirtation and amusing conversation, and had become an institution amongst the theatrical circles in which Gerald moved. He was always the centre of attention, and Muriel the gracious and well-organised hostess. There were liveried maids (in grey and white alpaca uniforms) who acted as waitresses, serving champagne and delicacies to a large and

varied mix of beautiful people. Angela enjoyed the relentless socialising. Daphne did not.

While Angela was beginning to grow up and learn about love, in
rather limited circumstances, Daphne was reading voraciously (Oscar
Wilde for a while was her favourite), still writing stories and thinking
a lot. At the suggestion of Tod, she had discovered Katherine Mansfield. Daphne declared her short stories the best she had ever read,
although they left her feeling melancholy, with 'a kind of helpless pity
for the dreariness of other people's lives'.[32] She identified with the
author as a sensitive outsider, but the expectations and hypocrisy of
the adult world alarmed and dismayed her, and sex seemed to be
fraught with menace. To Tod, she wrote:

> have you ever noticed, (I think its vile) that if one marries its
> considered awful if one does'nt do it thoroughly (you know what I
> mean) and yet if one does certain things without being married, its
> considered awful too. Surely that's narrow-minded, and disgusting.
> Either the Act of – er-well, you know, is right or wrong. A wedding-
> ring cant change facts. An illegitimate child is looked on as a sort of
> 'freak' or 'unnatural specimen', whereas a child whose parents are
> married is wholesome and decent ... Oh is'nt it all unwhole-
> some?[33]

She and Jeanne were exposed to another unwholesome aspect of
adult life when, at the beginning of 1924, their father took them to
Pentonville Prison. He was rehearsing *Not in Our Stars*, a play about
a man involved in the murder of his romantic rival, and wished to
investigate the experiences a convicted murderer would endure. It
was just a year after a sensational trial and double execution of Edith
Thompson and her young lover Frederick Bywaters for murdering
Edith's husband. Angela's new friend Beverley Nichols was a young
journalist on the case and he wrote about the awful tragedy that was
played out to a packed house at the Old Bailey, and the heartbreak of
the lovers' letters read aloud in court. All of London was talking about
it. The double executions were synchronised for 9 a.m. on 9 January
1923, Thompson's in Holloway and Bywaters's in Pentonville, the

prisons just half a mile apart. Rumours of Edith's grotesque last minutes on earth filled the newspapers.*

With the horror still raw, somehow Gerald thought it a good idea to take his young impressionable daughters with him to Pentonville. The girls were shown over the whole prison by the governor Major Blake; they saw the locked cells with their miserable inhabitants, the patients in their beds in the hospital wing, the condemned cell and the hanging shed, and even had the drop gruesomely demonstrated. The unmarked graves of the hanged added their own grim melancholy. Amongst them was wife-murderer Dr Crippen, the Irish revolutionary Roger Casement and, perhaps most poignantly, the twenty-year-old Bywaters, whose unfailing loyalty to his lover was remarked on by all in the press.

Daphne could not get the images out of her mind and sketched the cell and the hanged man's drop in her diary. This episode showed how peculiarly contrary Gerald could be. He was almost hysterically protective of his daughters and wished to keep them as children for ever, but then he was capable of taking Jeanne, just thirteen, and Daphne, seventeen, to see people at their most degraded and dangerous. He had even exposed them to the horror of the process and apparatus for judicial murder by hanging. Had Angela been there too it might well have elicited a fit of uncontrolled crying, but Daphne just digested the images and added them to her already jaundiced view of human nature and the harm people do each other. She wrote a poem in her diary and wondered later if it was inspired by the visit:

> Sorrow for the men that mourn
> Sorrow for the days that dawn,
> Sorrow for all things born
> Into this world of sorrow.

---

* Stories circulated of her mental disintegration, claiming she was drugged and had to be propped up to have the noose put round her neck and then in a final horrific detail, it was said, she had suffered a miscarriage as she fell through the drop. Her execution had not only haunted the witnesses, but also fuelled a great convulsion of outrage in wider society against the death penalty, and against killing women in particular.

And all my life, as far as I can see,
All that I hope, or ever hope to be,
Is merely driftwood on a lonely sea.[34]

Emboldened by her first kiss with a member of the Eton cricket XI, Angela next attempted to break out from the social straitjacket of home. Aged twenty, she developed a crush on a woman notorious for her lesbian proclivities. It showed a certain courage and boldness of character that this conscientious and obedient young woman should make a stand over this friendship. Her father was particularly hard to withstand. He was emotionally extreme and a practised actor and could work himself into a fit of temper that seemed close to insanity. Beverley Nichols had watched this amazing facility in action in rehearsal: 'He can precipitate himself into a state of hysteria with the speed of a sporting Bugatti, and the moment afterwards is playing a love scene with admirable timing and sentiment.'[35] When Angela persisted with her desire to see this forbidden woman, both parents raged and threatened. Angela resorted to asking the Almighty to intervene. 'Oh God,' she wrote in her diary that autumn, 'help something to happen to get them to change their minds.'[36] Their minds remained made up and Angela later reflected that this intensive control of her behaviour pushed her, from this time on, into subterfuge, secrecy and barefaced lies.

She did not name the focus of her desire in her memoir, but she was almost certainly an actress and most likely Gwen Farrar – the sensation of the highly successful revue at the Duke of York's Theatre, *The Punch Bowl*, that ran through 1924 and the following year. She was witty and lively, a natural boyish clown who attracted men and women alike. She was partnered in the revue by her partner in life, the more conventionally pretty Norah Blaney, a friend of Angela Halliday, who was to become a close and lifelong friend of Angela du Maurier's.

Daphne's eye had also been caught by the unconventional attractions of the crop-haired Gwen when she saw the revue and wrote a fan letter to the actress. She admitted this to Tod and begged her discretion:

I adored Gwen Farrar! I wrote to her last night (not a word of this) saying 'Dear Gwen, I think you are quite perfect, Daphne.' Shall I be drawn into the net too? I wonder. I hope she won't show the letter to anyone, or I shall be tarred with the same brush!

Being 'drawn into the net too' implied that someone else was in that net, and perhaps this was a reference to her elder sister, whose stormy rows with their parents over her unsuitable friendship could not have gone unnoticed. Daphne then added a significant coda: 'Life's no fun, unless theres' a spark of danger in it.'[37]

Angela did not relish the fights with her parents and, although she held out for a couple of months, in the end the force ranged against her was too much to withstand. She regretted her parents' slur on the reputation of this intriguing woman and the thwarting of her own longing for friendship with her: 'in all the weeks and months I knew her I never met anyone kinder, more generous, more amusing and so utterly uncontaminating in influencing the impressionable girl I was'. Angela's diary at the end of October 1924 relayed the rollercoaster of her life, the italics are hers:

> Dreadful scene with Daddy over X and Z (*another friend*) [possibly Gwen and Norah]. He stormed like a madman. Went to the dentist, awful time as he injected me with cocaine and jabbed a colossal needle into my jaw. Extraordinary feeling. Lilian and Joyce to lunch (*Lilian Braithwaite and* [daughter] *Joyce Carey*). Spent rest of day making frock. Polling Day – exciting results on wireless.[38]

What Angela, and no doubt her family, considered 'exciting results' was an increased majority for the Conservatives and a rout of the Liberals under Asquith.

Gerald perhaps decided it was time to divert his eldest daughter's energies away from unsuitable love affairs and into some kind of suitable career. Out of the blue he suggested that she play Wendy in the annual Christmas and New Year performance of *Peter Pan* at the Adelphi. This was a daunting role for someone who had never been trained as an actress. *Peter Pan*, however, was so well known to the du

Maurier sisters, and loved by them all that each was word perfect in every character. Daphne did not envy her one bit. To appear before an audience, even in such a special play, she said, 'would be agony'.[39] Angela, more extrovert, trusting and naïve, did not hesitate. She could have 'jumped over the moon with glee'. This was always her part in the family shows and she had not missed one of the professional productions since she was first taken at the age of two. Highly professional and famous actors were hired to co-star with her. The lovely Gladys Cooper was Peter Pan, Mrs Patrick Campbell was Mrs Darling, and Hook and Mr Darling were played by a young South African actor, Ian Hunter, for whom Angela had already conceived a crush.

There were rehearsals all day and Angela was still socialising at night. She had always found attending rehearsals generally fascinating and enjoyed nothing more than sitting in the darkened stalls watching her father tease performances out of his company as they brought a play to life. This time, Angela struggled with the director's vision of *Peter Pan*, which contradicted her own childhood memories of how it should be played. She also struggled with the acting. After weeks of work, her diary for late October 1924 lamented:

rehearsal all day 3rd act morning. Daddy came down and I was very bad. Lisped worse than ever, spoke quickly and forgot my words. Lunched Jill [Esmond, who was playing Nibs]. Last act afternoon. Ian so sweet, I had to prompt him and he said, 'Bless you.' I am a fool.

The middle-aged Angela wrote of her youthful sense of folly: 'How true, how true!'[40] In retrospect she realised also that she had been parachuted in ahead of all the other young actresses who would have hoped for the part. Jill Esmond for instance, although younger, was fully RADA-trained and merely had a minor part. The nepotism involved in her selection and Angela's lack of training, together with her naïve belief that she could just reprise her nursery performances, all set her up for a fall. Unfortunately it was a literal and almighty one.

Each actor who was required to fly had to don an uncomfortable harness and then be lifted into the air and manipulated by a man pulling wires in the wings. In the last act Wendy, John and Michael all flew through the window back to their nursery, alighting in the middle of the stage. But Angela was flown too vigorously and crash-landed on the footlights. She was catapulted into the orchestra pit, taking the double bassist and his instrument with her. There was an appalled hush from the audience: no one knew if she would emerge alive. She was dazed and in pain but recovered enough to creep under the stage and reappear as Wendy in her bed in the nursery. 'The ovation which greeted me was almost frightening. The audience stood and clapped and yelled, and with tears running down my face by then (from emotion not pain) I blew them all a kiss and then the play went on.'[41]

Angela dined out on the story of her flying debacle so many times that the family and her closest friends coined the phrase 'an orchestra' to mean a long tale of melodramatic disaster. After this mishap she realised she hadn't the mettle to be a proper actress because she did not believe that the show had to go on regardless. She was much more inclined to take to her bed if she felt under the weather. But although she was battered and bruised, her nerve shattered, Gerald insisted she return to the theatre the next day, conquer her fear of flying, and perform in the afternoon show.

Angela's careering flight was one of the few outside incidents to merit a mention in Daphne's continuing angst-ridden correspondence with Tod, who was living in some splendour at Burrough Court in Leicestershire, tutoring Averill the daughter of a rich, recently widowed businessman, the 1st Viscount Furness. Daphne teased Tod by suggesting that her much-loved governess should become the next Lady Furness. In fact, the Viscount's taste unhappily ran on rather more exotic lines as he was already engaged to one beautiful American socialite, and would end up married to another, who promptly became the mistress of Edward, the Prince of Wales.

Daphne's adolescent introspection and sense of the pointlessness of life was about to be challenged. At eighteen it was her turn to go to finishing school in Paris, the city of her imagination. She was not bound for the Ozannes', where Angela's experiences had been mixed, but to a school run by Miss Wicksteed at Camposena, some five and a half miles south-west of the city. Miss Wicksteed, or 'Wick' as she was known by the girls, was a reassuringly solid middle-aged Englishwoman with white hair and a no-nonsense manner. On 16 January 1925, after a blast of Christmas parties and dances, Daphne headed off to Paris for what would be the defining experience of her life.

Jeanne was now nearly fourteen and life for her was changing too. She was enrolled in Francis Holland School at Clarence Gate near Regent's Park to start in the autumn term a more formal education with art and sports on the curriculum. Having had generous notices for her Wendy the first time round, Angela contracted to do one more season of *Peter Pan*, but the critics this time sharpened their quills. Already ambivalent about her future as an actress, exhaustion, demoralisation and a stage fight with real swords, in which her nose was almost severed, put paid to her faltering ambition. Her famous theatrical name was both a boon and a liability. If she was to be an actress as a du Maurier she would have to be particularly dedicated and particularly good, and she feared she was neither.

During her run as Wendy, Angela had been conned by a well-known elderly photographer into posing for him in the nude, and been appalled and embarrassed by the results. A happier experience was provided by their young friend Cecil Beaton when he asked Angela and Daphne to be models in two of his earliest photographic experiments. They were shown into his old nursery where he had set up his props and various cameras and tripods and, with the help of his elderly nanny, and a great deal of laughter (and ineffectual fiddling around it seemed to the girls), produced his inventive portraits of the sisters: 'Daph's and my heads appearing magically under wine-glasses.'[42] Stilted and ludicrously artificial to the modern eye, the photographs were considered by Angela later in life to be the most flattering portraits of them both ever created. Hers hung in pride of place in the Italian house of her great friend Naomi Jacob, until the Germans arrived in the Second World War and either purloined or trashed it.

Angela could never confide her hopes or fears to her parents and without prospects of a career she drifted rudderless and ill-equipped for independent life. Years later she mused on how celebrity affected those closest to it:

> I wanted to be a good actress, and with a name like du Maurier I could not afford to be a bad one ... Possibly too much is expected of the children of the great; I would definitely say, in fact, that both as an actress – admittedly of only one part – and as a writer, I have found my name as big a handicap as ever it was a help. As Wendy I was Gerald du Maurier's daughter – and it had been an amusing 'stunt' to try me out in a star part straight off ...[43]

Her lack of training and the chance to work her way up from the bottom had also robbed her of the opportunity to graduate to being a producer, which was where her true talents possibly lay, though as a young woman gazing into the unknown she could not have been aware of this at the time. Girls of her background and education did not aspire to have serious careers apart from becoming actresses and the wives of famous men. While Angela waited for the man she would marry, the parties continued. In a private room at the Garrick, Gerald occasionally invited an eclectic group of friends and acquaintances to lunch. One memorable gathering on 23 October was recorded by Angela in her diary, and also by her old crush, Roland Pertwee.

The party was organised to wave off in style on an Australian tour their friends and colleagues, the actor-director Dion Boucicault Jnr and his actress wife Irene Vanbrugh. Apart from Muriel, Gerald, Angela, Roland and the Boucicaults, there was also (with Angela's comments in italics) 'Dame Nellie Melba (*most excited about [her] for whom I had (rightly) boundless admiration*), H. G. Wells (*too sweet*), Augustus John (*overawed by him and sat far away*), Sir Squire Bancroft,' and the sisters' lifelong heroes, John Barrymore and Gladys Cooper. Roland continued the tale:

> half-way through lunch Irene said to Melba: 'Tip us a stave, Nellie.' And Nellie Melba, over a loaded fork, for she was a hearty trencherman, opened her throat and sang like a lark.

That lunch, which started at one fifteen went on until seven thirty, when John Barrymore rushed off to appear as Hamlet at the Haymarket, and gave one of the most sensational performances of his career.[44]

This was the kind of glamorous world that the du Maurier sisters inhabited, some of them more happily than others. Angela, still child-like at twenty, was standing tentatively on the edge of this world she was reared to join, while Jeanne was allowed to remain a girl for a few years more. Daphne, who had been so reluctant to grow up and did not care for her parents' kind of high society or attitudes to love, was back in Paris in the heat of her first real love affair. This time she would give her father real reason for outrage. Luckily, he never knew.

4

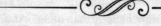

Love and Losing

I for this and this for me.

DAPHNE DU MAURIER, *Growing Pains*

DAPHNE HAD NEVER before been away from home and everyone expected her to be homesick – after all, Angela's time in Paris had been spoiled by a heart-clutching *nostalgie*. But Daphne suffered not one twinge. Why would she? She already adored Paris, not for its shopping and its shows, but for its possibilities, the ancient alleyways, the hidden squares, the imaginative connection with her ancestors, and the dark stories embedded in its stones. Daphne had found life at home limiting, her parents' suspicions claustrophobic, and she had never been happy with the relentless socialising expected of her in London. She had grown up with a sense of her own exceptionalism, something her father's attention had encouraged, and always felt separate and alien, and quite unlike other people.

Desperate to escape the envelope of make-believe and good manners that had maintained her in a suspended state of childhood, Daphne could not have chosen a better springboard for her flight. Paris between the wars was the most exciting city in the world, a City of Light that cast her home town distinctly in its shade. Intellectuals and artists were attracted to its vibrant energy, where the revolutionary movements of Cubism, Surrealism and Dadaism evolved from the studios of painters like Picasso, Matisse, Giacometti and Chagall.

American jazz was the thrilling accompaniment to the modernist experimentations that energised intellectual debate and transformations in design. Excitement spilled from the cafés and bars of the Left Bank – a favourite haunt of Daphne's all her life. Her pulse could not have failed to quicken to its beat.

Daphne's only concern was that she had to go to school and her fellow pupils would be a dull lot, as she wrote to Tod, adding revealingly, 'I know so few girls that I will probably think them all fools at first.'[1] She was accompanied by Doodie Millar, the daughter of another Hampstead family. Doodie, a lively, good-looking girl she had known from childhood, had already been to boarding school and so was sanguine about the whole experience. The house at Camposena was cold and far less comfortable than Cannon Hall but was situated in fine parkland close to the small town of Meudon, and a short train trip from Paris itself, which more than made up for its lack of luxury. The bedroom she and Doodie shared was barely furnished and bitter even in October, and Daphne thought the girls looked as dull and boring as she had expected. However, she liked the mistresses, and one in particular. She wrote to Tod, her faithful confidante, 'the head kind of mistress, Mlle Yvon, is obviously "Venice" [her code for lesbian], many of the girls, & one mistress, are mad about her. She has a sort of fatal attraction about her, I feel I shall fall for her before too long!!'[2]

During her flirtatious skirmishes with Cousin Geoffrey, Daphne had learnt of her singular power to attract: having been the sister who had always drawn the most attention, she was not used to having to compete with others for favour. She was stung by the school's assessment of her as being merely middling in her abilities, placing her in the B stream. The elite A girls, who clustered around Mlle Yvon, were privileged to choose where they sat at dinner and – the height of excitement – could follow her afterwards to a special room, the *salon du fond*. Here they played an uncomfortable game called 'Truths' that would reduce a few of them each night to tears. The atmosphere was febrile with girlish intrigues and emotion, encouraged by the green-eyed, soignée Fernande Yvon.

Daphne was determined that she would somehow penetrate this inner sanctum and claim her rightful place as favourite at its centre.

Despite remaining in stream B and therefore outside the charmed circle, she showed her father's chutzpah when one night she picked up her book (a French classic by Edmond de Goncourt whose *académie* had founded the most prestigious literary prize *Prix Goncourt*) and strolled nonchalantly into the lionesses' den. The girls greeted this uninvited interloper with surprised hostility, but Mlle Yvon appeared to be amused by her presumption and motioned her to sit at her feet by the fire. 'My triumph was complete,' Daphne wrote, recalling her heroic boy-self, 'even Eric Avon, bowing to the crowd from his balcony above Lord's cricket ground, had never achieved such a victory.'[3]

But this kind of power was heady and dangerous and, as with Cousin Geoffrey, the thrill of a clandestine and forbidden connection exerted its own power to enslave. Fernande Yvon, in her thirties, unmarried and with limited prospects, inevitably enjoyed the influence that her position as *directrice* of an exclusive finishing school gave her, and the devotion of well-connected girls brought its own rewards both socially and emotionally. There was little doubt that the teacher set out to seduce her new pupil, but also that the pupil was ready to be seduced, or certainly desired the power that being favourite bestowed. Daphne wrote to Tod:

I've quite fallen for the woman I've told you about – Mlle Yvon … She's absolutely kind of lured me on, and now I'm coiled in the net! She pops up to the bedroom at odd moments (Venice – what!!) and is generally divine. She's most seductive when coming back from the Opera. I get on the back seat with her, & she puts her arm round me and makes me put my head on her shoulder. Then sort of presses me! Ugh! It all sounds *too* sordid and low, but I don't know – it gives one a sort of extra-ordinary thrill!

Having her own feelings for Daphne, perhaps Tod found these letters rather hard to take. Daphne wrote extensively in her diary and letters of the romantic crush that became an obsessional affair, lasting almost two years, while their subsequent affectionate friendship lasted until Fernande's death. For this girl, who had always felt herself unloved by her mother, her need for Mlle's approval was 'as insidious as a drug'.[4] Her sensible friend Doodie tried to reassure her by saying everyone had crushes, and promptly decided to attach herself devotedly to a little red-headed teacher. Daphne thought she knew all there was to know about crushes, having seen enough of Angela's fleeting and, to her mind, vaguely ridiculous passions, but this, she insisted, was different. She added a further paragraph in her letter to Tod, revealing how cool, detached and watchful she remained, even while in thrall to her first grand passion:

> I hope I haven't got 'Venetian' tendencies! Already some of the girls are jealous which makes life somewhat uncomfortable … Life is queer, I can't make it out … It will be fun, when I get back from the hols, imitating everyone here and laughing at it all. Even when I'm feeling most 'épris' of Mlle Yvon, there is always something inside me laughing somewhere.[5]

Daphne's idea of courtship was theatrical and gleaned from the way her father behaved towards women: exaggerated chivalry alternated with studied indifference. When, for instance, Mlle Yvon dropped a handkerchief, Daphne swooped on it and hid it away; later, in Paris, she bought a bottle of scent, sprinkled it on the linen and then in front of her rivals in the *salon du fond* presented it to the object of her desire, 'with all the gallantry of Sir Walter Raleigh spreading his cloak in the mud before Queen Elizabeth'.[6]

The du Maurier sisters had a horror of 'the L word', as they referred to lesbianism. They were brought up by Victorian parents who, although steeped in the theatrical profession and surrounded by people who both covertly and openly expressed their less than hetero sexuality, were adamantly homophobic. Gerald particularly was virulent in his disapproval, perhaps because he himself exhibited a strong feminine streak, as Daphne recognised. Society and the Church's views contributed to this fear. Although the 1920s saw great social changes, male homosexual activity was still considered so despicable and contaminatory that it remained a crime for another forty years, and to this day is considered a sin by most of the major religions.

Homosexual women were at least free of the fear of criminal proceedings, but were categorised as deviants, or 'inverts' as Radclyffe Hall famously characterised herself, and others like her. This was a frightening thought, encouraged by the early sexologists Havelock Ellis and Krafft-Ebing who considered homosexuality a pathological state, along with other deviations from the norm such as necrophilia, coprophilia and bestiality. As always, the well-off, influential and upper classes were better insulated from the law and social ostracism. However, the hounding to death of their grandfather's friend Oscar Wilde, whom even celebrity and genius could not protect, was a chilling warning of how even the golden songbird could be crushed by prejudice and fear.

Considering the atmosphere in which the du Maurier sisters grew up it was all the more remarkable that Angela, in her mid-twenties and still clearly in the grip of her family ethos, should court controversy and parental outrage by writing her first novel, *The Little Less*, in which the central theme was the love of a young woman for another. With great boldness her heroine makes an impassioned plea for the normality of such feelings, and forcefully insists that sexual desire is indeed part of this love. Angela also took up the cudgels in her early memoir, published in her mid-forties, insisting on the naturalness of schoolgirls' passions for older girls and mistresses, deploring the Victorian mentality that thought the subject 'unhealthy' and inappropriate as subject matter in novels. She heartily recommended two works that dealt truthfully with the subject, *Mädchen in Uniform*, a novel by Christa Winsloe that became the first film to deal openly with lesbianism and double standards, and Julia Strachey's novel *Olivia*.

Perhaps thinking of her eighteen-year-old sister's affair with a charismatic teacher many years her senior, Angela did make one proviso, 'the only unhealthy matter is when an older woman battens on a young girl's adoration and cruelly persecutes her mind by maliciously seeing how far her power will reach'.[7]

If she was thinking of Daphne and Mlle Yvon, however, Angela had underestimated just how much power Daphne exercised in all her relationships, this first serious one being no exception.

All Angela's youthful tolerance and crusading zeal would seem to dissolve with age, just as her religious feeling increased, along with concern with what her local church and community would think. In her later memoir, written in her early sixties, Angela metaphorically pursed her lips and, after a lifetime of emotional and sexual relationships, mostly with women, harrumphed defensively:

> Far too much is talked about homosexuality nowadays, and when it comes to discussions about it on the radio and television I despair, because anything *new* is interesting to youth, and an innocent-minded boy or girl may learn by these means of homosexual friendships and, prompted by curiosity, set out to discover for himself or herself what it's all about.[8]

This did seem rather close to her father's opinion that had caused her so much grief as a young woman, tiptoeing towards some kind of awareness of herself and how to live in the world.

Daphne's attitude was much more complex. So much has been written since her death about her ambivalence towards her own sexual identity; she had written about it too in personal letters and public memoir, attempting to apply meaning to her inner life and explain herself to those closest to her. She too recoiled from 'the L word', and later expostulated in a letter to Ellen Doubleday, the wife of her American publisher, after describing her youthful love for Mlle Yvon, 'by God, and by Christ, if anyone should call that sort of love by that unattractive word that begins with L, I'd tear their guts out'.[9]

When Daphne was enthralled by a woman friend, she did not see herself as a woman in love with another woman: she did not personify herself even as a man, but as a boy, that creative, brave adventurous boy who had shadowed her through childhood. In some ways she did not even think of herself as human and driven by animal passions, but instead as a disembodied spirit. And in this, perhaps, she was closest to the truth, because the important love affairs in Daphne's life were conducted largely in the imagination. People inspired the stories that she then wove around them, but the living being she used as her 'peg', with inconvenient feelings and needs of his or her own, was barely considered. Daphne was fascinated by the way her own creative mind worked and she evolved a theory of her own self.

Some years later, she articulated this first to Ellen Doubleday. Ellen would become one of the most important women in Daphne's life, the first who needed nothing from her, but was an equal, and immune to manipulation. Instead she offered something of the unconditional affection and acceptance she sought. After their first meeting Daphne had felt it safe to confide in her. Metaphorically, she took a deep breath and let her secret out:

> Hold on, brace yourself, see if a McCarter [Ellen's maiden name] can take it! Go right back into the past and see D. du M as a little girl … very shy, always biting her nails. But never being a little girl. Always being little boy. And growing up with a boy's mind and a boy's heart, and a boy's love of adventure. So that at eighteen this half-breed fell in love, as a boy would do, with someone quite twelve years older than himself who was French and had all the understanding in the world, and he loved her in every conceivable way up to the age of twenty-three or so. And by doing so, learnt almost all there is to know about that complex thing, a woman's heart … And then the boy realised he had to grow up and not be a boy any longer, so he turned into a girl, and not an un-attractive one at that, and the boy was locked in a box and put away forever … but when she found Menabilly and lived in it alone, she opened up the box sometimes and let the phantom who was neither girl nor boy but disembodied spirit dance in the evening when there was no one there to see.[10]

Daphne admitted in a memoir that she was almost adult before she finally learned the true facts of life and how babies were conceived, probably from her fellow students in Paris, or from Mlle Yvon herself. It was also possible that bawdy conversations between the girls involved talk of sex toys that might have given her the idea for her very early short story, 'The Doll'. This was written when she was just twenty-one and featured a mechanical male doll, described in macabre detail, and which the female object of the narrator's desire preferred to him. However bold the talk, these well-bred girls, so carefully groomed to make good marriages, were most probably still completely lacking any experience of intimacy with men. Daphne, who had always been alarmed by the nature of men's relationships with women, remained cynical about the possibility of love.

The extent of sexual ignorance and unhappiness in marriage in society as a whole at the time was significant. This was more than twenty years before Kinsey and the results of his experiments into human sexuality burst into public consciousness. Marie Stopes's revolutionary sex manual *Married Love* had been published a few years earlier and become an underground success but was officially dismissed (and banned as late as 1931 by the US customs) and unlikely to get into the hands of the carefully brought-up youth of the du Mauriers' acquaintance. Heterosexual Victorian and Edwardian men – and women – were largely ignorant of women's sexual physiology, and barely acknowledged their needs and responses. Angela's panic when she was eighteen that a chaste kiss could make a woman pregnant was not an isolated misapprehension amongst girls of her class and upbringing. Her admission that she was twenty-five before she connected romantic love, kisses, the conception of babies even, with sexual desire was perhaps rather extreme, but both sexes were inhibited by ignorance, shame, shyness and lack of frank and easy communication on the matter with doctors, friends or partners.

The unhappiness and dissatisfaction in marriages at the time existed mostly due to this ignorance, not only between the sexes but also because well-brought-up women were encouraged to deny in themselves any erotic nature. It was said that Vita Sackville-West, aristocratic writer, gardener and conquistador in love, educated and thereby transformed the erotic expectations of the married women with whom she had affairs, so much so that they were loath to return to the marital bed and the usual wham, bam, thank you ma'am. And Vita was active in the generation between that of the du Maurier girls and their mother.

Early sexual experience, particularly perhaps for a girl, could set the template for life. A clumsy and bungling introduction by an inexperienced or uneducated man could encourage a young woman to think of sex as an unhappy duty – particularly as there was enough propaganda to that effect already. Daphne's first sexual experiences were with a woman and, although she continued to find both men and women attractive, she was never entirely to enjoy the complete heterosexual experience, as she admitted in a letter many years later. When her teenage daughter requested information about birth control, Daphne launched in. 'Well, anyway, I don't mind warning you, here and now,' she told her, 'that although kissing a person and what *I* call making love can be absolute heaven, the actual performance, so-called, is the shilling [family code for anything disappointing or worthless] of all time.'[11]

It seemed that Angela too was rather keener on kissing than anything more, and even then it was the *romance* of it all that mattered. 'All I ever aspired to in my thoughts were lovely marvellous, rapturous kisses.'[12] Certainly, her fictional alter ego in her first novel, *The Little Less*, was repelled by the rough advances of a man who could not believe she was as innocent and naïve as she appeared: 'Never, never, never again would she even speak to a man if this was what happened … She could still feel his hot horrible kisses on her mouth, his hungry hands exploring her body …'[13]

Although they were very different in character, Angela, Daphne and Jeanne shared so much more in being sisters in a family that considered itself as set apart, and touched with genius and fame. Jeanne and Daphne shared a room until Daphne married. 'We three got on so well, we never quarrelled, and could discuss every subject under the sun,'[14] Daphne remembered. Jeanne, being so much younger, was always amenable to Daphne's direction in her fantasy adventures, but it was Angela and Daphne who shared most of their secrets and theories of life with each other. Angela looking back on their relationship recalled, 'Daphne and I shared secrets, and still do. I certainly tell her everything; as a wife and mother she cannot of course go all the way.'[15]

It was therefore not surprising that in Angela's first novel the arguments she put into her heroine's mouth, about the hypocrisy of most marriages, were almost identical to Daphne's plaint in a letter to Tod, written when she was seventeen. In this she had pointed out how irrational it was that in the eyes of the world a wedding ring seemed to change everything, and yet most of the reasons for marriage were mercenary or dishonest. The elder du Maurier daughters seemed to share a certain disenchantment with marriage, as they saw it practised in their own home and in the homes of their friends, and they discussed what they saw.

In the heat of her obsession, Daphne felt she could not live without Fernande Yvon. She had persuaded her parents not only to let her stay a further two terms at the school in Camposena, turning down a chance to join the family for a holiday in Italy, but also to accompany her teacher in the summer to the spa at La Bourboule in the Auvergne. Having been so heavy-handed with Angela over her desire to have a friendship with an 'unsuitable' actress in London, it was remarkable that Gerald and Muriel's hypersensitive sapphist alert did not begin blaring an alarm. Looking back in middle age, Daphne was surprised by their permissiveness, or blindness.

While staying at the spa town, reading a great deal of good French literature, writing letters, and exploring the surrounding countryside in the afternoon, Daphne was in heaven. She had the object of her desire all to herself and was treated by this apparently sophisticated Frenchwoman as her confidante. Ferdy, for so she became, related dramatic stories of her life in which sudden death and thwarted liaisons largely featured. Daphne listened entranced. When her heroine, however, withdrew into moodiness, refusing to explain why, Daphne felt scared and guilty: the insecure, unloved daughter reared her head and she wondered again if it was all her fault. But she never lost her creative detachment. Despite all the turbulent emotions that buffeted her on the surface, she believed, 'buried in the unconscious of the eighteen-year-old, must have been the embryo writer, observing, watching, herself unmoved, noting the changing moods of a woman dissatisfied with her mode of life and temporarily bored by her young companion. The seed of an idea ...'[16]

It was inevitable that on this holiday Daphne's relationship with Fernande Yvon progressed. It was probably here that Daphne 'loved her in every conceivable way',[17] as she admitted in her letter to Ellen Doubleday. She also wrote in her diary when away from Ferdy of the disappointment of waking up alone. Certainly, when she had to return to England for the last part of the summer, Daphne wrote letters to her every day and confided to her diary that she could think of little else. But life had a way of intruding even on obsession. Aunt Billy had brought her a typewriter from the theatre to encourage her to write more short stories, or even start a novel. Daphne did try to be industrious but gave up at the first technical difficulty of changing the ribbon. There was horse-riding on the heath and tennis with Jeanne and Daddy and the usual social distractions of London, with numerous plays and films to attend and family gatherings she could not avoid. But the return in October to Paris and Ferdy was all that really mattered.

However, even Daphne's will to remain at the school was not able to resist the tenacious grip of pneumonia. Languishing in the chilly house at Camposena, Daphne began to lose weight quickly. The family at home were concerned enough to depute a rich American friend, who lived in the swanky Crillon Hotel in Paris, to take their daughter into her care. Margaret Miller had been married to Gilbert Miller, an American theatrical impresario who managed for a time the St James's Theatre in London. She was generous and sophisticated and much loved by Angela, but this time came to the aid of Muriel and her problematic middle daughter. She extracted a reluctant and sobbing Daphne from Mlle Yvon's care and installed her in her own luxurious suite at the hotel, complete with a steam room to treat respiratory ailments. Unfortunately, she also engaged the ministrations of her own personal doctor, who turned out to be a dangerous quack.

Daphne was booked in at the doctor's clinic for a daily injection of what turned out to be *sal volatile*, the active ingredient used in smelling salts. Daphne pleaded that Mlle Fernande should be allowed to visit, but Margaret Miller was not entirely welcoming. Poor Ferdy's discomfort inspired one of Daphne's – and the du Mauriers' – favourite expressions in their private language: as she sat bolt upright on a hard chair, while conversation flowed back and forth but did not include her, 'hard chair'[18] entered the du Maurier lexicon for that sense of offended exclusion.

The treatment continued, but Daphne's health declined further and she lost more weight, eventually weighing less than seven stone. An anxious Muriel and Jeanne travelled to Paris through the December snow to visit her, with the suggestion that a cure in the rarefied air of Switzerland might be the thing. But Daphne did not want to consider this without having Fernande Yvon with her. Much to Daphne's consternation her mother and Mlle Yvon were due to meet for the first time for dinner at the Crillon. What would Muriel think? How would Daphne's feelings for Ferdy change once exposed to the chill reality of home? Despite feeling sick with apprehension, her fears were not realised. She wrote in her diary, 'everything goes off successfully'[19] – though not altogether smoothly, as her journal also records a flaming row between daughter and mother. Daphne had told Muriel she intended returning to Paris after Christmas to continue the treatment, knowing full well it was not working but determined to be close to Ferdy. Daphne won the argument and it was agreed she could return and be cared for by Mlle Yvon until the start of the spring term. Then Angela would take over.

These obsessional, love-struck diary entries embarrassed Daphne when she read them again fifty years later, and it was probably then that she decided to put a fifty-year embargo on their release to the general public, although she used much of their material for her memoir of life before she married. During this period in France, Daphne wrote many letters to Tod and to her sisters. There was no doubt that Angela and Jeanne would have known of the transformation in their sister's emotional life, although Jeanne at only thirteen might not have recognised the source. Certainly Angela, no stranger to emotional tsunamis, would have sympathised, although none of her crushes had so far been reciprocated or lasted as long.

After she had finished her second and final season in *Peter Pan*, Angela was dispatched to Paris to care for Daphne. The smelling salts injections recommenced, but now garlic was added to the bizarre mix and Angela was shocked by the sorry sight of her once robust tomboy sister. 'She was the colour of a banana, smelt like a Calais porter and burst into tears over the smallest matter.'[20] Not even the offer of a month's holiday for the sisters on the Riviera with friends, the hotelier

Sir Francis 'Uncle Frank' and Lady Towle and their daughter Mollie, could arouse any enthusiasm. When she just burst into tears again, Angela realised that she had to get her sister home.

Daphne felt torn from Paris, the city she had made her own, the city she shared with her grandfather George du Maurier, the city where she had found love. The beauty and sophistication of the buildings and their inhabitants and the proximity of modernist artists and writers working in a shared fever of experimentation had resonated with the spirited girl on her own adventure with life. But particularly its cultural, geographic and emotional distance from parents and home allowed her a heady freedom she had never before enjoyed. Now her education was 'finished' and she was 'out' in the world, officially an adult, the future seemed limited and alarming. She could not be content, as Angela appeared to be, to hang about at home, living off her parents' allowance of £150 a year.* She did not care to pass her time in going to parties, theatrical first nights and country house weekends. She had written in her diary on the eve of the new year, 1926, 'the finish of security. Doubt lies ahead. *Adieu les jours heureux.*'[21]

Once out of the clutches of the mercenary doctor, Daphne began to regain her health, but moped around Cannon Hall being moody and difficult. Her room-mate Jeanne still continued with her fantasy of being schoolboy David Dampier, but Daphne could not conjure much enthusiasm for their old games. She only felt free and almost happy riding her horse on Hampstead Heath; the confines of home reduced her to 'a silent frenzy, and a mist of hate comes over me for it all'.[22] She dreamt of being a collie rounding up sheep on the moor. Learning to drive Muriel's car and getting herself a dog of her own, Jock, her second West Highland Terrier, provided some consolation. Driving a car in those days could often be quite literally a rather hit or miss affair: there were no formal lessons, no test, just jump in and

---

* The equivalent of £22,300 if calculated on the Retail Price Index; £95,500 if compared with average earnings.

off you go. Not surprisingly, there were accidents, but Daphne revelled in the freedom and was unfazed by skidding on the London streets into a passing car. She would borrow her mother's Calcott, a distinctive little car manufactured by a small British firm of bicycle makers which had just been taken over by the American company Singer. Jeanne too was involved in a road accident, but at the receiving end, when she was knocked down in the street, but was not badly hurt.

That spring a trip with Jeanne, Muriel and Jock to the Lake District awakened a new kind of ecstasy, for wild country, water, mountains, sky. When their mother had to return to London to care for Gerald, who was rehearsing a new play, Ferdy joined Daphne and Jeanne for the last week. This visit had been much anticipated by Daphne. Parisian allure, however, did not survive so well the mud, gorse and hills of Cumbria, for Daphne no longer felt quite so besotted. It rained a lot and Mlle Ferdy was not very keen on the inhospitable outdoors; accompanying Daphne as she scrambled up chilly becks, and struggled through the rain to the top of a windswept hill, was more in terrier Jock's line.

Daphne's vague disenchantment with her French mistress continued when Ferdy found, on returning to London, that she had been summarily sacked and suggested to an appalled Daphne that perhaps she could start an acting career, with some help from her pupil's distinguished actor-manager father. Had the down-to-earth proprietor, Miss Wicksteed, finally had enough of the divisive favouritism practised by her head teacher towards her pupils? Or did she in fact suspect something more scandalous? Perhaps even Gerald and Muriel had a hand in the matter – certainly Gerald would prove himself capable at the end of the year of threatening to ruin the career of an actress who seemed to be getting too close to his wayward, favoured daughter. For whatever reason, Ferdy suddenly was out of a job and Daphne had the awful dawning thought that her teacher's relationship with her had been nurtured by some hard-headed self-interest. Her father was influential and famous and perhaps Ferdy had always thought that one day she might need his help. Nevertheless, Daphne never lost her affection for Mlle Yvon and, wishing to help in her plans to start another finishing school, offered her the interest due on her war bond that amounted to £95. This Ferdy declined.

While Daphne, Jeanne and Jock scampered over the hills of Derwentwater, Angela had taken up with alacrity the Towles' kind invitation of a month in a luxury hotel on the French Riviera. There, in the Belle Epoque splendour of the Bristol Hotel in Beaulieu-sur-Mer nestling exquisitely on the coast between Nice and Monaco, she restored some of her hurt pride after the failure of her embryonic acting career. Between playing tennis and lotus eating, her heart unfurled in the spring sunshine. She turned twenty-two while in the hospitable embrace of the Towle family and, as if on cue, her prince arrived, or at least a prince's courtier.

This was a grand passion to rival Daphne's. The young man was a member of the immensely impressive and still highly formal entourage of Prince Chichibu of the Japanese Chrysanthemum throne. Many Japanese still considered their royal family to be divine beings and anyone in the prince's entourage had a certain theatrical glamour that Angela found hard to resist. Embellished with these exotic trappings, he seemed to the ecstatic young Englishwoman to be a god-like creature, and he was going to be hers: 'This was IT at last … For two months life was at its most blissful, and Casanova himself wrote no better letters I'll swear.'[23]

Angela's exuberance had got the better of her. But this time she had jumped the gun and pressed an engagement ring on him, he possibly too politely Japanese or hamstrung by courtly etiquette to demur. In her dream of marriage to the demi-god she had already decided on delphiniums for her wedding and pictured Betty Hicks and Daphne accompanying her and Daddy up the aisle. But once again her hopes, so brightly coloured and quickly inflated, were vulnerable to the unwelcome prick of reality. After just eight weeks of happiness, the unnamed and unofficial fiancé declared he could not marry her and disappeared from view, possibly back to Japan; the seductive letters ceased and Angela was left feeling duped and bewildered. Angela told no one in the family except Daphne that she had been jilted, as she saw it, and endured her heartache and humiliation in silence. Such were the shared confidences of the sisters it is very likely that this episode of emotional cross-purposes and piercing betrayal in Angela's life may well have been the inspiration for one of Daphne's recently discovered early stories, 'And His Letters Grew Colder'.[24]

Angela's family were great dog lovers and had always had Pekineses, little imperial dogs that were considered to be largely Muriel's pets. Daphne had had a succession of more sporty hounds, from her favourite West Highland Terriers to various mongrel mutts whose independent way of life had courted death a few too many times. There had been many tears shed in the family over the untimely loss of animals, mostly belonging to Daphne. Now Angela, still in a state of shock and grief at the undoing of her dream of marriage, one day found herself in Selfridges and there, gazing back at her in the Pet Department, was a tiny Pekinese puppy, for sale for the princely sum of six guineas. She immediately bought her and called her Wendy – or, in full, Wendy Pansy Posy Lollypop Stone-Martin – and puzzlingly 'Penelope-Anne' for short. And there began, with her first Pekinese, one of the more enduring love affairs of her life.

The du Maurier family were very lucky in the creative partnerships that Gerald managed to forge with remarkable men. First there was J. M. Barrie, whose plays he produced and starred in to great acclaim. Then there was the business genius of his partner Frank Curzon whose natural astuteness conjured huge sums of money from theatrical enterprises that funded for years the extravagant du Maurier way of life. Then in 1926 a towering personality burst into their world. Edgar Wallace was in his mid-fifties and already famous as a journalist, crime writer and playwright. His creative energy was phenomenal: he was reputed to have dictated a whole crime novel over one weekend. His publisher boasted in the 1920s that a quarter of all the books read by an avid British public were written by him. He had a clumsy childlike personality full of energy, exuberance and fun. In fact as a character he resembled his most famous creation, King Kong, though Kong was yet to be born when this powerhouse of activity whirled into the du Mauriers' view. Wallace wanted Gerald to produce his new play, *The Gaunt Stranger*. Gerald was canny enough to recognise that this story of a legendary assassin motivated purely by personal revenge, and which somehow managed to keep the suspense going to the last act, would be a sure-fire hit. The only proviso he made was that Wallace change the name to *The Ringer*, which he promptly did.

The whole Wallace family became firm friends of the du Mauriers, and Pat, his clever, lively daughter, 'with glasses, and an amount of intelligence and brain that was almost startling',[25] was just a year younger than Daphne, and became a particular friend of the sisters. Angela wrote about Edgar Wallace with gratitude and affection. She found him inordinately generous, sometimes frightening, the most compelling storyteller, and the kindest of men.

The play's first outing was on 3 May, the night before the start of the momentous General Strike of 1926, when nearly two million workers downed tools in support of the miners' struggle with the government to protect their wages and prevent the conditions of their lives becoming even harsher. Daphne wrote to Tod in Australia, 'nothing much happened beyond the fact that buses & tubes were driven by good-looking undergraduates in plus-fours but no body knows or cares what it's all about'.[26] The du Mauriers' main interest was whether the theatres, restaurants and parties could continue through the strike.

Edgar Wallace threw an extravagant first night party at the Carlton Hotel. London was about to grind to a halt but his glittering guest list ran into the hundreds and everyone, dressed to the nines, sat down either side of a very long table to eat, drink and toast a long run. Despite the chaos in the country and the temporary closing down of the transport systems, *The Ringer* was a terrific success, as Gerald had predicted it would be. And thanks to Wallace's generosity in sharing the proceeds, further riches poured into the du Maurier coffers.

The play brought various friends into the family's circle, but one in particular was of the greatest importance to Angela and would remain so until she died. Betty Hicks, her childhood friend, was playing the ingénue and shared a dressing room with the character actress, author and extraordinary personality, Naomi Jacob, known to one and all as Micky. In the play, Micky had to portray a drunken old charwoman, and she played the part with gusto. She was a Catholic, Jewish

Yorkshirewoman and liked to point out that she embodied all the romance and true grit that that hybrid implied. Short and stout and dressed in a gentleman's suit and tie, her hair a short-back-and-sides, she was completely comfortable with the fact that she was not made for marriage or conventional femininity. On the other hand, she exhibited an enormous capacity for nurturing and love: a bossy Jewish mother to all her many friends. Micky and Bet's dressing room at the theatre was suddenly the focal point for anyone in the production, or out of it, and the talk and laughter that emanated from that small room warmed the hearts of everyone who gathered there.

At the Wallaces' first night party, Angela had been riveted by the sight of Micky, at ease in the midst of all the evening dresses and jewels, wearing a velvet dinner jacket, her hair closely cropped to reveal 'a head like Beethoven'.[27] In later years Naomi Jacob was to become famous for her writing and radio broadcasts and had legions of fans; she cherished the letters she received, one of her favourite from a man who had seen her photograph and not surprisingly mistaken her for a man, for whom he felt some solidarity: 'The Catholic faith is only suited to actors and servant girls. It is no faith for a gentleman.'[28] This piece of fraternal advice was greeted with Micky's hearty great laugh.

While visiting Betty Hicks in her dressing room, Angela met this remarkable woman for the first time. She was still hurt by the flight of her Japanese phantom fiancé and was in need of solace. Beneath the surprising gentlemanly exterior, she recognised Micky's lion heart and larger than life personality that could accept and love her for whom she was. Here was someone who, like her, adored Pekinese dogs, opera and Italy; someone who thought she was wonderful – and best of all, *pretty*. Micky wrote about her first sighting of the diffident twenty-two-year-old:

> One hot afternoon, I remember she made her first visit [to the famous dressing room], a small, exceedingly pretty little girl, in a flowered dress carrying a parasol, Angela du Maurier, who one likes on sight, and loves when one knows her.[29]

She recognised Angela's vulnerability and tucked her under her wing. And there she remained, visiting Micky when she was in London in her flat in Harrow Road every week for tea (Micky wrote in her diary 'A.T.4' and it became a ritual that both relied on). They wrote when they were apart and Angela visited Micky when she moved to Italy for her health. For almost forty years Micky was 'my comforter and help and adviser and tear-wiper on more occasions than I care to remember'.[30]

The du Maurier parents were having a difficult time steering their daughters into conventional adulthood. Gerald did not want this natural transformation to happen, while Muriel hoped to marry the girls off with society weddings to wealthy, well-bred men. Instead, their eldest was falling for unsuitable men or cosying up for tea with an unashamed lesbian, twenty years her senior and dressed flamboyantly like a man. Jeanne had yet to set off any parental alarm; Daphne, however, was even more troubling to them. As the girl who had often felt an outsider and uneasy in social situations, the growing recognition of her power of attraction was thrilling and she was to spend the next few years fine-tuning her capacity to disturb men and women alike.

The next focus for her interest, after Ferdy, was a svelte, shingle-headed young actress called Molly Kerr, whom she met in June as part of the cast in a Galsworthy play, *Escape*. Ironically, this play of gentleman prisoner-on-the-run was to be filmed in 1930 with Gerald as the lead, two years before John Galsworthy was awarded the Nobel Prize for Literature. Earlier in the year Molly had returned from New York having triumphed as Bunty Mainwaring in Noël Coward's new play, *The Vortex*, in which she had caught the great theatre critic James Agate's eye with her 'vanity, and her sleek aristocratic head'.[31]

Daphne found Molly Kerr so attractive, she told her diary, that she could easily lose her head over her. With her newfound sexual confidence, she did not leave it merely as a crush conducted from afar, but pursued the relationship and continued to see her, causing great consternation to both her parents and pangs of jealous hurt to Mlle Yvon. Even dancing with the Prince of Wales at a select party thrown by Lord Victor Paget was not as exciting: Daphne at barely nineteen dismissed the Prince, thirteen years her senior, as rather a pathetic little figure.

In the middle of July she went on an outing with Molly, perhaps taking a picnic, to Richmond Park. Something significant happened between them and Daphne, on her return, had to prevaricate to suspicious parents as to where she had been and what she had been doing. After this visit, she wrote the poem that previous biographers have been sure was written about a man:

> 'Oh, we played halma [a board game], talked, and read,
> After all, one has to live.'
> This is what I vaguely said
> To those who were inquisitive.
> But more beautiful, less drear,
> Was the vision in my mind
> A greater risk, a happy fear,
> Halma of another kind,
> Crushed ferns amidst a haze of blue –
> The sun, egg sandwiches – and you.

The poem was written on the back of an unsigned letter that again, it was surmised, came from an unknown man. This letter was rather feminine in its expression and is much more likely to have been a letter from Molly Kerr, referring to the incident in Richmond Park that Daphne mentioned in her diary. The letter read: 'Just got home from leaving you to your bluebells – very late – very quiet – I never want to wake from the trance into which I shot suddenly. Don't ever wake me and don't put it in your diary – oh, that diary! Dangerous, indiscreet and stupid.'[32]

This relationship with Molly survived two quick visits Daphne made to France to be with Ferdy and a trip by the young actress to New York for the play *Loose Ends* that opened on 1 November at The Ritz on Broadway. Certainly Daphne's parents were rattled by Daphne and Molly's friendship, oddly much more than they seemed to be by that with Mlle Yvon. Gerald, in one of his draconian father moods, threatened to ruin Molly's acting career if Daphne did not give her up. If he meant it, it was an outrageous threat, but showed just how much the whole business distressed him, and just how much power he thought he had.

Part of his rage might also have been fuelled by his public spat in 1924 with Noël Coward, the new crown prince of British theatre. *The Vortex* was Coward's first big commercial success and had just finished a triumphant run on Broadway. The author played the frenetic juvenile lead, and Molly Kerr his girlfriend. The subject matter had genuinely shocked Gerald. He did not see theatre as a mirror of all aspects of human life and in this play Coward had unapologetically flaunted the seedier elements of high society: cocaine addiction, suppressed homosexuality and incestuous feelings between mother and son. Scandalised by the airing of such 'filth', as he called it, Gerald was alarmed too at the thought that the theatrical tide was turning against his kind of plays, his style of acting, and that he would be left washed up on the shore, out of date and disregarded. After all, he was in his mid-fifties and already growing tired of the whole show. It was galling that Coward, this mannered, sleekly sophisticated young man who scintillated as playwright, producer, actor and singer/songwriter, was only in his mid-twenties, and already too confident, too successful, too clever by half. Unwisely, perhaps, Gerald publicised his disapproval of what he insisted was 'dustbin drama' and Noël Coward struck back in a newspaper article with even greater venom and unerring aim:

> Sir Gerald du Maurier, having – if he will forgive me saying so – enthusiastically showered the English stage with second-rate drama for many years, now rises up with incredible violence and has a nice slap all round at the earnest and perspiring young dramatists.

He then turned Gerald's rather pompous call for reticence and reverence back on himself with the cattish dig: 'Sir Gerald's reverence so far seems to have been devoted to the box-office.'[33]

Molly's career continued but her name did not occur again in Daphne's 'dangerous, indiscreet and stupid' diary. But then this episode with Molly Kerr, as she suggested in her poem, had been a

game, an experiment with her sexual attraction that remained something separate from her real self – the watching, analytical writer
ready to process experience through imagination, to create the
fictions in which she truly lived.

Despite her recoil from masculine sexuality, Angela was already
longing for conventional marriage and children, perhaps provided
through immaculate conception. Jeanne, so much younger and still
enjoying her male persona as David Dampier, was at school in
Hampstead where, Daphne told Tod, she 'appears to get top marks for
every lesson'.[34] Like her elder sister, Daphne was now officially
launched on society and therefore considered in need of a husband,
although she had no desire for a marriage like those of her parents
and her friends. While with Ferdy in Brittany that August she had
written a poem reflecting her long-held beliefs, using the metaphor
of a property much like Cannon Hall, with the house enclosed by the
walled garden complete with tennis court and croquet lawn:

> If to be happy one must needs be chaste
> Dull and neglected, middle-class and kind,
> Surrounded by a garden and four walls
> Croquet and a tennis court behind,
> Surely one would choose then to be sad …[35]

Her clever, scheming parents, however, had realised after the Ferdy
and Paris experiences, and the battle over Molly Kerr, that they could
not control their headstrong daughter with direct confrontation.
They decided instead on the counter-seductions of the sea and countryside. The money from *The Ringer* allowed them to afford a holiday
house and Muriel thought they should head for Cornwall. The
parents said that it was necessary for Daphne's health but, given their
anxieties about her activities in Paris and London, and their express
desire to have her somewhere, 'where they could keep their eye on
her',[36] it was just as likely to be her moral health that concerned them.

In September 1926, the journey to Cornwall that would change all
their lives began. The three sisters and their mother boarded the Great
Western train at Paddington, heading for Looe. Disappointed with

the town, they hired a car, piled their baggage into the boot and drove a few miles westwards, towards Fowey, arriving on the other side of the River Fowey at the Bodinnick Ferry. From here they could gaze across the harbour to the houses that rose from the opposite water's edge. They were all overwhelmed with the beauty and fascination of the place and, almost as if fate took a hand they thought, there to the left of them, by the ferry landing, was a For Sale sign. It was attached to a ramshackle building that looked like a Swiss chalet and clung to the granite cliff just above the waves. When they enquired, they discovered it was certainly for sale, and was called Swiss Cottage. The ground floor had been an old boatyard with a sail loft above and the only living accommodation was on the third floor. Muriel was known for her intuitive feel for houses, and for her interior decorating skills. She showed her vision and strength in neither taking fright at the state of the property nor at the amount of work involved to make it habitable. Instead, she seemed to share her daughters' excitement that here they would find paradise. Angela's diary entry was breathless and prosaic:

Motored to Fowey which we fell in love with directly. To Bodinnick first, *adorable* … Saw over perfect little place to be sold. Lunched at Fowey Hotel and have taken awfully nice rooms there. Motor-boated to Polperro for tea, very nearly sick. *Quite* heaven on earth, no words to describe it. Motored back, perfect scenery.[37]

Daphne could not wait to explore and her sisters followed her lead in storming the property. Angela and Jeanne entered by the gate near the ferry that led to the boatyard while she climbed the cliffside to the terraced garden and stood beneath the jutting top floor, looking out on the activity of the harbour. Small boats were skiffing over the water, bigger yachts lay at anchor and then the thrill of a big ship approaching with its escort of tugs, to moor just beneath where she stood. Daphne's own diary entry was just as enthusiastic as Angela's, but abrupt and concise. In retrospect, writing many years later, she recognised the epiphany of this moment:

Here was the freedom I desired, long sought-for, not yet known. Freedom to write, to walk, to wander, freedom to climb hills, to pull a boat, to be alone … I remembered a line from a forgotten book, where a lover looks for the first time upon his chosen one – 'I for this, and this for me.'[38]

She was, like Julius, the extraordinary eponymous character in one of her great early novels, stretching out her hands to the sky. And his question, that throughout her conscious life had been hers too, 'Who am I? Where from? Where to?'[39] was answered by the ancient spirits of the place.

From this moment, the lives of each of the sisters would become entwined with Cornwall and the West Country. Angela was to live in the house almost until her death, content with a life and with loves very different from those she had expected when she first came to Fowey. Jeanne would become part of the artists' colonies of St Ives and Newlyn and end up living for the rest of her days with her painting, her animals and her partner in an ancient house and remarkable symbolic garden in the heart of Dartmoor. And Daphne would prove that her parents' ruse had worked. Her feelings for Ferdy cooled into lifelong friendship and her obsession became deflected to a place and a house with which no mere human could compete. With Cornwall as her focus, her restless, aimless life in London was swapped for independence, real contentment and hard purposeful work by the sea. Here in the solitude and beauty of the place, her imagination could take flight. Fowey would eventually bring her marriage too, and halt for a time her disruptive need to exercise her power of attraction over others.

5

In Pursuit of Happiness

I do not blame my parents, they over-indulged us, that was all.
There never were sisters who wished so ardently to eat cake and
have it.

ANGELA DU MAURIER, *It's Only the Sister*

BEFORE THE SISTERS could begin to explore their Cornish retreat,
the ramshackle building their mother had bought in record time had
to be renovated. Its name, Swiss Cottage, sounded too suburban to
their sophisticated London ears so it was changed to the equally
literal-minded Ferryside, for indeed it sat just above the ferry that
plied between Bodinnick and Fowey. While the builders knocked
down walls, reroofed, damp-proofed, partitioned, plastered and
painted, the elder du Maurier girls continued the hedonistic life of a
generation born with the right to play.

After a jolly family Christmas at Sandwich in Kent, Angela and
Daphne set off with Pat Wallace to join the Wallace parents and rest
of their entourage at the Palace Hotel at Caux in Switzerland for a
winter sports holiday. Edgar presided over a vast array of friends who
met for lunch and dinner parties after spending the daylight hours
skiing, skating and lugeing down the bobsleigh run. For Daphne it
was a revelation that she could enjoy the company of people of her
own age and of both sexes, although she still felt drawn towards the
more grown-up members of the party. Her competitive spirit and

need to be as courageous as the next man meant she launched herself flat out down the bob run; 'people say it's astonishing for my second day'.[1] The *après ski* extended well into the night with games and dancing, and both sisters got carried away with flirtations.

Angela's affections alighted on a young Oxford undergraduate who seemed to return some at least of her enthusiasm and Daphne felt 'menaced' (the du Maurier word for attracted) by Edgar Wallace's secretary, a woman called 'James'; equally confusing was the fact that Edgar's vivacious second wife was called Jim. The two elder du Maurier sisters confided fully in each other, Angela admitting, 'I have always told everything to Daphne.'[2] Years later, Angela told her friend Betty Williams that until Daphne's marriage changed the dynamic of their sisterly relationship, Daphne loved her 'passionately, from head to toe',[3] a closeness that would increasingly exclude Jeanne.

They had an uninhibitedly good time in Caux, although the worst of their transgressions would have been no more than a daring kiss or two with the object of their crushes. Daphne shocked Ferdy when she mentioned in a letter that she stayed up late at the bar drinking brandy and soda. The older woman's disapproval might have been as much for the company she kept as for the murder of a good cognac. Daphne, however, seemed unaware – or unconcerned – that Ferdy was suffering some jealousy as she felt her influence in Daphne's life wane.

In 1927, Jeanne was only sixteen and considered too young to be let loose on the wider world and its temptations. She was still at school but sometime in the following year or so she persuaded her parents that she did not want to follow her two elder sisters to Paris to be 'finished', but would rather go to art school. Whatever Gerald's old-fashioned ideas about raising his daughters, he did recognise that his youngest daughter needed to express her considerable talents in painting and drawing. Viola Tree, always a dynamic and influential friend to him, would certainly have encouraged the idea as she had allowed her own daughter, Virginia, a school friend of Jeanne's, to attend the Slade School when she was only sixteen.

Jeanne's formal artistic education began at the Central School of Arts and Crafts – a monumental building on the corner of Southampton Row and Parton Street in London – where she was lucky enough to be taught life drawing by Bernard Meninsky. Twenty years her senior, he was a brilliant figurative painter and draughtsman who was skilled in all media, but sadly his experiences in the Great War had led to a nervous breakdown and to fragile mental health. At the school, Jeanne also learnt drypoint techniques and etching. Perhaps she had already decided what was to be her life's work, for she followed this up with more study later at St John's Wood School of Art. Here, P. F. Millard taught painting in the huge studios decorated with amusing murals by famous old students like Byam Shaw. Eventually, Jeanne would get her own studio in New End Square, opposite Ye Olde White Bear hostelry, just a five-minute walk down the road from Cannon Hall. It was the studio in which Mark Gertler, genius boy painter on the margins of the Bloomsbury Group, had painted some of his most famous paintings, including, in 1916, the pacifist *Merry-Go-Round*.

Jeanne's elder sisters also had begun their search for a way to bring meaning and purpose to their lives. In their parents' circle, daughters did not consider middle-class careers as teachers or secretaries, although it was perfectly acceptable for a girl from the theatrical elite to become an actress. But Angela felt her lack of conventional beauty had disqualified her from the romantic lead and ingénue roles, although she allowed that if she had been more realistic and better advised then she might have made a career eventually as a character actress. However, the underlying problem was her chronic lack of confidence and the necessary ambition and tenacity to make her way in a tough profession. She would love the theatre all her life and liked nothing better than to read scripts for her father, picking out the good ones, and listening to him learning his lines. As long as she had her parents' allowance that just about covered the essentials of life for a young woman-about-town, then she did not have to consider other less glamorous work. But later she could not help wondering, what if?

If only one had been less flighty … I often think that in spite of the colossal hard work, I should have enjoyed musical comedy! I could have sung, I could have danced – but I couldn't have looked!!! (And I should have hated to have been the Funny Woman, even if I had brought the house down!)[4]

Most actors would be delighted to have the kind of power and attention that could 'bring the house down', but in this aside perhaps Angela was expressing her hurt pride at always being the butt of the joke in her own family, the plain woman who, like Micky Jacob, was not offered the romantic lead but the character part.

Out of the blue, Angela and Daphne were asked to do screen tests. The play *The Constant Nymph* had been adapted by its author Margaret Kennedy from her bestselling book and in 1926 had been a great success on the stage. Central to this was a young actress Edna Best who broke the hearts of her audience every night with the poignancy of her portrayal of a teenage girl hopelessly in love with a man called Lewis Dodd (played on stage by Noël Coward) who eventually marries her cousin. Angela was rapt and declared no one could have given a more touching performance; Daphne wept profusely, imagining herself at the heart of the emotionally charged plot: 'Cousin Geoffrey [as] Lewis Dodd to my fourteen-year-old Constant Nymph.'[5] A film was mooted and the director, rather foolishly perhaps given Edna's heart-wrenching performance, had suggested that a completely untried and untrained girl should be cast as the Constant Nymph. Whether it was this part that they had in mind when Angela was called in for her screen test was not clear, but she felt very underqualified for any role on film: 'I was short, plump, not at all photogenic, certainly not pretty ... and needless to say, nothing came from nothing.'[6]

When Daphne was called in for her screen test, the role of the Constant Nymph was definitely in mind. Although she had the looks, she did not in any way have the temperament or desire to be an actress. In her diary she wrote, 'Simply awful. I have to try and do a little scene. I was too frightful, I know, and felt such a fool.'[7] Where her sister's test had caused not even a ripple of notice, Daphne's, despite her deep embarrassment and utter lack of interest, caught the eye of the film's star, Ivor Novello. In the balance of sisterly justice, this was doubly unfair. Ivor was the epitome of male beauty and natural charm. Both sisters knew him as a family friend and thought him handsome and effortlessly glamorous, as indeed he was, and each determined as a schoolgirl that they would marry him, unaware then that he was unlikely to marry any woman. Not only was it Daphne who caught Ivor's professional eye, but acting had been the career that Angela had attempted and flunked. Now her younger sister, with great reluctance and without even trying, was about to be offered the chance of a lifetime: the starring role opposite Novello in a film directed by Basil Dean.

Despite pressure from her mother, father and Viola Tree, Daphne was having none of it. 'A little money and a lot of gush, and tiring, tedious work. I'm not at all keen,'[8] she wrote in her diary. The film was made in 1928 as a silent movie, with the experienced young actresses Mabel Poulton and Benita Hume cast as the young women in competition for the divine Ivor Novello.

Approaching her mid-twenties, Angela was still set on marriage. But she was aware that while she waited for the future father of her children to come along, the parties and first nights, the high days and holidays should be leavened with some Good Works. She turned what energies remained towards the RSPCA, for whom she had become honorary regional secretary, responsible for the wider reaches of Hampstead. This involved entering the various cases of cruelty to animals in a ledger, probably splashed with tears, and then writing an annual report. Her main contribution, however, was collecting money door to door, which she did with dogged determination, pounding the streets with her Peke, Wendy, in valiant and panting support.

She also was inducted into politics when she met Peter Macdonald, MP for the Isle of Wight, at the first night party for her father's play SOS. He enrolled Angela as a Young Conservative under an equally young Conservative, the Hon. Everleigh Leith, who was to become a well-known balletomane and recreational alpinist. Angela was dispatched south of the Thames to darkest Southwark. For this sheltered Hampstead girl it was a shock to find how many other Londoners lived. She set to addressing envelopes and canvassing support for the Conservative candidate in the council elections, and for the upcoming general election of 1929 she canvassed again for the Conservatives. It was an uphill battle, and she would understand for the first time the attractions of socialism. So appalled was she by the poverty and squalor that greeted her as she knocked on doors (and had many slammed in her face) that when a man shouted that he voted Labour and always would, she sighed in sympathy and said, 'Yes, so should I.'

The need to work at something was becoming more urgent for Daphne too. The idea of living at home, entirely dependent on her parents was particular anathema to her. But it was only writing that captured her imagination and she was determined somehow to make it a paying career and her path to independence. Daphne was trying to rediscover her enthusiasm for writing short stories. She had been encouraged by her cousin Gerald Millar, elder brother of the raffish and unreliable Geoffrey, who worked for the publishers Heinemann. He had read her poems and a blank verse play she had worked on intermittently and, although he and his colleagues had not felt able to publish what she had shown them, he urged her to embark on some more short stories. Angela and Betty Hicks had also encouraged Daphne when they had surreptitiously read a story of hers entitled 'Lundy' and reported that they thought it really good and worth her perseverance. But sitting in the dull room above the garage at Cannon Hall, lit only by a skylight and recently appropriated as her 'room of one's own', she struggled for inspiration.

Viola Tree, deputed by Gerald to take his daughter in hand, set off with Daphne to Cambridge to show her undergraduate life. Daphne had a terrific time. With her sharp questioning intellect and love of research she would have benefited from a university education and the life of the mind, but families like hers did not think of educating their daughters beyond the cultural skills necessary to enter society and make a supportive wife for some great man. The highlight of Daphne's visit was tea at Jesus College with Sir Arthur Quiller-Couch, or 'Q' as he was universally known, famous Cornishman, Professor of English and writer of poems, novels and literary criticism. Daphne was twenty-one and 'Q' was well into his sixties, but she was charmed by him and particularly delighted to learn that he had a house in Fowey. He, no doubt, was charmed by her. Certainly she intended to get to know him further and left Cambridge clutching a copy of his *Studies in Literature*.

* * *

The move to Fowey in early May 1927 was an exciting distraction for the du Mauriers, although it involved Angela and Muriel and the indomitable Tod, who had returned from Australia, in a great deal of organisational work and physical effort. They managed to get Ferryside shipshape in three days.

Daphne, meanwhile, was in France, approaching the end of a three-week stay with Fernande in Paris, where she had managed to exert her influence over Mlle's fierce wolf-like dog Schüller until it followed her meek as a lamb. She enjoyed the challenge of walking him in the Bois de Boulogne without the usual massacre of small furry innocents. This was another example of the comfort of power. Daphne read more French literature and sipped lemonade through a straw at various cafés in the Boulevard Montparnasse. But soon it was farewell Paris! Cornwall would be her new love and she set off on 9 May to join her family there, taking Daisy the maid with her.

The house was pronounced perfect. Daphne and Jeanne once more shared a bedroom but, in Daphne's eyes, they had the best – the room she had first discovered that led into the garden and had the fine view down to the harbour. The wooded cliffs were full of bluebells; the water was endlessly fascinating with its lapping tides and boats that plied back and forth, the big ships silently heaving into view. And the town of Fowey awaited. It could not have been more laden with promise and the sisters knew that in this place began the better part of their lives.

But the pleasure of discovery for Daphne was crowned by the rest of her family plus the maid returning to London five days later, leaving her alone (except for the cook, a local woman named Mrs Coombs): 'Oh, the happiness of those weeks!'[9] She learnt how to sail with Adams the boatman, she fished, she explored Fowey and climbed the steep cliff paths and rowed to the coves that unfolded around the coast. She dug and weeded the garden – and ideas for stories crowded into her mind: 'Another quite different story, about a smart vicar in London ['And Now to God the Father'], which would be fun to do and would make D[addy] laugh, if he ever read it. Yes, to work, to work … The time flashing by.'[10]

Adams the boatman was to prove a significant companion for Daphne in all her seafaring adventures. He was a brave survivor of the calamitous Battle of Jutland, fought against the German fleet in the early summer of 1916, when more than six thousand British seamen had perished in the North Sea. He was full of stories of this and his time as a spirited lad in Fowey, brimful of local knowledge of the land and coastline that was his home. Many weeks were spent in each other's company and, with his guidance, Daphne was transformed from dissatisfied city girl into a happy sailor, beachcomber and highly competent boating hand. Most importantly, it was Adams who gave Daphne the seeds for her first novel, *The Loving Spirit*, by telling her the story of the *Jane Slade*. This was an abandoned schooner with a magnificent figurehead that lay beached up Pont Creek and belonged to his own wife's family, the Slades, from the neighbouring village of Polruan.

While Daphne was messing about in boats, Angela was once more on the London stage in a Forbes Robinson production of *Twelfth Night*, but only in a walk-on part and only fleetingly as she cut her hand on a tin during the dress rehearsal and fainted dead away. Before she could even get to first night, she suffered a far worse accident at home at Cannon Hall when she slipped on the polished drawing-room floor and the corner of a wireless she was carrying smashed into her side, rupturing a kidney. In agony, she was pumped with morphine and sent to bed for two weeks. These two experiences, combined with her dive into the orchestra pit while impersonating a flying Wendy in *Peter Pan*, together with nearly getting her nose sliced off in a sword fight in the same part, she took as a warning that her health and happiness lay not on the stage but elsewhere.

The gay London Season continued with her attendance at every opera, ballet and major sporting event. At Wimbledon she saw the US tennis champion Helen Wills dominate in the finals and at the Derby witnessed Call Boy, owned and trained by Gerald's partner Frank Curzon, win against huge odds (earning a fortune for Gerald and no doubt much more for Frank). Then down to Ferryside with Wendy to spend a week with Daphne and accompany her reluctantly back to London. By the end of July, Daphne was back at Ferryside but this time with Jeanne as her companion sister, to greet Bingo, her new puppy, half-spaniel, half-collie, a dog blessed with boundless energy and good humour.

Angela's accident-prone stage experiences were matched by the poor survival rate of Daphne's dogs. All of them thus far had died prematurely, but most traumatically perhaps was the drowning of her West Highland Terrier, Jock, in a water butt at Cannon Hall into which he had slipped while in pursuit of a cat. The running down by a laundry van of his successor, a golden retriever called Phoebus, came a close second. Phoebus was in Angela's charge and, distressingly, bled to death in her lap. Understandably, Angela was even more distraught than Daphne for Angela empathically suffered with the dog and felt herself responsible, while her sister, although saddened by the news, thought it had a more universal significance: 'Another sacrifice. But why? For what reason? Must this always happen to animals I loved?'[11]

The rest of the family descended on Ferryside for the summer, everyone very nervous about Gerald's reaction, for this was the first time he would see the house and the area. As he generally hated being away from London, his home and his club and was hypercritical of anything that did not please him, he was quite capable of cancelling the holiday if the mood so took him. Luckily, Viola Tree was with him when he arrived. She had such natural exuberance and a clownish capacity for slapstick and jokes that no one could be glum for long in her company. Angela recalled the introduction of Gerald and Viola to Fowey as being one of her funniest memories of the time.

Viola arrived by motorboat and fell straight into the harbour, fully clothed and with a very smart hat on her head. Completely unfazed by her unceremonious dunking, and watched by a crowd of people including Gerald, she turned tail with bravado and set off, swimming out towards the sea, her hat becoming more and more rakish as the water lapped at its brim. She made it seem the most natural way to go for a swim. Sadly she did not have the last laugh this time as she caught a terrific chill and within a week was desperately ill with pleurisy.

In France, Fernande Yvon was feeling neglected, sensing that her place in Daphne's affections was slipping: 'Now your letters are so full of Fowey you won't want to come and stay in Paris again.'[12] Daphne felt the claustrophobic pull of others wanting something from her, when all she wanted was freedom. 'I'm Prometheus Unbound!' she declared in triumph in her diary. She dashed over to Ferdy's new house in the Paris suburb of Boulogne-sur-Seine in November, intent on spending a month before returning to Ferryside for Christmas with the family. It thrilled her to feel at home in Paris and she claimed her French blood with pride. But the month was slightly spoiled by the presence of Joan, an older ex-pupil of Fernande's, who was in constant attendance and appeared to dislike Daphne. Both the young Daphne, who wrote her diary at the time, and the seventy-year-old who reread the entries in preparing her memoir, seemed puzzled by this dislike. A possible reason for this antipathy was that Joan was another of Ferdy's lovers and felt some rivalry and resentment at the arrival of Daphne, a more recent former pupil and intimate who took her ascendancy in the household, over both Fernande and the dog, for granted.

Angela and Muriel went ahead of the family to Ferryside to get ready for their first Christmas there. Daphne was left in Hampstead in charge of Gerald, which she found quite a chore. It was significant how much her newly won independence had relieved some of the intensity of her relationship with her father. She and Angela had both written about how his emotional intrusiveness and extravagant suspicions, his possessiveness and dependence, made them reluctant to confide in him, as he so wished they might. This time he drank too much at Gladys Cooper's birthday party on 18 December and was left an emotional wreck. Breaking down and hysterically weeping, he behaved so irrationally that Daphne felt incapable of getting him to Bodinnick alone. Even with the help of Cousin Geoffrey and Uncle Coly, Aunt May's widower, she described the journey as still 'something of a nightmare',[13] suggesting Gerald may have been suffering some kind of psychosis. He only recovered under Muriel's motherly ministrations, combined with bed rest. Daphne showed scant sympathy for him in her diaries, and very little curiosity as to why he appeared to be going through some sort of collapse. Instead she was left thinking 'what a tie married life must be – I hoped it would never be my lot'.[14]

1928 stands as the midpoint between the end of the Great War and the looming shadow of the Second World War. Alongside the curses of unemployment, poverty and inequality, this was a period of real improvement in standards of living for the employed and in education and general health. Above all the interwar years saw an increase in leisure and a flowering of entertainment of all kinds. 1928 was the year in which Mickey Mouse strutted into film and Professor Alexander Fleming had his chance encounter with penicillium mould. The genie of female power had well and truly escaped from the lamp, and in this year British women over the age of twenty-one won the right to vote, at last. Angela would be one of these new women and it helped propel her into volunteer political work. One of the most significant events for her, however, amongst all the first nights and general jollity, was the publication of Radclyffe Hall's sensational novel, *The Well of Loneliness*.

The book shocked the male establishment which launched a concerted, at times hysterical, attack on the book. The clarion call came from the editor of the *Sunday Express*, James Douglas, who in the middle of August's 'Silly Season' for newspapers with substantial stories thin on the ground, wrote an overheated leader article declaring the book should be banned. In the midst of a great deal of grandstanding rhetoric, he thundered: 'I would rather give a healthy boy or a healthy girl a phial of prussic acid than this novel. Poison kills the body, but moral poison kills the soul.'[15]

The novel was so discreet about love between the two women that the only explicit lesbian action was a kiss on the lips and the only sexually suggestive text was the phrase, 'and that night they were not divided'.[16] Radclyffe Hall and her lover Una Troubridge were glamorous friends of Micky Jacob, and Angela, who spent time with them later in Italy while visiting Micky, might well have met them during the turmoil of the campaign against *The Well*. Hall was already a well-known and successful author and had written her book with the express purpose of bringing her kind of love into the open in the hopes for greater tolerance.

As a devout Roman Catholic, she made her female protagonist, Stephen Gordon, melodramatically petition God and the rest of mainstream society: 'Acknowledge us, O God, before the whole world. Give us also the right to our own existence!'[17] Without the campaign against it and the subsequent high-profile obscenity trial, few people would have read the book, and the general populace would have remained largely ignorant about the subject matter. The *Express*, and the trial, made sure the subject was a matter of discussion over most of the nation's breakfast tables – or behind the backs of disapproving parents.

Certainly the operatic emotion in the novel was entirely to Angela's taste. The subject of love and sex was excitingly taboo but, no doubt, had been discussed to some extent with Micky Jacob at their weekly teas. Daphne too would have been part of the chatter, for she sought with her sister some insight into her early exploratory relationships with Cousin Geoffrey, Mlle Yvon and Molly Kerr. After all, this was the book Angela admitted had had more impact on her than any other work by a woman writer, and it had disturbed her. It was this, perhaps, which would give her the courage to embark on her first novel whose subject matter was equally subversive and brave.

1928 was also for Daphne a highly significant year for, at the age of twenty-one, she had encountered the love of her life: Menabilly. This was the house of her imagination, the captor of her soul, but it would take fifteen years until she could possess it for herself. She managed to live in Menabilly for a precious twenty-five years as if it was her own, before it was extracted from her grasp, reclaimed by the family who had owned it for more than three and a half centuries.

All three sisters had enjoyed a glorious summer of freedom and exploration at Ferryside while their parents were mostly busy with a new play in London. At the end of the holidays, Jeanne and Muriel returned to Hampstead and Angela and Daphne had just two weeks more before they too had to drag themselves away.

One afternoon in late October, Angela and Daphne, accompanied by the dogs Wendy and Bingo, set out at last to find the mysterious great mansion hidden in the rhododendron woods on the cliffs about two miles west of Fowey. It was already a house with a dark glamour. Stories about it abounded: it was ancient, abandoned and unloved by the Rashleigh family, protected by an almost impenetrable jungle of trees, bushes and undergrowth gone wild. Still furnished, it was suspended in time by some enchantment, like a sleeping beauty.

Daphne had met the Quiller-Couch family in Fowey that summer and had been delighted by Q's eccentric daughter Foy. Their stories of Menabilly's history in its heyday were the most compelling of all. Built at the end of the Elizabethan era, completed by a Stuart royalist, the house was battered and broken in the English Civil War, its past rich with ghosts and the skeleton of a cavalier. It had an atmosphere so powerful that it changed those who strayed into its domain.

With their heads full of these romances, the two sisters started to walk up the three-mile drive. Hours seemed to pass and the path became fainter and more overgrown. The trees grew taller and to Daphne's eye more menacing, the undergrowth encroached more and more and they eventually lost their way. Angela grew increasingly nervous: 'an eerie and most ghost-like atmosphere pervaded these uninhabited acres, and we threshed backwards and forwards, this way and that, falling into holes and over submerged tree-trunks, realising only too well that we knew neither the way to the great house nor yet the way back to Fowey'.[18] The light was beginning to fail and the unseen owls were hooting and screeching in the trees overhead. The stink of fox drifted on the air and the dogs, much subdued, their tails no longer gaily waving, clung to their heels, starting back occasionally and staring into the gloom. "'I don't like it," said Angela firmly. "Let's go back."

"But the house," I said with longing, "we haven't seen the house.'"[19]

Daphne dragged her sister onwards but then even she was daunted by the dark vegetation that loomed above, encircling them in the gloom as twilight turned to night. They beat their way out of the woods and emerged at a distant cove that they recognised with relief. The great house was nowhere to be seen. Daphne was sure it was guarding its secrets from them and did not want to be disturbed.

Angela was less starry-eyed about the expedition. She had been scared and exhausted and was much more willing to believe the local stories of a haunted house that had lost its soul. However, after a good night's sleep, she was prepared to be persuaded by her determined younger sister, who would not now give up her quest. They set out early and tried a different approach. Driving their mother's little car to the entrance gates at West Lodge, they parked before heading into the forbidding woods. This time they emerged unexpectedly in a clearing, and there Menabilly stood, grey, silent, almost suffocated by the dense creeper that covered its face, the probing tendrils invading the stonework and even the great sash windows. It was an early autumn day and the sisters stared at their prize in the cool morning light. Angela was both disappointed and frightened by what she saw. The grimy windows were shuttered, making the house appear sightless and closed off from the present. She thought it lonely, gloomy and filled with ghosts. In some trepidation they approached and pressed their faces to the dirty glass. The fact it was still furnished, with pictures on the walls, heavy Victorian furniture and a dusty rocking horse in suspended animation, added to the sense of pathos, of other times, of other worlds.

Daphne's emotions were entirely different. Here was her own enchanted princess whom she alone was destined to wake. In her memoir it was striking how she referred throughout to the house, a great, austere mansion built of granite, as 'she'. Daphne noticed the ugly later wing, the altered windows, 'but with all her faults she had a grace and charm that made me hers upon an instant'. Angela realised that from this moment an obsession formed in Daphne's mind: she would somehow, someday, make Menabilly her home. 'This house which had taken complete possession of her heart and soul should one day be hers.'[20]

They returned to London for the usual rounds of parties and first nights. Daphne was more determined than ever to earn money from writing so she could escape her bondage to parents and the city, but Angela and Jeanne seemed happy enough with the life they led there. Angela, however, like Daphne, was beginning to think of writing as a career. With her grandfather's example before her, she thought that a sensational novel might do the trick. Her interest had been caught by *The Well of Loneliness* and its scandalous subject matter. Here she had the theme, but could not have alighted on a more attention-seeking debut as a novelist.

While this idea brewed, she continued with more mundane matters – collecting RSPCA subscriptions, helping her mother with the traditional Sunday parties at Cannon Hall, serving on the Actor's Orphanage Committee, and enduring the rudeness of one of their regular guests for Christmas dinner. Bunny Bruce, the actress wife of the actor Nigel Bruce, declared over the turkey and stuffing that Angela was fat and 'a disgrace'. Angela had never thought of herself this way, although she did realise that at five foot two inches and weighing over ten stone she would not be mistaken for a sylph. She had always felt lumpish compared to Daphne's finer beauty and boyish figure, but being dubbed a disgrace was rather a blinder. The awful thought began to lurk that the reason for her lack of romantic success with young men might be her disgraceful fat. It did little to bolster her confidence. She might have forgiven Bunny – 'obviously she believed in the method of being cruel to be kind'[21] – but she did not forget.

As Angela and Jeanne entered once more into the fray of London society, Daphne could hardly bear the contrast with her life at Fowey. Her sisters, and her diary, bore the brunt of her dissatisfaction:

I think I've been born into the wrong atmosphere. Take Sunday, so typical of all the Sundays I have ever known. People to lunch, to tea, to dinner, and endless discussions of plays, of actors, and criticism of everything. I have to become an unnatural Sunday person and be part of it all … I'm selfish and I admit it, but I know that no person will ever get into my blood as a place can, as Fowey does. People and things pass away, but not places.[22]

Daphne's answer to being exiled from her new love was to immerse herself in books, including many on seamanship and practical boating skills such as navigation. Amongst these handbooks, however, she made particular mention in her diary of an oddity, *De L'Amour Physique*, by a prolific French poet, novelist and critic, Camille Mauclair. The book's thesis was radical, even shocking, for the times. It had been first published in 1912 and had been a great success in France. Mauclair argued that men and women should be treated equally in matters of their sexual needs and consequent behaviour, suggesting that just as men could visit prostitutes without shame so women too should be allowed to pay for sex with men, instead of being 'condemned to a comedy that overlays with sentimentality the purely physical satisfaction that she desires'.[23] This unorthodox thought may well have contributed to Daphne's idea of the chillingly mechanical relationship her female protagonist had with a male sex doll in her striking early short story, 'The Doll', written in its first draft the year before. The idea that women should be free to live like men would also have had a huge attraction to a young adventurous girl like Daphne, who resisted the narrowness and passivity of the female life she was expected to follow.

Perhaps more relevant to all the du Maurier sisters, who had so resented the artificial sexual innocence their parents had tried to enforce in their childhoods, was Mauclair's chapter 'L'Ignorance Sexuelle'. He agreed with them that ignorance was highly destructive but, where Angela had thought it made them scared of men and sexuality and Daphne had felt utterly unprepared for life, he argued something more complex – that ignorance fuelled the imagination, enforced dishonesty and corrupted and distorted natural desires.

Curiosity in children was natural, he declared, but then they had to learn hypocrisy in order to cover up their inevitable investigations and experimentations. He believed that imagination became necessary to fill in the gaps in their knowledge and this combination of curiosity, hypocrisy and an overheated imagination (all the results of being kept in the dark) led to eroticism, '*avec sa consequence directe et terrible chez les enfants: l'onanisme* [with the direct and terrible consequence to children of masturbation]'.[24] Perhaps it was a peculiarly French perversity to deplore masturbation yet to argue for unsentimental sex between prostitutes and their clients, of either sex.

In a letter to Tod, Daphne gave sexual ignorance as the reason for the mess men and women made of their emotional lives, a thought that perhaps resulted from her recent reading alongside her collected works on boating for beginners. 'If only they were brought up to know about sex like they know the rain falling from the sky, half the battle would be over. It's all the mystery and giggle-behind-the-hand that causes the trouble.'[25]

However, as Mauclair developed his argument further, there was a psychological truth that may have found further resonance with Daphne. In her first erotic stirrings with Cousin Geoffrey she had recognised that it was the hidden, secret aspect of her relationship, rather than the man himself and his hand-holding, that was arousing. The excitement of the secret and forbidden, Mauclair believed, would end up so distorting one's taste that the natural act of sexual intercourse could only be disappointing. Instead, the thrill of taboo, together with the power of the imagination, made a young woman return continually to her first sexual experiences, for 'in the mind of the child keeping secret something so disapproved of gives the act an immense and fatal importance'.[26] Daphne agreed with Mauclair, and D. H. Lawrence, when she said, 'that one is brought up to believe sex is "Nature's dirty little secret"'.[27] This book's message explained that secret's erotic charge.

In January 1929, Daphne set off once more with Pat Wallace to Switzerland, to join Edgar and the rest of the Wallace family and friends at the Caux Palace Hotel for a New Year's winter sports and partying. It suggested that her reading of *De L'Amour Physique* might

The sisters' grandfather George du Maurier, celebrated artist and author of *Trilby*, sitting at the desk on which he drew his cartoons for *Punch*.

The sisters' father Gerald du Maurier as a young actor in the early 1900s.

The sisters' mother Muriel Beaumont as an ingénue actress before she became Mrs Gerald du Maurier.

Jeanne, Angela and Daphne with their
father outside their London house at
24 Cumberland Terrace, opposite
Regent's Park, about 1914.

Gerald du Maurier at Westminster
Cathedral for Sarah Bernhardt's
memorial service on 10 April 1923,
the year after he was knighted.

Jeanne, Muriel and Daphne on a stone garden seat with their terrier Brutus, in 1922 when Jeanne was eleven and Daphne fifteen.

Daphne, Jeanne and Angela circa 1917, only a few months before they sat for the large group portrait of the sisters by Frederic Whiting (reproduced on this book's jacket and in the colour picture section).

Gerald playing the possessive father with Daphne, at nineteen already in secret rebellion.

Jeanne studio portrait about 1923, aged twelve.

Angela studio portrait taken in the early thirties, when she was beginning to find purpose and love.

Mlle Fernande Yvon, 'Ferdy', the directrice at Daphne's finishing school near Paris, and her first love; here circa 1928, when she was running her own school and had become a friend.

Twenty-year-old Angela playing Wendy Darling in the production of *Peter Pan* at the Adelphi, with Gladys Cooper as Peter.

Naomi 'Micky' Jacob, 'with a head like Beethoven' – actress, writer, radio personality and stalwart friend of Angela's until Micky's death at her home in Italy in 1964.

The darling
PUFF!!
From Beb.

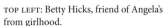

TOP LEFT: Betty Hicks, friend of Angela's from girlhood.

LEFT: Anne Treffry, photographed by Angela at Place, Anne's house in Fowey.

BOTTOM LEFT: Bo Foster, photographed by Angela.

BELOW: Brigit Patmore, literary mentor, photographed by Angela during her visit to Ferryside.

The actress Mary Newcomb, photographed by Angela in the garden at Stinsford, Mary's country house in Dorset where Angela spent many months in the thirties.

'Little and Large': Angela with Angela Halliday, her 'twin' and lifelong friend.

The South African actress Marda Vanne with Angela at Marda and Gwen Ffrangcom-Davies's country cottage at Tagley in Essex.

Betty Williams, whose long-term friendship with Angela began after she wrote a fan letter to her about her memoir, *It's Only the Sister*.

The actor Geoffrey Millar rehearsing at Wyndam's Theatre. Cousin of the du Maurier sisters, he was twenty-two years older than Daphne, and became infatuated with her when she was fourteen.

Carol Reed, the son of Sir Herbert Beerbohm Tree and Daphne's first boyfriend, here in 1929, aged twenty-two, like her. Later he became a film director famous for *Odd Man Out*, *The Third Man* and *Oliver!*, for which he won the Oscar for Best Director.

Henry 'Christopher' Puxley, romantic 'soul mate' of Daphne's during the Second World War, spur to her imagination in writing *Hungry Hill* and *Frenchman's Creek*.

have released some inhibitions, for she enjoyed herself even more than two years previously when she and Angela had surprised themselves with how much fun their contemporaries could be. This time Daphne had greater skills at the sporting activities by day, and discovered how successful she could be with the young men at night. The most daring it got was dancing cheek to cheek, light-hearted kisses and late nights at the bar, but she felt compelled to boast to Ferdy: 'I was kissed by two young men at the same time ... and another man, married, kissed me outside in the snow.'[28]

Daphne drew men like moths to her flame, but their amorous attentions did not mean much to her, except for the excitement of the power it bestowed. The person she most fancied, she confided in her diary, remained Edgar's female secretary, James, who had caught her eye during their last holiday with the Wallaces. But the most attractive of the young men who fluttered about her was not going to be put off. He was Carol Reed, an illegitimate son of Sir Herbert Beerbohm Tree, and thereby a half-brother of their much-loved friend Viola Tree. Only six months older than Daphne, his persistence would make him the first important man in her life, after her father and Geoffrey. Reed was charming and talented, an actor turned producer/director, who would be responsible for the masterpieces *The Third Man* and *Odd Man Out*, eventually winning an Oscar for *Oliver!* and a knighthood for his services to film. He could not have been a more suitable suitor.

Ferdy was not amused by Daphne's light-hearted, confessional letter, and wrote to Aunt Billy relaying her niece's licentious behaviour in Switzerland. Like wildfire the news spread to her parents and the Wallaces. Edgar, feeling his relaxed hospitality had been taken advantage of and that it reflected badly on him, did not welcome Daphne back into the family fold for many months to come. When she eventually returned to Cannon Hall, via Ferdy and Paris, her reception was cold. It grew colder as Carol Reed followed her to London and they pursued a youthful love affair, under Gerald's increasingly paranoid glare.

But more importantly to Daphne, she was writing short stories again with the excitement and intensity of old. The thrill of hurtling down the icy slopes of a Swiss mountain was translated into the swift adrenaline-filled dash of a story about an actress. She also copied out another story, 'East Wind', which she had written when she was nineteen – a strange brutal story of murder, madness and sexual awakening conjured up in a remote and peaceful fishing community by the relentless blowing of the easterly wind. The sexuality in the story was no more overt than the mention of moist lips and the pressing of warm flesh, and this may have been all that happened between herself and Carol Reed, both young and inexperienced as they were. They were inevitably wary of pregnancy and outraging social mores. He had wished he had played the hero and clambered up to her window one night and Daphne seemed half-relieved he had not: 'It would have been awful, I suppose, if he'd been seen.'[29]

Gerald's jealousy and suspicions had him cross-examining Daphne at breakfast, making her squirm with the intrusiveness and inappropriateness of his questions. He was back on his midnight vigil at the landing window, waiting, watching, twitching the curtain as he strained to catch his daughters kissing their beaux goodnight. Daphne was to use these humiliating memories to sinister effect in her third novel, *The Progress of Julius*, written three years later, about a father's murderously possessive desire for his daughter:

> 'I saw you,' he said. 'I saw you from the window. Out in the square with some fellow. You were in that car eight whole minutes [in her diary she mentioned kissing Carol in the car for five minutes], and then you got out and I saw him kiss you. You bitch!'[30]

In the novel, the daughter enjoyed taunting her father, patronising him as a fool, as someone getting old and losing his virility, while she remained masterful with the magnetism of youth and sexual attraction. For Daphne, there was a similar excitement at discovering the power inherent in her beauty and desirability and in the exercise of it: 'Knowing you can attract people … really is more heady than champagne.'[31] This realisation had begun covertly, with her own father's dependence and favouritism towards her somehow entwined with Cousin Geoffrey's suppressed desire. Her growing sense of power was greatly boosted by her success in overthrowing all competition for Mlle Yvon's attention and affection, and now, with Carol Reed, a young man of her own generation and background, she once more held the upper hand. It was an exhilarating feeling, this sense of conquest and control.

But she did not herself become enslaved to love or desire. While in the throes of this new romantic relationship with the besotted Carol, Daphne was capable of fantasising about the actor Leslie Howard, who embodied some kind of creative peg for a story, or fulfilled some need in her for a doe-eyed man. But she did not want to be tied down at all. Recalling the primitive male energy she captured so well in her story, 'East Wind', Daphne wrote in her diary: 'What a pity I'm not a vagrant on the face of the earth. Wandering in strange cities, foreign lands, open spaces, fighting, drinking, loving physically. And here I am, only a silly sheltered girl in a dress, knowing nothing at all – but Nothing.'[32] In her imagination and fiction, however, she could become whatever she chose to be, that vagabond boy, that free spirit, untrammelled by the limitations and expectations of family and the rest of the world.

For Daphne there was panic too that her parents, in their very different ways, sought to contain and control her. It exasperated her that when she at last turned up with a young man of her own age, and from the right background, they still made as much fuss as they had about her relationship with Ferdy, and her passing attraction to the actress Molly Kerr. Something of this frustration went into her portrayal of the mother in *Julius*, set by her husband in deadly competition for his love with her own threateningly seductive daughter whose power, she fears, can only be defused through marriage:

> … hoping with bitter, grim tenacity that the girl of eighteen would wake up suddenly and throw away her crude, unbroken, dangerous charm and fall in love and lose her individuality. Then only would she be harmless and natural; the wife of some man – or even his mistress … possessed and held at last.[33]

As Muriel's main concern was Gerald's peace of mind and happiness, and he was far from happy with his daughters' slipping the surly bonds of family, she could not rejoice that Daphne, now in her early twenties, was interested at last in such a nice, eligible young man, with impeccable theatrical provenance. This jealousy of the carelessly beautiful daughter who came between her and her husband, transmuted into an unexpressed hostility. All her life Daphne remembered with a shudder, her mother's 'cold awful *suspicious* look at me, after I had come in rather late, having been out in Carol's Lagonda'.[34]

Gerald's paranoia about his daughters' behaviour was stoked once again by his elder daughter Angela, who had always seemed more conformist, but also appeared to be hellbent on steering a romantically dangerous course. In 1929 she met the man who came closest to marrying her. 'I had at last found what novelettes are pleased to call Mr Right.'[35] She did not name him, but mentioned he was almost as famous as her father, was married to another and almost certainly a good deal older than she was. They met while she was involved with canvassing for the general election: a socialist, he was at that time in the opposing camp to herself, a cradle Tory.

Love brought Angela into the exciting turmoil of politics, and this election was a critical and interesting one. She and her generation of women under thirty were added to the electoral roll and for the first time they would be able to make their interests known via the ballot box. For this reason it became known in some quarters as the Flapper Election. The Conservatives were in power under Stanley Baldwin and had presided rather ignominiously over the General Strike three years before. Millions were out of work, poverty was rife; there was widespread disillusionment with a ruling party that seemed old and tired.

Angela's job was a difficult one. She had to persuade the poor and disadvantaged people of Southwark that voting Conservative would improve their lot, as they shouldered the brunt of high unemployment and low wages. She attended a huge rally, where Baldwin gave his electioneering speech, and was greatly impressed by the excitement and theatricality of the whole event. She was delighted he was an Old Harrovian 'like Daddy!'[36] He was, however, up against the charismatic new Liberal leader David Lloyd George, and Ramsay MacDonald who pledged that a Labour government would tackle as its first priority the rising tide of unemployment and the cost of living, where there were still taxes levied on staple foodstuffs.

Angela and the new 'love of her life' argued their opposing politics during surreptitious visits to the zoo or out-of-the-way restaurants, and planned how they could somehow make their lives together. When Angela eventually confided her feelings to her parents they were horrified and deeply disapproving, and attempted to freeze the relationship out by refusing to talk to or entertain Angela and her man friend. She never forgot how bitter and miserable she was made by their lack of sympathy or understanding. Most unforgivable, she felt, was her father's outburst of anger. 'How little cause my father had when he called me a whore – virgin as I was – when I told him I was in love with X, and that X loved me.'[37] This was a shocking accusation towards any daughter, but particularly one as conscientious and highly emotional as Angela. She was all the more shattered by his reaction as her love for this man had not been consummated. This violent and unjust response was no doubt relayed to Daphne and added by her sister to her memorable portrayal of paternal cruelty in *The Progress of Julius*, where the father was quite capable of spitting, 'You bitch! ... You bitch!'[38] at his daughter, when she showed interest in another man.

The general election was not only the first time that Angela, as a woman, was allowed to vote but it was to prove the watershed of her romantic life. Her first and last real love affair with a man had unfolded during the hard work that preceded it, but with the election of a Labour government at the end of May came the end of any hope she had of marriage. 'We had a superstitious gamble on the issue [of the election]: if the Conservatives won all would be well with us; if Labour, then all would be over. It was the first time I'd had a vote, and a great deal of my heart went into the ballot box.'[39]

Angela was not, however, as dutiful a daughter as she appeared. Rebellion was growing in her heart. Despite her 'Mr Right' being married, she declared she would have been prepared to run away and live with him, and face the opprobrium this would have called down on their heads: 'In those days it would have needed untold courage on both our parts, as he was nearly as well known as my father and we would have courted censure from the world we knew.'[40] She also decided this was the last time she would be honest with her parents about where she went at night, what she got up to and what her feelings were about anything that mattered.

Angela's fictions were pretty closely tied to her own and her friends' experiences and preoccupations. Her doomed love for this man was perhaps immortalised ten years later in her first published novel, *The Perplexed Heart*, where her heroine, Verona, falls in love with a champagne socialist, Maxwell Harris, who has a 'genuine Christ-like attitude towards the poor'.[41] For an intelligent and serious politician he also has a callow and theatrical way of speaking: 'I couldn't bear you to look old. Awful old frights you conjure us up as! We must both die young, gallantly, and very thrillingly. In an air-smash I think.'[42] It could almost have been her father speaking in one of the light, drawing-room melodramas he produced at Wyndham's. In a much later novel, *Reveille*, published in 1950, Angela re-entered the socialist versus Conservative debate. Her socialist anti-hero, who is in love with a heroine who, had she married well and pursued her political ambitions would have borne a striking resemblance to Angela, owes something to this forbidden love. 'He had a slow cynical way of talking, was inclined to a biting and sarcastic wit, and embarrassed the wrong type of person by suddenly quoting poetry, which he spoke beautifully.'[43] Needless to say, Angela's fictional self did not marry the man, but he loved her until his bitter, self-inflicted death.

In real life, Angela was stricken with grief at the loss of her dreams of happiness. In the middle of all this, she ended up having an emergency operation to remove her appendix. Thereupon the wronged wife of 'Mr Right' became convinced that the procedure was really an abortion, an accusation that was doubly distressing to a heartbroken Angela. This was the painful and ignominious end to what was to be her last attempt at living a conventional life with a husband and children. She was not yet twenty-five years old. The lack of children was to prove a lasting regret for her but she was to fill her life with friends and dogs, and to find happiness in the love of women.

Two people who became good friends to her at the time were Rita Jolivet, the beautiful Anglo-French actress, and Stafford Bourne. Rita had made world news by being a brave survivor of the *Lusitania*, torpedoed by the Germans in 1915 (she had stood at the bridge as the liner went down). In the summer of 1928 she had married, as her third husband, the immensely popular Jimmy Bryce Allan, a rich and well-connected Scottish landowner and socialite. They invited Angela up to their grand gothic castle, The Cliff, at Wemyss Bay in Renfrewshire, and there began an emotional connection with Scotland that was to last most of her life.

In between her two visits to the smart nursing home where first she had her tonsils out and then that controversial appendix, Angela was introduced to a young man not much older than herself who was recuperating from his tonsillectomy. Stafford Bourne was the son of the Bourne half of the great West End store Bourne & Hollingsworth, and there began a chummy friendship with lunches at The Ivy, weekly visits to the theatre and country house weekends at his mother's grand house, Garston Manor in Hertfordshire. When he married and had children of his own and took on more responsibility at the store, their lives inevitably diverged, but the friendship remained, in a more diluted form, with the whole family.

The Wall Street Crash that autumn reverberated round the world. The sense of doom and approaching economic depression affected Gerald in his working and personal life. He owed money he did not have to the Inland Revenue, his daughters were growing away from him, and in the theatre he was thrown back on tired old favourites like Barrie's *Dear Brutus* that he had made so triumphantly his own twelve years before. That Christmas he also returned for the first time to *Peter Pan* and to the roles as Mr Darling and Captain Hook that he had fashioned so successfully for himself it became a template for the actors who followed him.

Despite ceremoniously attending the production every year, this was the first time his daughters saw their father bring to life the great mythic characters he had helped create. Luckily, having heard so much about his brilliance and how he had had no equal, Gerald managed once more to spring across the stage, almost as athletic as he was of old, and conjure the pathos and menace of Hook. He was superb, Angela loyally declared. But Gerald was getting tired of it all and Daphne realised he had long ago lost his enthusiasm for capering about on stage in a Charles II wig, brandishing a toy sword. Anyway, he admitted, 'it plays the devil with your back, your voice, and your temper the next morning'.[44] Never one to enjoy modern life, living always with a nostalgic backward glance to his father and brother Guy and the youthful times that would always seem more golden, he felt a weariness and lack of sympathy with the world. He was now in his late fifties, had far outlived his hero brother and was getting close to the age when his beloved father had given up the fight and abandoned them all for death.

Daphne recalled how Gerald, always in need of distraction and entertainment, happiest when at the centre of things, was growing increasingly sad and lonely. He mourned his lost elder daughters:

> Gerald was hungry for companionship; he longed for Angela and Daphne to tell him everything, to discuss their friends, to solve their problems, to share their troubles; but the very quality of his emotion made them shy … he was so changeful, so inconsequent a man, a judge intolerant and hard one day, and human, all too human on the morrow. They were never quite sure of him, never certain of his mood, and they walked away from him.[45]

In an attempt at throwing off Carol Reed's attentions towards his daughter, Gerald organised for Daphne to join the party on board Otto Kahn's luxury yacht for a three-week cruise in the Baltic, through a Mr Fixit, the writer and theatrical impresario Rudolph Kommer. If he had had a clue about his daughters' private lives, he might have realised that Daphne's morals were far less likely to be compromised in her continued romantic friendship with the shy and honourable Mr Reed. Instead, in her current mood of newfound sexual allure, she was let loose on a boatload of strangers.

Otto Kahn was a vastly rich and charismatic investment banker, philanthropist and patron of the arts. He was older even than Gerald, suave and easy-going in temperament and used to having his own way. Although reluctant at first, Daphne loved the cruise, amazed by the luxury of the boat and thrilled by the scenery. She was amused too by the changing configurations among the ten varied guests, but she was possibly the only member of the party who enjoyed herself so much. At the end of the holiday, she was told by the man at whom she had initially set her cap (a gentle beardy like Tennyson, she thought) that she had ruined the cruise for all five of the other women present. Daphne, oblivious to the effect of her behaviour on others, seemed nonplussed. 'A little horseplay, neither more nor less,'[46] was how she responded. After all, she had entertained in her cabin a besotted wing commander called George, purely to tease, but had not realised this would upset his wife no end. Although the beautiful German girl who had come along as Kahn's companion was sidelined by the host's increasing interest in Daphne, it was hardly her fault. While alone with Kahn on the banks of a spectacular fiord, she had evaded his increasingly amorous approaches by stripping naked and diving into the crystal cold water in front of his astonished eyes, apparently unaware that this might inflame his passions further. At their next stop he offered to buy her a fur coat, but she asked for a dagger instead.

By now, Rudolph Kommer was regretting taking on Gerald's wayward daughter. Her faithful diary records this analysis from its emotionally blinkered owner:

> I think we are all getting on one another's nerves. Kommer hasn't spoken to me for two days, I don't know why. The women are on edge. Irène got blind drunk at lunch. She's lovely to look at but such a crashing bore, perhaps that's why Kahn went off her and the other men didn't fall. As for George [the Wing Commander] he is at the moment lying on my bed, purely to rag, as the poets would say! As long as he doesn't start snoring I don't care.[47]

But the faithful diary could not offer a little psychological insight in return. It was perhaps significant that Daphne, now grown-up at twenty-two, showed little solidarity with the other women, and less sense of concern for the ease and enjoyment of her fellow guests, with apparently scant understanding of why they might have felt discomforted.

Absorbed in her own experiences, exploring her own ideas, this seemed more of a kind of emotional blindness in Daphne than any malice. With the insouciance of a novice she was exercising the undeniable power of her sexual attractiveness, unaware of how this unsettled the men and upset the women. Years later she recalled the excitement of her youthful experimentation at the Wallaces' skiing holiday and her experience on Kahn's yacht: 'I wildly remember [being promiscuous with my kisses] for a few months, thinking I had Power when I was about twenty-one – because it's like putting on too much lipstick, one suddenly doesn't know when to stop!'[48]

Upbraided by Ferdy for being weak and selfish like Cousin Geoffrey, Daphne knew her detachment from normal human feeling and her selfishness were necessary to her writerly self: 'the writing me is different from the living me, yet they're both mixed-up. If writing goes there would be no longer any reason for living. It's the opposite extremes that makes the conflict.'[49]

Daphne's fatal attractiveness may have blighted everyone else's holiday, but she came home refreshed and empowered and she stored the cruise experience away in her memory to reprise it in *I'll Never Be Young Again*. To write, to write, this was what she most wanted to do, but still had not found her way. Uncle Willie, her mother's brother, had published in his magazine *Bystander* her much-edited short story, 'And Now to God the Father', and she had earned £10. Celebrations indeed! He had also introduced her to the literary agency Curtis Brown, and to Michael Joseph, the man who ran their fiction side. Michael Joseph suggested she write a novel before trying to get a collection of short stories published, just as Daphne was thinking about writing about Jane Slade and her Cornish family. She admitted she did not yet feel up to the task. Continue with the stories then, was his sage advice. Having fled once again to the warm embrace of Paris and Ferdy, Daphne found a constellation of new ideas for stories suddenly crowded her mind. She began to write.

If the young Daphne had any muse it was Katherine Mansfield, whose stories she so admired and longed to emulate. It had excited her very much to hear that when the du Maurier girls were children, Katherine lived in the next road to Cannon Hall and used to watch them playing on Hampstead Heath and longed to talk to them. She was not quite twenty years older than Daphne and had died tragically young of tuberculosis when Daphne was fifteen. Discovering this connection had made her believe that something of Katherine's creative spirit had entered her soul. Now grown up, Daphne was suddenly desperate to visit Katherine's grave and Ferdy organised a taxi to take them to the old forest cemetery at Avon near Fontainebleau. After some trouble they found the overgrown headstone. There was something poignant and pathetic about the fact her husband Middleton Murry had never visited it, and Daphne wished she could afford to pay to have the site tended. On the simple stone slab was inscribed Hotspur's words from Shakespeare's *Henry IV*, words he had used when being warned of the riskiness of his plan, words that Katherine had loved and lived by: 'I tell you, my lord fool, out of this nettle danger we pluck this flower, safety.'

Ferryside beckoned for the summer but the house was too full of family and friends coming and going for Daphne to have the concentration necessary to start her novel, but by autumn everyone returned to London and she could begin. Luckily Carol Reed was busy, although his plaintive letters told her how much he longed to see her. Cousin Geoffrey, older, seedier, divorced again, his life pretty much washed up, plucked at her coattails too. But Daphne was not interested enough in either. Carol was her son-like acolyte and Geoffrey the weakling brother: neither was important enough to her for any sacrifice of Fowey and her writing life.

Jeanne, having made her decision that art was to be her future, was now eighteen and had brought her friend Elaine with her to Ferryside. Together they and Daphne, and a cousin Ursula, Uncle Willie Beaumont's daughter, set out to find Menabilly again, from the difficult eastern approach. This time they made their way through the wild woods that had turned Daphne and Angela back the first time. They still seemed sinister and impenetrable but they did manage to find the house and enter it by the derelict, unfinished north wing. Excited, and yet also daunted by the dust and debris and the weight of the past, they climbed back to the present through a downstairs window. As Daphne secured the catch, a great white owl flew out of an upstairs window.

The sisters were keen sea bathers and loved to swim naked from the secluded coves that proliferated around Cornwall's south-east coast. One day, lying in the sun, salty from the sea water, Daphne felt overwhelmed with an urgency to write: 'Sometimes my book comes so strongly on me that it's like a restless urge within saying "Get on! Get on!" I want silence more than anything, the peace of solitude, long hours for reflection … No striving after cleverness, nor cheap and ready-made wit. Sincerity – beauty – purity.' A line from 'Self-Interrogation', a poem by her favourite Emily Brontë, was suddenly vivid in her mind: 'The Loving Spirit' was what she would call it.

Angela too was quietly considering her future now that she felt her best hopes of marriage had been thwarted. Could she also write a novel? But her ambition was more tentative and secretive than Daphne's. Just as her father and mother were the actors in the family, Jeanne was the artist, and Daphne the writer, Angela knew it would take some extra confidence in her to trespass on these territories already marked out by her family. Love was everything to Angela, and if she was to write that would be her theme, despite her limited personal experience.

Love, or rather to be the object of love, was paramount for Gerald too. His creative powers might be failing and his power over his daughters on the wane, but he nevertheless continued his restless flirtations and inconsequential conquests. While he was obsessing over Angela's and Daphne's morals, a popular limerick was doing the rounds:

> There was a young lady called Gloria
> Seduced by Sir Gerald du Maurier,
> Jack Hulbert, Jack Payne,
> Sir Gerald again
> And the band of the Waldorf Astoria

But then Victorian fathers and their twentieth-century daughters were bound to find that a gulf opened up between them on the matter of sex, bridged if at all with many misunderstandings, but widened by double standards and hypocrisy.

6

Set on Adventure

Oh, the utter joy of looking across the harbour once again. Blue
smoke curling from the grey houses opposite, the haze over the
water, the noise & smell of ships … What more on earth should I
want but these things? I'm here, I've always been here, and yet the
me of the past is still going on …

DAPHNE DU MAURIER, *Growing Pains*

THE 1930S WERE a very different era from the glamour and carefree
exuberance of the previous decade. The Jazz Age was becoming the
age of austerity. The Wall Street Crash and ensuing worldwide depression brought a new mood of anxiety, and belt-tightening gloom. The
popular press no longer followed the antics of the privileged young
with slavering admiration. As working men marched for jobs, and
hungry children ran shoeless in the streets, there was a growing
disgust at flamboyant wastefulness and wanton excess. Uncle Willie's
weekly magazine, *Bystander*, recognised the mood had turned against
the feckless rich. When a 'Red and White' fancy dress party (the host
in white silk pyjamas, long kid gloves, ruby and diamond bracelets
and a muff made of white narcissi) coincided with a march of the
unemployed, it thundered its disapproval. 'When such ill-bred extravagance was flaunted, as hungry men were marching to London to get
work,' it asked, who could be surprised if people turned in revolt to
communism?[1]

The dancing was over too for the du Mauriers. Gerald, approaching sixty, was becoming increasingly disenchanted with everything. He missed his brilliant theatrical partner Frank Curzon who had died in 1927 at not yet sixty. He had managed to leave the world in his customary style, dying a month after making his last trip to Epsom racecourse, against doctor's orders, to see his horse Call Boy win the Derby. Gerald had lost too his business partner, the irreplaceable conjuror Tom Vaughan. Together these men had been father figures, oiling the wheels of Gerald's work and home life and effortlessly, it seemed, keeping the fountain of gold sovereigns flowing. Now both were dead he felt abandoned, his daughters were growing up and did not need him, and the Revenue was still pursuing him. His last success in the theatre was *Cynara*, made memorable by the magic of acting once more alongside Gladys Cooper who played his betrayed wife. Celia Johnson made her triumphant debut as the luminous shop girl, whom Gerald's character was meant to prefer to this legendary beauty.

The paucity of successes in the theatre and the need for money made him turn with reluctance to film. Their old friend Basil Dean, who had wanted to cast Daphne as the Reluctant Nymph, now cast her father as the fugitive hero in *Escape*, a movie shot at Elstree and on Dartmoor. British film-making in its infancy was a long way from the luxury of being a celebrated actor-manager in your own West End theatre in its heyday. Gone was the civilised luxury he craved and a leisurely start to the day. Now Gerald had to rise early and then hang around until needed to clamber over the moor's rocky outcrops, and clamber again, and repeat *ad nauseam*, until Dean had perfected the take. If two performances a day in the theatre was a chore then mindless repetitions of a scene, while the light changed or camera angles were adjusted, was almost unendurable. For a man with a very low boredom threshold, the experience of film-acting was close to purgatory. The youthful technicians did not hold him in the same affectionate awe as did his faithful staff at Wyndham's and, although Muriel was there to soothe him, he felt himself a dinosaur from another age.

He returned to the stage with another dull melodrama, John Van Druten's *Behold, We Live*, but this was made significant by the fact that his co-star was the great Gertrude Lawrence. As mercurial and mischievous as Gerald himself, she became 'the last of Daddy's actress loves'.[2] She was so similar to him it was like Narcissus gazing at his own reflection in the pool. Fascinating, highly strung, quicksilver in her moods and repartee, ravenous for male attention, she was a woman who lived life at such a tempo that, like Gerald, she defied and feared old age. In fact, as they were to both die well before their allotted span, both managed to evade the decline they dreaded.

Another great friend of Gerald's, and a different force of nature, died young and without warning: the unexpected news of Edgar Wallace's death at fifty-six shocked the world. He was in Beverly Hills, working on the original screenplay for a 'gorilla picture' that was to become *King Kong*. For such a gargantuan personality, so vastly energetic and prolific in output, it had been impossible to think of him slowing down, let alone dying. Pure willpower had driven him on, despite any unacknowledged failures of his body. When he had a late diagnosis of diabetes so serious the doctors could not believe he was still functioning, the realisation of his mortality overwhelmed his will to live. Within days the creator of Kong was dead. He was never to know just how iconic the great gorilla was to become.

For Gerald, the death of Edgar was a terrific blow. Another titan of his past was gone. He had been such a large-spirited friend, the creative and energetic engine of so many collaborations. The whole du Maurier family owed him much, for his brilliance and generosity had helped finance Ferryside, the house that would transform all three sisters' lives. His death reinforced Gerald's sense of futility. To be a theatre actor was to know that your life's work was evanescent, that nothing remained of your triumphs except in the fading memories of others. Life too seemed to flee before him and film, the medium that captured something for posterity, seemed to him such a poor two-dimensional thing, and tedious beyond belief.

But both he and Gertie needed to pay off the taxman and they embarked together on another film, *Lord Camber's Ladies*, with the family's friend Nigel Bruce as Lord Camber and a younger friend, Alfred Hitchcock, as producer. It was slight and inconsequential, a quota quickie, about an aristocratic love affair, a poisoned wife, false accusations of murder – all tied up predictably in a bow.

The film did not improve Gerald's mood. Existential boredom and despair meant his habitual reliance on endless practical jokes to enliven and dominate proceedings got increasingly out of hand. He had as his partner in crime his mischief-making co-star Gertie. Hitchcock's appreciation of cruelty and control made him an ally too in the worst of Gerald's jokes. Daphne realised how desperate was this need in her father for distraction, and for maintaining his role as the arch manipulator, yet how trying it all was for the other members of the cast. It was also another example of how, despite being extremely sensitive and touchy about his own feelings, he could be oblivious to the discomfort and embarrassment he inflicted on others:

> with his pockets full of tricks and practical jokes that he let fly amongst the feet of cameramen, electricians, and directors in a sort of desperate effort to relieve the tedium. Practical joking during these months developed to a pitch of positive frenzy ... hardly a moment would pass without some faked telegram arriving, some bogus message being delivered, some supposed telephone bell ringing ... It was a game that could be carried too far, and settling as it did into a daily routine, ceased before long to be genuinely amusing, and almost developed into a vice.[3]

While for Gerald work had lost its lustre, for his daughters it was just beginning. Their adult lives lay before them, full of unknown possibilities. Having found it difficult to start on her novel about Jane Slade and her shipbuilding family, suddenly, in the autumn of 1929, Daphne began. On 3 October, with a rug around her knees, she sat at her desk in her cold bedroom at Ferryside looking out on the busy harbour, and wrote in capitals the title of her first novel, which had been conceived of on the beach: 'THE LOVING SPIRIT'. The poem from which it came seemed to express something of what Daphne felt for the abandoned schooner with its great bleached figurehead, symbolic of human endeavour and the family from which she came:

Then art thou glad to seek repose?
Art glad to leave the sea,
And anchor all thy weary woes
In calm Eternity?
Nothing regrets to see thee go –
Not one voice sobs 'farewell';
And where thy heart has suffered so,
Canst thou desire to dwell?
Alas! The countless links are strong
That bind us to our clay;
The loving spirit lingers long,
And would not pass away!

The du Maurier family had all left after a hectic social summer at Ferryside and the house was shut up. Daphne lodged with Miss Roberts who lived in The Nook, the cottage opposite, and cooked and skivvied with endless good humour, leaving Daphne to dispose of every hour of her time just as she wished. She could write, take a boat out and go exploring in the company of Bingo, her faithful Cornish mongrel. She longed for nothing more. Every day she would let herself into Ferryside and work there in her room before returning to Miss Roberts'. Sunday supper with the Quiller-Couches at The Haven, their house on the Esplanade in Fowey, became a regular and welcome date, for no one knew more about Cornwall than 'Q'. He was a much-loved character and Kenneth Grahame claimed him as the inspiration for his immortal Ratty, the friendly and relaxed, if stubborn, water vole in *Wind in the Willows*, who believed 'there is nothing – absolutely nothing – half so much worth doing as simply messing about in boats': it was 'Q' to a T. His daughter Foy was as distinctive a character and just as much an attraction for Daphne, for she was a boon companion in any adventure.

The affectionate relationship with Carol continued, he keener than Daphne but luckily as taken up with his work as she was on her book. He mentioned marriage half-jokingly and she said if it meant she could not continue her lengthy retreats to Fowey it would never work, so better think no more of it.

Daphne trespassed in Menabilly again in late autumn, taking with her Foy Quiller-Couch and a torch. The ghosts were once more disturbed and the dust and cobwebs gave up a few more secrets. With each visit the house and its attendant spirits took greater hold of her. She had to return to London for a family Christmas and once more chafed under the strict restrictions put on her movements. It was so ridiculous, she thought, that she was watched and reined in, while it seemed to her that Angela was free to do as she pleased. 'Whoopee ad lib!'[4] Angela had told her sister with glee and, despite Daphne's sense of unfairness, she had had to laugh. By the new year, Daphne had escaped her parents and returned to Miss Roberts', and once more was writing at full heat.

Angela meanwhile was in love again – this time with Capri. She and her parents had set off in January 1930 for Naples but had ended up in the island resort for artists and writers and bohemians of all kinds. She may have wept bitter tears as she left on a steamer, bemoaning the fact that falling for a place was doubly unsatisfactory because you could not even hope for letters from an island, but it proved another turning point in her life. She had met the successful English novelist Francis Brett Young, who had lived there for the past nine years with his wife Jessie, and whose novel *Portrait of Clare*, the last in his Mercian series, was a favourite of hers. As she sat on a pile of old rope in the stern of the boat, Angela at last felt confident enough to embark on her own book.

Just prior to this trip she had met another novelist, the successful and now forgotten Edward Holstius, who had been the first person to seriously suggest to her that she should write and offered what advice and encouragement he could. Having been cast down and hesitant for so long, Angela now felt ready to trespass on her talented younger sister's territory. She was flouting an unspoken sisterly rule, and so she kept her new writing project secret from her family.

She had been entirely at home in Capri and longed to be left there, while her parents steamed home to Britain without her. The climate, the rocky terrain, the social mix and the sexually tolerant atmosphere she found so attractive, could well have emboldened her in her choice of subject matter for her first novel. Capri had become a centre for creative artists of every nationality and kind, but was also an appealing haven for homosexual men and women who settled there in villas in the verdant hills. The novelist Sir Compton Mackenzie lived there for some years with his wife Faith. She had an affair with another Capri resident, the Italian pianist Renata Borgatti, who then became the lover of the American painter Romaine Brooks. Mackenzie's inside knowledge of the intrigues and latticed liaisons of the lesbian community of Capri inspired him to write his satirical novel *Extraordinary Women*. This was published in 1928, the same year as *The Well of Loneliness* and Virginia Woolf's *Orlando*, her playful love letter to Vita Sackville-West, but only Radclyffe Hall's book faced prosecution.

Rather than it being the subject of shame, scandal and vituperation, Angela learned that, in certain communities in Capri, lesbianism was relatively commonplace, tolerated and unremarkable. This was a revelation that freed her emotionally and creatively. The world at large, however, was not Capri, or even Hampstead. Compton Mackenzie's *Extraordinary Women* attracted double-edged praise. The *New Statesman*, a left-leaning paper known for its socially liberal perspective, published an article commending the book for shining a light on what it considered to be the modern disease of sapphism. It was interesting to see what the educated, mostly male, public thought of female homosexuality at the end of the 1920s – if they thought of it at all – and the kind of snake pit Angela would be entering with her own novel. 'Twenty years ago,' the article argued, 'such a topic could have seemed outrageous and completely unacceptable for a novel; but it is impossible to overlook it in this post-war world populated by girl boys and boy girls.' It went on to blame the epidemic on the rise of the suffragette movement, Mrs Pankhurst's hatred of men, indeed the shortage of marriageable men after the war; all played their part in forcing women into each other's arms. Sapphism, it continued, was 'a modern social disease ... a minor illness ... a factitious passion that will pass like all fashions in our society ... more a matter of fancy than of facts, *easily dissipated by the arrival of a man worthy of the name* [my italics]' – the latter a pompous variation on the age-old theme that all these confused women needed was a jolly good seeing-to!

The argument ended with the damning conclusion that lesbian women were in some way morally polluted. The novel 'suggests that women cannot fall in love with other women while remaining healthy and decent beings'.[5]

So, at much the same time that her sister was writing the title of her own first novel, Angela wrote in capitals at the head of a pristine piece of paper her title: 'THE LITTLE LESS'. She knew she was entering dangerous territory. She was not only about to step on sisterly toes, but also potentially disgust her parents and outrage the world. Like Daphne she had taken her title from a line of a favourite family poem, this time 'By the Fire-Side' by Robert Browning. In it he celebrated his love for his wife and for Italy, having experienced 'the little more', while Angela's novel explored the taboo love of a woman for another, who in the end could only offer friendship, in other words, 'the little less':

— Oh, the little more, and how much it is!
  And the little less, and what worlds away!
  … Friends – lovers that might have been.

By her own admission Angela was very young for her age and still in thrall to influential Daddy. This made it all the more astonishing that she could show such open passion and crusading zeal about a subject barely spoken of in polite society. Angela wrote with frank emotion about this outlawed, unrequited love. Here her heroine, Vivian, explains her feelings for Clare to Richard, the man who wishes to marry her, but had thought women incapable of sexual passion:

'D'you think I don't know what it is to go hungry day and night, for a look, a word, gathering the least crumbs in such greed that a starved beggar would be a king in comparison? To lie awake at night, telling oneself that such hopelessness must be a nightmare? To have to be ordinary, amusing, talk about everyday affairs when all you can think of is the poetry in your mind and the music in your heart, when you want nothing but to take them in your arms and give them the treasures of the world; and when every kiss you get back is worth more than every king's ransom since the world began?

'… I'll marry you Richard. But – and it's a hell of a "but" – if ever Clare does send for me I must go to her.'

And as Vivian spoke she knew she'd given herself away …

'I suppose you'll hate me now, look upon me as so much offal. That's the way the world does look on that kind of love.'[6]

The scene continues with an emotional plea from Vivian for the normality of sexual feelings between women. When Richard declares that such an idea would revolutionise society and suggests, patronisingly, that her passion for Clare was all in the mind, Vivian replies:

'I'm afraid you're wrong, Richard. If you love someone completely and utterly you can't keep physical feelings out of it. To me it's all beautiful; I refuse to desecrate it by calling it rotten, unnatural, vicious.'

Richard then retreats to the cocktail cabinet to get them both a stiff drink, but still sees it as his mission to marry Vivian and cure her from her sickness. After the violent death of Clare, the object of her desire, Vivian sinks into a lukewarm marriage to Richard, gives birth to a precious son and embarks on an almost love affair with another man. The novel ends with womanly resignation as the heroine accepts that, for the sake of her son, she should hope for nothing now beyond her conventional, passionless marriage.

Angela had already encountered the malevolence towards lesbianism that was aroused in good decent people whom she knew and admired. Agnes Mackay and her sister Lil were unmarried sisters of the Canon of All Saints Church near London's Oxford Street, known for its Anglo-Catholic services. Angela thought the sisters, 'like stalwart saints in a medieval age', and was impressed particularly by Agnes and her good works, including visiting inmates at Holloway women's prison. The older woman who showed such a Christian tolerance for prostitutes and thieves, however, shocked the young Angela with her vitriolic denunciation of divorcées and lesbians. '"As regards the latter," she literally snorted, "I can smell them a mile off. Dear child, why do you *know* such people?"'[7]

Despite this, Angela admitted she adored Agnes for her clarity and her uncompromising faith – and rather riskily imported her character into this first novel as Flora Macdonald, the Scottish spinster militantly spewing out hatred against such women who expressed their true natures, natures in fact like hers, if she had only been less frightened and repressed to accept it.

Both Angela and Daphne put a great deal of themselves and their experience into their novels and short stories. Daphne was frank about the autobiographical impulses in her work, and Angela left in hers many clues to her life and thoughts. Noël Welch, who knew all three sisters well, pointed out that although Angela's novels lacked the compulsive page-turning excitement of Daphne's, they were full of warmth and human feeling: 'She certainly betrays herself more, utterly, sometimes. One is taken aback by the outrightness.'[8] Although she could be reserved and guarded in person, in writing, whether letters or novels, Angela gave everything of herself, and this exposure was reckless and courageous in equal measure.

In her memoir of the sisters, written when Angela was respectably middle-aged, Noël Welch pointed out that the eldest du Maurier daughter had enjoyed a wild bohemian past that had alarmed her father: after a youth of crushes on men and women and a couple of attempts at romanticised relationships with the opposite sex had ended in tears, Angela's turbulent emotions found outlet elsewhere. One of her first loves in her adult life had been the American actress Mary Newcomb. In 1929, Angela, along with half of London, had fallen for her, dazzling as the wronged wife in *Jealousy*, a play by Eugene Walters. Angela's feelings of shy, barely expressed desire for a heterosexual woman, for Mary, were written, almost unfiltered, into her novel.

Mary was in her mid-thirties when Angela, eleven years her junior, first made her acquaintance. She was married to Alex Higginson, an American millionaire whose life as a country gentleman and lover of field sports, particularly hunting with hounds, was entirely funded by his indulgent multi-millionaire father, a supremely successful entrepreneur. Apart from supporting his son's passion for hunting and hounds, he had also founded and funded the Boston Symphony Orchestra and much of Harvard University's expansion. Alex was almost two decades older than Mary, his third wife, and they had no children, but lived in a country house in Dorset where he became Master of Foxhounds of the Cattistock Hounds, while she pursued her acting career in London.

Another admirer who met Mary Newcomb at the time was the music critic and writer Francis Toye, who explained her attraction: 'She was famous and much sought after; she was beautiful, she was distinguished, she was rich.'[9] He added that not only did she have a wonderful body, shown off to great effect by expensive clothes, but she walked with such sexy grace that all eyes were drawn to her. She reminded him of Vergil's description of Venus: '*vera incessu patuit dea*' – she was revealed as a true goddess by her gait.[10]

Angela not only used her own feelings for Mary as the mainspring of the novel, she found herself writing poetry as a more immediate way of expressing the *coup de foudre* she had experienced when in her company. This was the first poem in a book of love poems hand-written by Angela and addressed to some of the most important women in her life, each identified with just their initials. Although subsequent poems became more sophisticated in technique, this prosaic one had the narrative drive of a short story and was full of suppressed feeling:

> Your voice called 'Hullo' –
> You were dressed in black,
> Together we sat
> Through the three hours show of Maugham and Garbo –
> You smoked incessantly
> (Lucky Strikes)
> And you suddenly said
> You wished you were dead,
> – And talked of suicide –
> Do you remember the Savoy,
> Later?

You drank champagne, I beer.
And as evening wore on Fear
And excitement seized hold of me.
Oh little you knew at that juncture
The volcanic unrest
You caused in my breast –
We talked, you and I,
Of what? & why?

But our souls lay bare
To each other –
But you were sad
And I felt mad,
So you made a vow –
And I wondered how
I had lived these years without you –
We talked religion,
We talked love.
We discussed almost everything on earth
And above.
My world toppled & crashed that night,
And you set a light
That kindled a flame
And put to shame
All others.

Another significant woman arrived in Angela's life just as she was writing her first novel in secret in the summer of 1930. Angela Halliday was a great character, valiant and generous, and would remain a confirmed spinster all her life. She was to become a special friend to Angela du Maurier but also a friend to her other two sisters, and Muriel too. She did not merit one of Angela's love poems, but was hailed as her spiritual twin. It amused them that both were exactly the same age and shared a birthday, mothers with Muriel for a first name, Old Harrovian fathers, nurses called Pearce and childhoods spent in Regent's Park. If they were twins, however, they made a comic pair as

Little and Large, with six-foot Angela Halliday (nicknamed Shaw) towering over a diminutive Angela du Maurier.

That summer, the glamorous Furnesses once more captured Daphne's interest. One of Lord Furness's conquests had been an American beauty and actress, Julie Thompson, who for a while seemed set to become a stepmother to his unfortunate daughter Averill. Tod had met her and relayed her impressions to Daphne. Suddenly and incongruously this exquisite creature turned up at a rented cottage at the idyllic Readymoney Cove, at the mouth of the River Fowey, with a new aristocratic boyfriend in tow, Eddie Fitzclarence, who would become the 6th Earl of Munster.

All the sisters were intrigued, not least because they found Julie herself so alluring, and Daphne begged Tod for more salacious gossip on her and the Furness connection. By the summer of 1930, 'Fiery' Furness had indeed married again, providing Averill with a stepmother, not Julie, but Thelma Converse, a rich American divorcée with an aspirational eye for glamorous princes. She had already begun her romance with the Prince of Wales and was to introduce him, and lose him, to her friend Wallis Simpson. To restore her wounded pride she moved on to Prince Aly Khan.

At a time when divorce was still shameful and Cousin Geoffrey was the only member of the du Maurier family to have gone down that shady path, the sisters were aghast at the number of divorces that littered the Furness story. Julie was perfectly brazen about hers and mercenary too, when she told a shocked Angela that she did not want to marry Eddie as it would mean she would lose her alimony from Thompson. This was all grist to Daphne's cynical view of relationships between men and women. She even wondered if Julie's friendliness towards them was merely a sham, and the real focus of her interest was Gerald and what he could do for her career.

Daphne was always more single-minded, hard-working and dedicated to the profession of writing than Angela, and finished writing *The Loving Spirit* at the beginning of the year. Within two months her agent Michael Joseph had sold it to Heinemann, the firm that she and

Angela had decided, as girls, would be their first choice as publishers. She was delighted. This deal proved she could be an independent working woman. At last she had some kind of public validation for her sense, since childhood, that she was born to be a writer. She had been handed a cheque for £67* as an advance on royalties and told her parents, somewhat to their surprise, that from now on she would support herself by writing and did not need their allowance. Throwing off all obligations and restraints, Daphne was truly free at last. The feeling was exhilarating and, energised by this new belief in her creative powers, in mid-May she plunged into her second novel, *I'll Never Be Young Again*.

This time Daphne did not need the isolation and inspiration of Ferryside but was able to write in London, using a room where their Aunt Billy worked as Gerald's secretary in Orange Street in the heart of Theatreland. This was conveniently close to where Carol Reed was working so that snatched secret lunches with him were possible. Their relationship continued happily but with little real excitement, on her part at least. She did enjoy the long kissing sessions in the car on the occasions he ran her home to Cannon Hall in his Lagonda. There is little reason to believe that they ever got much beyond the petting stage in their relationship; Daphne admitted years later that she had always enjoyed most the foreplay in a sexual relationship and was not much bothered with the rest. Writing mattered much more to her than romance, and fortunately Carol was busy too. With intense concentration and relentless work, she finished her second novel well before her first was published.

For a young woman of twenty-three still learning her craft, Daphne's confidence and versatility was astonishing. *I'll Never Be Young Again* was quite different from the more conventional family drama of her first book. Dick, her male narrator, the first of many, had a series of page-turning adventures before ending up in Paris with the woman who enabled him to fulfil his destiny as a writer. But his compulsion to write, and the almost sexual excitement and

---

* Worth just over £3,000 using the Retail Price Index; nearly £13,000 if compared with average earnings.

satisfaction it gave him, alienated his lover who eventually left him for a musician called Julio. It was perhaps significant that this erotic competitor shared the same unusual name as the grotesque sex mannequin in 'The Doll', the most original of Daphne's earliest short stories. The doll Julio had also claimed the sexual interest of the woman whom the male narrator desired.

This novel dramatised Daphne's long-held opinion that uniting love and sex was fraught with difficulty in relationships between men and women; perhaps she believed it was even impossible. This cynicism most probably emerged from watching her beloved father's behaviour towards a wife he obviously adored and without whom he could not function. Yet, this most important man in Daphne's life had numerous affairs with his 'actress loves', discussed with his young daughters with ribald lack of respect, even ridicule. His influence was obvious in her third novel, *The Progress of Julius*, in the coruscating struggle between a father and the daughter he intends to possess, even to death. The more lovable side of Gerald popped up as Pappy Delaney in *The Parasites*, crying easily and protesting to his children, 'You're all going to leave me one by one.' But all Daphne's relationships in life were transmuted into her fiction, combining the force of lived experience with the alchemy of her imagination and visceral understanding of dramatic tension.

In *I'll Never Be Young Again*, the relationship between Dick and Hesta had something of the dynamic of that between herself and Carol Reed, where the dissatisfied lover accuses Dick (Daphne) of being selfish, caring more for writing than anything or anyone else, and upbraiding him for habitually shying away from seriousness. Through the medium of her male narrator, Daphne describes the pleasures of writing, and the almost orgasmic climax of finishing a novel at last:

> My heart was beating, and my hands were trembling for no reason.
> There had never been anything like the thrill of writing the last word,
> of drawing a line at the bottom, of blotting the page. The breaking up
> of tension, the culmination of excitement, the supreme effort of the
> final word.[11]

Daphne also has Dick struggle, as she did, to separate herself from her famous father: 'I wanted to win through on my own merits; I hated the idea of trading on my father's name, of getting my things read just because I was his son.'[12]

Daphne herself stalked through both novels. Janet Coombe, the central mast of *The Loving Spirit*, shares the same conflicts as her creator; she wishes she was born a man and longs to live unfettered, at one with the elements and in mystical symbiosis with the sea. Daphne drove the story forward with a terrific sense of narrative drama and a Brontëan belief in the animistic power of landscape. Colourful characters, improbable situations, high emotion, all made reading it a theatrical experience. Daphne revealed her provenance as the child of actors who had grown up on stage, never knowing quite what was true; be it at home with her father's histrionics or in the theatre audience aware that real life and make-believe were confusingly blurred. She understood the dramatic propulsion of cliffhangers and shock denouement. Unsentimental about her characters, she was more than willing to have them betrayed, denied happy endings, and killed off without regret.

The main idea of her favourite novel of her grandfather's, *Peter Ibbetson* – that with imagination and will one could make things happen – excited Daphne as a girl and continued to fascinate her throughout her life where she found evidence in her own experience. She was disconcerted and yet strangely thrilled by what she saw as a connection between the fatal shipwreck she described in *I'll Never Be Young Again* and the news that summer that a yacht had been wrecked on the rocks at Lantivet Bay in Cornwall and six people drowned. In her diary she wrote, 'Another body has been found at Lantivet Bay. There is something queerly allied in all this to my story … Yet mine came first.'[13]

With her longing to possess Menabilly, she was already practising the power she believed she had to conjure this desire into being. She wrote to its owner Dr Rashleigh to ask permission to walk in the grounds of the great house, so that she no longer had to trespass, and he had agreed. Though it would take quite a few more years before she would manage to complete the dream and move herself and her family into the house itself, the very effort of will demanded to do this would prove that she, like Peter Ibbetson, could achieve everything she wanted.

Daphne had finished two novels by the summer of 1930 but, never one to ignore a friend's invitation or the chance of a holiday abroad, Angela was still writing her first. While Daphne generally shunned society, Angela collected friends and acquaintances wherever she went. She threw herself with enthusiasm into having fun with her new pal, Angela Halliday: 'It was a most exciting business getting to know each other, for we shared many interests and had even more in common than twin sisters.'[14] Then, in July, she accepted an invitation to go and spend some time with the actress Faith Celli on the isle of Seil, just off the west coast of Scotland.

Faith was almost old enough to be Angela's mother, as were many of her closest women friends. Perhaps they offered some of the love and acceptance she had craved and never quite received from Muriel. Faith's charm and beauty had won her a husband who was a war hero and heir to the Viscount of Elibank, Arthur Murray. Together, at their house at An Cala, they created a renowned coastal garden. Angela's ecstatic discovery of this beautiful part of Western Scotland found its way into her novel, as did her other loves, Devon, Cornwall and Capri.

Like Daphne, she employed in her writing their grandfather's concept of 'dreaming true'. *The Little Less*, however, was a very different book from her sister's. This novel had little compelling adventure, much less narrative drive, and was instead an emotional voyage of discovery for a young woman growing up and finding her place in the world. Full of feeling, there is a great deal of internal musing about love and loss and what it was to be a woman at the time she was writing. Strongly autobiographical, the main character of Vivian is a young woman so ignorant of life that at eighteen she asks a friend to explain what it is to be a virgin (as had Angela at the same age) and is put off men and sex by a rough attempt at seduction that gets as far as a 'brutal kiss' and some fumbling with her clothes. Nonplussed by the carefree behaviour of a bisexual woman friend and her louche circle, Vivian wonders, 'I wish I could understand how people feel about these things … How can they call all this mucking about love?

I thought love was just devotion, and wanting to be with a person. But all this funny business …'[15] This was very close to Angela's responses in her youthful diaries.

In the novel, Vivian longs for 'the little more', to offer all of herself and live with her lover for ever as a protective, husbandly presence. Inspired by her feelings for Mary Newcomb who, like the love interest in the novel, is unhappily married, Angela and her heroine knew that if she wanted to remain in the orbit of the woman she loved, she had to keep her real self hidden. This sense of ecstatic but unfulfilled feeling, and the need for absolute secrecy, was an emotional state that Angela had come to know well, having lived in thrall to passion under the proscriptive and mocking gaze of her father.

She may have employed the family concept of 'dreaming true' by making her heroine experience the ghastly premonition of her loved-one's death, but Angela also managed, through fiction, to redress a little of the balance of power between herself and her middle sister in life. Her heroine, with whom she so closely identified, eventually marries a widower who loves her more than his first wife, a pretty young woman prematurely killed off by pneumonia, whom Angela decided to call Daphne.

Of all three sisters, Angela was by nature the most nervous and conformist and yet here she had written something that potentially courted the world's, her parents' (and the aunts'), scorn. In its quiet if hyperbolic way it was also an emotional polemic for greater tolerance and understanding of homosexual love:

> Vivian said lifelessly, 'How can there be wrong in the love I have for Clare, which is all the best of me, the most unselfish, the most beautiful? She's everything that makes life beautiful, to me. These mountains, the sunsets, the lovely thrilling glory of an evening sea in winter, they're Clare to me, not just water and rock and red sky. Are you going to tell me that's all wrong? All beastly?'

Sometime in early 1931, Angela finished her novel, knowing how exposing this would be of her inner feelings. This may have been one of the main reasons she did not show the manuscript to her family or even mention the fact she had completed her first book. Instead she sent *The Little Less* to a series of publishers. The timing was unfortunate. After the notorious case against Radclyffe Hall's *The Well of Loneliness*, publishers were disinclined to take on an even more explicit book. Their letters of rejection variously mentioned that she could certainly write, but the subject was 'too unpleasant'.[16]

Angela recalled what a blow this was, all the more so as Daphne's first book, launched on 23 February that year to extensive and enthusiastic reviews, had been immediately accepted by the publisher both sisters considered the best. *The Times* claimed: '*The Loving Spirit* is a fine, widely sweeping romance of family life over four generations, of strong sentiment, lively episodes, Cornish locality, sea-life, and domestic vicissitudes,'[17] and it was soon reprinted. The American edition carried a selling quote from Rebecca West, already the most admired woman writer on either side of the Atlantic, 'a whopper of a romantic novel in the vein of Emily Brontë'.

None of this much impressed Daphne. 'I couldn't feel excited about it,' she wrote, for her attention and creative energies were newly centred on the idea for her third book, 'the life story of a French Jew'[18] – *The Progress of Julius*. When Gerald rang, however, to say he had read *The Loving Spirit* and liked it very much, she was surprised and pleased: his low boredom threshold meant he rarely read a novel through to the end; and it was gratifying too to get a letter from Noël Coward congratulating her on her achievement.

Angela's first attempts to be published had been far less heartening and as a personality she was already easily discouraged. How grateful she would have been for a scintilla of the positive attention that Daphne so carelessly tossed aside:

> [the rejection of my book] was a great disappointment, for I had laboured long … all through life I have needed encouragement in whatever field I have striven, whether the end product be the role of Wendy, a game of tennis, the writing of a book, or a dish of Irish Stew. So when *The Little Less* came back from the third or fourth publisher I put it away and never really imagined I would write again.[19]

In fact, she would not write again for nearly ten years, a gap that all but sunk her chance of momentum in her career. *The Little Less* was eventually published in 1941, somewhat pruned and modified, as her third novel, but by this time the only du Maurier who mattered in the literary world was Daphne. Angela's book was dedicated rather boldly, '*To* MUMMIE *With Dearest Love*'. Years later a friend of Angela's was reading the book on the lawn at Ferryside while Muriel reclined on a steamer chair in the sun. When the friend held out the book and asked if she had read it, Muriel, with a small shudder, admitted that she never read any of her daughters' novels because she could recognise all the main characters, and it made her uneasy. She then avoided further conversation about a subject she found distasteful by pulling the fabric canopy on the chair down so that it covered her face, obscuring sight of the book affectionately dedicated to her.

The city of Paris, combined with Mlle Yvon's intellectual encouragement and tender care, still exerted its pull on Daphne. Since her schooldays, she had managed at least one extended stay each year with Ferdy, sometimes two. At the beginning of 1931 she and Jeanne set off to stay with Fernande and once again the distinctive combination of the city's history and its evocative atmosphere and a kind of race memory set Daphne's imagination alight. Always intrigued by existential debate, ideas for short stories kept surfacing in her mind and then suddenly Julius Lévy, her third novel's protagonist, arrived like a genie, fully formed, to dominate her waking thoughts. 'I saw him as an old man first, dying, and then as a child … Where on earth had he sprung from into my mind? I didn't know. He was there. He was suddenly alive.'[20]

Daphne returned to London fleetingly. She went to a grand evening party at the American embassy, thrown by Nelson Doubleday, her American publisher, and then with Angela to a party given by Micky Jacob, and was underwhelmed by both. Micky's party was full of lesbians and pansies, Daphne reported, and she wondered what Ferdy and Foy, the two most important women in her life at the time, would have thought of them. Fernande was lesbian in her proclivities and practice but her position as schoolmistress and then directrice of her own school, and her devout Catholicism, made for a prim reticence. Foy Quiller-Couch, as the intellectual and eccentric daughter of the academic and unworldly Sir Arthur (who found Daphne's second novel shocking enough), was unlikely to have been comfortable in, let alone comprehending of, the metropolitan milieu of Micky Jacob and her friends. The thought of these disparate aspects of her life colliding amused Daphne.

Carol Reed was still on the scene but marriage seemed even more remote, while Cousin Geoffrey, once golden and glamorous, was ageing without grace and had completely lost his lustre. His spontaneity now seemed closer to fecklessness and his charm had turned tawdry: failure stared him reproachfully in the face. Daphne was irritated by him for the first time in her life when, at lunch, he was rude to the waiter in an attempt to impress her. By spring she had left London for Ferryside without a backward glance. She wrote to Tod that summer, before the family descended, about how she loved her life in Cornwall, filled with boating, gardening, walking and writing. She could keep herself and a cook for £2 a week and for intellectual enjoyment and adventure she had the Quiller-Couches across the river in Fowey. 'I'm happier than I've ever been in my life! Not a "crush" on the horizon.'[21]

As Daphne worked away in Cornwall on her third novel, free to pursue her own thoughts and interests, to come and go as she pleased, her thoughts turned to the constraints that relationships put on a woman. In *Julius*, she explored the damage done by possessive, controlling, perverted love, and it made her appreciate all the more her single carefree state. To the faithful Tod, who loved and never judged her, she could be honest about her true feelings:

> It's all great fun – the sheer *selfish* joy of living alone and being dependent on no one, as I imagine you relish as well as me! Thank heaven I hav'nt got to cater for a grumbly husband who is snappy about the bacon at breakfast! When all is said and done one doesn't miss much in that line. Sex may be very exciting, but so it is to sail a boat in a spanking breeze ...[22]

Little did she know that about the time she was writing her paean to the solitary creative life, a handsome youthful major in the Grenadier Guards was reading *The Loving Spirit* and, mad about boats and the sea, had thought it the best book he had read for years. He determined to set off from the Isle of Wight in his own boat, *Ygdrasil*, and head for Fowey and the coastline evoked so lyrically in the book. He asked his best friend, the Cornishman John Prescott, to come with him, and had a vague hope he might even meet the young author herself.

The young major was not alone: everyone seemed to be converging on Fowey intent on invasion. The sisters descended on Ferryside at Easter with friends in tow, Angela bringing her special new friend Angela Halliday, in Shaw's sporty little MG car, while Jeanne brought once more Elaine. Muriel and Aunt Billy joined them all a little later. The family gathered again in the summer with Gerald and the Cannon Hall maids too, and picnics and expeditions in boats and cars were in full swing.

Daphne and Foy visited Clara Vyvyan, a woman closer to Muriel's generation but who could not have been more different, and she caught Daphne's imagination. A most intrepid traveller and successful writer, Clara had married late in life the elderly 10th Baronet, Sir Courtenay Vyvyan, owner of the magnificent Trelowarren Estate, situated on the Helford River in a protected microclimate so mild that tropical plants could be grown in its renowned gardens.

But Cornwall could not contain Angela. She was planning a romantic adventure with her new best friend Shaw and Wendy, her Pekinese, to the west coast of Scotland and the Isles of Mull and Skye. In mid-July they set off in the MG Midget. Bowling merrily along the Great North Road, they had reached as far as Yorkshire when they were hit broadside, and without warning, by a much larger car that shot out of a crossroads at speed. The tiny MG was shunted off the road and upended, tossing Angela over a hedge while her friend Shaw and dog Wendy ended up in a ditch. The car was so badly damaged it is possible the two Angelas and Wendy only survived because it was open-topped and they were thrown clear.

Angela was badly concussed and unconscious and the rescuers at first thought she was dead. Her first slurred words were to ask about her dog. Shaw, conscious throughout and in agony, having badly smashed her collarbone, never let Angela forget how revealing this was of her heart's priorities. They were taken to Ripon Cottage Hospital, where they stayed for a week in the empty children's ward, with Wendy in a child's cot by Angela's bed. Apart from the concussion Angela's back was damaged and she and Wendy 'vomited constantly', while Shaw, in extreme pain and for some reason refused morphia, cried out through the night: 'I've come to the end of my tether.'[23]

Shaw's family were quickly roaring up the Great North Road in their motors, but Angela, anxious not to disturb her father's holiday at Ferryside, made light of the incident. Not even Daphne knew how close they had all come to death, for she wrote in her diary at the time, 'Angela & Shaw have car accident on way to Scotland, neither injured.'[24] It was probably Angela's and Muriel's joint decision not to tell the family and upset Daddy's holiday for it was generally accepted that Gerald's interests came first in everything. It did not stop Angela, however, from feeling bereft as she languished alone and in pain, while her friend in the next bed was surrounded by concerned relations.

By the time Angela and Shaw had made their battered way back to Ferryside, the handsome Guards officer, and fan of *The Loving Spirit*, had eventually arrived in Fowey in his motor cruiser and booked himself into a local hostelry. It was Angela who first spotted this good-looking stranger in the town's post office and excitedly reported her sighting back to Ferryside. Daphne was busy finishing *Julius*, working on the shocking murder scene, and did not at this point take much notice. It was mainly Angela who hung out of the window of the house with Gerald's bird-watching binoculars. She plotted the progress of this romantically solitary figure as he daily cruised up and down the estuary on some unknown quest, and pointed him out to her sisters: 'There's a most attractive man going up and down the harbour in a white motor-boat … Do come and look!' They took turns watching him and speculating on what he was up to. Local gossip relayed his name as Browning and that he was the youngest major in the British Army.

Ferryside was shut up and everyone headed back to London for Christmas in varying degrees of expectation. Angela was panicking about how once again she had overspent her allowance and was overdrawn with barely sixpence to last her to the end of the year. Her extravagance was on a par with Gerald's and a source of some friction with the parents, so had to be kept deadly secret. Daphne had spent almost the whole year in Cornwall, had finished her book and was expected to join in with 'the usual festivities ... worse luck!'[25] Once again Carol Reed was much in evidence. He had shown his devotion a few months earlier by driving down from London to Bodinnick overnight just to see her fleetingly before driving back again the next day – a round trip before motorways of well over five hundred miles. But such seeming devotion did nothing to heighten Daphne's romantic interest in Carol, rated still in her mind at the level of a son.

Daphne was interested in the imbalance of affection and need in all human relationships; her earliest experiences of longing for affection from her mother were as damaging to her as the excessive and demanding love of her father. His intense attention had shifted to Jeanne, still living at home, still studying at the Central School of Arts, and a more discreet character than her spirited elder sister. Gerald was delighted by Jeanne's artistic ability, another connection he made with his father. Though Daphne found her father's needy love oppressive, discovering the beam of his affection now turned on her younger sister was unsettling. Yet, unapologetic about what she considered to be her selfishness, Daphne was happiest when she could live unfettered from the ties that bind one to another. Above all, she recognised how much she needed freedom and the solitude that allowed her to inhabit her imagination, and make real the people and worlds she created, through the alchemy of words. She was aware that both her father and Ferdy and Carol Reed wanted so much more from her than she was willing to give.

Angela was the sister to whom Daphne most naturally turned in their adulthood and it was she who accompanied her to Brighton in the early spring of 1932, as part of her younger sister's recuperation after an operation to remove her appendix in January. Daphne then headed off to Paris to be further cosseted by Ferdy, but this time Carol followed her there and pursued his romantic interests in the cafés of the Left Bank. An English girl who was at Mlle Yvon's finishing school remembered Daphne at this time as highly self-possessed and rather awesome to the younger women there, struck by, 'her manly stride and unusual clothes – her boyishness, but great fun'.[26]

But nothing could keep Daphne from Cornwall for long and by April she was back in Ferryside. Her second novel *I'll Never Be Young Again* was published to distaste and alarm amongst her family and closest associates. 'Prepare for a bit of a shock,' she wrote to Tod, 'the family are all a trifle staggered. What is known as outspoken …!' In fact her hero Sir Arthur Quiller-Couch was more than staggered: he was appalled by the worldliness and cynicism and banned this book, and her next, *Julius*, from his library, considering the human relationships she described and the attitudes towards sex to be corrupting of young minds. Angela, alone of those closest to her, thought *I'll Never Be Young Again* a triumph and years later declared it to be her favourite.

After the success of her first novel, Daphne was paid £125 for her second, significantly more than for *The Loving Spirit*, although her publishers did not expect it to sell as well. She was fulfilling her life's desire to live independently by her own pen. However, within a week of arriving in Fowey she was told by the boatbuilder's wife that Major Browning was back. His boat was on the water again and he wished to meet Daphne. She was flattered. A letter from the dashing major arrived the following day, pointing out that their fathers had met and in fact shared the same club, the Garrick. As Angela made clear, this meant it was perfectly proper for him to call on Daphne, despite the fact she was unchaperoned and living alone at Ferryside.

On 8 April they met for the first time, on his boat, and set off into a brisk breeze. Both were in their element and charmed to have found someone who felt the same way about boating and the sea. Major Browning explained that to his company he was 'Boy' Browning, that his family called him 'Tommy' and he would like Daphne to call him that too. He was fascinated by Norse mythology and hence had named his boat *Ygdrasil*, after the great Norse Tree of Life. So together they battled through the choppy sea, drenched with spray and exhilarated by each other's company. Daphne asked him back to Ferryside, lit the fire and they talked on into the night.

Both admitted to each other that 'it was a case of mutual "love at first sight"'. 'How's that for romance?' Daphne triumphantly wrote to Tod, describing the focus of this instant love as 'the best-looking thing I have ever seen, 35, lives for boats and all the things I live for … The sort of person who has always liked being alone, up to the moment, like me, and hates a crowd.'[27]

Love at first sight is an interesting phenomenon that always implies an element of narcissism. Daphne and Tommy were gazing at intriguing versions of themselves: lean, handsome, heroic, happiest in boats, away from society. He was even a sporting hero and had competed in the bobsleigh at the 1928 Winter Olympics, a sport Daphne had tried in Switzerland and had, by her own description, been 'astonishingly good at'. Here was the personification of Daphne's masculine alter ego, her boy-in-the-box, Eric Avon – with knobs on. No wonder he seemed so familiar. 'He's the most amazing person … and I feel I've known him for years,'[28] she wrote in her diary, having just met him. Even his nickname in the Army, that was to follow him all his professional life, was 'Boy', with all the delightful resonance of a youthful, carefree personality, a true match for Daphne's identification with Peter Pan.

It was easy to fall for this charming Guards officer, in his old boating clothes with the wind in his hair and sunburn on his cheeks. But alike as they were on the surface, their characters and the experiences of their lives were dramatically different. Daphne could not know the real Tommy, the Tommy who was gregarious and good fun in company but nervous and prone to depression, with an iron discipline that kept him from the abyss. Unbuttoned, carefree and tousled by the sea breeze, this Tommy was a far cry from his professional persona as a ferocious stickler for discipline and the most immaculately dapper man in the Army. He was an old Etonian, an intelligent and sensitive man who had had the misfortune to be part of the generation that went off as teenagers to face the horrors of the Great War, and fought as a young officer of eighteen on the Western Front.

He had been instrumental in the battle for Cambrai in 1917 – his brigade ordered to take the strategically important Gauche Wood

– and it was here that 'Boy' Browning found himself dodging sniper bullets and fighting hand to hand with bayonets drawn. All the officers apart from three were killed or wounded in this operation and, in this hell of dead and dying men, Browning found himself the last remaining officer in the wood, charged with leading what men remained. Under continuous shelling they battled equally youthful Germans, face to face in deadly combat, with men falling to left and right of them. The unexpected responsibility for so many living and wounded men, and the prolonged stress and horror of the situation, changed his life for ever.

It was for this action that Tommy received his Distinguished Service Order, an award hard-won and rarely given to a lieutenant, proudly worn alongside all the other distinguished medals he was to receive throughout his active service. But he was only twenty when this experience took possession of his life, and for the rest of his days he suffered nightmares that would jolt him awake with a scream. The tension in his perfectionist, highly strung nature was wound so tight it could never return to resilient normality. None of this was evident to Daphne as she thrilled to the handsome windswept sailor beside her in the boat on the Cornish seas.

While twenty-year-old Tommy was being strained beyond endurance in the cauldron of war, Daphne, the pampered daughter of one of the most glamorous theatrical families, had found herself ecstatically exploring Cornwall and visiting Paris for creative inspiration and the loving care of Fernande Yvon. All her life Daphne had been the special one who had never had to accommodate anyone else's needs and always got what she wanted in life. She had at an early age been singled out by Gerald from her sisters; their governess Tod adored her always, as did Cousin Geoffrey. Everyone she met offered admiration, loyalty, even love. Only Muriel did not fall under Daphne's spell and this, although a lasting grief, was managed by ignoring her as much as possible, and seeking sympathetic mother substitutes elsewhere.

In those first exciting weeks when Daphne only saw the heroic figure, a masculine clone of herself, Tommy too had fallen for the image of a robust and beautiful young woman, as much fun as a male companion but with the added frisson of her strikingly attractive femininity. It did not occur to him that the elusive spirit to which he had responded in her novel and saw in its element in Fowey, was just that. Daphne was not someone who could be contained, made to nurture, and sacrifice her own interests for the needs or comfort of others.

The fact Daphne had fallen in love with this handsome, interesting, distinguished man was not at all surprising. She had had passionate and obsessional relationships before and of all of them he was the most deserving of her interest. That *she* had asked *him* to marry her, within ten weeks, much of them spent apart, knowing little about him and less about marriage: this was the interesting conundrum.

In her letter to Muriel, even Daphne sounded puzzled by her own decision: 'Don't know quite what I'm doing myself, it all seems so extraordinary, and I never thought I was the sort of person who would get married …'[29] She had been adamant to her sisters and to Foy that she would never marry. Her sisters were kept in the dark until after the event and Daphne obviously felt some embarrassment at telling Foy:

> I have burnt my boats and thrown my cap over the hills, and have followed the drum. Tommy and I are going to be married … I never thought or intended this should happen to me, or if it did would have lived carelessly in Walmsley fashion [the writer and war hero Leo Walmsley, who lived nearby at Pont, was a great friend] but he is trying to teach me that these ways of living are messy and stupid and very very young.[30]

Daphne's decision to propose to Tommy, a fundamentally conventional man, was an extraordinarily unconventional act at the time; her power of imagination had brought this hero into her sphere of influence, her beauty and strength had kept him there. By taking the initiative Daphne retained the power and control that had been hers so far. Years later, Tommy admitted he had never regretted accepting her proposal, 'though I was a bit scared at the time and was too much of a gentleman to refuse you!!'[31]

Daphne agreed that she would try and live in a different way, 'to have a shot at living "unselfishly" for the first time in my life'.[32] She must have wobbled over her decision soon afterwards, for when she went to Pirbright, the Army camp where Tommy was stationed, and saw him for the first time resplendent in his uniform and medals, she realised a little more of what Army life entailed. She was reminded by Tommy's friends, the Dorman Smiths, however, that his career would be compromised if they lived together without marriage. Having boldly taken the initiative and proposed, Daphne suddenly was uncertain about what she had willed into being and the kind of life that would now be hers.

She was not a quitter and her response was to insist on having as little ceremony as possible. She told Foy she was a reluctant bride who could only manage the wedding if no one was looking. She was terrified of having her essential self changed by the experience, by appearing different: a married woman. It had to be as close to an impromptu event as could be, no engagement, no announcement, no sisters, neither of Tommy's parents – despite his being their only son – none of the aunts, no Quiller-Couches or any other close friends. Only Gerald, Muriel and, peculiarly perhaps, Cousin Geoffrey, would be there, and for best man George Hunkin, the boatbuilder.

The marriage itself was as romantic and secretive as an elopement. Daphne was dressed in an old blue coat and skirt, carefully ironed by her mother the night before. According to Aunt Billy, Muriel had dreamed of her daughters marrying in grand society weddings. But on 19 July 1932 at 8.15 in the morning, 'so nobody was about', she and her mother and father with Geoffrey climbed into her boat, the *Cora Ann*, and proceeded up the creek to Lanteglos and the remote small Norman church that awaited them. Tommy and George Hunkin followed in *Ygdrasil*. Once the service was over and breakfast quickly eaten, Daphne and Tommy changed into their old sailing clothes, climbed into his boat and set off for the open sea. The newly married couple pointed the prow towards the Helford River and Frenchman's Creek. Daphne's diary ended with this romantic view of a new beginning: 'We couldn't have chosen anything more beautiful.'[33]

Daphne hoped that by marrying she would create a 'fuller life'. Was this need for a new adventure encouraged by a romantic scandal that hit the headlines both sides of the Atlantic involving Averill Furness? Daphne had told Tod that the dynamic in the Furness family provided part of the inspiration for her psychologically bleak novel, *The Progress of Julius*. She had always been fascinated by Tod's charge, who was only a year younger than she, and the stories her old governess told of the shenanigans (some of them royal) in the multi-million-pound Furness menagerie. Averill had been the girl to whom Daphne had proffered advice over her hopeless passion for her cousin. She was also perhaps a girl who, like Daphne herself, suffered from an unhealthily close relationship with a possessive and powerful father. In this way she had found her way into Daphne's imagination and into the book. But from poor little rich girl, Averill had sprung to independence and celebrity as the heroine of a high romance of sex, class and dangerous wild animals. Just a few weeks before Daphne fell in love 'at first sight' with Tommy, news of Averill's elopement had the world, Tod and the du Mauriers, agog.

At the age of twenty-three, while on safari with her father in Kenya, Averill had secretly married his white hunter and zebra trainer, Andrew Rattray. One year older than her father, Rattray was a handsome, romantic figure, completely at home with wild animals and big game in Africa, and irresistible to well-brought-up English women who longed to escape their destiny. He could not have been less like the scion of an aristocratic family that her social-climbing father and stepmother would have hoped for her as a husband. 'Fiery' Furness had been in the bush, shooting lions, when he was told of his daughter's elopement and his roar of fury and disapproval could be heard across the Maasai Mara.

Did this unconventional match make Daphne realise that romantic love and adventure could co-exist in a marriage? That she too could marry a hero and live an expanded life with an eye to the distant horizon, rather than shrink into conventional bondage like all the other wives she knew? It would explain her triumphant comment to Tod when she told her of her instantaneous attraction to Tommy,

'How's that for romance!', for she had a hero every bit as handsome and remarkable as Averill's, and she intended to live just as unconventional a life.

The fathers' reactions were slightly different, however. Marmaduke Furness roared in possessive outrage and curtailed all further association with Rattray; while Gerald, on hearing Daphne was to marry, burst into tears and cried, 'It isn't fair!'[34] And so the Alpha Male rampaged and Peter Pan wept – and then gave the young lovers one of the cottages at Cannon Hall to live in as a wedding present, thereby keeping his precious daughter within the family compound. Most grand passions have a tragic coda and the same was true for poor Averill's. Rattray died just a year and a half later from some tropical disease. After nursing him devotedly, Averill, heartbroken, soon followed him to the grave, apparently having drunk herself to death. She was just twenty-seven. Daphne's reality was more a prolonged disillusionment, as she and Tommy returned, with mixed feelings, to their solitary lives.

Their marriage would prove a great mismatch of expectation and experience. Daphne thought she was marrying someone strong and self-sufficient like herself, a natural nonconformist in most things. Their carefree courtship in Cornwall, largely conducted in a boat, was not an accurate precursor of what was to come. Daphne was completely unprepared for any kind of conventional wifely role, let alone to become the supportive spouse of an exacting military man destined for glory. She was horrified and shocked by the night terrors Tommy suffered and recoiled from his naked need of her reassurance and comfort. The last thing she wanted was any vestige of a clingy, weeping man like her father, or a marriage like her parents', where Muriel's every waking thought was directed towards making Gerald's life easy and less stressful.

Tommy later told Daphne he always looked for something of his devoted mother or sister in women. Although she was a terrific companion in any adventure and a fascinating and generous friend, womanly nurture was not Daphne's strong suit and Tommy, lonely and disconsolate, would ultimately seek comfort in alcohol and the affection of other women.

Daphne had written a poem 'The Writer' when she was nineteen, before she started her writing career. Yet it was uncannily prescient about her destiny:

> …
> Mine is the silence
> And the quiet gloom
> Of a clock ticking
> In an empty room,
> The scratch of a pen,
> Ink-pot and paper,
> And the patter of the rain
> Nothing but this as long as I am able,
> Firelight – and a chair, and a table.
>
> Not for me the whisper in the ear,
> Nor the touch of a hand,
> And that hand on my heart,
> Nor the quick pattering of feet
> Upon the stair, nor laughter in the street,
> Nor the swift glance, intangible and dear.
>
> Not for me the hunger in the night,
> And the strength of the lover
> Tired of his loving.
> Seeking after passion the broken rest,
> Bearing his body's weight upon my breast.
>
> Mine is the silence
> Of the still day,
> When the shouting on the hills
> Sounds far away,
> The song of the thrush,
> In the quiet woods,
> And the scent of trees …[35]

Nothing could deflect Daphne for long from the irresistible need to write, the longing for solitude and freedom to explore her characters and inhabit her imaginary worlds. This was to prove difficult to combine with wifeliness, and motherhood. As Dick, the male narrator in *I'll Never Be Young Again*, declared 'this power of writing [is] more dangerous than adventure, more satisfying than love'.[36] This was Daphne's own voice speaking of the central impulse of her life.

7

Stepping Out

A lot of people say I have suffered because of Daphne's fame and
success, in the same way as I had to stand for greater and stronger
criticism on the stage, being Gerald du Maurier's daughter. I am
still – and know I always shall be – asked 'Are you the writer?', and
I still – and always shall I suppose – reply, 'I'm the Sister'.

ANGELA DU MAURIER, *Old Maids Remember*

THE SISTER WHO had been most vocal about not marrying had now
deserted the sisterhood and done just that, and kept her marriage
secret from both sisters. Daphne was a little sheepish, and perhaps did
not enjoy relinquishing her place as the most individual and nonconformist du Maurier. 'How Puff [Angela] and Queenie [Jeanne] will
jeer,'[1] she wrote in a letter to her mother. In fact, she told her sisters
nothing and the first that either heard of it was through a letter from
Muriel to Angela in Italy. The news took both sisters by surprise.

Jeanne had never entertained any thoughts at all of marriage. From
girlhood it was obvious to her Hampstead schoolfriend Elizabeth that
she had quite quickly left girlish friendships behind and 'moved on to
various lady friends'.[2] As the 'most boy-like of them all', and despite
her sweet and docile manner as a child, she had from a young age
'quickly become startlingly independent in thought and action'.[3] At
twenty-one she was already on her path to becoming an artist. In this,
she continued to be encouraged by Gerald, the full light of his

expectation now falling on her. Her talents in music and sport created other bonds with Gerald: she played the piano and for a time the violin too; she was a powerful tennis player, 'able to hold her own as a girl playing with three good men',[4] and a passably good golfer, a game her father enjoyed and could also play with her as his partner. Angela thought Jeanne initially suffered from having too many talents, but it was painting that finally claimed all her creative energies.

The college she had attended, the Central School of Arts and Crafts, had been set up in the late nineteenth century with the specific aim of encouraging the traditional handicrafts and industries. But it was also very forward looking, embracing new developments in design and manufacture and blending tradition with the excitement of the new. Students and teachers flourished in the lively and enlightened atmosphere of innovation, experimentation and debate. When Virginia and Leonard Woolf visited in the late 1930s, Virginia wrote in her diary how she liked the cheerful, free-and-easy atmosphere and compared it favourably to the stuffiness and formality in Oxford and Cambridge colleges at the time.

The life-drawing classes that Jeanne attended were run by an eclectic collection of practising artists, most notably the Vorticist painter William Roberts and Bernard Meninsky, a painter who responded most to the warmth and light of the Mediterranean. Roberts's art was powerfully felt and compellingly modern. A war artist during the Great War, he had depicted its hell in his searing *The First German Gas Attack at Ypres*. But it was the more expansive Meninsky who made the strongest impression on Jeanne. His charisma as a teacher inspired generations of students at the Central, where he taught on and off from his youth, on the eve of the First World War, until his suicide in 1950. Morris Kestelman was a scholarship student, not much older than Jeanne, and he too became a renowned artist and teacher at the Central. Recalling his time as a student, shortly before Jeanne herself was attending Meninsky's classes, Kestelman evoked the thrill of his teaching:

[Meninsky] was gifted with brilliant powers of demonstration accompanied by lucid exposition of what he was about. What held me was the intensity of his concentration in the act of drawing, remarkable feats of improvisation from the model. It was a fascinating exercise to watch, and it related to you as a student … He talked very well, constructively and clearly, and would establish a strong personal relationship, watching your reaction. Then he would produce a stub of a pencil … and with extraordinary directness proceed to produce, on a corner of your sheet, one of those remarkable drawings which students would later cut out and mount. As he drew, he talked.[5]

Unsurprisingly given the quality of the teaching, the drawing classes at the Central were increasingly highly regarded and well attended. Drawing was considered the skill that underpinned all the other crafts taught at the school, from textiles and costume, silversmithing, stained glass and book production, through to furniture-making and architecture. Before Jeanne could enrol in the life classes, she had to go through the general drawing classes, where students were expected to spend many hours drawing from the vast collection of plaster casts of everything from classical statues to bits of English cathedrals. After this apprenticeship, she could move to the life classes at the college and spend a day a week in the studio drawing the human form from the life models employed to pose for them. When drawing naked models the classes were segregated. Men and women were not allowed to work alongside each other while contemplating the curve of a buttock or a breast. If the model was 'draped', however, either in ordinary clothes or some wonderful theatrical confection loaned from the costume department, then the classes were once again mixed.

The models were paid half a crown an hour and posed from ten in the morning to three in the afternoon, with three fifteen-minute breaks and an hour for lunch, before everyone went home at four. For this course, with teaching one day a week with inspirational teachers, Jeanne was charged £3 a term.

The landscape and light of the Mediterranean proved irresistible to the artists who taught Jeanne and her fellow students and she, like many artists before and since, would be drawn south for inspiration. Europe, and particularly France, was still the powerhouse of art and design and Paris was the flame at the centre that attracted artists from all over the world. The scintillating concentration of talent there between the two world wars was characterised by the creative independence and brilliance of artists such as Modigliani, Chagall, Marie Laurencin and Picasso. Most were still working in Paris when Jeanne began her life as an artist; some embodied the romantic vision of a creative bohemian, indulging in an excess of life and love, yet always in obsessive thrall to their art. This creative vitality streamed across the Channel to fizz in the corridors of the Central School. Even the students who had never been abroad were enthused by their teachers with artistic innovation and fervour.

The stimulus of the teaching was more than equalled by the liveliness of student life. The annual Chelsea Arts Ball was held in the Albert Hall and students were encouraged to attend in fancy dress by being offered tickets at half price. Bizarre costumes were often inspired by famous paintings. These, especially the classical references, were used as an excuse for extravagance, hilarity and, sometimes, near nudity. Given a theme each year, for decades the ball was one of the social highlights of artistic London. General exuberance, however, got increasingly out of hand until, in the 1950s, a smoke bomb was set off causing some of the revellers to require medical treatment, and the ball was eventually banned.

It was in this febrile, unfettered atmosphere that Jeanne pursued her art, while maintaining her image as the youngest, most placid sister. Her surprisingly independent spirit was beginning to strain at the carapace of conventional family life.

Angela too was baulking at the narrow role assigned unmarried women of her generation and class. She was twenty-eight and, as the hope of a husband and children of her own receded, the marriage of her younger sister confirmed her in her spinsterhood. She would refer to herself with some poignancy when she was middle-aged as an Aunt Jessie, but she was an Aunt Jessie with a wilder and more bohemian private life than any of her sisters. Beneath the tweeds and sensible shoes beat a passionate and unconventional heart. Part of the problem for Angela's generation of women was the very real lack of marriageable men after the catastrophe of the Great War. Angela was fourteen at the outbreak of hostilities, and the young men she would have expected to marry were the eighteen-year-olds plucked from their schools and universities and sent across the Channel to fight, be wounded and die.

It is probable that Angela would have been most happy in a theatrical marriage, much like her parents' own. Facing the increasingly likely fact of her spinsterhood, however, she had to find some kind of genteel voluntary work to make use of her time, while turning to relationships elsewhere to satisfy her highly emotional and romantic nature. During her canvassing in the poorer parts of South London, Angela had begun to question her family's lack of political engagement and their acceptance of the status quo that made them natural Tories. With direct experience of how most of her fellow Londoners lived, she could not remain unmoved: 'The conditions of the poor filled me with unspeakable pity … turning me into a rabid socialist for quite a long time.' 'Mr Right', the unnamed married man she had once longed to wed, had also been a socialist and it was to the left that she leaned until after the Second World War when, wishing to reward Winston Churchill for his wartime leadership she said, she returned to the Conservative fold. She became more strongly Tory as she aged and, looking back on her youthful idealism, wrote, 'I was foolish enough to imagine that only a Labour government could put these conditions [of widespread poverty and inequality] right.'[6]

Her great friend from her debutante days, Betty Hicks, had joined the Red Cross and proved herself an instinctive nurse, which Angela did not. Bedpans, dirty linen and unsightly diseases that needed hands-on treatment were all beyond her. However, she did love the scruffy little urchins who came to the children's clinic and she would burst into tears in sympathy with them. So, turning her back on the nursing side of the work, Angela was encouraged by Shaw, ever the robust and adventurous spirit, to become a VAD with her.

Voluntary Aid Detachments had been founded in the Great War by the Red Cross to provide supplementary aid to the Territorial Forces Medical Service, working in convalescent hospitals and helping with clerical and kitchen duties. They were a volunteer force mostly of women drawn from the middle and upper classes. In the interwar years their duties were much less onerous and Angela, largely employed with distributing cups of coffee to spectators at Society events like the royal wedding of Princess Marina to the Duke of Kent, enjoyed the brushes with royalty and high society this entailed. Unfortunately, the Red Cross enforced a strict no make-up rule and more than once a virago bore down on her wielding methylated spirits and stripped the lipstick from her face: 'good gracious, du Maurier, who do you think you are? In the chorus? ...'[7]

The women VADs even had their own club, in a palatial house in Cavendish Square that used to be Marshall Thompson's Hotel, used by Thackeray in *Vanity Fair* as inspiration for the grand hotel where Captain George Osborne takes his new bride, Amelia. Conveniently close to the draper John Lewis, it was an extremely popular club for ladies, run on much the same lines as the gentlemen's clubs but more economical. Lunch was one shilling and threepence and a six-course club dinner was only the equivalent of twenty-six new pence. It was managed by a series of resilient and resourceful women and, during the extreme food shortages just after the Second World War, the main source of protein offered up at club mealtimes would be the ever-adaptable London pigeon.

Angela and Jeanne were still living with their parents at Cannon Hall and Daphne and Tommy had moved into a cottage on Well Road adjoining the main house's garden, so sisterly friendships and support continued uninterrupted, although Angela was aware of an inevitable shift in allegiance. She still felt she could tell Daphne everything, but she accepted that since her marriage, Daphne could not be as completely confiding in her. Another intimate family relationship was altered too. Muriel, uneasy with Gerald's obsessive relationship with Daphne throughout her girlhood, recognised that this difficult and beautiful daughter created less disturbance now she was wed and Gerald had been forced to finally let go. The unspoken maternal hostility that Daphne feared from childhood dissolved a little and the two women tentatively began to share an occasional solidarity over how best to deal with emotionally needy husbands. Where Muriel seemed to accept her wifely role as mother, cheerleader and nurse, Daphne resisted any demands for nurture. Despite her remarkable imagination and ability to inhabit the personae of her fictional creations, she only had occasional flashes of empathy for the feelings of the living and was largely uncomprehending about their suffering. She could not attempt to enter sympathetically the experiences of the young men and officers, like Tommy, whose terrible experiences of war were far from imaginary.

Daphne was forced to adjust to life with another person whose needs and expectations encroached on her free-wheeling independence, demanding that she live in a world not entirely fashioned to her own designs. Although she loved Tommy and thought him 'the most charming person in the world', she found his night terrors, moodiness and irritability trying. Overall she declared to Tod that life was 'very pleasant all round',[8] and more full and interesting than her single life had been. After all, it was all still a new adventure.

Part of this idea of an expanded life involved children and Daphne wanted lots, as many as six – but only sons. Within three months of marriage she was pregnant and was certain she would have a boy. It did not occur to her that she was just as likely to be carrying a daughter. The nursery at the cottage was painted blue and the name 'Christian' inscribed on the cupboard doors. This was another occasion when she would exercise her power to 'dream true'. Through force of will and desire, she could imagine anything she wanted into being; throughout her pregnancy she was certain she would manage what her mother had failed three times to do, to produce the longed-for son.

The surge of hormones in pregnancy temporarily slowed Daphne down and took the edge off her ambition to write. *The Progress of Julius* had been published during this time to respectable reviews but, like her second novel, it did not sell as well as *The Loving Spirit*. This was demoralising as Daphne thought her subsequent novels better than her first, and Angela thought *Julius* 'a brilliant affair'.[9] If the hormones of pregnancy dulled Daphne's disappointment at the becalming of her reputation as an exciting new novelist, they also made her more keen 'to wax', her code for making love.

She made few concessions to her state and, at a time when heavily pregnant women tended to hide themselves away, she continued to stride over Hampstead Heath and, even well past her due date, attended the annual ritual of the Eton and Harrow cricket match with the family. This was a century-old institution and had become part of the Season, along with Wimbledon and Henley. Current and past Etonian men and boys watched the two-day match in their customary top hat and tails. The du Maurier family had always rooted for Gerald's school, but now, in 1933, an old Etonian, in the handsome guise of Tommy, had arrived on the scene. On 14 July, Harrow won the toss and elected to bat. At the end of the day's play, Daphne went into labour.

Daphne was naturally physically courageous and not easily scared. Contemptuous of conventional female squeamishness and any show of weakness, Daphne had approached her impending labour in a gung-ho spirit. But even she was shocked and humiliated by the visceral power of childbirth. This was one process she could not control through willpower alone. Her body took over and in the process reminded her of its primitive, ruthless femaleness, even though she liked to think her heart and mind were male.

The labour continued into the second day, and Tommy and Gerald duly went off together to watch the conclusion of the cricket match. While the contest ended with an unsatisfactory draw, Daphne's baby came into the world: not the expected son but a daughter – a similarly disappointing outcome. They decided to call her Tessa after the heroine in *The Constant Nymph*, the play with which Daphne had identified so closely as a girl. A month later Daphne wrote to Tod:

All the old wives' tales about 'childbirth' are true! Of all the hellish performances – so beastly degrading too, lying on a bed with legs spread eagled and feeling exactly as though one's entire inside plus intestines and bowels were being torn from me! Pheugh! It makes me sweat to think back on it.[10]

Daphne managed to feed her baby herself and, although she had some pride in the fact, denied it gave her any pleasure or sense of intimacy. She did, however, feel some protective impulse towards her child for, when Tommy wanted her to go boating with him in Fowey, she felt that at a month old Tessa was too young to be left with a nurse. Any sign of tenderness and soft-heartedness she tended to label sentimental, a characteristic she recognised in Angela but, from very young, rejected in herself. ('I never was sentimental!'[11] she reminded Tod.) And quite quickly the baby was handed over pretty much full time to Nanny, while Daphne went back to her preferred life of writing and the imagination.

If she was underwhelmed by the whole experience of new motherhood, Daphne, not yet married a year, also soon became disillusioned with sex, telling her old governess, half in jest, that it was 'grossly overrated as a form of amusement', and certainly the resultant childbirth and baby was an exorbitant price to pay 'for a momentary flash in the pan'.[12] She was deeply disappointed that she had produced a girl, having never really rated the female sex, and vowed she would put off any further attempt to conjure herself a son for at least two and a half years. Was Tessa's birth not just a disappointment but also a challenge to Daphne's long-held belief in her power to 'dream true'? Perhaps the birth of a daughter rather than the much-willed son made her question her power to control *everything* in her own universe, as she did in her fiction, and led to a momentary loss of confidence. This was the first time in her life that Daphne had not achieved what she had set out to do.

Angela, who had inherited much of the sentiment that Daphne felt she lacked, was enchanted by her new niece and thought her 'an adorable baby and a most amusing little girl',[13] and most importantly, for a du Maurier, very pretty. Jeanne was never to show much interest in children and even less in babies; animals were where her sympathies found expression and she did not relish being an aunt as much as Angela. Daphne chose as godmothers not her doting elder sister but the other Angela, her sister's best friend Shaw, possibly because being so masculine she seemed unlikely to marry and have children of her own. Tessa's other godmother was Countess Atalanta Mercati, a glamorous woman the same age as her sister Angela, and married to the celebrity author Michael Arlen, made famous by his novel, *The Green Hat*, that became both a play and a film.

Just as motherhood and conjugal love disappointed Daphne, so too did the kind of socialising that her new husband occasionally enjoyed. Weekends away in country houses filled her with dread and a certain amused scorn. She had few if any domestic or maternal duties, care for the house and her baby being undertaken by paid staff, but she longed for solitude and time to herself and even the presence of a husband and baby and having to consider them in this new life was intrusive on her need for imaginative space. Daphne had married with the hope that she would be entering into a richer, less selfish way of living, but the constraints dismayed her and she began longing for her former life of self-centred freedoms. Her new nanny was taken aback at how little interest Daphne had in Tessa and how detached she was both mentally and emotionally. This was more complicated perhaps than post-natal depression, as Daphne's lack of empathy for her young daughters remained throughout their childhood and even the beloved son, when he eventually arrived, could be ignored when his needs clashed with her own, to write and be alone.

The family had long been aware that Gerald was losing his zest for life. He no longer had a theatre of his own, the triumphs of the Wyndham's days were long behind him; he was still acting but in rather nondescript plays. Having not toured since he was a young man, he decided to take to the road again with *The Ware Case*, a rather improbable murder-drama with which he had had such success at Wyndham's in the mid-twenties. This last tour was a modest success, but wearying to body and spirit. For quite a while he had been complaining of not feeling very well and went from doctor to doctor, none of whom appeared to know what was ailing him. Then suddenly there was the shocking news that he had to have an operation. The family's history of operations was rather a morbid one: they feared that any du Maurier who went under the knife would somehow fail to recover, although both Angela and Daphne had survived having their appendix removed. In fact in du Maurier parlance hospitals were known as 'slaughterhouses'. Certainly the sisters' first sight of their father in his hospital bed after a 'successful' operation was alarming. His pale and haggard face filled them with foreboding.

Gerald was operated on to remove cancerous cells from his colon; it had seemed to go well but his health declined further, despite the care of a top-flight nursing home. In less than two weeks he was dead. He was barely sixty-one when he died on 11 April 1934, his thirty-first wedding anniversary. Muriel was so prostrated with grief that Daphne felt an unaccustomed pity for her and for the first time was able to comfort her physically, without fear of rejection. Angela declared it 'the saddest and most horrible [day] I had ever known'.[14] Still shocked and grieving she, as his firstborn, stepped into the role of spokesperson for the family, answering the phone and speaking to the press.

Daphne just could not believe it. She was cavalier at killing off the characters in her novels and short stories, and actually enjoyed the frisson it added to the narrative, but, as she admitted many years later, 'it is only when death touches the writer in real life that he, or she, realised the full impact of its meaning. The deathbed scene … becomes suddenly true. The shock is profound.'[15] Even in her memoir of Gerald, written at speed soon after he died in an attempt to keep him alive to her, she did not deal with his death. Instead she ended the book with her father, on the eve of his trip to hospital, gazing out on the Hampstead night seeking to draw consolation from his long-mourned dead brother and fond memories of his family.

Daphne refused to attend Gerald's funeral and instead took a basket of caged pigeons up to Hampstead Heath and set them free. From her father's belongings she claimed the camel-hair trousers and jacket that, 'poor darling Daddy wore in the nursing home before he died', and by wearing them kept something of him close. She wore these clothes for years. 'There's sentiment for you,'[16] was her wry comment to a friend, as she changed into them for the umpteenth time, a decade and a half later.

Gerald's sudden death altered everything. He had always lived beyond his means and when his debts threatened to catch up with him just worked harder or organised another tour. He had made little provision for the future and long-term security of his family, so pretty soon it was clear that Cannon Hall would have to be sold. Muriel and her two unmarried daughters would move into the pair of Queen Anne cottages at the bottom of the garden, one of which had been occupied by Daphne, Tommy and baby Tessa and Nanny. Tommy had been given a new posting as second in command of 2nd Battalion, the Grenadier Guards, stationed at Aldershot, and the Browning family had moved to the Old Rectory at Frimley in Surrey.

Muriel's talent for house renovation was once more in action and she turned both cottages into one charming house which they named Providence Corner. Unlike Daphne and their father, who loved large houses and theatrically proportioned rooms, Angela was always drawn to more modest affairs and admitted the house their mother created 'stole my heart from the moment it became our home'.[17]

Gerald's death brought fundamental emotional changes too in his daughters. From black-and-white drawings that had echoed her grandfather's iconic work for *Punch*, Jeanne's growing freedom of artistic expression meant she began to experiment more with colour and paint and allow the influence of the modern artists her father deplored to infiltrate her work. Angela recalled that Jeanne only really started to use paint after Gerald's death. With much less surveillance and intrusion into her private life, she could discover her own path in the world.

Having not engaged in any substantial writing during her first year of marriage, Daphne was energised by her need to keep Gerald alive still and close to her, and decided almost immediately to write a biography of him. Within a month of his death she had signed a contract with a new and dynamic publisher, Victor Gollancz, that began a remarkably affectionate and fruitful relationship with Victor himself, lasting his lifetime. After four intensive months of writing, she finished *Gerald* and it was published before the year was out. Her warts-and-all portrait upset a good many of Gerald's Garrick Club friends, who thought no daughter should be quite so frank about a father's weaknesses, delineated unapologetically alongside his charms. Angela, ever loyal, insisted that Gerald would have given it his blessing and been delighted with the result. Despite the snorts of various old clubmen, most of whom Angela insisted had not even known their father, the book was enthusiastically received by the critics and sold well.

Angela had striven so hard during her youth to please her parents and be the responsible and good elder sister. All her life so far she had sought her father's love and respect. Perhaps even more than her sisters, it was Angela, at thirty years old, who most needed release from Gerald's values and view of the world. His powerful prejudices encompassed homophobia and a bathetic suspicion of every man who ever showed an interest in his daughters. With his death, she could break away from the stultifying demand that she remain a naïve, sexually ignorant girl. At last she could put away her propensity for fantasy love affairs with people who could never reciprocate her feelings. It was time to grow up at last and find a more honest and satisfying outlet for her febrile emotions and overactive heart.

Confused and grieving, she set off for Italy to visit her great old friend and mother substitute Micky Jacob. Micky had settled in Sirmione, the home town of the poet Catullus, nestling in breathtaking medieval splendour at the southern edge of Lake Garda. Here Micky dispensed comfort food and warm wisdom to friends who came to stay. It was here too that Angela met Una Troubridge and Radclyffe Hall, who were still having to live with the fallout that followed the scandal over *The Well of Loneliness*. In Angela's photo album there was Micky, as stout and jolly as a Toby jug, alongside a chic and shingled Radclyffe Hall, numerous Italian children and assorted Pekes. Incongruous in this company was a snatched photo of sleek, well-groomed men at lunch round a long trestle table covered with a white cloth. Angela's caption, 'Fascists Dining', showed a glimpse of a darkening Europe. Hitler was about to become Chancellor of Germany and Spain's unrest was escalating into civil war.

By the mid-thirties, Mussolini's vision of Italy as a resurrected Roman Empire, with him as *Il Duce*, was becoming more radical. Military expansionism into Africa and glorification of an exalted masculinity and traditional hierarchical values was growing ugly and dangerous for anyone who did not fit the iron-clad glove. Jewish, liberal, lesbian, thespian Micky, and her motley friends, were too obviously the types of decadent individual so vilified by this emergent fascist order that sought to create the new *uomo fascista*. In barely four years, with the outbreak of the Second World War, Micky would have to leave her beautiful retreat on the shores of Lake Garda and head for the relative safety of England. When she returned to 'Casa Micky', after peace eventually came, she was given the warmest of welcomes from her Italian neighbours, delighted to see her home.

But while Angela was with her, it seemed there were just a few clouds gathering on the distant horizon. The everyday pleasures of Italian life continued. After some days of rest under the supervision of Micky's motherly care and consolation, Angela was ready for adventure again and encouraged by her to accompany two very camp gentlemen friends of hers, Roland and George, to Venice. This was Angela's first visit to the city. She filled her photo album with timeless images of narrow, inky canals, bobbing ranks of gondolas for hire, the importunate pigeons of St Mark's Square and tourists, including herself with her beaming, well-fed companions, posing on the Lido. Despite rather limited experience, Angela declared Venice 'the fairest city on earth', adding that it was 'unutterably beautiful and still unspoilt'.[18]

She was experimenting with her own viewpoints and friendships that would never have been countenanced by her father:

> I began to meet and make exciting friends of my own. Hitherto they had for the most part been culled from my childhood and from Daddy's plays and productions. But now … I began to discover for myself people belonging to the profession who were to be my own friends. I was to be Angela, and not merely Gerald's daughter (nor, as yet, 'only the sister'!).

Her growing confidence, and the company of more interesting and worldly women, moved her romantic relationships into the erotic: her writing was spurred on by these relationships, her poems and novels became gifts to the women she loved.

In the December after Gerald died, Angela went alone to see Mary Newcomb in George Bernard Shaw's *Saint Joan* at the Old Vic. Mary was the woman and actress for whom she had felt such an admiration and attraction when she met her after her dazzling performance in the play *Jealousy* some six years before. This time Mary was the star in the Old Vic season and went on to dazzle again as Cleopatra in Shakespeare's *Antony and Cleopatra*. In an up-to-the-minute production, striking for its modernist set design, the great theatre critic James Agate thought Mary portrayed Cleopatra as 'a brilliantly clever, highly complex, neurotic lady of our times'.[19] And her physical charms were not lost on Leslie Rees, an Australian writer working in London as a critic on the theatrical weekly *The Era*, who noted Mary's glamour and beauty and, 'her long leg-stride [that] reminds you of Garbo'.[20]

Now that Angela no longer had her father looking over her shoulder she felt emboldened to move from infatuated fan of Miss Newcomb, the actress, to become a loving friend of Mary, the woman. Mary and her elderly husband Alex Higginson had just moved into Stinsford House in an idyllic part of Dorset, nestling low beside the parish church with its churchyard in which Thomas Hardy's heart was buried. This was the village and the countryside that had inspired Hardy's *Under the Greenwood Tree*. 'I was to know Stinsford in all its seasons,' Angela wrote, and recorded a privileged life that had hardly changed since Hardy's day:

> In the winter, gay with hunt balls; in the early autumn, when I lazed abed in a high haunted room covered in antique Chinese wallpaper while Mary would be out cubbing;* and in the spring when narcissi, daffodils, tulips and wallflowers made one wonder whether after all the youth of each year was not the best.

Alex, immensely rich and able to live the leisured sporting life as Master of the Cattisford, indulged his passion for hounds and

---

* Cubbing was a form of autumn hunting aimed at teaching young hounds how to hunt and kill and dispersing young foxes from their usual territory into a wider area.

hunting and other country pursuits while supporting a household replete with many servants, whom he would summon with his hunting horn.

Mary tried to be as good a consort as she could, but her natural predisposition leant much more to the theatre and the arts and here she found a sympathetic ally in Angela who was more than happy to be with her. Indeed, she spent so many months in this lovely setting over the next couple of years that Stinsford became what Angela described as her second home, the whole experience 'a time of very great happiness'. The gardens were particularly romantic: herbaceous borders in summer overflowed with roses and delphiniums, and the sultry scent of wisteria and heavy, waxy magnolia flowers wafted from the creepers surrounding Mary's bedroom window. Angela succumbed to the languid beauty of a lovely English house and garden, irresistibly combined with American standards of luxury and comfort: 'Happy warm summer days in Dorset … with bees humming, and the sound of a lark high in the sky above the lush meadows beyond.'[21]

Mary not only took Angela under her glamorous wing but she also introduced her to the pleasures of poetry, particularly of Walt Whitman, the great American humanist poet who dealt earthily and erotically with matters of the heart. Guided by Mary's enthusiasm for this writer, Angela thought him 'a poetic giant' whose work she found more heady than any wine. This was an epiphany for her. She recalled, 'I never really read much poetry till I fell in love … indeed it was not until I had reached my thirties that I "fell" for poetry in a big way as they say, both reading it and writing it.'[22]

Lazing in this beautiful garden, Angela wrote poems of her own, focused on love and desire, entirely reflective of her own state of mind at the time, and dedicated them to Mary. She expressed in poetry everything she felt she could not say in person. Mary was a sophisticated, experienced woman of the world, twice married and firmly heterosexual. Given the leisurely weeks and months they spent together, however, it would have been remarkable if Mary had not realised the true nature of Angela's feelings for her. She was in her early forties while Angela had just reached an emotionally immature thirty, but growing up fast. Mary's triumph as Cleopatra inspired this poem, a real-life version of the central theme of *The Little Less*, Angela's most personal novel that rejection had made her shut away in a drawer:

> *M.N.H. as [Cleopatra]*
> If I were asked where'ere I'd been
> Who was the loveliest vision seen,
> I would reply with haste, I wean
> Why Clementine, my Clementine.
>
> … Her dimpled chin & roguish eyes
> Fill me with wonder & surprise,
>
> But she will n'er my thoughts surmise
> Will Clementine, my Clementine.
>
> For friends am I, & only such
> Who would alas! Be more by much,
> But I must not so much as touch
> My Clementine, – my Clementine.
>
> What would I give to so possess
> Such bounty as thy dear caress?
> Thinkst thou, thou couldst thyself demean
> To grant such pleasure, Clementine?
> If thou dost know what sweet delight
> Is mine when in my arms you lay
> Perchance when even turns to night
> Thou wouldst not spurn me with a 'nay'.
>
> For kisses sweet I fain would rain
> Upon thy breasts & ears & lips
> And take them back to give again
> To eyes that launch a million ships.

Although Angela here was still pursuing, as in her youth, love affairs that could not be consummated, Mary's calm, motherly presence allowed her to come to terms with an emotional nature that would have brought out the overwrought bully in her father. After all, she had been called a whore by him for chastely falling in love with a married man; what would she be called if she had declared her love for another woman? Mary valued Angela's company, accepted her love and reassured her fears. In doing so, she provided Angela with the bridge into her adult emotional life.

One of Angela's last poems to Mary was much more sophisticated, deftly amusing, and played on the du Maurier sisters' code, 'I have other fish to fry' (meaning 'I am pursuing forbidden love affairs') which they used to deflect their prying parents:

> *To M.N.H. On Losing the Desire to Fry Fish*
> I am no longer int'rested in fish
> Since you provided me another dish.
> A wealth of fruit; forbidden, – it is true;
> But who would look to Neptune's realm when you
> Are by?
> Not I.

Daphne was certainly kept up to date on Angela's emotional flowering for, in generously sharing some of her royalty money with her sisters, she wrote to Angela, 'The only condition I make is that it does not go on "flowers" for Mary Newcomb, etc!!'

The intensity of Angela's feeling for Mary dissipated with her friend's trip to America on tour in 1937. But Angela had already moved into a new and exciting circle of friends. She had been introduced, by the actress Phyllis Terry, to the gaily adventurous Caroline 'Lena' Ramsden, a racehorse owner, sculptor, writer and large-hearted *bon viveur*. Lena's extrovert personality attracted an array of theatre people, artists and writers into whose orbit Angela was flung. These included the actresses Gwen Ffrangcon-Davies and Marda Vanne, and Martita Hunt, actors John Gielgud and Dave Burnaby and the playwright Dodie Smith. The writer Marguerite Steen and her lifetime partner the artist William Nicholson also circled on the periphery of this group.

Everyone congregated in Lena's handsome studio home, 8 Primrose Hill Studios (Arthur Rackham lived at Number 6), decorated in her racing colours of royal blue and white. Here Lena threw lavish parties – one to celebrate the success of one of her horses lasted for three days. There were always lethal cocktails, a piano being played and voices singing, or declaiming to the assembled throng. For cosier and marginally less wild times, people climbed further up the hill, to Gwen Ffrangcon-Davies and Marda Vanne's cottage at Holly Place, Hampstead.

A love of small distinctive dogs also bound these new friends to Angela. She had her Pekinese Wendy and her mother's Pekes too, while Lena had a French bulldog called Napoléon and Gwen and Marda a little pug, Snuffles, 'a dog of extremely strong character and completely devoid of charm', but doted on by Gwen and Marda who gave him Marda's surname and treated him like their child.[23] On at least one of many occasions Lena had a raging row with her close friend, the actress Martita Hunt, who for a while lived in a flat at 7 Primrose Hill Studios, this pretty mews peopled by huge artistic egos. Lena feared her love affair with Martita had been ruined for ever and, in floods of tears, rang Angela and Gwen for solace. All three women, and their dogs, ended up on Hampstead Heath and walked and laughed until perspective returned once more to the world. Lena explained it was impossible to be close to Martita and not have occasional fights, 'unless your argumentative attributes were no better than those of a doormat'.[24] Angela was learning that the company of interesting, unconventional women was fun and rewarding in all kinds of ways.

Gwen and Marda were an intriguing couple. Lifelong partners despite occasional separations, they were poles apart in character and in the way they practised their art. Gwen was hailed as the best Shakespearian actress of her day. Her luminous portrayal of Juliet was heart-wrenching and unforgettable to anyone lucky enough to see it. She was striking looking with a lovely speaking voice and an emotional truth that animated everything she did. Gwen was already quite well acquainted with Angela's father, having acted with Gerald in J. M. Barrie's play, *Shall We Join the Ladies?*, a one act murder-mystery in which Gerald played the butler, Dolphin. It proved to be a popular play and Gwen and Gerald appeared together in at least three revivals between 1925 and 1932, with John Gielgud joining the cast in 1929. So Angela entered the circle of friends trailing clouds of theatrical glory.

Marda Vanne (short for Margaretha van Hulsteyn) was five years Gwen's junior and a handsome and headstrong South African, whose family were part of the Afrikaner elite. Her father, Sir Willem van Hulsteyn, was a Dutch born lawyer who had been knighted for services to the British Empire in 1902. With her wonderful rich voice and a talent for comedy Marda was determined to be an actress. She was already becoming established when she married an eminent lawyer, Johannes Gerhardus Strydom, while still very young. Marda barely lasted a few weeks as the conventional wife of a man whose uncompromising toughness in his political career became legendary. When she bolted from the marriage it became a scandal in the highly conservative world to which they belonged, and Marda, barely twenty-two, escaped for England to further her acting career. Her ex-husband eventually, in 1954, became Prime Minister of South Africa and an intransigent proponent of apartheid. Marda never took his name, kept her own but shortened it to Vanne, and barely mentioned him again. He, on the other hand, apparently never stopped loving her. At the end of 1926, when she was thirty and Gwen thirty-five, these two remarkable women met and their lifelong relationship began.

When Angela first got to know them in 1935 she entered a vibrant, relaxed world of actresses and artists. But it could not have been more different from her du Maurier upbringing in Hampstead, just half a mile further up the hill. She was familiar with the excessive emotionality that characterised her father and his friends, but the fact that the norm here was love between women and candour about sex was a startling liberation. The free-and-easy mores, the falling in and out of bed and the apparent lack of jealousy, was remarkable. The women who circled Gwen and Marda were all successful or wealthy, and independent of men and marriage. They enjoyed interesting, creative lives with a racy group of varied artistic friends. However, their emotional and sexual lives were entangled and, despite the love and support between them, there was also a high degree of neurotic obsession, casual sex and unrequited love.

Angela had been invited into a ménage in which Lena was in love with Marda, who was living with Gwen, but obsessed with the elusive playwright Gordon Daviot. Gordon Daviot was born Elizabeth Mackintosh, and yet to become the hugely successful mystery novelist Josephine Tey. As Josephine Tey, she immortalised Marda as the character Marda Hallard in a number of her major novels. The real Marda was not only pursued by Lena but also by an actress Toska von Bissing, with whom she engaged in dangerous liaisons, while longing for the company of others.

For Angela, the lack of shame of these women and their frankness and light-hearted enjoyment of sex was an extraordinary revelation. Lena held erotic cocktail parties in her bedroom, 'for one or two especially nice folks selected from the adult members of the community', and lubricated by loads of alcohol. Lena ended a love letter to Marda with the touching, 'You make this already grand world even grander', and then added a P.S.: 'Would you like me to shave Pussy? I'm told it's customary!!! P.P.S. You *are* a cave woman!' Toska, a baroness and an actress, was also besotted with Marda and sent her sizzling love letters, including one with an anatomical drawing of her vulva with x marks the spot, where Marda had bitten her. This was a whole new world to Angela, where women were in charge of their lives and, through both pain and pleasure, pursued their own romantic destinies.

Various presents also passed between the friends. Lena remarked that Marda seemed mostly to give her girlfriends watches. Marda wrote in her diary that in reply she 'murmured truthfully that I had given five young cuties wristwatches',[25] while Lena admitted her favourite gift for a girlfriend was the trouser press. Marda asked her what if they don't all wear trousers? But Lena was undeterred; this was the perfect gift in the circumstances. Lena lavished not a trouser press but a fur coat on Marda, who immediately felt ashamed that she had accepted such an extravagant present in exchange for sexual favours. This made her 'three-quarters skunk', she feared, and 'one-quarter angel'; Lena pandering to the skunk and Gwen to the angel. Her self-disgust was mitigated by Angela saying: 'Well darling, so long as you have it, what the Hell does it matter who gave it to you? You will look lovely in it & I shall see you.' She thus consoled Marda who subsequently felt that she and Angela shared a certain sensibility. Gwen's response to her moral dilemma was more practical and less reassuring: 'Well, thank God you won't borrow mine now.'[26]

Fear, confusion and shame over sex were the salient emotions in Angela's girlhood and suddenly she found herself among women who revelled in one another's bodies and, best of all, thought she was charming and desirable too. She had entered this bohemian world with excitement and some alarm. She was clear in her memoir how her father's death had allowed her to explore her own friendships and an alternative way of living in which she was not expected to play the role of supportive wife, so faithfully enacted by her mother, and now so chafed against by her beautiful and brilliant middle sister. Angela had been born and brought up to practise 'the magic and delicious power of reflecting the figure of man at twice its natural size'.[27] She would have followed her mother's peerless example if a willing man had presented himself. Without that man, however, her ecstatic, worshipful nature turned her reflective powers on women instead. And unlike Mary Newcomb, Marda Vanne was more than ready for the gift.

Naturally timid and law-abiding, at thirty Angela had found the courage to make her own way at last, freed from the constraints of her family's ethos and the harsh judgements of the world. To be engaged in something generally considered deviant and transgressive was to be cast out of the mainstream into an often lonely struggle for self-acceptance. The circle around Gwen and Marda made her feel less aberrant and alone.

Marda was energetic and adventurous. She poured her energies into her work as an actress, writing letters, diaries and poetry, and was generous with her sexual favours – a fact that caused much grief to Gwen but one she came to accommodate. In fact Marda valued herself most as a sexual being. 'What does it matter if I fail as an actress? I shall have raised sweet-peas, made my friends happy, & given satisfaction to my lovers.'[28] The effect she had on her numerous young women, however, made her uneasy. Too predictably they imagined themselves in love with her and were hard to shake off once the romance had gone. Marda was remarkable for her clear-sightedness and unflinching honesty, and suggested the cause: 'My desire for power which has been thwarted on the stage, comes out in my relations with these unhappy young ladies ... now this is a ghastly thought. I have no conscious wish to hurt or maim.'[29]

By the time that Angela arrived on the scene, Marda and Gwen's relationship was subsiding towards the loving companionship that it became. Where Mary Newcomb had introduced Angela to contemporary poetry, Marda continued her education by encouraging her to read Shakespeare and Milton. In response, Angela now turned her poetic efforts towards the sexually experienced Marda. Angela's first effort ('To M. v. H.' Marda's maiden name with the 'v' underlined to differentiate her from Mary 'M.N.H') was an unfinished fragment that expressed her acceptance that Marda loved Gwen, while being in love with Gordon Daviot:

> If to be loved is Heaven
> Then I indeed at Heaven's
> portal stand.
> Seeing that your heart
> Whereof I have the Key
> Is locked to mine –

It seemed that generous, insightful Gwen understood Angela's longing to be loved, and Marda's keenness to comply, at least for a time. Gwen was also possibly exasperated by Marda's continued unrequited longing for the absent playwright and hoped that a dalliance with Angela might distract her for a while. For the last week of July 1935, she sent them both off alone, without the housekeeper, to their house in the country. Gwen and Marda had jointly bought Tagley Cottage, near Finchingfield in Essex. This had originally been two attached cottages but was now a delightful retreat with about an acre of gardens. It was to Tagley that their friends would come, pouring out of London at weekends which, when Gwen and Marda were in a play, started on Saturday night and lasted until Monday afternoon. The area was becoming a popular retreat for writers and actors. John

Gielgud had a house locally, as did the actress Diana Wynyard, and Dodie Smith, with her Dalmatian Pongo, and her bestselling novels yet to come.

Angela and Marda were dropped off by Gwen. She knew that neither woman cooked, so deposited them with a roast leg of mutton. 'What memories [it] evokes,' Angela wrote in her memoir, recalling her time at Tagley: 'Gwen once sent Marda and me alone there for a week, we were to do the cooking between us …We survived and so did our friendship. So these new Gerald-less days passed.'[30] Perhaps it was significant that she should think of Gerald as she recalled her first consummated love affair. Angela had always thought it was foolish to be ignorant about sex, 'one of life's pleasures', and although she agreed with her father that 'to be shop-soiled at sixteen is a tragedy', she departed from him when she declared 'but to be white as the driven snow at thirty is just damn silly'.[31] Perhaps it was also significant that her initiation into sexual love should happen when she was thirty. Marda, however, was less sanguine about this proposed week of love, as she confided to her diary, 'being in no condition for dalliance … nothing in or out of the world will induce me to touch anyone when I have spots on my face'.[32] But Angela reassured her that she was not in the least put off.

In fact the week turned out to be much more successful than Marda feared. The beauty of the countryside, the woods full of pink whorls of ragged robin, the birdsong and the sweetness of Angela's company, all made her relax: 'I forgot my spots & all my other ailments, & my face, full of grease, took on grace … I take back all I said about my young lady's silliness. She is gay & gallant & has a nice wit.' Cooking was still a challenge and Angela, with ill-founded confidence, set about making a bacon omelette for their supper. Marda had to intervene when she saw her young companion frying the bacon in dollops of beef dripping.

The week ended happily, as Marda noted, 'We dined together in mutual admiration. Greek acknowledged Greek & the suburban twins, tenderness & respect were conceived.' Later, Angela caught the midnight sleeper train to Cornwall. The love affair lifted Marda's spirits but they evaporated with the return to everyday life at the house in Holly Place: 'If my young lady had been here I should have gone to Goodwood [races], danced all night, & swum in Kenwood [Hampstead] at six the next morning without turning a hair. I suppose I must be one of those women who are good for one purpose only – bed.'[33]

Angela was based at home with Muriel and Jeanne and, although Gerald was dead, she still had to navigate Muriel's disapproval of the unconventional women whose company her eldest daughter enjoyed. While they were staying in London, Angela learnt quickly not to confront but to deceive:

> I had certain friends who were not always approved of, so I found the best thing to do was to lie when I was with them and say I had been somewhere else, and although at thirty I had to 'clock in' to my mother's bedroom at whatever the hour of my return, I discovered there were ways and means of inventing some story of one's evening pleasures.[34]

The true story would have given Muriel sleepless nights and would have had Gerald turning in his grave. Angela described her life at the time in a poem to Marda, 'With Apologies to Milton'. A parody of his sonnet 'On His Blindness', she cast herself, ironically, as Milton with Gwen, personified as Patience, giving advice on how to best manage Milton/Angela's struggle to express love for God/Marda:

> When I consider how my life is spent
> Dashing 'tween Hampstead, Bayswater, South Ken.
> Dishing out to women 'stead of men
> Some perquisites of nature (which I meant
> To give but Marda.) I am afraid –;
> Tho' she's no axe to grind & I no stranger –
> 'treat me as Greek & be not dog in manger'
> I supplicate. But Gwen will upbraid
> That murmur & reply 'Marda's no need
> Of coats, pyjamas, tears. And if you pine
> To gain her favour gitter not. Her state

Is Sap[p]hic. Thousands at her bidding speed
Up hill to Holly Place but cry and whine –
They sometimes – come – who merely lie & wait.'

In fact Angela did try and unite her life as a daughter and sister with her new transformative romance and invited Marda to stay at Ferryside for a fortnight in September. Marda confided to her diary: 'I do not look forward to meeting her rather frightening family.'[35] The du Maurier reputation was still awesome. Gerald was not long dead and Daphne had published three well-received novels and her acclaimed biography of their father was just out. *Jamaica Inn* was about to spring into vivid life. In fact Marda cried off from this visit to Cornwall at this point because she and Gwen had an opportunity to go away together, and she thought this a less daunting prospect.

Marda was already uneasily aware that this love affair had gone to her young lover's head. Angela considered herself deeply in love while for Marda this was a delightful but passing diversion. Angela bombarded her with letters, poems and invitations. She gave her a bottle of gardenia scent and three pairs of pyjamas, while all Marda wanted was the distraction of sex. Nearly a decade later, and with the intervention of war, Angela was still writing to her, admitting that her current love thought Marda 'the person that has meant most to me in my life. Well, well, well. I fear you'd be highly amused at the times your name crops up.'[36] There was an inevitable gap in emotion between Angela, who had discovered a whole new world in which she could belong, and Marda, the experienced, world-weary actress, pursued by lovers but held at bay by the one woman for whose love she longed. Marda was above all honest, and wished she could be frank with Angela who was already imagining making a life with her. Instead, she wrote her the letter she could never send:

Thank you for your two letters which I received today. They distressed me because it seems you expect me to feel more than lust for you. Is not lust a decent honest thing? I have told you the limits of what I gave when I said the words of that song we heard together. 'You're lovely to look at, delightful to hold, & heaven to kiss.' And that is all. I do not think about you now you are away [in Cornwall], nor long for your companionship, but I do long for the illusion of apple blossom you give me in bed. You're clean, & fragrant, & damn silly; & you make, & will make, me proud of my body. Therefore, stop writing I pray you, & when you come back to London let us fall to love making without the ado of words. Yours, gratefully, Marda.[37]

By November, Marda was referring to Angela as her 'ex-young lady', but, unusually for her, their relationship continued as an affectionate friendship for many years. Their loving friendship's longevity said a great deal about Angela's warmth and generosity of spirit. When she came to write her autobiography some fifteen years later, Gwen commented to Marda that Angela's 'memoirs I fear will have to be so censored as to be a little dull!'*[38] Marda eventually met Lady du Maurier for lunch with Angela in November and felt uncomfortable about it but, good actress that she was, reported she managed to stop her hands and lips from trembling and did not give the game away. She seemed to arouse great affection and loyalty in her lovers, for when Angela told her, with a flourish, that she had made her the beneficiary in her will, Marda related to Gordon Daviot that Angela was the third young woman to do so. It embarrassed her, but she knew they were young, time would pass and the will would be changed again (as indeed it was).

One of the more interesting couples Angela met through these new friendships was the novelist and bull-fighting aficionado Marguerite Steen and her much older lover, the distinguished painter William Nicholson. Delightfully youthful and dandified in his dress, William welcomed Angela to his famous London studio in Apple Tree Yard. Rich with the divine clutter of a working painter, the studio was converted from stables just behind St James's Square. Full of mischief and rapid-fire repartee, he was an artist of wide-ranging ability and brilliance, and in recognition of this was knighted the following year. Yet one of Angela's fondest memories of him was when she took Jeanne round to see him one afternoon at the studio and 'with strange

* Angela did heavily censor her autobiography but it turned out far from dull.

humility he showed Jeanne and myself picture after picture as though we were Duveens or Kenneth Clarks'.*[39] Of all the famous men she had got to know well in her life, and this must have included her father and all the eminent actors of her acquaintance, she considered William Nicholson to be the only really great man among them.

Angela was enjoying her newfound liberty to be herself with a group of women (and the occasional man) who did not judge her plain, disgracefully fat, or undesirable, and whose lives as single, liberated working women of independent means seemed to be far more interesting and adventurous than their married counterparts. In the mid-1930s, once a woman married she lost much of her autonomy and independence and was expected to defer to her husband on all the important and practical matters such as money, how to vote, and even sometimes what to think.

Daphne was struggling with just this very constraint as an officer's wife in Surrey. Tommy was tolerant and understanding of his wife's need for freedom, but he was conventionally brought up and subject to the social conventions of the time. He also had to maintain his authority and face in a very conventional, masculine world where officers' wives were expected to be attractive and amenable and very much the secondary partner. A wife who went her own way ran the risk of undermining her husband in his relationship with his men and fellow officers, where it might be wondered how he would control his troops if he couldn't even bring his wife into line.

Daphne started out determined to do her best, but had never been exposed to the harsh deprivations of working-class life and visiting the wives of the squaddies under her husband's command was a shock. How could women live like this, she wondered, with so many children, no servants, little money and poor living conditions, and yet

---

* The Duveen brothers were extremely successful (and controversial) art dealers responsible for helping to build some of the great American private collections. Kenneth Clark was a leading academic, writer and art historian, eventually made world famous by his epic series for the BBC, *Civilisation*.

be so happy and uncomplaining of their lot? 'I must say, though,' she wrote to Tod, 'the poor things are cheerful on the whole, and clean.'[40] The 'and clean' revealed her detachment and lack of natural empathy with women whose men would fight and give their lives under her husband's command. She could not identify on a human level with these wives and mothers and their hard-pressed families, but intellectually she knew how privileged she was and how she had some duty to them as the commanding officer's wife. She set to letter-writing to help claim benefits due to them, and was always kind and polite, if rather remote.

Daphne may have found the lives of the ordinary soldiers and their families incomprehensibly difficult but she was, for different reasons, just as horrified by the wives of the officer classes. Again to Tod she confided: 'I dread the picture of paying calls, and watching polo, and hearing Mrs So-and-So whisper in Mrs Such-and-Such's ear ("Of course you know she had a terrible reputation in England – drinks like a fish – and they say the little girl is'nt her husband's at all ....") What a life!'[41]

However, the Army wives' loss was literature's gain, for the grimness of Army wifedom spurred Daphne on to blissful escape into her imagination and work. Her dismay and contempt for most human society precipitated her with increased energy into the worlds she created in her novels, peopled with characters utterly under her command. After the success of her biography of her father, Daphne set to with a will to write a novel that expressed all her love of the wildest most mysterious aspects of Cornwall, a novel of gothic adventure and suspense with wreckers, countless murders and brutal reversals of fortune. The atmosphere of the sea and the moor was so vividly conjured that Cornish mists seemed to rise from its pages.

The previous autumn, Daphne and Foy Quiller-Couch had set off for Bodmin Moor and, sheltering from the swirling fog and sheeting rain, stayed a couple of nights at Jamaica Inn. She had first come across this ancient coaching-inn the previous November. The women had undertaken an expedition on horseback and got lost on what seemed so mysterious and sinister a moor, only finding their way back when they dropped their reins and relied on their horses' instincts for home. From that point the place lived on in her imagination. This second visit with Foy, and a chance meeting at the inn with a diminutive local pastor, provided a hook for a story that would not let her go. 'What seed was dropped that night into the subconscious? I shall never know.'[42]

The seed grew into *Jamaica Inn*, and Victor Gollancz was determined to publish it, thereby poaching her from Heinemann, her previous fiction publisher. He offered Daphne the princely sum of £1,000 as an advance with generous twenty per cent royalties up to the first 10,000 copies sold. With Tommy only able to draw on his military salary, Daphne was aware that she had become her family's main breadwinner and was proud of the fact, enjoying the independence and power it brought. Although she was not one to spend money on herself and cared little for clothes, she valued the freedom that money bestowed and was gratified at being the sole provider for her family with the same kind of largesse that had characterised her father's approach to life.

Margaret, the nanny, looked after Tessa virtually full time and Daphne had a cook and a cleaner so her day was almost entirely her own. She continued to escape as much as she could to Cornwall, the land that fired her imagination and fed her spirit. Writing with intensity and discipline, she managed to work five to six hours a day and, by the beginning of 1936, was writing her last paragraph of *Jamaica Inn*. She made her heroine, Mary Yellan, eschew the conventional female yoke of support and subjection, and choose instead an uncertain future with her disreputable lover in his vagabond life. The novel was complexly plotted with terrific twists and turns to the melodramatic tale.

Daphne's own response to the visceral power of Cornish sea and landscape and the pull of the past made her story thrillingly affective, and her dysphoric view of human nature permeated it, with menacing and brutalised characters denied redemption. The most disconcerting revelation was that her villain was not the murderous but tragic thug who terrorised the neighbourhood, but the albino vicar who admitted he was a 'freak in nature', someone from whom her heroine Mary instinctively recoiled: 'In the animal kingdom a freak was a thing of abhorrence, at once hunted and destroyed, or driven out into the wilderness.'[43] In Angela's novel, *The Little Less*, she too made much of society's reaction to 'freaks of nature', as homosexuals were described at the time, and their fear of misunderstanding, contempt and ostracism. Gerald's long shadow still loomed over them.

Published with confidence and flair by Daphne's new publisher, within just three months *Jamaica Inn* had sold more than her previous three novels put together and Daphne and Gollancz had a bestseller on their hands. Daphne had her family to thank for an unerring sense of the dramatic. Even home life with Gerald was like an extended pantomime, with extremes of histrionic emotion, intense intimacy alternating with almost hysterical rejection. Although difficult to cope with in real life, it stimulated Daphne's sensitive understanding of all the dramatic tricks used so memorably by her father in his acting and theatrical direction. The excitement of the cliffhanger, the volte face, the unmasking of the unexpected villain and the terror of the other, hidden self, all served her brilliantly in her fiction.

But rather than please her new publisher by capitalising on this new vein of English Gothic, Daphne wanted to return to the subject of her family once more and suggested instead that she write about grandfather George, at the centre of a group biography on the du Mauriers. She was someone whose active curious mind was excited by research and particularly fascinated by her own family and its romanticised roots in France. Her position as Tommy's wife, however, was set to make its first intrusive demands on her life. Her husband was now a lieutenant colonel and in sole command of 2nd Battalion, the Grenadier Guards in Alexandria in Egypt. Daphne recognised her duty was to go with him.

Life in Alexandria as Mrs Browning was almost unendurable for Daphne. She could not bear the heat, recoiled from the locals and loathed the social life of cocktail parties and gossip with the other English ex-pats, whom she looked down her nose at as 'horrible Manchester folk'. Just as she was taught as a child to have perfect

Edwardian manners, Daphne behaved with old-world courtesy, but also as their father had encouraged his children to mock behind people's backs, her vitriol against the people she met was expressed in letters home. At fifteen on holiday in Algiers, she had been fascinated by the Arab traders, but that curiosity and interest was not now extended to the Egyptians. She thought them filthy and was irritated that they could not understand the English language. The English people in Egypt she found petty-minded and second-rate and she could not wait to leave.

Daphne ached with longing for England, but specifically for Cornwall, and swore she would never again stray 'east of Looe, or west of Par', a promise to herself she pretty much managed to keep. But, in her professional, hard-working way, Daphne slogged all through the heat of an Egyptian summer working on her book on the family, at times wishing she had never contracted to do it. She finished at last, but slumped into a depressed listlessness. Pale and low spirited, she had lost her appetite for food and life. The energy of three-year-old Tessa, even though she was in the full-time care of the redoubtable Margaret, still seemed too much for her mother to bear. Nothing seemed to be right.

Daphne had never become emotionally attached to her young daughter, although at times she was shocked by sudden feelings of protectiveness towards her. As a mother she always appeared kind and even-tempered, but puzzled by why anyone should delight in the company of one's children. Daphne was proud of the fact she was not 'one of those mothers who live for having their brats with them all the time',[44] and seemed incapable of empathising with her daughter who, like herself as a girl, longed for love from an attractive, elusive mother. Daphne was so sensitive and articulate about the damage done to her by her mother's remoteness, yet it never occurred to her that she was repeating the same pattern in her own relationship with her daughter. Rather, she chose to dilute Tessa's intimate connection to her by insisting her daughter was more a Browning than a du Maurier, but also more like Angela than herself, both these descriptions emphasising the little girl's inferiority and separateness from Daphne and Gerald, who by her reckoning were quintessential du Mauriers.

When Daphne was eventually seen by a doctor and diagnosed as being not ill but pregnant she was horrified. She did not want another baby at this point in her life. Even Tommy, trying to lift her mood with the jokey speculation that she might be carrying twin boys, failed to raise her spirits. Daphne wrote to Tod, who was living in Baker Street trying to make a go as a hat-maker, trusting her old governess to understand and sympathise: 'The worst. Another infant on the way!! This was really rather a knock-out blow, as you can imagine.'[45]

Depressed that life seemed to be alarmingly beyond her control, Daphne could not know that her career and fortune were about to be transformed by a serendipitous creative relationship with the young film-maker and friend of her father's, Alfred Hitchcock. Their stars would rise together as he took three of her most compelling works of imagination and turned two of them into iconic works of cinematic art. Her stories would help propel him into Hollywood and immortality and he would make her one of the most famous and high-earning writers in the world. But bereft of inspiration and feeling powerless to command her own life, Daphne faced only the encroaching demands of marriage and maternity.

Angela was living a completely different life and, as great letter writers, the sisters were aware of how much their experiences were diverging. Her social life had expanded dramatically through her intimacy with Marda and Gwen and their Hampstead friends. They were an intellectually lively and creative, unorthodox group concerned with the arts and the world at large and Angela, although as sheltered in her upbringing as Daphne, was more able to sympathise with people less fortunate than herself. Her work with the Red Cross and VAD had made it inescapably clear how the majority of her countrymen and women struggled. Angela had a sympathy for the lives of others. She also felt some outrage at the injustices in England at the time, hence her parting from family tradition for a while and becoming a socialist. Even that aberration, however, was sparked, as with every big decision in her life, by love.

England in the mid-thirties was still struggling with the effects of the Depression. Society was deeply divided by class and region and Daphne was not alone in being ignorant of or uninterested in the two million unemployed, most in the industrial north, and how they managed to live on meagre dole money, food handouts, with little hope of work or progression. For those who did have jobs, however, there were numerous innovations that people with money could enjoy. Car ownership (and fatal accidents) increased dramatically, and cinemas and lidos were being built in the more prosperous suburbs and towns. The 1930s was seen retrospectively as the decade of depression and yawning inequalities. Yet, by the middle of the decade, economic prospects appeared slightly rosier, while the political landscape in Europe grew increasingly dark.

Angela remembered the sense of grief that engulfed the country on the announcement on 21 January 1936 of the death of King George V. She and Daphne watched from the balcony at St James's Palace the impressive funeral procession: 'So much scarlet down below us worn by the troops lining the streets, and the unrelieved black of the mourning civilians, and the hushed quiet throughout the long hours of waiting for the cortège, and when it came, the gun carriage … with field-marshal's helmet and baton … his sons following … the new King.'[46] In fact, the glamorous new King, Edward VIII, promised so much, and lifted the mood of the nation. Although it was in part a calculated play for a good press, he seemed to understand the plight of the poorest of his subjects, endearing himself to the Welsh miners when he toured their depressed villages, where so many were out of work, and famously declaring that 'Something must be done'. Little did any of his subjects know, however, the turmoil in his private life that meant before the year was out he would turn his back on duty, and on them all, for love.

Angela's life was becoming more brave and expansive. She bought her first car in 1936 and this marked a new stage in her life as an independent single woman. There was something confident, defiant even, about choosing a bright green sporty two-seater Morris Eight. This

The du Mauriers: Angela, Jeanne, their mother Muriel and Daphne – the model of a glamorous Edwardian family, circa 1912.

A particularly large group painting of the sisters with their dog Brutus by society portraitist Frederic Whiting (painted in 1918, purportedly on Hampstead Heath, but actually in his studio). Angela never liked the way she was portrayed as rather shapeless and with a shiny nose, to be compared unfavourably for ever with her younger sister: 'Daphne looking rather like a flaming shining Jeanne d'Arc.'

MISS DAPHNE DU MAURIER

The second daughter of Sir Gerald and Lady du Maurier, who has inherited much of the literary genius of her grandfather, George du Maurier, the famous "Punch" artist and the author of "Trilby." Her short story "And Now to God the Father" is published in this number.

This cartoon of Gerald du Maurier was drawn for *Vanity Fair* by Leslie Ward, known as 'Spy', the most celebrated *Vanity Fair* artist and cartoonist of the time. This appeared in the Christmas edition of 1907, the year Daphne was born, with Gerald's career on a rapid upward trajectory after the triumph of playing Raffles, the gentleman thief, and Brewster in *Brewster's Millions*.

Daphne's appearance on the cover of *The Bystander* on 15 May 1929, the week of her twenty-second birthday, to celebrate the publication of her short story 'And Now to God the Father' (written to amuse her atheist father), emphasised how much their famous name and a well-connected family helped the sisters' early careers. Uncle Willie Beaumont had just been appointed editor of *The Bystander*.

A controversial painting: the exhibition label on the back declares it to be a portrait by Jeanne du Maurier 'of the artist's sister Daphne', the exhibition dates 1936–1939. This painting was bought by a dealer from a London auction house as part of a collection of pictures. Neither Noël Welch nor Kits Browning thought it to be a work by Jeanne. But Ann and David Willmore, Daphne du Maurier enthusiasts and owners of Bookends of Fowey, now own it and consider it authentic. Jeanne is, after all, an unlikely artist for anyone to forge.

The Bird Cage and *Mimosa*, two of
Jeanne's paintings bought by the
Royal West of England Academy
in Bristol, *The Bird Cage* in 1979,
Mimosa in 1963.

Gerald du Maurier and Gertrude Lawrence, his 'last actress love', in John van Druten's play *Behold We Live* performed at St James's Theatre in 1932. Gertrude was thirty-four and Gerald fifty-nine with only two more years to live.

THEATRE WORLD SOUVENIR
"*September Tide*"

ALDWYCH THEATRE

Lawrence starred in *September Tide* in 1948, Daphne's play that explored her own fascination with Ellen Doubleday. Initially dismayed by the casting of Gertrude, 'a hardened dyed haired tart', Daphne's obsession for Ellen became partially transferred to her leading lady during the rehearsal and run of the play.

Daphne with Kits, and Flavia in the background, at a window at Menabilly, the house near Fowey she loved. She lived there from 1942 until the summer of 1969.

Daphne, Kits and Flavia picnicking on Menabilly Beach at Polridmouth Bay in 1947.

The view from Ferryside of Fowey, Polruan and the estuary leading to the sea. This was the house that changed the sisters' lives, that offered freedom and creative inspiration and began their lifelong love of Cornwall and its coast. As Daphne wrote: 'The lights of Polruan and Fowey. Ships anchored, looking up through blackness. The jetties, white with clay. Mysterious shrouded trees, owls hooting, the splash of muffled oars in lumpy water … All I want is to be at Fowey. Nothing and no one else. This, now, is my life.'

was a car for a bold woman about town, not the demure miss, waiting for her prince to come. She was to become a highly competent driver who prided herself on her assertiveness and speed, a better driver than most men. The heroines in her novels were also good, fast drivers at a time when it was quite racy for a woman to have her own car and bowl around the countryside on her own, or only in the company of a sister or female friend.

While Daphne was sweating through the Alexandrian summer, struggling to finish her du Maurier family biography, Angela and Jeanne set off on a holiday to Majorca with their mother, Aunt Billy and the actress Jill Esmond, who was due shortly to give birth to her first child, Tarquin. The hotel was inferior, the weather bad and the lavatories smelt. Jill knew that her husband, Laurence Olivier, was already under the spell of another, the tragic enchantress Vivien Leigh. Nobody enjoyed the holiday except for Angela, who loved travel and revelled in the louche company at the café they frequented, whose 'inmates and habituées might have been drawn from the type of novel one does not leave lying about in the schoolroom. (As I have remarked, I enjoyed the holiday).'[47] That arch comment in parentheses in her memoir says a great deal about her new freedoms to choose. Muriel and Aunt Billy were rather shocked by the clientele, but Angela, recently so naïve and in thrall to her parents, now embraced this gay and carefree scene. How much Marda and Gwen and their circle had taught her. She made new friends and stayed drinking into the night (apricot brandy, wine and Chartreuse) before stumbling back to the room she shared with her sister, thoroughly drunk. She woke up Jeanne who was not best pleased, but backed up Angela's lie to Muriel that her illness the following day was due to a surfeit of octopus.

Triangular relationships can be full of tension and strife. Angela's last poem to Marda seemed to express the impossibility of passion without responsibility for others:

The sun has ceased to shine
upon your head & mine
Because of love we have
too much partaken.
For Passion like a sweet & poisoned wine
Has blinded us to leave ought
else forsaken.

Marda had taught her how natural and carefree love could be, regardless of society's attempts to control and constrain it. She had shown her that she was lovable and attractive, after thirty years of feeling both these qualities had passed her by to alight instead on her sisters. But above all, Marda had offered Angela honesty and loyalty and a true friendship that endured their separation and love for other women. Angela's letters to her continued to start with 'Darling' and end with 'your devoted Angela', and so they remained through the years of their friendship.

But into her life had come another influential woman who was to inspire her to write novels again, and for that Angela would always be grateful. Brigit Patmore was a flame-haired phenomenon. Already into her fifties when she and Angela met, Brigit had packed so much experience and heartache into her life she exuded hard-won wisdom and good humour. She was drawn particularly to poets, had married the grandson of the poet Coventry Patmore, then lived with the imagist poet Richard Aldington. It was rumoured, she had an affair with another imagist poet, Hilda Doolittle, who became Aldington's first wife. Brigit was a friend and confidante to many writers – Ezra Pound, T. S. Eliot and D. H. Lawrence among them – and she explained what she found so attractive about them. This was also the source of her gift to the writer manqué in Angela: 'People haunted by sounds or words – especially words – were irresistible to me, and I liked best to meet them at the beginning of their search, when frustration made them silent or a frenzy of hope made them voluble.'[48]

Angela first met Brigit Patmore in William Nicholson's magical studio. She had been a great beauty but hardship and sorrow had made their mark on her fine skin, and the bright magenta of her dyed hair accentuated her pallor. It was the garish hue of her hair that first attracted Angela to her side, 'and then I realised she had eyes like zircons. She lay on a sofa and seemed to me one of the most romantic women I had met.'[49] Marguerite Steen was a good friend to Brigit and pointed out that she was always described as a beauty long after her looks had fled. Her loveliness, however, was still to be found in the sweetness of her expression, and in her tranquillity and grace.

Angela would be attracted to older women throughout her life. The motherly mentor figure remained most seductive to this woman who still felt she was a girl, longing for the kind of love and appreciation that would draw her from her sisters' shadows, a girl with so much still to learn. If Tod and Ferdy had educated and encouraged Daphne, then Angela's female friends too educated her taste in literature and spurred her on. Brigit introduced Angela to the poetry of Yeats, to a range of modern poetry, and poets, she had never read before. She encouraged her to write her own poetry, to read boldly and widely, and Angela was a keen pupil. She wrote a poem for Brigit after they had been to Ferryside and had visited one of the lovely lonely Cornish coves the family knew so well. In it she acknowledged the confidence and encouragement that Brigit's generous spirit brought to hers:

> … A breeze sea-laden & salt bespewn
> Blew past our lips & bade depart
> the honeysuckle-scented air –
> Meditation held my soul
> And all I asked of Life – your hand in mine,
> And turning, found it there.

From this point, Angela began to collect an anthology of her favourite poems, writing them out longhand in two manuscript books, and hoping that one day they might be published. They all had personal reasons for inclusion. There was a great deal of Whitman, Mary Newcomb's favourite, many of Shakespeare's sonnets, Marda's contribution to her education, and lots of Yeats and Coventry

Patmore – and Richard Aldington, of course – the result of Angela's love and admiration for Brigit.

Neither Brigit nor Angela were strangers to the misery of the love-lorn and the anguish of frustrated desire. Brigit had endured it when the love of her life, Richard Aldington, left her for her daughter-in-law Netta Patmore, while Angela's heart, until Marda, had been on a rollercoaster of impossible dreams. Even Marda was ultimately unsatisfactory as a lover because she always belonged with Gwen and could never be truly hers. With Brigit's example, Angela hoped to live by one of the sonnets by Gerald Gould that she had carefully copied out in her collection of much-loved poems: 'For God's sake, if you sin, take pleasure in it/And do it for the pleasure.'

So, encouraged by Brigit's brave and vivid life, and with her hand in hers, Angela started a new novel, for the first time in almost a decade. As with everything she did, she needed great encouragement and, as with all her writing, the impulse was personal. 'I wished to help a friend of mine,' she explained as she set out to tell the story of a woman, labelled by some disapproving critics as a nymphomaniac, and her disappointed life, full of unwise sexual conquests, drug-taking, misunderstandings, criminality, snobbery, religion, homosexuality and death. Angela called it *The Perplexed Heart*, a phrase taken from one of Rupert Brooke's poems. And she dedicated it to Brigit Patmore 'with dear love'.

A Transfiguring Flame

Chapter III. Married, and so to Manderley. The house, the rooms,
determined to do well. Mrs Danvers, such opposition. 'It is a little
difficult, madam, for us. You see we were all very fond of Rebecca.'

DAPHNE DU MAURIER, *The Rebecca Notebook*

AT THE BEGINNING of 1937, Daphne returned from Egypt to England
to give birth to her second child. The nostalgic longing of the exile for
her country, for Cornwall, had been the predominant emotion while
away, and now at last she was home. She spent an exhilarating couple
of months at Ferryside. Even the imminent advent of her unplanned
baby seemed a small price to pay for the cliffs and coves and green
fields she had missed so long.

On 1 April, Daphne and Angela moved into a flat in St Anne's
Mansions near St James's Park to await the birth. The day after the
move Angela decided to take Daphne out for a drive in her racy bright
green two-seater. She would later blame herself for bringing on her
sister's labour, two weeks early. The car's suspension left much to be
desired, and the constant jolting seemed to start off labour. If Angela's
driving had anything to do with it, at least she had precipitated a
much easier birth, for it was all over in a few hours. Daphne wrote to
Tod, 'the child literally whizzed out!' It was another daughter, but
Daphne continued cheerily, 'Don't really mind half so much this time
about not having a boy. Third time lucky?!!'[1] Somehow the

disappointments in real life were much easier to bear when she had an exciting new idea for a novel. Already Daphne was mulling over her next book, 'a sinister tale about a woman who marries a widower … Psychological and rather macabre', and it was thrilling to begin inhabiting her newly created world as she worked out the characters and plot.

Tommy had really missed his wife and finally returned to England a month later to be reunited with his family and meet his new daughter. He had chosen Flavia as her name, inspired by the heroine of one of his favourite books, the impossibly romantic and swashbuckling *The Prisoner of Zenda*. She was a peaceful baby who grew into a very pretty toddler. 'With eyes like periwinkles and corkscrew curls, and terribly, terribly feminine,'[2] was Aunt Angela's verdict, while her father's first words on seeing his daughter were, 'Hmm, she's plain.'[3] In a family where good looks were mandatory, this verdict would resonate through her life, despite her evident beauty.

Daphne had been looking forward to Tommy's leave but, as she confided to Tod, reality never lived up to the dream. The summer holidays at Ferryside also disappointed. She felt pulled in too many directions by the needs of husband and small children when all she wanted was the peace and intellectual space to pursue her new idea. Daphne's compelling fictions were spun from her own observations and experiences. This time her jealousy of Tommy's previous fiancée, the exotic and enigmatic Jan Ricardo, was the spur to the novel she would call *Rebecca*, after the mysterious and bewitching first wife who in death acquired unassailable psychic power. Daphne had found a bundle of Jan's old love letters to Tommy and was haunted by the fact that her defection had left him bereft, and her place in his heart was preserved for ever by her suicide under the wheels of a train. Daphne identified with the unnamed second Mrs de Winter, tentative about her own womanliness and fearful that she was not successful enough as a wife, increasingly intimidated by the shadow of her predecessor. Rivals we can never meet grow in the imagination into something superhuman and invulnerable, and so it was with Jan Ricardo/Rebecca.

Social demands and family responsibilities were anathema to Daphne when she was working, for she inhabited fully her own created worlds and could only release herself through writing; her fictional people and plots she created held far more interest and thrill for her than her relationships in the material world. Even when she became obsessed with people in the real world it was largely as inspiration for her work. They became the 'pegs' around which her fictions were constructed, sometimes causing her emotional confusion and stress and doing damage to the person who became the focus of her imaginary recreation. Daphne explained that only by transforming the obsession into fiction did she become free.

Angela's novel was spurred on by Brigit Patmore, who managed to encourage her to believe in herself as a writer and the resultant *The Perplexed Heart* owed a great deal to Brigit's tumultuous life and personality. Women and love were once more Angela's subject matter, but unlike her first novel, her main character – a 'female Don Juan' was the description from at least one disgruntled reviewer – struggled to make sense of heterosexual love while cutting a romantic swathe through a motley collection of unsuitable men: a leading socialist politico, London playboy, married Lothario, troubled clergyman, jailbird, and an extra few young men on the side.

Angela began with good intentions, but as ever found life too distracting. Her great friend and 'twin', Angela Halliday, had stayed on in Majorca after she, Jeanne and Muriel had returned to England in May 1936. Now in the height of summer she was forced to evade the Spanish Civil War that had arrived bloodily on her doorstep. The Republicans had begun a daring bombing raid on Palma and Cabrera in an attempt to reclaim the island. Angela was on tenterhooks following the astounding news in the papers and waiting for any word from her friend. Eventually she received a letter saying that six people had died in Palma the previous day and all foreigners were being evacuated by a British battleship to Marseille. Shaw, like all the other evacuees, was completely penniless and had to rely on the British consul at Marseille to bail her out and pay her bills. She had not lost her sense of humour, however, for this six-foot-tall, mannish woman, who was not in the least interested romantically in men, added as her postscript: 'Imagine me with two thousand sailors!!!'[4]

Meanwhile, Angela du Maurier was meeting another courageous woman who did not fit the conventional feminine model, and was to become *the* most important love of her life. Every summer for the last six years she had travelled north to stay with her friend, the actress Faith Celli, at her house and garden, An Cala, on the west coast of Scotland. And every summer she had looked across to the island of Mull and longed to go there. She thought it 'a tall dark far-distant Shangri-La' that called to her highly romantic spirit. This time Faith greeted her with the magical words: 'We're going to Mull. I'm going to take you to Torosay, to meet Olive Guthrie.'[5]

They caught the ferry from Oban, passing islands, rocky islets, distant mountains and the magnificent, forbidding bulk of Duart Castle, the Maclean clan's thousand-year-old ancestral seat where their seaborne power was based. Then suddenly she glimpsed the Castle of Torosay sitting at the centre of its tree-fringed bay. Built in the mid-nineteenth century in grand Scottish baronial style, it was a large, turreted country house with twelve acres of formal gardens extending to the shoreline of Duart Bay, where dolphins and otters could be glimpsed at play. Olive welcomed them to her magical castle with coffee, 'wearing a very old tweed coat, an equally old (man's) tweed hat (from which poked honey-coloured curls), her cigarette (which she was never without) in a holder, and she spoke in a voice that fascinated me from that first moment of meeting'.[6]

Angela and Faith only stayed for three days but they were days extended by so much talk, walks with breathtaking views (the best being from the estate's dogs' graveyard), the fascination of the castle with its wonderful pictures, Fabergé treasures, and Olive's Pekinese Impy, and a parrot. The parrot had started off below stairs with the faithful old butler; when it graduated to living upstairs, every time it heard a bell ring for the servants it muttered in the butler's broad Scottish brogue, 'Let the old bitch wait!' which did not seem to disconcert Olive at all, and caused her family and guests much mirth.

Olive Guthrie was thirty-two years older than Angela, older even than Angela's mother, but hardly a motherly presence and certainly the complete opposite of Muriel. She was the proudly Irish daughter of the pre-Raphaelite painter Sir John Leslie and aunt to the flamboyant diplomat and writer Sir Shane Leslie. Sister-in-law too to one of the glamorous American Jerome sisters, Olive was thereby an aunt to Winston Churchill, who visited her at Torosay. She was widowed young and had to gather her considerable forces of energy and character to take on the management for a while of her husband's merchant bank, Chalmers, Guthrie & Co, with offices in Dundee and the City of London. She was involved in politics and the arts and was a director of the Chelsea Book Club, the first bookshop to stock Joyce's *Ulysses*, but a club also that provided lectures and exhibitions in its premises at 65 Cheyne Walk. Olive was just as at home with the sporting pursuits of a great Scottish estate and was a superb shot, better than most men. Cosmopolitan, well-connected, politically savvy, she had a wonderful capacity for storytelling and anecdote (she recalled playing on the floor with Angela's father when they were children – George du Maurier and Sir John Leslie being fellow artists and friends). This fascinating woman of the world would provide the next stage in Angela's education in politics, literature and love.

Angela returned south at the end of summer, bowled over by Olive's personality and charm and the glamour of Torosay. The three days spent on Mull were a dreamlike interlude that she thought was unlikely to come again. London held its attractions too. Angela Halliday was back from her brush with a brutish civil war in Majorca and Angela's own new friendships with Marguerite Steen and William Nicholson, Marda and Gwen picked up again now that the holidays were over. Angela also felt excitement at the feast of concerts that awaited her that autumn. She loved Sir Thomas Beecham and his series of Sunday concerts at Covent Garden, and was there when the immaculate Malcolm Sargent conducted one of his first performances after recovering from a near-fatal attack of tuberculosis. She saw Richard Strauss conduct the Dresden State Opera and Rachmaninoff play the piano. All her life, Angela would remember Barbirolli conducting the maestro Horowitz playing Beethoven's Emperor Concerto, a piece of emotional bravura entirely to her taste, and was lucky enough to hear Myra Hess's celebrated interpretation of

Brahms's second piano concerto. In these highly charged performances, Angela never forgot her first love had been music and her first longing had been to be an opera singer.

Her Primrose Hill friends introduced Angela to another woman who would broaden her musical tastes and offer her love. Until she met Bo Foster, Angela had thought that ballet came a poor second to opera as a musical and emotional experience. But now, with Bo as an experienced guide, she became a devotee of the various Russian companies who had formed after the break-up of Ballet Russe on the death of Diaghilev. Together they saw most of the great Russian dancers of the time. Particularly impressive was Tamara Toumanova, the choreographer Massine's favourite ballerina, nicknamed 'the black pearl of Russian Ballet', a reference to her dark beauty and extraordinary dramatic performances that marked her out in an already scintillating company. Angela saw so many extraordinary performances but *Les Sylphides*, the shimmering nymphs in diaphanous white as weightless as thistledown, was outstanding, 'danced by a corps de ballet in which every dancer was worthy to be a prima ballerina'.[7] Angela was hooked.

But Angela, it seemed, was also attracted to Bo Foster. She was an interesting cultured woman, a devout Catholic and a Tory activist. She was nearly ten years older than Angela and they met after Bo's long, turbulent love affair with the poet Valentine Ackland had just come to an end. Valentine's description of Bo mirrored a photograph in Angela's photo album of Bo gazing into the distance, looking bulky in a tweed suit and tie, with her hair in an unforgiving crop: 'her rather heavy face, with its noble seventeenth-century nose and the beautiful arch of forehead (or is it brow, just above the eyeball?) looked most grave, most moved as she stared out of the window'. They were listening to Hahn's song, '*L'heure exquise*', that had supposedly made Verlaine weep.

Valentine had met Bo Foster when she was a troubled teenager of seventeen and still called Molly McCrory. She was two years younger than Angela but had packed a great deal of frantic living into her life so far. Valentine's relationship with Bo lasted for six years, through her impetuous and unconsummated marriage to a homosexual youth, and various other febrile affairs with women, and a few men. It finally ended when Molly met and fell in love with her life partner, the erudite poet and writer, Sylvia Townsend Warner, in 1930.

When Molly changed her name to Valentine she put on trousers to mark her new identity. She was nearly six foot tall, as thin as a couturier's model and strikingly androgynous. At this time for a woman to wear men's clothes and crop her hair as short as a boy's was a bold advertisement of her independence from men and from male desire, and the constraint put on women by the expectations of others. Valentine, like many young people before and after her, was told by her father that loving someone of your own sex was 'the filthiest, the most unforgiveable thing', and that her 'unnaturalness' would make her go mad and blind. 'I believed this,' she wrote in a memoir, 'in a kind of cold reasonableness, I tried to teach myself to type and play the piano with my eyes shut … But the madness I could not think how to prepare for …'[8]

Just two years before Angela met Bo, a small book of poems celebrating erotic love between women had been published by Valentine and Sylvia as joint authors, causing a stir among the alternative intellectual set. It was called *Whether a Dove or Seagull* and, like Wordsworth and Coleridge's *The Lyrical Ballads*, refused to attribute the poems to either one of the poets so that readers came to them without preconceptions. It was also a generous act from Sylvia who wanted to encourage a wider publication and readership of Valentine's work and used her name to do so. It certainly encouraged Angela.

Bo Foster, or 'BF' as Angela identified her in her poetry book, asked Angela to write a sonnet dedicated to her. Angela, in her less flamboyant way, was as brave as Valentine Ackland, if not as skilled as a poet. She was, however, just as unafraid of her subject matter:

> …
> It ought to be terribly easy
> To sing to the woman you love
> in villanelles, sonnets, & such like
> Without asking help from above!

When you've given me all that I crave for? And have lain in my
   arms till the dawn
And I've kissed you from midnight till daybreak? Perhaps I
   shall not be so torn As to how to compose for you sonnets?
   Comparing your eyes to the stars,
Your breasts to two exquisite hill-tops
You Venus in fact, & I Mars!

In brackets she added an alternative last stanza:

Shall I tear you asunder with worship?
Will you faint 'neath my burning caress?
If I ask you to yield to my passion
Will you ever surrender, – say 'yes'?

This interesting, independent, sexually free group of people with
whom Angela was now mixing were exactly the friends that Noël
Welch alluded to when she wrote of the sisters in middle age: 'I have
seen photographs, curled at the edges, blurred and hastily snatched
away, showing a wilder Angela than the one I know, though sometimes in a sudden flash of humour, a ribald remark, one gets glimpses
of a bohemian past that alarmed her father.'[9]

Angela and Daphne were in close communication, the intrusive
suspicions and exaggerated protectiveness of their parents having
enhanced their closeness as confidantes, something that lasted
throughout their lives despite Daphne's necessary discretion about
the trials of her own marriage. It was clear that Daphne knew about
Angela's explorations of love with women, just as Angela had
known about Cousin Geoffrey, Ferdy, Molly Kerr and Carol Reed.
By midsummer of 1937, however, Daphne was no longer
experimenting with love but had returned to Tommy and
Alexandria, having left Tessa and four-month-old baby Flavia in
England with Margaret under their aunt Grace Browning's watchful
eye. Instead, in stifling temperatures, she was struggling to bring to
paper the ideas that teemed in her head. Her only escape from the
heat and frustration was to imagine herself back in her beloved

Cornwall, and Menabilly and its cool dark woods became an almost transcendent object of desire. 'What I'd give to be at Fowey!'[10] she wrote despairingly to Tod. This longing for the powerfully envisioned world in her memory and imagination became the driving force of the book.

Her passion for the dreamlike Menabilly, decaying in its enchanted, encroaching woods, combined in her imagination with her long fascination with the even grander Milton, where she had stayed as a child, to create the most haunting and desirable character in *Rebecca*, Manderley itself. Daphne's own unease in the social roles expected of the wife of the commandant, her inability to run her household efficiently, even though she had servants to do every bidding, all fed into the character of the diffident outsider, the second Mrs de Winter. Her lack of a name just underlined her fugitive sense of self. As Daphne struggled to recover her old fluency and speed, she feared too for her own identity, for without being able to write she was nothing.

After nearly five months away from England and their children, Daphne and Tommy returned home, Daphne with only about a quarter of *Rebecca* in her luggage. She was impatient to get to Cornwall and desperate to work, but she feared the presence of two small children, from whom after so long she had been emotionally disengaged, would interfere with that. She made the surprising decision to continue the estrangement from her daughters by leaving them with Nanny for Christmas. She and Tommy then headed alone to Ferryside to join the rest of the du Maurier family. Daphne feared it appeared ruthless and unkind, particularly with Tessa, aged four and old enough to know what was going on and express any feelings of missing her mother (although she recalled later that she enjoyed herself anyway). Daphne was full of justifications. It would be better for the girls, she said. 'I do so *dread* [Tessa] becoming too precocious and for the next few years want her to lead as quiet and nurseryfied an existence as possible,' she explained to her mother. The real reason, however, eventually emerged, 'I should get no work done.'[11]

Her writing proceeded slowly over Christmas. The children were reunited with their mother in January and by the spring, Daphne had settled herself, the children and servants into a charming new Army house, Greyfriars, near Fleet in Hampshire, close to Tommy's work at Pirbright Camp. She was suddenly writing again with real concentration and pace and was enjoying herself tremendously. Her imaginary world had come alive. By April, *Rebecca* was finished and, although she had eventually found writing it a pleasure, she felt it was too grim to be a bestseller and that the psychological scaffolding might not be appreciated.

Her publisher Victor Gollancz knew better. Here was an exceptional, atmospheric novel full of drama and suspense. His editor thought it an exquisite love story. Daphne always baulked at being considered a writer of romances. She was far more concerned with power and identity than love, and instead thought this new novel full of hatred and fear. *Rebecca*'s mutability, its capacity to draw very different responses from its readers, ensured it would be solid gold for Gollancz's beautiful young author, and a terrific boost for his own young publishing company.

More than any critical reaction, Daphne cared most about how much the book would earn. Though she had the responsibility of being the family's main breadwinner, she liked the way this altered the balance of power in her marriage. Daphne was now free to choose to spend her money how she liked, and eventually to decide where and how they lived. Earning so much more money than her husband bought her the freedom to write, and to decline most of the usual duties of an Army wife and mother. It was central to her sense of herself as a creative, hardworking, boyish spirit who could be bold and adventurous in both her real and imaginary worlds, where she answered to no one. Money freed her from dependency and service, the condition of most women's lives in her and previous generations, and one that filled her with horror, fuelling some of her most searing fiction.

Rebecca was published in August 1938 to wide, if at times patronising, acclaim. The predominantly male reviewers stressed the book's popular appeal and some its boldness and strangeness. All agreed that its author had written an unusual bestseller and Daphne was delighted – with the numbers of copies sold and monies earned more than with the opinions of strangers. Within a month of publication, Victor

Gollancz could answer her anxious question by telling her she had made £3,000, including her original advance.

The book's American publication by Doubleday in the autumn brought another cascade of reviews, again some rather carping, suggesting *Rebecca* was a poor relation of *Jane Eyre*'s, or invoking the spirit of the Brontës, not always to Daphne's credit. All of this fired the excitement, and the novel soared away once more to great success. The most crucial accelerator of Daphne's fame and fortune, however, came when her nascent career as a writer was hooked up to the rocket of Alfred Hitchcock's genius. Her extraordinary imagination, combined with his complex understanding of fear and cinematic brilliance, for a while propelled them both on a blazing trajectory to world recognition and acclaim.

The producer David O. Selznick had bought the rights to *Rebecca* and hired Hitchcock to direct the film. It was due to be Hitchcock's first Hollywood movie, after plans to film a story of the sinking of the *Titanic* were scrapped. Before he left for Hollywood, however, Hitchcock was offered the chance to direct Daphne's earlier novel, *Jamaica Inn*. This was a nightmare to direct, the whole process riven with problems, the biggest of which was its temperamental star, Charles Laughton. When *Jamaica Inn* was eventually released, the critics complained of its melodramatic clunkiness, but the audiences loved it and turned it into box office gold.

Hitchcock began his career in Hollywood buoyed by this success. His second great stroke of good luck (and Daphne's too) was that Selznick was too absorbed in finishing *Gone With the Wind* to interfere or oversee his new protégé's work on *Rebecca*. They had already cast two fine actors in the main parts, Laurence Olivier for Max de Winter and Joan Fontaine as his tormented wife. Hitchcock made the film as close to Daphne's story as he could, except the American censors would not allow Max to get away with intentionally killing Rebecca and so her death had to be accidental. Even so, he made the film entirely his own. The result was sensational and the film won an Oscar for best picture and another for best cinematography. Hitchcock's global reputation was made and Daphne could look forward to lifelong financial security.

Her anxiety that she might not be able to shoulder the household expenditure was stilled; she and her family could continue to live as she had as a child, with the necessities of space and live-in staff that left her free to pursue the only thing that mattered, the creative life of her imagination. She may have taken on her father's mantle as the high-earning breadwinner, the moral paterfamilias, but she was nothing like as extravagant and was determined not to squander the cornucopia that suddenly seemed to shower into her lap.

But just as her career took off, unbeknownst to Daphne, the subterranean unhappiness of her two daughters began bubbling to the surface at home. Neither girl had received any sense of her importance in her parents' lives, and neither had received enough love and attention from their mother, the one person they longed to affect. They knew, with the instinct of small children, that they made little impression on her emotional radar, although she was concerned and conscientious about their physical welfare. Where there is not enough love to go round, children invest great significance in any signs of affection or favouritism.

Tessa, as the eldest, had lived longer in this atmosphere of unrequited longing and her baby sister can only have been a threat to the already inadequate portion of love that was hers. According to Flavia, the flashpoint that marked the unhappy breakdown between Tessa and herself came when she inadvertently broke her elder sister's precious and much-loved doll, a present from her glamorous godmother, Atalanta Arlen. The relationship between them deteriorated from there, with Tessa unhappy and resentful and Flavia uncomprehending of the reason for this sibling friction. Tessa's irritation with her younger sister evaporated once she had escaped into her own life, with friends and love to sustain her. In a sensitive memoir, written many years later, Flavia recognised the tragedy when a precious sisterly relationship was spoiled: 'We are now close and the best of friends, but I often think both our lives would have been quite different if we had got on well as children.'[12]

Daphne's phenomenal success with *Rebecca* not only altered the balance of power in her marriage, it also utterly dominated her sisters' forays into their own careers. All three sisters had grown up aware that the world knew them as the daughters of Gerald du Maurier, some even thought of them as the grandchildren of the more notable George. Their surname was distinctive and singular to their family, but with their father dead, his claim on the name began to fade in the public's memory and for a while they were seen as discrete individuals in their own rights.

Once Daphne's name was united with the most successful and highly rated film of 1940, her meteoric fame meant that from this time Angela and Jeanne would be known as sisters of Daphne. They were much less famous, much less successful – and less strikingly attractive too. Gallingly perhaps, Daphne only endured the fame as a spur to her earning capacity. She valued power and autonomy and shrank from publicity, from any kind of public show as the famous author. Daphne was even cavalier about her own good looks, recognising them as a means of gaining what she needed in life; to feel in control, to bolster her fragile self-esteem and to win her freedom to write. Even her evident beauty, however, was not enough to make her feel confident in unfamiliar social situations.

The comparisons between herself and Daphne were more invidious for Angela. She was the eldest and naturally felt some advantages should have come her way. Coming off worst in all the comparisons was bad enough, but most difficult of all was the fact that she aspired to be a writer too. She recognised this last barrier in a memoir written in late middle age:

> A lot of people say I have suffered because of Daphne's fame and success ... I am still – and know I always shall be – asked 'Are you the writer?', and I still – and always shall I suppose – reply 'I'm the Sister' ...[13]

It was to her credit that she continued to write in the increasing obscurity of Daphne's shadow. Initially critics thought she was published because she was Daphne's sister. They then compared her unfavourably to her younger sister, and finally ceased paying much attention at all to her work, even though by the end of her life she had published eight novels, a collection of short stories, one spiritual travelogue and two books of autobiography.

Angela's rackety social life with the bohemian set in London was suddenly interrupted in the late summer of 1937 by an invitation out of the blue. Olive Guthrie had written, asking her to come to stay at Torosay. She needed help with her rhododendrons, she said. Angela was 'astounded' that Olive had remembered her. There had been those three blissful days the previous year and her one letter of thanks and no other communication since.

She arrived on Mull during a brilliant autumn and was initiated into the life of a great Scottish estate: stalking deer on the hillside, an activity that had her winded before she had managed half a mile, duck shooting at dusk, collecting mussels from the rocks for the evening *moules marinières*, and daily sawing of rhododendron branches where the invasive bushes suffocated the natural undergrowth.

Angela was also introduced to the cries of the wilderness, the call of the heron and 'the low thrilling sound of the stags' roar in the forest, to me the most exciting noise on earth'.[14] Despite the fact that Olive's daughter, 'Bobs' de Klee, much the same age as Angela, was staying along with other sporting friends, some sympathetic understanding between Olive and Angela sprang up that autumn. 'Daily one became more fascinated by Olive's wit, and the general charm and the enveloping tendrils of Mull closed slowly around me.'[15]

They decided to meet again in February when Angela would once again go to Torosay. This time the lovely landscape of Mull was shrouded in snow and the sunny days were crystal bright, the air astringently cold. The castle was freezing and Olive and Angela spent the days together in the library trying to keep warm by a great fire, enjoying their meals there, playing bezique and reading. It was perhaps at this time that Olive invited Angela to share her bed, a routine that happened on each subsequent visit, even when other visitors were there. When Olive's daughters remonstrated Olive, unperturbed, pointed out that the castle was so cold and damp it made sense to sleep together. This was undoubtedly true, but Olive did not offer to sleep with her other visitors who were left to shiver in their beds alone. It was accepted in the family, but not approved of at the time, that Olive and Angela's relationship was 'physically intimate'.[16]

The honesty and frankness of these two women about their unorthodox relationship showed a courage and freedom from the judgemental social mores of the times. It was certainly easier for Olive to live as she pleased; she was much older and more worldly than Angela. Having been happily married, had children and been widowed, she was allowed greater sexual freedoms than those extended to an unmarried young woman. Most telling, however, was the fact that Olive was a woman of high social status, chatelaine of Torosay Castle and its estates, with a backbone already stiffened by being born to the proudly independent-minded Irish Leslies. Angela had none of these advantages. She was brought up to mind very much what others thought of her by a conventional mother and an overbearing and influential father. She was also vulnerable as a single woman without an independent career, and so reliant on her family's allowance to live. Her refusal to hide her feelings for Olive, or to prevaricate in the face of Guthrie family disapproval, said a great deal for how much her association with her open-minded and welcoming London friends had helped her overcome her shame and live more openly as she pleased.

Angela's first poem to Olive Guthrie was shy and rather clumsily expressive of her gratitude for the love of a remarkable woman who suddenly was of great importance in her life:

> ...
> And all I ask is this
> your daily kiss.
> To hear you call me friend
> would be the end
> Of troubles great & small.
> For you are all
> That's beautiful & fair,
> A being rare
> That fills my heart with love ... Some benediction new
> Is born through you.

It was the beginning of 1938 and the mood in Europe was ominous, though at home things seemed less grim. Daphne's husband Tommy, along with many of the military men and politicians in the know, was full of foreboding of what he considered an inevitable war. But the country at large, with its island mentality, appeared more sanguine and hopeful. After all, it had survived the crisis of the abdication of Edward VIII and, with the coronation of George VI the previous summer, had welcomed a new royal family with two young daughters full of youth and promise. Not even a generation had passed since the end of the last war and for men like Tommy, young enough to fight in both world wars, the prospect of another global conflict was daunting.

As war loomed closer, Angela embarked on what she considered to be the great love affair of her life. She tried to capture something of Olive's unique attraction, already in her sixties when Angela fell in love with her:

> She was the most remarkable woman I ever knew … She had the ability and integrity of a man, the fascination of a woman, the enthusiasm of a child and the imagination of a fairy … she had led the most surprising and wonderful life, had known people in every walk of life – kings, statesmen, poets, bandits, singers, writers – had travelled the globe from one end to the other in strange and unconventional ways, had herself worked in the City doing a man's job as Chairman of a great bank … she had a fund of stories and anecdotes unparalleled, which only an Irishwoman such as she was could have told with just the right amount of wit, or pathos, or credulity.[17]

Angela considered that Olive's life had been so varied and rich it needed a whole book to do it justice; instead she used it as the inspiration for her third novel. In 1938 she was to spend more than four months in Olive's company and every year until 1941 spent anything between three and nine months of the year at Torosay.

Angela and Olive left the island of Mull on 3 March and parted at Dover, Angela bound for a hospital in Germany, recommended to her by a friend as the best place to go to have her periodic abdominal pains diagnosed and treated. Olive was heading for Athens and due to meet Angela a month later, after she had spent some weeks with her mother and Jeanne, holidaying in Italy. With Angela pursuing love in London and the Isle of Mull, and Daphne in Hampshire with her family, Jeanne had become their mother's main companion. Widowed mothers expected to be looked after by their unmarried daughters and, apart from Jeanne being her youngest and favourite, it seemed natural to lean on her. Jeanne, however, still managed to conduct her own painting life and friendships independent of Muriel, and to break away from her allotted duties, to the irritation at times of her older sisters.

At their parting, Angela wrote a poem for Olive that she copied into a specially commissioned leather-bound book, their two sets of initials embossed in gold at either corner of the front cover. Entitled 'DOVER March 1938' it read:

How can I brave the long forsaken hours
That beckon me with weary leaden hands
Jeering with ghoulish joy that other lands
Have taken to their midst my well-belov'd …
How may I count the days that one by one
Appear unsmiling, greeting me at dawn
With laggard footsteps, pitiless forlorn
Sunless with your absence & my tears …
How shall I bear the loneliness of sleep
When nightly by my side your body lay
Slaked with my love yet bidding me to stay
To crown you with the passion of my heart …
Your little whispered words … your woman's smile
The mistress in you, – & eternal child,
Which has so utterly & well beguiled
Your lover's heart for ever & a day!
Cannot a ghost or shadow – you return
To lay a head upon my outstretched arm
And comfort me & tell me that no harm?
Can come upon you while we are apart?

Angela and Olive were to meet up again in May and spend the month travelling to some of Europe's most romantic places, Venice, Lake Garda and eventually Paris, in what would become a kind of honeymoon tour. But first Angela had to endure the efficient but, she felt, unkind treatment of the medical staff in a German clinic as they passed tubes into her stomach, gave her every kind of internal and invasive examination ('revolting treatment they forced on me') and x-rayed her from all angles, but still did not ascertain the source of her pain. While she was there the Anschluss, Hitler's annexation of Austria, occurred and the horror of her experience at the hands of the medical staff felt amplified by the Führer's harsh rhetoric, crackling from every hospital radio. She escaped 'Hitler's minions' without any kind of diagnosis and met up with Mary Fox, one of the theatrical Fox family and a great friend of Jeanne's. They travelled together to join Jeanne and Muriel at Portofino, a beautiful and then still unspoiled fishing village on the Italian Riviera.

Mary Fox and her family grew closer to the du Mauriers during the war when they lived nearby. Her mother was the actress Hilda Hanbury and her brother became the famous theatrical agent Robin Fox, whose children, actors Edward, James and Robert Fox and grandchildren Emilia and Laurence, continued the tradition. Mary was a 'twin' with Daphne, sharing her birthday, just as Shaw shared Angela's, and was to be an important friend to the du Maurier sisters, but particularly to Jeanne with whom she shared for a while a market garden during the coming war. The four women lived in a villa near Portofino's Castello Brown, made famous by Elizabeth von Arnim, who wrote her bestseller, *The Enchanted April*, while staying within its romantic walls.

Restored to health, Angela left Portofino and set off for Venice where she met up with Olive on her return journey from Athens. The first time Angela had seen Venice was after Gerald's death, when Micky Jacob had sent her off with a couple of her gay friends. Angela then was lonely and bereft. This time she had been through a sea change: she was meeting the woman she loved. Arriving late at night, she was met by Olive in a gondola, 'and quietly, in the light of a full moon, we slowly drifted down the side canals to the hotel'.[18] They ate in different hotels or cafés every day, had drinks at Florian's, the famous mirrored bar on the Piazza San Marco, and dinners at Fenice, the exquisitely embellished opera house. Olive and Angela travelled always by gondola, silent through dark and mysterious canals, a thrilling backdrop to their romance. Remembering this time in Venice, Angela wrote discreetly: 'What a week we had.'[19]

San Vigilio on Lake Garda followed and then Paris in May, with the chestnut trees and lilac flowering in the streets, scenting the air. There was the added luxury of an embassy car put at Olive's disposal and the women purred from delicious meals to exquisite shops and then off to the theatre. Little did they know what horrors and indignities were about to befall France and Paris, its precious jewelled heart. They were enjoying the glories of Europe before it re-entered the dark ages, and they rounded off the experience with a few days in London. She and Olive spent one of the best evenings Angela could ever remember at Covent Garden where Richard Strauss's savage opera *Electra* held her spellbound, as Sir Thomas Beecham once again lorded over the orchestra pit.

For the next three and a half years Angela could hardly bear to be away from Olive Guthrie and Torosay. Shortly after returning with her to England, she once more headed back to Mull, and signed herself in to the visitors' book on 11 June as 'Tommy'.

This adoption of a masculine nickname was obviously very significant but it was difficult to know for certain what exactly she meant by it. It was quite common at the time for lesbian women to adopt male soubriquets. When Angela was a young woman and had first met Naomi Jacob, everyone accepted that Naomi preferred to be known as Micky. Radclyffe Hall was an androgynous response to her overtly feminine given name, Marguerite; and Valentine Ackland had chosen her similarly androgynous first name when she left 'Molly' behind, along with her abandoned petticoats. Marda and Bo, Angela's previous inamoratas, were also adaptations of more obviously feminine first names. Perhaps the fact that Angela adopted this masculine nickname when she was staying at Torosay marked her public acknowledgement of her love for Olive, for every visitor and member of Olive's family was free to see it clearly written there.

More surprising was the actual name that Angela had chosen for herself. Tommy was Daphne's husband's name, one by which he was universally known in private. Why choose this rather than Freddy, or Billy or Will? Given she was a du Maurier, could it have been a joke? But if so, it would have been a joke only she and possibly Daphne would have appreciated. Was she so identified with Daphne that she desired to be part of her intimate life by sharing a name with her husband? Was it a subliminal way of getting closer to the sister who already outshone her in most things? Of course, Angela had seen 'Tommy' Browning first as he motored his boat in the harbour at Fowey, and, although she had found him interesting, once again it was her little sister who had won the prize of his attention, love and eventual hand in marriage. Was calling herself Tommy somehow a way of imagining what might have been if Daphne had not been on the scene? Angela would certainly have felt that, had she married, she would have been a more committed and supportive wife and mother than her sister could ever be.

Angela spent most of the summer at Torosay working on her novel. Brigit Patmore had provided the spark and Olive now nurtured the creative flame with love, admiration and care, amid the extraordinary beauty of the gardens and landscape that surrounded the castle. Finally, with her completed manuscript in her suitcase, Angela returned to London. There she spent many hours at the home of Michael Joseph, who had now started his own publishing house and, after a full day's work at the office, gave up his evenings to help his young protégée by closely editing her book. 'I owe much of its success to him and his brutal blue pencilling,' Angela recalled, paying tribute to his dedication: 'together we took line by line, scratching this, deleting that, until I was so despondent and miserable that I asked him why he bothered to publish the damn thing at all. He said he believed I would one day write a good book …'[20]

Angela dedicated *The Perplexed Heart* to Brigit, for it was she whose encouragement and colourful life had inspired her to begin again in her quest to become a recognised author. Published as her first book in February 1939, she inevitably attracted attention because of her name, but the timing could not have been more unhelpful. Daphne's phenomenal success with *Rebecca*, burst upon the world just the previous year, was still very much in everyone's mind. It was already public knowledge that Alfred Hitchcock would be filming it and titillating debate ensued as to which actor would play Maxim de Winter and who, of a range of Hollywood beauties, would win the battle to portray his wife.

Angela's rather leaden offering, with an unsympathetic heroine driven by her passions to no great effect, meant any comparisons between the two du Maurier sisters could only be to her detriment. This was already a well-established pattern in their lives and by now Angela expected it. She was indignant at the idea, mooted by friends, that she should write under a *nom de plume*. 'Why should I? I am proud of being a du Maurier, and having never parted with my name for love of a man I am not likely to let it go for a possible success story.'[21]

The best review in England was perhaps the effusive offering of Philip Page, drama critic of the *Daily Mail*, who declared theatrically, 'the du Maurier family gives us another brilliant writer', and suggested the book 'was illuminated by something very near genius'. In America, where reviewers were less sycophantic, Angela was published by Daphne's publisher Doubleday, and again this intensified the cruel comparisons. Virginia Kirkus had started an influential magazine that specialised in advance reviews of most of the trade books published in the United States, taken notice of by the whole literary world, the libraries, booksellers and film agents. The verdict on *The Perplexed Heart* was frank and damning: 'second rate, and if Angela du Maurier was not the sister of Daphne, the book would not get to first base'.[22] The *Saturday Review* gave Angela's book more space, but the ghost of her sister's *Rebecca* haunted all the reviewers' minds and this one reached a similarly downbeat verdict:

> If Rebecca herself, and an adoring cousin, had alternated in telling Rebecca's story, it might have read like this first novel of Daphne du Maurier's elder sister. But ... Verona herself is not enough of a person to make her life worth writing. If Miss du Maurier had been able to

analyse her thoughts and emotions more deeply, Verona might have stood for the restlessness of the modern woman and the strange paths along which it sometimes leads her ...[23]

Angela had realised early in life that her surname was a double-edged sword. It brought notice and opportunities where otherwise there may have been only struggle and obscurity. Although she would nearly always be unfavourably compared with her younger sister, for an extrovert and born performer like herself, some attention, even adverse, would always be better than being ignored. Her name also brought old friends of her father's willing to trumpet the glories of his offspring. Dennis Wheatley tootled, 'I say, without hesitation, that its publication will establish Miss du Maurier as an important novel-ist immediately ... the book [is] so outstanding ... Angela du Maurier is a consummate artist ...'[24] Despite radically divided opinions on *The Perplexed Heart*, publication brought her name to an interna-tional public and she was excited by being noticed at last for some-thing she had done, rather than merely her relationship to a more famous du Maurier, 'for suddenly I was in the news ... and let's face it – enjoying the fact'.[25]

Angela had returned again to Olive and Torosay in the autumn of 1938, travelling up on the train in the company for the first time of her Pekinese Wendy. Her mother and Jeanne were due for two weeks in October, their first and only visit, while Angela herself would stay on until the middle of November. Her heart was light, she was head-ing north to her beloved's castle on a magical island, she had finished her novel at last, and, it seemed, Neville Chamberlain had triumphed in Munich and brought home 'peace for our time'. Despite the catas-trophe that followed and his subsequent vilification, Angela remained a champion of Chamberlain's all her life. One of his daughters told her some years later that on that fateful trip to Munich, the Prime Minister had packed a copy of *Rebecca* in his luggage, to take his mind off the momentous business he had to conduct. All her life Angela would be known for her loyalty to people and ideas.

1939 was marked by her with a hectic round of socialising. In February, Angela was taken by Olive for a month's visit to Castle

Leslie at Glaslough in County Monahan in Ireland, the Leslie family's stately and rather forbidding Victorian pile. Here dinners, balls, and shooting parties, where Olive showed off her prowess with shotgun and rifle, rotated with card and musical evenings and visits to the other grand houses of the neighbourhood. The hospitality of the Leslies, and the Irish generally, was legendary. Olive had promised to take Angela to visit Yeats, but that was the one treat denied her for the great man of Irish letters had died just a couple of weeks before.

She returned to London in March just in time to watch, from Carlton House Terrace, the spectacular state visit of President Lebrun of France with Herr Ribbentrop in attendance. The whirl continued as Angela dashed to Mull and Olive at Torosay and spent a month there before returning to London at the end of May for the Season. Looking back, she was surprised how unreal the looming cataclysm felt as the privileged classes reeled from Covent Garden to Wimbledon, Henley, Ascot, cricket at Lord's, and the Richmond Horse Trials. All the established social events of the summer continued as if the approaching hurricane was nothing but a refreshing continental breeze that barely ruffled their programme notes.

Even Olive, so worldly wise and politically sophisticated, seemed oblivious. Or perhaps the febrile activity of that summer was just a desperate desire to live life to the hilt before darkness descended. Olive travelled down to Bodinnick to stay with Angela and her family and then in July, as Jeanne accompanied Muriel to the annual Buckingham Palace Garden Party, Angela and Olive set off for a tour around Cornwall and the West Country. They were even then, as Angela recalled, unaware 'that within two months the great fear would be a Fait Accompli'.[26]

Daphne's vivid internal life had always detached her from the world, unlike her sisters who were more sociable and interested in events. As a fundamentally solitary individualist, she had never seen the need for religion. Neither had she been interested in politics. However, she was living with Tommy who, as Commanding Officer, was putting his elite unit of Grenadier Guards through a regime of strict discipline and training to prepare them for war. He was full of gloom about the unpreparedness of the British Army generally and explosive frustration at the complacency of so many of the top brass to the imminent conflagration. Daphne could not continue to live in her imagination, protected from the anxieties and privations of everyday life, while her husband, at the centre of the action, was full of fearful concern.

Awoken from her reverie, Daphne attempted to find some kind of philosophical framework to help her better understand herself and her place in the world. Although not formally educated, she had an intellectual cast of mind, was fascinated by ideas and, in seeking answers to the eternal metaphysical questions, picked eclectically from the Greek myths, bits of current psychoanalytical thinking, and even from the Bible. In this questing state, old family friends seemed to offer some solution. The tennis star Bunny Austin, and his actress wife Phyllis Konstam, were long-time friends of the du Maurier family and part of the Sunday lunch crowd at Cannon Hall. Considered by the press to be a celebrity couple, in 1938 Bunny was a finalist in the Gentleman's Singles at Wimbledon (although soundly beaten by the tall American Don Budge) and Phyllis was an established actress who had acted in four of Hitchcock's films. The spiritual solace they offered came wrapped in the controversial banner of 'the Oxford Group', the brainchild of a Swiss American Frank Buchman who, as war approached, renamed his movement, 'Moral Re-Armament'.

For a while, Daphne was inspired by its followers' message of personal responsibility, self-examination, confession and restitution (a message that became translated into the personal commitment that characterised Alcoholics Anonymous). There was reason to think that Angela, Jeanne and Muriel, all more conventionally religious than Daphne, might have been affected by their old friends' zeal too. It was a branch of Protestantism that concerned itself with the individual, and his or her own perfectability and journey to redemption, rather than wider social justice and society at large. Understandably, it appealed to the educated and better off. Like all 'cultish' movements, it gave its adherents the comfortable sense of their own superiority as the enlightened in a benighted world.

Daphne came to feel embarrassed about her association with the Oxford Group, but for a while did her best to try and live less selfishly, with greater self-awareness, and offered to put her skills to the cause as part of her war effort. She was asked to write up stories of ordinary people whose lives had been enriched by following the Moral Re-Armament precepts of God-centred self-awareness. Furnished with the facts of these people's lives by an MRA insider, Garth Lean, Daphne's moral stories, with titles like: 'The Admiralty Regrets'; 'George and Jimmy'; 'Over the Ration Books'; 'A Miner's Tale'; 'Spitfire Megan', and 'A Nation's Strength', were meant to stiffen the resolve of the British as they entered yet another world war. The tales were placed by Garth Lean in various local newspapers and were eventually collected into a booklet entitled *Come Wind, Come Weather*. Published in the summer of 1940, it sold almost three quarters of a million copies during the fearful early years of the war.

Doubleday, Daphne's publishers in America, decided to publish it too, where it was read as gentle propaganda, pointing out how the plucky little islanders would manage to repel the ravening wolves of Nazism through sheer goodness and bulldog grit. The subject matter and style, however, never sat very easily with Daphne's interests or skills, and within a few years she was gently extricating herself from the MRA movement. Some seven years later she explained why:

> One just is'nt selfless, one just cant give up life and all its possibilities for the Brave New World of Bunny Austin and his earnest friends. I don't want to fight for Christianity, or save the souls of people, or even go round in the train of Princess Elizabeth being a good wife, which I ought to do. I want to dance alone in my monastery, and every three years or so write a book, just as one would give birth to a baby![27]

The success of *Rebecca* had made her lazy, Daphne said, as her brain was not yet fizzing with another idea for a book. If *Rebecca* was her biggest baby so far, then this was the post-partum of recovery and reward. She had embarked on turning her bestseller into a play and by the summer of 1939 her script was completed. Daphne had found it hard going and did not hold out much hope of it being produced. Domestic concerns also reared their demanding heads. Margaret the nanny was near collapse with ill-health and exhaustion and Daphne had to look after her daughters without help, until she managed to employ a temporary nursemaid to release her from the drudgery of two lively and needy young girls.

Tessa was six, intelligent and perceptive, and Flavia was a sensitive pretty toddler of two. Both continued to be starved of their mother's attention and sought reassurance with a clinginess Daphne found trying. She also had to organise moving house, as Tommy's career in the run up to war had gone from strength to strength. He was now in charge of the Small Arms School at Netheravon, where the troops were instructed in how to use modern weaponry, and anything from mines and mortars to machine guns. He was expected to live in the commandant's house at the headquarters in Hythe in Kent, at almost the closest point for an invading army, and so Daphne sent the children, for safety, to their grandmother Browning's house in Oxfordshire, or to Nanny's own cottage. Flavia recalled they did not see their mother for much of 1939.

Certainly the news from Europe that summer was terrifying. Fascism was rampant. Spain was bleeding to death under Franco's fist, Mussolini had invaded Ethiopia and the Germans had militarised the Rhineland, overrun Austria, the Sudetenland and most of Czechoslovakia. Hitler signed a 'pact of steel' with Italy, and then a secret non-aggression pact with Stalin that implicitly exposed Poland to German and Russian megalomania. On 1 September, a million and a half German troops in six armoured and eight motorised divisions swept into Poland. Two weeks later, Russia invaded from the east. On 3 September, war was declared in London and Paris.

In Washington, President Roosevelt announced US neutrality and an embargo on shipping armaments to any of the countries at war (amended two months later to allow Britain and France to buy arms from the US after all). Tommy's predictions all year, that war would be inevitable by the summer, were proved right. It was only just over twenty years since he, and hundreds of thousands of young men like him, had thought themselves lucky to survive the horror and slaughter of the Great War, or 'the war to end all wars' as they had been promised. Once again, they were facing another global war, young enough to have to offer their lives for a second time, in a conflagration that threatened to be every bit as bloody and destructive of Western civilisation.

As thousands of troops of the British Expeditionary Force returned to France and the news from Europe became even grimmer, Angela returned to Torosay Castle, signed herself in as 'Tommy' and hopped into Olive's bed for comfort. Her Pekinese Wendy had just died of meningitis and in tearing grief she had climbed into her car, and driven nearly eight hundred miles in two and a half days.

War was to etch very different experiences on the three du Maurier sisters. Angela evaded it as much as she could by living for large stretches of time with Olive at Torosay. She began her new book while she sat in the library there, a book dedicated to Olive, its plot a gift for the woman she loved and its setting her Hebridean isle. While Angela struggled with the unlikely story of a woman's first and greatest love being restored to her, despite his death and the ensuing years, Jeanne shouldered the responsibility for Muriel, now living mainly at Ferryside. Very soon, she was working long backbreaking days growing vegetables in a steep and difficult site near Pont as her contribution to war work. Daphne was protected from such hard physical labour by being a wife and mother of small children. She did, however, volunteer to be a 'gas decontaminator' at the first-aid unit attached to the local school, but found it hard to take seriously. However, she was assailed on all sides by Tommy's terrible reports from Europe and decided, in these first fearful months of the war, that she would try one last time for a son, 'although I am quite prepared for another lumping daughter!'[28]

9

Fruits of War

I am rather sad that you will apparently weed for hours the Passing
Glory of Torosay and don't consider you can be of import in what
may yet prove to be the Suttons of Cornwall. 'You don't – (sniff)
– mind what you do for Olive' ... It's been very wild weather again
– my poor greens have all had to be staked and I've been like Lob
practically kissing each sprout.

Letter from JEANNE *in Fowey to Angela in Torosay, 1940*

OF ALL THE sisters, Jeanne was the one who really committed herself
to the war effort. Anything she did she embraced wholeheartedly with
all her energy and spirit. For most of the war she cultivated, in very
tough conditions, a two-acre field at Pont, steeply sloping and a good
two-mile hike from Ferryside.

Jeanne took the new slogan 'Dig For Victory' and made it flesh,
with all the aching muscles, strained hernias and dropped arches that
ensued. The precipitous field had to be turned into a productive
vegetable garden that meant every tool, bucket of manure and water,
had to be lugged up by hand, and the produce brought down, again
in buckets and baskets, to sell. She had very little help with the digging,
manuring, planting, weeding, pest control, harvesting and even
marketing of her crops. Certainly, there were no men to shoulder the
heavier work. Jeanne's good friend Mary Fox and her younger sister
Pam toiled alongside her for a time, until both were drafted as Land

Army girls onto local farms, Mary at Lawhyre and Pam at Trevedda. She was joined periodically by a very reluctant Angela. But it was Jeanne alone who planned, worked and managed the market garden, eventually compromising her health in the process.

The passions of her life, painting and music, were put to one side for the duration of the war as she had neither the time nor the energy to pursue them. Even while her elder sisters were still free to follow their interests, Jeanne complained little and got on with her onerous tasks. The responsibility for Muriel also hung heavily on her, a responsibility shared with Angela at times when she was not at Torosay with Olive. Pam Fox recalled Muriel in late middle age as a still extremely pretty woman, stylishly dressed and always with her hair done and make-up immaculate. Her real flair for interior decorating and home-making ensured that every house she inhabited was beautiful, comfortable and welcoming. She could not cook an egg, but she could charm extra rations during the war from local shopkeepers and managed to get her cook, or any available local woman, to rustle up delicious meals while everyone else was making do with the dullest rationed fare.

Pam was amazed how a woman who could produce three daughters with rollicking senses of humour was absolutely devoid of any herself, and in fact was quite bemused by humour in others. Muriel's driving caused her daughters endless merriment as she never learnt how to reverse, and rarely shifted the car out of first gear. She also insisted on driving with a blanket over her knees, which inevitably would get tangled up in the foot pedals. It was a testament as to how few cars there were on the roads at the time that she did not cause herself or any others serious injury, mutilation or death. Muriel was remembered by many as being selfish and rather cold, but somehow her charming manners and beauty meant she largely got away with it.

When the war began, Muriel was 'secretly terrified that she would be landed with evacuees', and asked the Fox sisters to come and live with the family 'indefinitely'[1] at Ferryside. They complied for a short and stressful time, but then made other arrangements and decamped. The fear persisted, however, and Muriel, who had turned sixty in

1937, suffered from a series of ailments, some possibly as a result of anxiety and depression.

There was much to be anxious about. Both Cornwall and the far-flung Isle of Mull, sheltered on the extreme westerly margins of the kingdom, no longer seemed quite so protected from the advancing threat across the Channel. June 1940 seemed a moment of unremitting despair with the evacuation of the British Expeditionary Force from the beaches of Dunkirk. The news that the German army had reached Paris and marched triumphantly up the Champs Elysées was the final humiliation. But there were darker hours to come. Events in Europe were moving so fast that Britain was learning the true and terrible meaning of *blitzkrieg*, as London was nightly bombed by relentless flights of German bombers. Daphne, in the east of the country, justifiably felt more exposed to the threat of invasion and sent her daughters down to Cornwall for safety. They stayed with Nanny Margaret in a cottage in Fowey and came across to Ferryside for meals with Angela, Jeanne and Muriel. It was unsettling for the children, as every evacuation would be. Angela had an abiding memory of Flavia, aged three, lying in bed silent about her distress, except that a single tear welled from a cornflower blue eye and rolled down her cheek. Even this far west there was danger with Plymouth, a couple of headlands east, one of the most heavily bombed cities in the blitz and evacuees billeted on households in Fowey. A bomb fell in the garden of the cottage next door and another in the harbour, but Daphne did not want the children moved to a more remote spot unless she or one of her family were with them.

In the early summer of 1940, Angela once more hightailed it up to Mull and Olive, still signing herself in to the visitors' book as 'Tommy'. She intended to spend a month at Torosay but ended up staying for nine. This was the height of their love affair. She had already spent a month in the early spring, leaving three days after her thirty-sixth birthday on 1 March. On that visit she had written a poem on the castle's headed notepaper, entitled 'Hold on to Happiness', that ended with the lines:

Hebridean sunsets – bitter-sweet –
Peace & free from yearning
A road that has no turning
Leading to an end where I shall meet
She who owns my heart-beats
Now & evermore
Friend & lover, husband, sister, wife
We shall stand together
Link'd by Muillach's* shore
Joy & sorrows shared in future life.
Hold on to happiness …

She later copied it into the leather-bound book, embossed with her and Olive's initials and containing the fair copies of her love poetry to Olive, and gave this poem the explanatory title, 'Lines written on Birthday, 1940 at Torosay'.

It had a sense of reckoning. Angela was halfway through the allotted lifespan of three score years and ten. Certainly, at that point she would not have expected to live to almost ninety-eight, the age she died, for the du Mauriers often reminded themselves they were not a long-lived family. The future seemed to be in retreat. The war was not going well, and there was no certainty that the country could continue to withstand the German advance: it was more than a year and a half before the Japanese attack on Pearl Harbor forced America into the war alongside a weary, bombed-out Britain. Angela, like the rest of the population, grasped what happiness she could and lived for the day, never knowing whether there would even be a morrow.

She could rationalise her long absence from her family duties caring for Muriel and her neglect of Jeanne – so clearly in need of domestic and horticultural help – by pointing out she was gardening full time at Torosay, although admittedly tending to the delphiniums rather than the vegetables. She also undertook some knitting of scarves and balaclavas for freezing sailors as a contribution to Olive's war work for the merchant seamen based at Oban. But most pressing

---

* *Mullach* or *Mullagh* is Gaelic for Mull.

of all was her desire to finish her third novel, her gift for Olive. She was determined to call this *Weep No More*, but to her chagrin had to defer to her English publishers who insisted on calling it *The Spinning Wheel*, a title she complained had no meaning for her whatsoever. Having been set on her path as a novelist, she had found a surge of creative energy and self-belief through her love affair and was working almost as concentratedly as Daphne.

Angela managed to publish four novels in four years. Sadly for her, *Weep No More* (her American publishers retained her original title) was met with little enthusiasm. Her weakness as a novelist, and one of her real differences from Daphne, was her propensity to pour all her highly charged romantic longings into the story. Her books were often a direct tribute to her current love and this hobbled her narrative drive with a too literal importation of her own or her lover's emotional lives. Daphne had always insisted that her own strength lay not in emotion but in imagination. In each book she recreated herself and, through writing, inhabited that imaginary self and controlled the actions of others, 'clothing some unfortunate human being with my own misguided fantasy'.[2]

Neither sister was a great stylist but both responded deeply to the spirit of place, and it was Daphne's sharp eye for disturbing or illuminating detail that made her evocation so atmospheric and compelling. Most tellingly, Angela lacked her sister's macabre imagination and ability to inhabit her misanthropic worlds, in which complex plots unfolded with a ruthless psychological logic that kept the reader enthralled. Perhaps Angela's most successful novel was her fourth, *Treveryan*, a melodramatic gothic tale that was appreciated as an overwrought pastiche of her sister's *Rebecca*, and other Cornish novels.

Weep No More proved to be one of Angela's least convincing novels. The story was deeply personal and the heroine embodied both women's qualities: Olive's nobility, valiant spirit and once flaming red hair; Angela's loyalty and girlish sentiment. Olive's first marriage to Murray Guthrie had been a very happy one, cut short by her husband's premature death. He was buried at Torosay at the spot where he used to look out on one of the most breathtaking views on his estate.

Touched by Olive's experiences of loss, Angela attempted in this novel to restore to her heroine the long-absent love, in the person of a young artist friend of her heroine's son who shared his bizarre first name, Sirion. In America, an influential reviewer found it all too much to bear:

> 100% romanticists might be tricked into enjoying this lush novel of reincarnation, ineptly set in Europe of the World War, the Austrian Anschluss and the submarine warfare of the present crisis. But to the hard-headed average reader, the story is unreal, – sublime, perhaps for the heroine, but ridiculous for the audience.[3]

As a girl, Angela had wilted under lack of appreciation and given up her singing and acting careers at the first hurdles. Now in the warm acceptance she found at Torosay, with encouragement and time to work, she cast off the poor reviews and continued to write, even beyond the three novels she had initially promised Michael Joseph. In his treatment of Angela, in the teeth of unenthusiastic reviews and indifferent sales, Michael Joseph was the exemplary supportive publisher. She was lucky he was, as there was no doubt that she did not want to return to her life as an unmarried and dutiful daughter, based largely now in Cornwall. She was happy enough to leave Jeanne shouldering everything while she continued her much more congenial work, writing and gardening, under Olive's accommodating wing.

From childhood, Angela may have felt disadvantaged in looks and love compared with her sisters, but throughout her life she always insisted on her particular rights as the eldest – 'Esau-ing' as Daphne called it. In likening her sister to Isaac's elder son, did Daphne realise that Esau lost his birthright as the first-born to the trickery of his younger twin? If Angela's birthright as heir to du Maurier celebrity was lost to her, it was more due to the fickleness of fate and her early defeatism than any conscious plan on Daphne's part.

An example of Esau-ing occurred while Angela was at Torosay. Jeanne was struggling, not only with the market garden but also their mother's poor health. Muriel had had some teeth removed, was pole-axed by flu, had suffered a bad fall and was diagnosed with arthritis all in a short space of time. She was feeling very sorry for herself and her doctor suggested that the isolation of Ferryside might be contributing to her depressed malaise and it might be better to move across the water into a cottage in more-lively Fowey. Angela on her distant isle had not liked this idea at all, as it involved her leaving Ferryside too, and mentioned that she thought the decision Jeanne had made, to take a modest house on the Esplanade in Fowey, 'curious'. This provoked an exasperated letter from her long-suffering sister:

> I'm trying to be unbiased, but your letter rather gave the impression of what *you* wanted to do … Life *is* curious these days – it is curious that Mummie who once cared so much about changing for dinner doesn't any longer, that she carves only for herself and doesn't mind my hacking the joint under her eyes, curious that I am concerned more for it to rain for my Cabbage Plants than to fill the Tanks for Baths, that I have to peruse prices and lists of seeds in lieu of Tubes of paint, that one doesn't get shoes cleaned unless done by oneself …[4]

While Angela was busy writing, sustained by love and Olive's faithful staff in a Scottish baronial castle, and Jeanne was toiling in Cornish mud, Daphne, usually so concentrated on her writing and prolific in her output, was finding her 'Muse' had temporarily fled. 'I don't feel like "musing" myself. I don't think I could lose myself in a fictitious story whilst living in such uncertainty. I fluctuate between insanely deciding to join the WAAF (!) if Tommy goes abroad, or trekking for a Pacific Island and never mentioning war,'[5] she told Angela. What Daphne did not admit to her family until later was that she was pregnant with her third child – and pregnancy always made her dreamy and less ambitious.

By July 1940, Tommy was stationed in Hertfordshire and Daphne moved as a paying guest into a beautiful Lutyens house, Langley End near Hitchen, owned by Christopher and Paddy Puxley. The Puxleys were a charming couple in their early forties who extended their unstinting hospitality to Daphne – and Tommy on his infrequent leaves – and then to their children who joined the household later. They were childless and Paddy had thrown herself into voluntary work with the Red Cross and Women's Voluntary Service, and ran the house immaculately. When the Browning girls finally arrived there was an instant rapport. Paddy treated them as if they were special and interesting and Flavia particularly was thrilled to have so much motherly attention and affection directed her way. But Paddy Puxley's generous impulse towards this glamorous family was to have tragic consequences for her marriage, to which Daphne was oblivious at the time. Many years later, however, she did suffer a pang of remorse at how shabbily she had repaid Paddy's kindness and trust, but by then it was too late to repair.

Tommy was away a great deal trying to deal with the increasingly grim progress of the war and his country under continual threat of invasion. When Daphne did see him he was exhausted or fraught with the nervous strain of it all, magnified by the intransigence, as he saw it, of many senior military commanders and civilian counterparts in power. The handsome windswept sailor who had seemed, when she had first met him at Fowey, to have not a care in the world, was now short-tempered and weighed down with responsibility, with little time or energy for his wife.

Christopher Puxley, on the other hand, was charmed by his beautiful houseguest. Unlike Tommy, with the world's very real cares on his shoulders, he had been excused active service and had little to do all day but waft around his exquisite house and garden and tinkle on the grand piano in the flower-filled drawing room. Daphne too had nothing much to do. As a paying guest, she was freed from any responsibility for meals, servants, the domestic organisation that kept a large house running seamlessly, and freed too by Nanny from the daily concern of her children. 'I breakfast in bed and wander in the garden, and go for walks to my heart's content,' she wrote to Tod. She also lay languidly on a sofa in the sunlit drawing room while Christopher, looking like a young Compton Mackenzie she thought, ran his fingers thrillingly over the keys, entertaining her with Chopin's difficult *Preludes*.

The love affair that ensued was hardly a fully consummated sexual affair, for Daphne did not care for that and Puxley was rather lacking in vigour. It was more a romantic obsession, spiced up with some sexual foreplay, between a weak and unhappy man who lacked purpose and a powerful and beautiful woman who needed some diversion, and a spur to her imagination. She wondered if perhaps 'falling in love' was merely 'a fabricated compensation for lack of inner stability',[6] and for a while considered him a kind of soul mate who made her feel less solitary.

For Daphne, having a lover obsessed with her was a familiar and comforting condition to be in. From earliest childhood, she had known her father adored her above all others; then against some competition she won Ferdy's love and kept it for the rest of the Frenchwoman's life. She had practised her power to attract on Cousin Geoffrey, the actress Molly Kerr, tyro film director Carol Reed and magnate Otto Kahn. Then she captured the heart of a real hero in Tommy. His distance from her, now he was engrossed in matters of life and death and the very future of his country, made her feel she had lost her precious power, and with it a central part of her identity. Years later she was amused by the thought that women could be divided into three kinds:

> the ruling type, the ministering type, and the prostitute … I realise I started out in married life by trying to be the ministering type, and succeeded but at great mental disturbance to myself, and a squishing of the ruling type, who simmered. Came the war, and the ministering type began to fade, and the ruling type emerged, bringing a feeling of mental power to myself (and, I suspect, a feeling of squished humility to [Tommy]).[7]

Daphne often pointed out that she was the daughter of an actor and had herself been an actress all her life: this fugitive sense of self only gained substance in her imagination, and in the reflection of that recreated self in the reactions of others. Christopher Puxley reflected back at her a conquering and seductive spirit with the power to change lives. His life, diminished through alcoholism, was affected by her for the remainder of his days. He eventually died wishing to see only her, something in the end Daphne could not face.

What she did face in a confessional letter to a friend was the painful recognition, seven years after she first met the Puxleys, that she had played a significant part in the destruction of their marriage and in Christopher's further decline into alcoholism and ill-health. Daphne had insisted in previous letters that, as there were no children involved, she had little conscience over it all, but then suddenly burst out with, 'all D. du M. achieved in the great war was to keep her own home intact, but to break up somebody else's more successfully than an atom bomb could do'.[8]

Being pregnant, spending the summer lazing in a beautiful garden, flirting with her host while being educated in the beauty of Chopin's piano music, insulated Daphne somewhat from the realities of war. Tommy was back so infrequently now, and she rather dreaded his visits because of the grim news he brought and the shortness of his temper through sheer exhaustion and frustration with the bureaucracy of war. He had told her that he thought the British Army came nowhere near the professionalism of the German military machine and likened it to 'putting up an indifferent clubside to tackle Internationals at Twickenham'.[9] But protected by the champagne and roses of life at Langley End, Daphne could still watch a formation of twenty German bombers on their way to bomb Luton, only eight miles away, and see the beauty of them rather than the deadly menace they embodied. To Angela in Torosay, she wrote dreamily: 'It really was rather an exquisite sight, so remote and unreal, those silvery creatures like humming birds above us at about twenty thousand feet, whilst above them circled their own protective fighters.'[10]

But then she also was capable of patriotic outrage, noble lack of self-interest and some exasperation at America's continued disengagement from the war. Someone in the Doubleday rights department in New York wrote 'a silly letter' suggesting they could get her a great deal of money for serialising her next novel, if she would only let them know something of the plot. 'So I wrote a rather thick letter back, saying as the New York office was many thousands of miles away they perhaps did not realise that this country was faced with the biggest crisis in history and almost certain invasion … and that "vast sums for the next novel" seemed a little beside the point –!'[11]

Daphne's lazy summer was rewarded in November by a quick labour and the miracle of a longed-for son. After three tries she had her Christian at last (she told Angela that if the baby had been another girl she would have called her Gloria). She reported to Tod in triumph: 'Well, I've done it at last! For seven years I've waited to see "Mrs Browning – a son" in the *Times*!'[12] She had trumped her mother and wished her father had been alive to see his favourite daughter produce the son he had always wanted. In Gerald's absence, Daphne set out to turn her precious boy into a little Gerald, commenting how like his grandfather he was and setting out to spoil him as thoroughly as Gerald's mother had spoiled her youngest child, her 'ewe lamb'.

Realising that she may have been taking too great an advantage of Paddy Puxley's generosity, Daphne had moved to another house nearby called Cloud's Hill for her confinement. It was here that she gave birth, and astounded her family by the transformation in her maternal feelings. Tessa was seven and Flavia three and a half when their brother was born. Both were very aware that their much-loved but remote mother was suddenly behaving in a strange manner: 'She adored Christian Frederick du Maurier Browning from the moment she clapped eyes on him,' Flavia recalled, 'hugging and kissing him in a way which made Tessa and I stare in astonishment, for we had never received such treatment. We would watch him lying gurgling in her arms, her face buried in his tiny neck, and we would slip from the room, uncomfortable, knowing we were not wanted there.'[13]

Remarkably, Tessa and Flavia did not resent this newcomer, but came to be as enchanted with his sunny nature and funny little ways. It helped that their mother's love for her son did not alter her unwillingness to give up her routine of breakfast on her own in her room and uninterrupted writing time, regardless of what staff illness, child neglect and domestic chaos was raging outside her door.

By the beginning of 1941, the family had accepted the Puxleys' hospitality once more but now had to share their elegant house with a number of refugees taken in by their hostess. Daphne had begun *Frenchman's Creek* and told Tod it would be a 'Romance with a big R, to help you forget the war!'[14] She was fired up by her infatuation with Christopher Puxley and, freed from domestic duties, wrote it quickly, despite both her daughters succumbing to a severe attack of measles, and Nanny collapsing once more with nervous exhaustion. 'So great was my Gondal-Peg [imaginative recreation] urge towards the man,' she explained years later to a friend, 'that *Frenchman's Creek* absolutely *tore* along.'[15] Within six months, the book was finished and dedicated to the Puxleys. By early September she had advance copies and sent one to Tod, before heading off at last to Ferryside with Tommy for a week's precious leave.

Nothing Daphne wrote could really be called Romance with a capital R, if by romance one means inhabiting a fundamentally just and benign world in which the heroine gets her man, and love in the end prevails. Daphne provided all the props of romance, powerful and poetic evocations of landscape and place, adventurous or compelling situations, psychological suspense, but her heroes and heroines were unsympathetic and loveless. Her women were only admirable if they were women who should have been men, but even they in the end were thwarted in their lives or ended up murdered. Her men were just as unsatisfactory, either weak and ineffectual or brutish and bullying. But the dark and menacing relationship between the sexes she returned to time and again was fascinating and distinctively hers. *Frenchman's Creek* was the novel Daphne was least proud of, a swashbuckling adventure that moved between the high seas and a Cornish ancestral estate. She used her fabrication of Christopher Puxley's character as the cultured pirate, a heroic figure who almost managed to seduce the aristocratic heroine away from her husband and duty to her family. Years later, however, she admitted that 'anything less like the Frenchman, really, than that poor man, there couldn't be, but I Gondalled [imagined] him into it, and saw him that way!'[16]

But Puxley had for a while embodied that compelling psychological manifestation of a soul mate, a reflection of herself that made her feel less insubstantial and alone:

> she was filled with a great triumph and a sudden ecstasy … she had known then that this thing was to happen, that nothing could prevent it; she was part of his body and part of his mind, they belonged to each other, both wanderers, both fugitives, cast in the same mould.[17]

This recognition opened her aristocratic heroine up to a kind of ecstatic love she had never before experienced and, although her reckless adventure with her Frenchman did not last, she returned to a new reality changed by the experience. The story was also powered descriptively by Daphne's lifelong love for the mysterious beauty of Cornwall and the untamable Cornish sea. Her knowledge and fascination with birds, something she and her sisters all inherited from their bird-watching father, also added colour, for in this novel she had more than ninety references to birds, including fifteen different species.

Daphne had tossed into Victor Gollancz's lap another highly marketable novel, and film rights were soon sold. The critics hailed it as an excellent piece of escapist storytelling, and her growing public read it avidly as a welcome relief from the hardships and horrors of war. She was amused by two schoolmistresses who had written to her to say how the book had shocked them to the core because, 'you made immorality attractive'.[18] The film rights alone were so lucrative that Daphne, for a moment, thought her fortune made, but tax was swingeing at the time and she told Tod she was left with only £2,500 of the original £25,000. She was astounded to realise that her book's film rights, have 'given the Govt enough to build a Lancaster Bomber!'[19]

The idyll at Langley End of flirting, writing and listening to music, however, came to an abrupt end. Although the relationship between Daphne and her host had become embarrassingly evident to the nanny, Margaret, Paddy Puxley had not suspected a thing, until she unexpectedly came upon her husband with their houseguest in his arms. Appalled, yet civil to the end, all she said to Daphne was that she had thought she was her friend. In fact the betrayal went very deep indeed, for to a woman who had longed for and failed to have children, whose bloom was gone, Daphne represented beauty, youth, and most cruelly, fertility, careless of the gifts of her lovely daughters and triumphant at producing her son.

Daphne recognised it was time to move her family back to Cornwall. She rented a cottage at Readymoney Cove, and Christopher Puxley motored her down alone in his Bentley. The house was within a stone's throw of the sea, and a brisk walk from her sisters and mother. It was good to be back in the part of the world that was most congenial to her spirit, where her imagination ran free. Her daughters, Flavia in particular, mourned the loss of Paddy Puxley's company and affection, but Daphne dealt with the removal of Christopher Puxley by recreating her soul mate, and his family history, in her next novel, *Hungry Hill*.

During their romantic summer, Christopher had told her stories of the decline and fall of his Irish family that ended with the razing to the ground by the IRA of his ancestral home. She enthusiastically plunged into a world where the men were called John or Henry Broderick (her code for Puxley was John-Henry) and were relentlessly weak and incompetent, as they oversaw the rapid dissolution of the family's status and fortune. Cursed by a rival family who had once owned Hungry Hill, 'Copper John' Broderick had been warned to respect nature and the hill before tearing into it with his mines. His arrogant dismissal of the past and the claims of the land set in progress the inevitability of the Broderick family's downfall. Daphne could be ruthless in her dissection of even those she loved, and she was unsparing in her treatment of the Puxley/Brodericks. It did not really occur to her that the real family might recognise their ancestors in these wimps and wastrels and be unamused. Christopher Puxley's mother particularly objected to the depiction of the women, and Christopher himself would have had to gaze at the portrait of himself as 'Wild Johnnie', a reckless alcoholic lost to hope and happiness. It had a certain justice.

In the summer of 1941, *Frenchman's Creek* was not the only du Maurier novel to jostle for attention. After the retirement of Michael Joseph, Angela had decided to offer Peter Davies her first unloved manuscript as her third novel. *The Little Less* had carried all the emotional freight usual in a first novel but now, as an experienced woman of thirty-seven, she had looked at her youthful offering of more than ten years before and thought it needed some pruning. She had worked at it during the freezing winter months at Torosay. The woman whom her heroine had loved was based on Angela's feelings at the time for Mary Newcomb. Now in thrall to Olive, she made her red-haired, as Olive had once been. At last it was published. If the critics considered Daphne had produced a satisfyingly escapist yarn, they were much less pleased with Angela's clumsier, but bold and brave book.

The critics were either exercised by the 'abnormal sex relations',[20] that Angela had placed at the centre of her story or the more sophisticated dismissed it as 'lush mush'. In the *Saturday Review of Literature*, the reviewer was too worldly to overtly object to the subject matter, but found the writing uninvolving and the narrative 'banal'. He or she then went on to characterise the heroine Vivian, who was in fact a portrait of the young Angela herself:

> the author is eternally preoccupied with the beating of her heroine's heart ... motherless from birth, starved for affection, and doomed to a continual frustration. As a young girl, Vivian Osborne's early sensibilities are outraged when an older man tries to make love to her. She is not altogether a usual girl to begin with, and her emotions are deflected away from men by this unfortunate experience.[21]

Angela's heroine had then entered the path of continually thwarted love. The effect was to deny the possibility of any harmonious or lasting relationship between the sexes, a bleak view she appeared to share with Daphne.

The book was an eye-opener for Daphne too, who wrote one of her newsy and light-hearted letters while she was still in residence with the Puxleys. She had thought it unsuitable reading matter for Nanny, but all the other adults had been absorbed by it:

> [Paddy Puxley] like all fundamentally 'innocent and pure' women, expressed disapproval but nevertheless lapped it up with gusto, while [Christopher Puxley] a cryptic smile on his face has been positively gloating ... My newfound 'discovery' about you, as a writer, is that I believe you should write short stories ... I do wish you would write a funny book, you so obviously can ... I had a bit of fun out of the book

and think some other people will have the same … I feel it's only a matter of time before I'm asked, 'Does Angela know a lot of queer people?!'[22]

Of course, the answer to that question, as Daphne well knew, was yes. Underneath its own humour, this is an interesting letter for it reveals something of the dynamic between the sisters. *The Little Less* was in no way meant to be a humorous novel. Serious, even lugubrious, in its emotionality, any laughs (and there could be many) would only be at its expense. Daphne did not say anything supportive about the novel, whereas Angela was often effusive in her praise for her sister's books – with good reason, it was true. For instance, she had written to Daphne to say how much she had 'adored' *Frenchman's Creek*, and had been so engrossed she had read it in one sitting. On the other hand, for Angela to have her efforts at writing a deeply felt and serious novel about a difficult subject greeted by an admired and much more successful sister with the suggestion that she should try short stories instead, or indeed a comic novel, sounded rather less encouraging. In fact, her emotive and rather baggy style did not lend itself either to the comic or the more tautly condensed.

Angela's war work continued through the summer, helping Jeanne with the market garden at Pont. Jeanne complained to Daphne that Angela rather skimped her tasks and obviously had none of the dedication that drove her youngest sister on to such feats of endurance. After a hard day's work in sun and rain and wind, the sisters would go across to Fowey, dusty and sweat-stained with heavy baskets on their arms, to offer vegetables and fruit to their regular customers, and anyone else they encountered. There was some ill-feeling towards privileged women who could escape the worst of war work in the factories and farms, and Angela particularly had to endure some sour comments and poisonous letters from the locals.

The prize, however, for most dangerous and demanding war work by a civilian in their circle, would have had to go to Angela's redoubtable friend, Angela Halliday. Shaw worked in London throughout the Blitz as an ambulance driver in the Paddington area and was lucky to emerge from the war alive. She endured so much destruction and death, of friends, along with patients for whom she was caring, and strangers in the street, but her strong and optimistic personality saw her through. She sent wonderfully descriptive letters to her old friend, no doubt read out by Angela to the other members of the du Maurier family, and managed to transport the reader into the heart of the inferno. This one was written in May 1941:

By the grace of God I am still here. I suppose it was the most appalling night almost anyone ever spent. It started at eleven pm and J. and I were happily in bed. We tried to stick it out again but it was too hot and we went to the Mews shelter and played bridge until that became a farce and incendiaries were pouring all around us, so we seized bags of sand from various doorsteps and dealt with them. Fires were raging everywhere and H.E.s [High Explosives] screaming round us. As we got back to the shelter there was a God Almighty crash and tons of stuff and glass seemed to pour onto the roof. I went out to see what had gone and a crater about twenty feet deep and wide had appeared in the road by Albion Street P.O. where two minutes before J. and I had been ...

There is no glass anywhere except on the pavements. The window of the room I was to have gone to on Wednesday has been blown in – but anyway my tenant won't come here as there is no gas or water. Druces* is a crumpled mass of twisted iron and most of Baker Street is still burning ... I think every [fire] engine and ambulance in London must have gone out. Some of ours went out four times each ... Poor J. has gone on duty at eight this morning, and as we never closed our eyes at all all night, and she was violently sick before going, I can't think she'll be much good to-day ... I don't think one's nerves could stand many raids like last night's, and until I'm rung up for I shall try and get some sleep.[23]

---

* Druces Depository was a large furniture and textiles showroom on the corner of Baker Street and Blandford Street. The warehouse was full of antiques, furniture, bedding and carpets and was largely destroyed in this bombing raid and the pretty nineteenth-century façade reduced to a charred skeleton.

While Shaw drove ambulances through a burning London, Angela was tramping to and from the market garden near Fowey. As she planted, weeded and watered she worked out in detail the idea for another book. Just as Jeanne had no time or energy for her real love, painting, while she laboured on the land, so Angela too could not put pen to paper while she was digging potatoes by day, and at night easing her aching muscles into an early bed. By the end of the summer, she was desperate to write the novel she had closely plotted while she tied onions in bunches and collected apples for storage. Once the harvest was in, she begged for permission from Jeanne to return to Mull. Her mother was strongly against the idea. Perhaps Muriel thought her eldest daughter would disappear for another nine months, as she had the previous year (and possibly did not approve of the reason) but, despite disapproval at home, Angela headed back at the end of September to Torosay and to Olive. She was only allowed two months and set herself the task of writing, in that time, the whole of her fourth novel that lay like a spring waiting to be released.

Angela ignored the critics and her family's lukewarm interest in her writing and set to work with a will. She knew that soon her age group of women would be called up for compulsory war work, and when that happened she would not have another chance at writing anything longer than a letter. She worked eight hours a day, breaking only for meals provided by Olive's cook, and the daily tramp to a derelict cottage on the estate, Achnacroish, that she had bought off Olive's daughter 'for a song'. She dreamed one day it would become her paradisiacal home where, 'I could walk in unsurpassed beauty for ever.'[24] With fuel and fires rationed, she and Olive huddled together at night in the castle dining room, wrapped in rugs to keep themselves warm. The penetrating cold at bedtime involved even more layers: 'I remember quite well going to sleep under four blankets, an eiderdown, a fur rug, four hot-water bottles, wearing flannel pyjamas, a cardigan and a woollen rug!'[25] And there was also the human warmth of Olive.

This novel was an interesting one. *Treveryan* was Angela's attempt at a bestseller following the pattern of her sister's *Rebecca* and *Frenchman's Creek*, and in fact was dedicated to Daphne 'with much

Love'. It had the du Maurier stamp of lethal sexual relationships, a family with a fearful secret, a once-great estate, wild landscape, thwarted desires. But Angela rather over-egged an already melodramatic tale by throwing in incest, ancestral madness and murder. She set her sights high by starting her first chapter with a quote from a rather more famous tale of family dysfunction, madness and murder, Shakespeare's *Hamlet*: 'I could a tale unfold whose lightest word Would harrow up thy soul ...' This time film rights were sold quickly as film producers found the chance to replicate a past success almost irresistible. Here was a du Maurier story full of sinister intent, set in Cornwall – surely it had the makings of *Rebecca* Mark II? Angela was thrilled at the prospect and probably had cast the whole *personae dramatis* in her mind before the ink on the contract was dry.

The Romanian-born British film producer Marcel Hellman bought the rights and then asked Rodney Ackland, a successful playwright and screenwriter, to write the screenplay. Ackland struggled valiantly with the superabundance of 'strong' scenes, as he called them. The plot remained vivid in his memory:

> This novel I might say, begins with a devoted husband going stark mad and cutting his wife's throat during a ball [in fact he only tried to strangle her] and ends with a semi-demented spinster shooting in cold blood the half-brother for whom she has an incestuous passion, and being sent to Broadmoor. In between these two lurid episodes in high life, Miss du Maurier describes deaths from cancer, Lady Chatterley-like couplings in barns, miscarriages, illegitimate children palmed off on unsuspecting husbands and shadows of incipient homicidal-mania brooding over all.

After months of work, he was surprised to see the verdict on *Treveryan* from one of the exalted executives in the film company as, 'a fragrant little tale but rather thin'.[26]

The company had been determined to cast Lana Turner as the delicately nurtured Bethel Treveryan (her name was quickly changed to Eleanor Veryan). This casting did not fit very easily with Angela's portrayal of the eldest daughter of an ancient but cursed dynasty, forced to renounce love through fear of the mania stalking the family's genes. In the book, this conscientious eldest sibling grew increasingly bitter when she discovered the brother, whom she had always loved too well, had ignored the direst warnings, married against all family directives and, most heinous of all, begotten a potentially homicidal child.

If this film was to have any chance in America, however, Ackland was told that they could not have the heroine become a sour and murderous bitch, capable of killing her brother. Instead a screen heroine would have to become sweeter and ever more saintly, as she suffered the disappointments and renunciations of her bleak inheritance. Most crucially, if her brother died at her hand, his death would have to be accidental. In fact her brother must try and shoot her first, and she was to attempt to Save Him From Himself. A short trial and acquittal and then a happy ending with Lana Turner in the arms of her forsaken lover, would wrap the harrowing tale up with a bow. Oh, and the title would have to be changed from the apparently unpronounceable *Treveryan*, to *Yours For Ever*.

Angela had written a story full of drama, emotion and incident and considered this her favourite book. For once the critics seemed to agree with her and even Daphne was encouraging, writing to Tod, 'It's the best she's yet written though somewhat gloomy in theme, and a trifle over-drawn.'[27] In the Treveryans, Angela had recreated her own family, with some necessary exaggerations, but she had made the second of the three children a son called Veryan, as a present for Daphne who had always wanted to be that boy. Their mother was remote and vaguely hostile, particularly to Veryan, and the children were thrown on each other for love and entertainment.

Angela prided herself on her theatrical imagination and confessed she could always see her characters and their story as filmable, or at least on stage. After Ackland was sacked as screenwriter for being too highbrow (adding one word of Latin that the executives thought might as well be Greek to the average American), the second screenplay was also quietly shelved. The official reason given for this was that the powers-that-be thought, having invested in two full screenplays, that hereditary lunacy was not a fit subject for the screen after all.

Angela's hopes had been riding on this book. A blockbuster film would have made up for so much disappointment in her writing career so far, elevating her profile, so she could stand almost shoulder to shoulder with her sister. However, she managed to be philosophical about the collapse of her hopes and even claimed she was relieved that nothing came of the film, once she had read the much-bowdler-ised screenplay. She consoled herself with a tragic confession: 'The greatest compliment I ever had paid to me was when someone said, "I like Treveryan the best of Daphne's books"!'[28]

For a few months Ferryside was requisitioned by the Royal Navy as a headquarters base for the officers and was not badly treated for the duration of its official use. When the du Mauriers were allowed back, in the early summer of 1942, Muriel soon restored it again to a gracious and comfortable home. Living there, rather than in Fowey, made the trip to the market garden at Pont much less time-consum-ing and tiring for Jeanne and Angela. But soon Angela was directed to work at a farm upstream from Bodinnick at Mixtow and leave Jeanne to garden alone.

This was a blow to both sisters: Jeanne because her health was suffering and she badly needed help, and Angela because she had to work from nine to five cleaning out the cowsheds (she was frightened of cows and the smell of farmyard slurry made her retch), digging a field of potatoes, hoeing turnips, carting gallons of water and clearing pasture of thistles by pulling them out of the ground one by one. Daphne thought that there was some official malice in this posting, that the local bureaucrat had thought 'h'm – do that eldest du Maurier girl a bit of good to break her back. Been idling down here all this time.'[29]

Indeed the heaviness of the work was exhausting and strained Angela's back and body generally, and the loneliness of her solitary labour depressed her naturally companionable spirit. The best part of her time as a farm labourer was the twenty-minute row to work and back. All the du Maurier girls were competent at handling boats and even when she was in late middle age, Angela would row from her home at Ferryside to Fowey, always dressed in a sensible tweed skirt. After four months of miserable and not very efficient work on the farm (there was quite a lot of amusement locally at her ineffectual efforts and fear of farm animals), Angela's stomach pains returned and she was given time off her work for rest. She took the opportunity to hare up once again to Torosay Castle and throw herself into Olive's embrace to recuperate, restored by the familiar beauty of Mull in autumn.

While love and writing filled Angela and Daphne's days, Jeanne was steadfastly gardening her difficult plot through the cycle of seasons, in fair weather and foul, drought and deluge, harrowing and harvest. Exhausted as she was each day, she was not without love and friendship. Her great friend Mary Fox was a stalwart fixture in her life, someone who loved farming and could share Jeanne's dedication to horticulture and the land. Jeanne's letters were as lively and full of detail as her sisters', making light of her battle with rodents, whereby she rolled every pea she intended to plant in red lead and paraffin, and the backbreaking labour of laying hundredweights of new potatoes in the cold earth single-handed. The relentless struggle with nature, terrain and weather meant Jeanne occasionally lost heart. After surveying the damage done by some marauding bullocks that had burst through the top hedge, she found herself longing for her old freedoms to live as she chose, pursuing her life's work: 'God, what I'd give for m'warm studio, filled with the smell of paint, a kettle singing on the stove, and lights glaring through the uncurtained skylight.'[30]

Angela was a good companion when she was around, sharing a laugh, talking of their childhood and snatching the odd cigarette together to punctuate their labours. But Mary Fox was a more practical friend to Jeanne, for she truly loved working on the land and was capable and uncomplaining. When the war was over and Jeanne returned to her painterly and musical pursuits, however, Mary felt somewhat out of her depth; as Jeanne made new friends with painters and poets, the intimacy between the two old friends diminished.

The du Maurier sisters enjoyed each other's letters and Daphne, after reading an operatic account from Jeanne about work on the market garden and her elder sister's less than impressive efforts, wrote to Angela: 'Thank Bird for her priceless letter. I wish she'd take to the pen and make the third [of the 'Sisters Brontë']. It seems you are not entirely thorough with your hoe! How about her making me a birthday cake? ... I must rouse, it's nearly twelve and I'm still in bed. Sordid!'[31]

The war continued with its hardships, fears and deprivations at home. Every family knew someone who had been killed or injured and worried for those who were fighting abroad, or living in large English cities being bombed and burned in concerted German raids. No one could predict when it would end and what if anything of the old world order would remain. Because of Tommy's close involvement, Daphne shared the fear, with millions of other wives of fighting men, that she would receive the fateful communication that changed everything.

Tommy had risen fast up the chain of command and was now in charge of forming and commanding the Army's Airborne Division, responsible for training glider pilots and parachutists in their thousands. It involved superhuman efforts of organisation, persuasion and strategic planning and for years he had been living on adrenaline, his nerves taut with stress. The news on the radio alternated triumphs with disaster. The Americans and Japanese were now in the war, and the conflict was truly global with British troops fighting the Japanese in Burma, General Montgomery and his Eighth Army turning the tide in Africa against Rommel and his Afrika Korps, and the desperate battle for Stalingrad in inhuman conditions of cold and starvation.

Angela had been allowed to leave for good the farm at Mixtow and return to less onerous work as Jeanne's assistant at the market garden. She nevertheless managed to escape for a week's recreation in London with Olive Guthrie in March 1943, where they went to theatres and concerts every day. The Russian composer Sergei Rachmaninoff had just died in exile in California and they sat enraptured through his Piano Concerto No. 3, played by an incandescently fine young Cornish-born pianist Moura Lympany. 'It was the first time I had heard her,' Angela recalled, 'and both Olive and I were pulp by the end. That anyone – any girl so young too [she was twenty-six] – should have quite such power staggered both of us … she is a superb artist.'[32]

The social highlight of her week was meeting Olive's old friend, the exiled King George II of Greece. They had a few meals together, one evening in a restaurant (probably Greek) during a bombing raid, but the clatter of plates, the clamour, and rowdy dancing inside the building drowned out the war outside. The King was fifty-two and yet would live less than five more years, before dying in Athens, the monarchy having just been restored, in April 1947. Olive had another week in London and King George wanted Angela to join them at Claridge's, her favourite haunt when she was young. She had promised Jeanne she would only be gone a week and would return to help plant hundreds of onions, so instead she reluctantly left behind London's remnants of glamour to dig the claggy ground of Cornwall.

This time with Olive had been very much overshadowed by the news that Lieutenant David James, Olive's much-loved twenty-three-year-old grandson, was missing in action, presumed drowned. His motor gun-boat, operating out of Felixstowe, had been sunk in freezing waters off the Hook of Holland. In fact, against all odds, he did survive. He became a prisoner of war and wrote a gripping book about his experiences and eventual escape. David James went on to live a life of adventure, to marry and father six children, inherit Torosay and become a Conservative Member of Parliament.

Angela hurried back to Fowey and her onions. Her summer was spent weeding, watering and harvesting, often dressed just in shorts and a sleeveless vest and tanned by the sun and wind. Daphne was rather disconsolately settled at Readymoney with her children, Margaret and a new cook whom Nanny did not take to. Christopher Puxley still came down to see her for romantic trysts, staying in the annexe to the Fowey Hotel, but it was not satisfactory for either of them. Daphne was once again living in close proximity with her sisters and spent some time with them, even contracting to help Jeanne once a week at the garden, 'she puts me to weeding carrots with great sternness, or picking up onions, or some other equally backbreaking task', she wrote to Tod, 'the Madam [Jeanne] is a great task master these days'.[33] Although she was exempt from the war work that her sisters, especially Angela, found so gruelling, Daphne was aware that being seen 'lounging about in my corduroy pants', risked her receiving abusive anonymous letters about privileged women not doing their bit for the war. She certainly knew that Angela felt life was rather unfair on her, compared to her middle sister, and Daphne joked to Tod that the anonymous letters would be 'from the Puffin herself who will be sore with secret resentment!'[34]

Daphne was looking forward to the publication of *Hungry Hill* that summer. She hoped it would be a kind of watershed that established her as a serious writer, freed from the hated tag of 'romantic' novelist. Sadly, it did not live up to this expectation. It did become a bestseller, largely through the tireless efforts of her publisher Victor Gollancz, and a film was eventually made of it after the war. It was, however, an unwieldy novel with a confusing storyline and cast of characters – whose names alternated through the generations as John or Henry Broderick – and no unifying thread to which the reader could cling. The critics were disappointed and disappointing. They thought it would sell on her name alone, but showed none of the staying power of *Rebecca*, or even the popular romantic pull of *Frenchman's Creek*. Daphne was to be as haunted by the phenomenon of *Rebecca*, the novel, just as surely as her second Mrs de Winter never cast off the shadow of Rebecca herself.

In this lowish mood, Daphne was suddenly given the chance of something she had wanted more than anything in the world. Dr Rashleigh, the owner of her beloved Menabilly, appeared to be willing to let her lease the house and grounds for twenty years. Her work may suffer under the spell of *Rebecca*, but she would now have Rebecca's house and it would be hers alone. Menabilly was Daphne's Manderley and her love for it was more powerful than her love for any man. The thought it could be hers was exhilarating, and no amount of judicious advice or family opposition would put her off.

There was a lot that was off-putting. The house was so long uninhabited it needed restoration, certainly a whole wing was already derelict and dangerous to unwary visitors and children. You could open a door upstairs and teeter on the abyss where a floor once was, giving a whole new dimension to passage wandering at night. The lease she would be required to sign was a fully repairing one. Her own money would have to be used to restore the mansion to a habitable state and keep it maintained, without any ultimate advantage to her for the huge sums invested, other than the chance to live there for twenty years. 'I so much want to go there I'd rather be rooked than not go,'[35] she admitted to Tod, knowing this weakened her negotiating hand. There was no way she'd walk away, whatever was asked of her, and she knew that Dr Rashleigh knew that too. To solicitors and accountants this seemed a crazy scheme. To Tommy and family, who knew how many staff would be needed to run such a big house comfortably, it seemed far too ambitious: to Daphne who relished forbidden and heroic love affairs, it was absolutely irresistible.

She and Angela were with the children having a picnic in the grounds of Menabilly when Daphne decided to confide her plans to her sister. The children heard their aunt's distinctive hoot of laughter, and then a shout of amazement, '"You're mad, you can't,"' Flavia recalled, 'and we wondered what she meant and why they suddenly seemed so heated in their conversation.'[36] The house at this stage was so completely covered with ivy you could barely see the windows. Its dark presence, stillness and quiet was eerie. The overgrown gardens and woods were magical, but there was nothing to attract Angela, or Daphne's children, to the house as a potential home. Flavia remembered seeing her mother lean against the ivy-clad walls and kiss the stone and, when she turned, her slightly flushed face had a look close to ecstasy.

Once the lease was signed then Daphne was determined to move her family into the house for Christmas, but to keep it as a surprise for the children. Builders arrived to patch the roof and provide some functional running water in the place. Windows were cleared of ivy and rotten frames replaced. The nineteenth-century wing, riddled with sinister fingers of dry rot, was barred and bolted and left in peace to further decay. Daphne and Margaret disappeared each day to clear and clean two decades of dust, animal droppings, cobwebs and debris from the rooms the family was to inhabit. Walls were decorated and rooms minimally furnished. Light and life, if not warmth, began to seep into the unloved spaces, and the force of Daphne's determination and passion breathed life into the house again. Her enduring love affair with Menabilly was now consummated as she awoke it slowly from its long sleep.

Everyone was amazed at the transformation. The children were delighted with the adventure of its vast spaces and the fascination of the woods that surrounded it like a protecting reef. Tommy was home for a week over Christmas, shattered with fatigue but appreciative of the house and its miraculous metamorphosis, masterminded by his wife. Draughty and freezing cold when out of the narrow reach of an open fire, understaffed, haunted, infested with rats beneath the floorboards and flying battalions of bats at dusk (both families of creatures Daphne admirably insisted had as much right to live in the house as they did): this was a house that aroused strong feelings in every sentient being within its orbit. Flavia and Christian (known always as Kits) grew to love it in different ways and for different things; but Tessa, lonely and out of place, was frightened by the powerful atmosphere and the night-time skirmishing of an army of tiny rodent feet.

Angela managed her customary autumn visit to Mull, this time for only two weeks at the beginning of October. The war arrived at Oban when a squadron of German bombers discharged their cargo on ships at anchor. Some valuable thoroughbred horses were killed in the raid and Angela and Olive lay awake listening to the *crump!* of exploding bombs that shattered the deep silence of the Hebridean night. Returning to Fowey she found that the American navy had arrived and the town was seething with excitement and rumour. Her more than five-year romantic obsession with Olive and Torosay was about to be deflected by a new, very different, romantic interest.

There were many in Fowey who initially resented this American invasion. They did not like their houses being commandeered and US personnel billeted on them, and were outraged that their familiar town was overrun with a swaggering group of young, tall, well-fed and confident men. For the majority, however, these exotic creatures, so well-off compared to their British counterparts, so charming with their drawls and American courtesies, brought sex and glamour and the thrill of film star sophistication. Angela was part of the latter group.

The American invasion could not have got off to a better start, as far as the du Mauriers were concerned, for Gertrude Lawrence's husband Richard Aldrich turned up with his commanding officer, Lawrence Woodsworth Snell. The whole family liked Richard and, having just landed with their troops, it was natural that their first port of call was Ferryside. Angela, particularly, was charmed by Richard's boss, Commander Snell. Larry, as he quickly became known to them, had a great deal to commend him. He was the commanding officer of the US Naval Advanced Amphibious Training Sub-base at Fowey and his brief was to get his men ready and the landing ships and craft seaworthy for the coming invasion of Normandy. He was obviously efficient at his job and was awarded the Bronze Star medal for this coming D-Day operation. He also looked impressive in his naval uniform, complete with medals. Daphne had her distinguished war hero husband, away doing important and dangerous work for the safety of the realm; Angela now had the most distinguished American in uniform in Fowey paying her court. No wonder it went to Angela's head.

Larry had a way with the ladies. By the time Angela met him he had been married twice, with two sons from his first marriage. He was a graduate of the University of Michigan and was well known on the New York Social Register; his social ease and awareness of his status (his third wife complained that he treated her as inferior for not being like him, a 'blueblooded social registerite'[37]) would have charmed Angela, who had long given up hope of being charmed by a man again. Her nieces noticed how she giggled a lot in his company and eventually had a large signed photograph of his chubby shining face by her bed. Even Tod got to hear of her infatuation when Daphne wrote in some amusement: 'Puff having the time of her life with the US Naval officers, who are stationed in Fowey.'[38]

The war had lost its dreariness and suddenly become a lot more exciting. Angela wrote to Gertrude Lawrence to thank her for two packets of silk stockings that had just arrived and would now allow her to fit in better with Larry's idea of female glamour: 'No woman wears trousers … at home!' In this excited letter of thanks, Angela described how 'a comet from the sky, L[arry] appeared & blitzkreiged us out of our trousers into frocks & skirts & God knows what else!'[39] Gertie was still in America having triumphantly starred in the musical, *Lady in the Dark*, a great hit on Broadway and then toured for years. She had not forgotten, however, the hard-pressed women at home and, along with Angela's stockings, she had also sent nail varnish to Muriel, who was just as delighted with this unexpected luxury.

Angela joined the local Home Guard in an 'intelligence role', a fact that caused a great deal of chauvinistic ribbing from her fellow male Local Defence Volunteers. She enjoyed herself immensely, although she was still meant to be working on the market garden by day. On evenings off, instead of the drabness of a book, some cocoa and early bed, now she was helping forge, 'a kind of Atlantic Charter in a real but minor way',[40] in other words socialising and flirting with American naval officers in various private houses and drinking places round Fowey.

Given Angela's romantic and emotional nature, there was little doubt that, facing forty, a small part of her hoped it was not too late for her to love a man and be loved in return. Why should she not dream of marrying her Commander, to enter at last the life for which she had been bred, to be the supportive wife of an important and well-off man? Larry may well have let her think she had a hope. Certainly, they were extra friendly and affectionate together, and their friendship continued once Larry had returned to America.

The fact that he married for a third time, very soon after returning to America in 1945, would not have escaped Angela's notice. Larry Snell had fallen quickly in love with a glamorous Washington businesswoman, ten years Angela's junior, who went by the Chandleresque name of Marshall Adams. She was a radio talkshow host and a 'fashion arbiter', who organised fashion shows at foreign embassies. Larry was so bowled over by her that he proposed on their second date. Less than two years of marriage and a baby son later, Marshall was suing Larry for divorce, declaring 'he does not want to work … and prefers to loaf, have a good time, drink, gamble and cavort around the city',[41] and philander with other women.

In fact, Larry could not be entirely averse to work, as he went on to found an investment company in Wall Street, and sail close to the wind in his dealings in securities. Angela kept a sizeable photograph of Commander Larry Snell, in his naval uniform with tramlines of decorations – long after he had left the navy – with sad eyes and thinning hair, signed with love and dated Christmas 1951. Perhaps he was ruing the day he had married the tall blue-eyed, down-market blonde, having left behind his small, dark and unglamorous, but well-bred, English admirer.

In the days leading up to June 1944 there was an atmosphere of expectation in Fowey as the day of departure of their American visitors approached, although the actual date was kept a secret. Daphne at Menabilly was asked to give a party for the US war correspondents who were in the town incognito. No one was to know, even Daphne's servants were sent away on a picnic and Angela noted that 'negro naval staff' were bussed in, in unmarked vans, to replace them. Angela and Muriel were asked to be present as hostesses to the war correspondents, on what was meant to be the eve of D-Day (it was postponed at the last minute because of adverse weather). The party was a huge success and Angela, always more extrovert than either of her sisters, enjoyed herself immensely, even though it marked the beginning of the US Navy's mission to Normandy, and therefore the end of the American invasion of Fowey.

It was here that she saw close up African-Americans and appreciated their attractiveness, and that fear of their difference and the prejudice against them was purely due to the colour of their skin. Like most people of her generation, Angela was aware of Leslie 'Hutch' Hutchinson, a half-Grenadian pianist and singer, one of the most famous cabaret performers in London at the time. Daphne loved the way he sang *Sand in My Shoes*, and recommended it to Tod, and high society generally had taken him up enthusiastically. But scandal accompanied him everywhere. His attractiveness to men and women alike meant there were all kinds of rumours as to the celebrity of his lovers, among them the du Mauriers' great friend Ivor Novello and

Edwina, the wife of Tommy's colleague, Lord Louis Mountbatten. The rumours were made all the more salacious because of Hutch's colour and his legendary sexual prowess. Love between a white woman and a black man was as controversial an idea as love between women. Angela's next novel began to take root in her mind.

Jeanne's dogged determination to make her market garden as productive as possible finally took its toll on her health. While Angela was forging the Atlantic Charter in Fowey, Jeanne was off sick and ordered to rest with an umbilical hernia, caused by all the heavy lifting and carrying she had been engaged in on her unforgiving plot. Never had the idea of a studio and the smell of paint been more attractive as she lay in bed, hoping that Angela, whose horticultural work had hardly been as dedicated as Jeanne would have liked, would be left in charge. Luckily, she did not need an operation, but was told she must take three months off work.

She and Mary Fox headed off to St Ives for a holiday together and rented a small flat. They had been discussing buying a farm at Mixtow together, close enough to Muriel at Ferryside, but in St Ives, Jeanne was reminded of her true calling, not to be a farmer but a painter, and here began her belief that she could be a serious artist and live among other artists. It would be here that Mary realised the close friendship they shared in Fowey could not last in its original intensity, once Jeanne entered the painters' colony at St Ives.

While Angela was flirting with the Americans and Daphne was exultantly sorting out the house of her desire, Tommy was engaged in the most testing and tragic military operation of his career. He had been in charge of creating the British Army's 1st Airborne Division and, in August 1944 as lieutenant general, was put in overall charge of the First Allied Airborne Army, consisting of British, American and Polish troops and their commanders. This job was immense, with the potential to alter the progress of the war. He had to provide the 'Market' part of 'Operation Market Garden' in support of Field Marshal Montgomery's plan to encircle and control the Ruhr, Germany's industrial heartland, from the north. The expectation was that if this operation was successful, the war could be ended by Christmas. Fundamental to the plan was the airborne troops who were to be parachuted and glided in to the field of conflict. The men then would seize the bridges over the River Meuse and the Lower Rhine, so that Allied troops, the 'Garden' part of the operation, could pour through in armoured units into northern Germany.

This was to be the largest airborne operation ever mounted with nearly 35,000 men silently delivered by glider and parachute, in daylight from 17 September 1944. Gliders and parachutes were also used to bring in military vehicles, guns and ammunition, but the men by necessity were more lightly armed than those due to follow by land in their tanks. It started well, but German resistance was far more powerful and well organised than the Allies had expected. This meant Tommy's 1st Airborne Division were left without backup, trying valiantly for four days to defend one end of the road bridge at Arnhem, before being overrun by the Germans on the twenty-first. The rest of the company, trapped to the west of the bridge, had to be evacuated four days later. For the division created and trained by Tommy, this was a colossal tragedy. Only a quarter of his 10,000 or so airborne troops returned to Allied lines, the rest wounded, killed or captured.

The courage and resistance of the men fighting on the ground, often outnumbered four to one, was never in doubt. In fact, to have survived Arnhem became a badge of honour. But criticism of the high command began almost immediately. Analysis, supposition and blame circled them all and Tommy, as strategic planner of the 'Market' part of the assault, and commander of the airborne division, was most vulnerable. The controversy continues to this day, never to be categorically resolved. However much Tommy's strategic judgements may or may not have been instrumental in the failure, Browning himself, a man with sensitivities and empathy hidden deep behind his rigid upper lip, was full of grief and a guilt that would never be assuaged. Ever proud of him and fiercely loyal in public, Daphne sprang to Tommy's defence in a letter to the researcher for a forthcoming book, *A Bridge Too Far*, expressing something of the anguish with which her husband had to live for the rest of his life:

One thing I do know, although he did not talk about it, was that his grief at the loss of life at Arnhem was very deep indeed … this particular loss was something to which he could never become reconciled. He truly loved the men under his command, and the various regiments that combined to make up the Airborne Forces, his pride and his faith in them was tremendous, I would say – next to his family – the dearest thing in his life.[42]

Daphne and her sisters had been in Cornwall while the fateful hours of Operation Market Garden ticked tensely by. The news on the radio became desperate. Everyone knew Tommy was in the thick of it, having glided in along with his men. In his pack he carried three teddy bears and a framed print of Dürer's *The Praying Hands*. Suddenly Daphne's bubble of detachment at Menabilly was brutally breached by a phonecall from a newspaper reporter at six o'clock in the morning, demanding if it was true that Tommy had been taken prisoner. She knew nothing and for a while could find out nothing. Once she discovered there was no truth to the rumour, she wrote a sharp letter to *The Times* complaining about the cruel tactlessness of such a call.

Tommy wrote full of longing to come home to her and their familiar routines and was excited by plans for a new boat. Daphne, however, had grown used to being alone and liked it much better than having to accommodate another in her life. She had explored her forebodings in her play, *The Years Between*, in which a woman, deprived of her husband who is presumed dead, eventually thrives in his absence. She takes up his job and starts a new and more congenial relationship, only to renounce it all to return to her wifely role once more, when her husband turns up, very much alive. This gulf of experience was endured by tens of thousands of couples at the time, between the battle-scarred men and their wives whose independence and self-sufficiency had grown as they were freed from more conventional domestic roles by work and the need to cope resourcefully with the daily privations at home. It was difficult for them to share or even understand the full horror and deep camaraderie of war.

Daphne, too, seemed to be incapable or unwilling to imagine what her husband had been through, and, although unswervingly loyal when he was under attack, she found it hard to be sympathetic to the daily consequences in his own life and character, wrought by the extreme experiences he had endured in two world wars. As she contemplated with some misgivings the return of her soldier, Angela had waved goodbye to her American sailor, knowing this had been the last chance she had had of a conventional marriage. She was to immortalise him, however, by giving his name to the heroine and title of her fifth novel, *Lawrence Vane*. As war drew to its end, Jeanne managed at last to return to her love, painting, as she prepared for her first exhibition planned for the autumn of 1945 in St Ives.

10

A Mind in Flight

> Do you remember me saying to you once at Oyster Bay that I
> had found, through life, that just as one had reached a moment
> in time when everything seemed static, and one knew all
> the answers, suddenly – Bang out of the Blue – a sledge-hammer
> came and knocked one out? I feel rather like that now. And
> the sledge-hammer was not Mr Rosenshein … Work that one
> out if you can! (Go and look in the glass, it will save you a lot of
> time.)
>
> *Letter from* DAPHNE *to Ellen Doubleday, 4 December 1947*

AS THE WAR was drawing to its close in Europe, the news of victories,
surrenders and retreats tumbled out of the radio, 'faster and faster',
Angela recalled, 'like Alice'[1] sped up in an unreal momentum. Within
just over a week there was Mussolini's execution, Hitler's suicide and
then the once barely imaginable VE Day, declared on 8 May 1945.
Muriel caused her daughters much amusement by insisting it should
be VD Day – Victory Day – not for a moment understanding what
was so funny. The streets were suddenly heaving with people celebrating with an ecstatic and bone-weary relief. Londoners, who had
endured the worst of the bombing, thronged Whitehall and The Mall
and pressed against the railings of Buckingham Palace chanting, 'We
want the King!' and the young princesses Elizabeth and Margaret
were allowed to mingle with the crowds, experiencing first-hand the

euphoria of a nation that had prevailed against once apparently insurmountable forces.

A few days later, the du Maurier family en masse took over the front seats at Fowey's small cinema to watch *Frenchman's Creek*. Their pleasure was much enhanced by seeing old family friends Basil Rathbone, in a towering wig, as the dastardly Lord Rockingham and Nigel Bruce as Godolphin, a dimwitted aristocrat, in what was a sumptuous piece of overdressed derring-do. Joan Fontaine, who had made no secret of how unhappy she had been on set, shimmered as the beautiful Dona St Columb, the heroine who embodied something of Daphne's own fantasy of temporarily abandoning husband and children for a life of adventure, dressed as a boy, with a dashing lover who reflected herself.

In real life, dashing Lieutenant General Browning's duties were not yet over. At the end of 1944, Tommy had been appointed Chief of Staff to Lord Louis Mountbatten at South East Asia Command, a job he was not particularly pleased to have, and was soon off to Ceylon. Daphne felt ambivalent at the news, telling Tod that one was bound to get out of touch with such long separations and dreading the difficulties of 'beginning afresh'.[2] She did not really miss her husband, however, as her solitary life, in a house she had made entirely to her liking, gave her creative and spiritual solace: 'I do love my queer monastic existence. [Menabilly's] cold, and austere, but I belong to it, and the house is in league with me against the outside world.'[3] She particularly loved her bedroom, her space alone, and had asked Tommy if he minded having his own bedroom at Menabilly. He did mind, but did not complain when Daphne organised a room for him adjacent to hers. She was not yet forty when she closed the door on easy intimate relations with her husband.

This did not stop Daphne hoping for a romantic reunion when Tommy eventually came home from war. During their marriage they had been apart almost as much as they had been together and yet Tommy seemed to be sympathetic to the sacrifices made by all women left at home to await the return of those they loved. '[Daphne] and I seldom talk of those six years of practically complete separation,' he wrote to Ellen Doubleday, 'but my admiration for her in never giving a sign of how she must have felt is very deep.'[4] In that one sentence there was all the poignancy of the unexpressed and unexplored, the gulf between.

On his return in the summer of 1946, Daphne's hopeful expectations collided with Tommy's exhaustion, inhibition and sense of anticlimax on finally arriving home, and both were left disappointed and ever more distant. Daphne found it a shock to find he had changed and was not as dependent on her as he had been: 'So See Me [showy-off], rather boastful, and not a little boy any longer.' And she had changed too, the five years' separation had made her more independent again, she had become, 'the pre-marriage person who went her own way … Kits got the tenderness I had given before to Tommy'.[5] Moreover, Daphne's natural jealousy and insecurity in herself as a woman was quickened by the sudden appearance behind her husband of his beautiful personal assistant, Maureen Luschwitz. The uneasiness she felt had no foundation in fact but nevertheless, combined with Tommy's cool welcome, left Daphne feeling deflated and unattractive.

Her rather bleak play, *The Years Between*, dealing with this dilemma of 'beginning afresh' after a long separation, had been a quiet success during its run at Wyndham's, her father's old theatre. And she was writing another novel with great energy and enthusiasm, *The King's General*, spurred on by her discovery of the impact the Civil War had had on Menabilly when the house had been besieged by Cromwellian forces. A skeleton wearing remnants of Cavalier clothing had been found during earlier restoration work on the house and this added an extra fascination to Daphne's researches.

Daphne was imaginative but never fanciful and not prone to seeing ghosts, but Flavia remembered being told by her mother that before she even knew of this siege, Daphne had heard one night what seemed to be the galloping of horses and the jingling of their harnesses as they surged across the park towards the house. She even heard the scraping of metal and the stamping hooves of what sounded like hundreds of horses jostling beneath her bedroom window. When Daphne came to draw back the curtains and look out on the scene all she saw was the silent, empty drive starkly illuminated by moonlight.

The history of the house was inextricably bound up with the Rashleighs, the family to whom it had belonged since Elizabeth I's reign, whose unassailable rights over it would always thwart Daphne's dreams of complete possession. Dr Rashleigh had refused to let her borrow the family papers to research her story but, rather gleefully, she decided she could get copies of them through her friendship with the great Cornishman and historian A. L. Rowse. He did in fact help her with sources for her extensive research but did not care for the novel, feeling that non-historians could never authentically conjure up the period. Rowse, however, was a great fan of Daphne's and understood very well her reclusive nature. He appreciated too that her fundamental loneliness and shyness was masked by an affable, kindly manner, but her real longing was to be left alone with her imagination in the house of her dreams.

The heroine of this stirring tale is one of Daphne's rare strong women, Honor Harris, whose intellect and physical courage, despite being disabled by a riding accident, is the backbone of the story. Daphne's skill in weaving real historical fact with the compelling skein of fiction meant the battle for Menabilly and the ruthless but irresistible Sir Richard Grenville burst into her readers' imaginations. The confused and bloody events of the Civil War in the West Country were made all the more dramatic by Daphne's unerring sense of place and visceral love of landscape.

Daphne dedicated the book to her own King's General: 'To my husband, also a general, but I trust a more discreet one' – an act of appreciation that made Tommy slightly uneasy as it identified him with the charismatic but murderous and insubordinate commander who swaggered through his wife's novel.

In the midst of the fun of writing *The King's General*, Daphne was forced to take seriously the threat of having to defend herself against a suit of plagiarism involving *Rebecca*. This was brought against her in America by the estate of Edwina MacDonald, the author of a book, *Blind Windows*, published in 1927, and set in Louisiana. The two novels appeared to have a number of coincidental, or borrowed, factors in common, but it seemed there was some opportunism in the timing as the claim was only first made in 1942, after the phenomenal success of Hitchcock's film. Although Daphne knew her idea for the book had arisen out of her own jealousy of Tommy's previous love, she loathed the idea of being cross-examined about the entirely mysterious and secret elaborations of her mind, and she had no intention of revealing them to strangers. She felt the most private part of her self would be on trial. She was exasperated that neither Angela nor Muriel could understand this. They thought if she knew she was innocent why get so upset about the exposure: 'They just missed the whole point. What I write is me. It's inside myself. It's deeply, bitterly, terribly personal. And to have to stand up and talk about it was to me absolutely degrading … It was, to me, my own private day of judgment.'[6]

The day of judgement did come. In 1947, Daphne was summoned to appear before a judge in New York and it threw her into a panic. Her American publisher Nelson Doubleday and his wife Ellen were immensely hospitable to their English authors and had previously offered to open up their home as a safe haven to the Browning children during the war. This time, Nelson encouraged Daphne to make the best of an event she could not evade and invited her to come with the whole family to stay at his lovely house on the ocean in Long Island's Oyster Bay. This caused Daphne further anxiety for she felt singularly ill-equipped for the kind of gracious living practised by the well-connected and distinctly well-off Doubledays. Daphne hated to have to think about clothes and grooming and was always happiest wearing comfortable slacks and a shirt, tunic or fisherman's jersey. She could look strikingly glamorous when coifed, made-up and smartly dressed but always felt something of an impostor, longing to return to her comfortable anonymous 'jam-a-long' clothes.

Daphne had persuaded the ever-devoted Tod to return as governess to her children in the autumn of 1945. Tod loathed the cold and discomfort of Menabilly but it was a measure of her love for Daphne that she agreed, despite being well into middle age, to come and live once more under a grand, if leaking, du Maurier roof. She had struggled to keep her hat-making business going during the war and had resorted to being a paid companion to a rich widow, where at least she lived in some luxury and was always warm. But she loved Daphne and liked her children, who returned her affection, although the young Kits had some reservations as she was unlikely to indulge him as much as his mother.

Daphne decided she would take Tod and her two youngest children with her to America. Tessa was due to start boarding school and Tommy was involved in his new job as Military Secretary, living for the week in an austere flat in Whitelands House in Cheltenham Terrace in Chelsea. She hated being away from Menabilly, felt awkward anyway staying in the house of strangers and bitterly resented having to go to New York to answer such an obviously put-up case. She boarded the *Queen Mary* liner in November 1947, not in the most relaxed frame of mind. Flavia and Tod shared a cabin, and Kits was in with his mother. Greta Garbo was on board and was much amused by Flavia and Kits, galloping about the deck on all fours. Two days into the voyage there was a knock on her cabin door and it opened to reveal Ellen Doubleday.

Daphne's first sight of Ellen took her completely by surprise. She was struck by a *coup de foudre*, or as she described it, a sledgehammer poleaxed her, 'Bang out of the Blue'. Ellen walked in straight out of her dreams. For here was Rebecca, and Daphne, the faltering insecure second Mrs de Winter, felt immediately eclipsed by her sense of entitlement, competence and beauty. She had been expecting Nelson's wife to be a cross between Mrs Simpson and Mrs Roosevelt, but instead she was faced by a beautiful, elegant and charming woman whom she conflated too with the Mary Stuart of her imagination. Daphne's heroic boy-self wanted to be all the men who had loved her, 'Lord Darnley, and Earl of Bothwell in exact sequence (I think Bothwell had the best of it). Even the Italian secretary Rizzio ... who was murdered at Mary Stuart's feet.' She felt she was suddenly Eric Avon again, 'a boy of eighteen ... with nervous hands and a beating heart, incurably romantic, and wanting to throw a cloak before his lady's feet'.[7]

The boy she had wanted to be had been consigned to a box locked within herself and now, unexpectedly, had escaped – and it was thrilling and alarming to her in equal measure. For Daphne it was as if Peter Pan, the hero of their youth, had suddenly flown into her imagination to taunt the grown-up Wendy with what she had forfeited in choosing adulthood and the real world over the dreams and limitless possibilities of Neverland.

The friendship with Ellen Doubleday was to be the most important creative relationship of Daphne's life, conducted largely through Daphne's baroque imagination and her remarkable letters: funny, descriptive, confessional. Their infrequent meetings, especially when Ellen occasionally came to Europe, were often a disappointment. They were so utterly unalike as women, enjoyed such different things and Ellen, merely mortal – and a privileged American – had a much greater need for comfort and security (Daphne was scornful when Ellen checked herself into a Parisian hospital when she had a cold). The real Ellen could never live up to the curlicued creation of Daphne's fantastical mind.

Daphne hung all kinds of different personae round Ellen's neck – not just her own Rebecca and Mary Stuart, but the Madonna de la Esperanza and Eleanor of Aquitaine. This could be burdensome for a literal-minded, conventional and sympathetic woman like Ellen. Daphne saw her as a consummate woman, everything that she could not and did not wish herself to be. Ellen was undoubtedly beautiful but also soignée and groomed in a way that utterly defeated Daphne. She ran the Doubleday mansions and their numerous servants with social grace and iron discipline and entertained immaculately. She was the professional wife of a highly successful and difficult man, shouldering her role with the kind of flair and commitment Daphne had never been able to offer Tommy in his career. A motherly presence, she appeared to preside effortlessly over a happy brood of children.

But most importantly for Daphne, Ellen was to be the imaginative inspiration for two fictional characters. She was Stella, the mother in *September Tide*, a play Daphne began writing on her return to England, even requesting the name of her signature scent (Coty's L'Aimant) so that the actress could wear that on stage. More significantly, her idea of Ellen animated Rachel in *My Cousin Rachel*, the book she thought of as 'the most *emotionally-felt* book I had ever written.'[8]

Daphne was obsessed with Ellen during the first years of their relationship. She bombarded her with scintillating but demanding letters: by Christmas 1947 she pointed out that she had written six long letters to Ellen's measly two and requested the reasons for this dereliction. It did not occur to Daphne until later that the avalanche of demanding emotion and longing she directed towards her new friend would never be reciprocated and possibly even came close to harassment, so wrapped up was she in her own imagined world.

This was Daphne's first trip to America. Alarmed at the prospect of being subjected to impertinent questions that revealed her working methods and exposed what felt to her to be her very being, she most feared being forced to admit that the spur to her story was her jealousy of Tommy's former fiancée. This would have been a revelation of female weakness that the swaggering boy in her psyche found shameful to contemplate. She sat in the imposing gloom of the New York District Court on Foley Square, pale and slightly bowed.

Harrison Smith, one of the editors at the *Saturday Review of Literature* who was called as an expert witness on the case, watched her on the witness stand and thought she was obviously suffering and deeply embarrassed. The prosecuting barrister Mr Rosenshein read out statements she had made when writing about her father and forebears that implied the du Mauriers were sometimes loosely acquainted with the truth. He pointed out that at least one previous female ancestor had broken more than one of the commandments. Despite enduring having her own honesty and veracity impugned, Daphne conducted herself in a highly disciplined way and remained outwardly serene.

As part of his expertise, Harrison Smith had read every second-wife novel he could find and been amazed at how many there were and the similarity of their plots, with mysterious mansions, portraits of first wives with uncanny eyes, hauntings and madness much in evidence. However, as he told Judge John Bright, 'of them all, *Rebecca* was the most original and the most vital. Danvers, the grim housekeeper of Manderley, was an original conception, as was the entire section dealing with Max de Winter's murder of Rebecca … the evidence of the novel's originality was plain for anyone to see'.[9]

Daphne suffered by day, feeling flayed by lawyers in the courtroom, and then returned to the balm of Nelson and Ellen's luxurious hospitality each night. Barberrys, the spacious house specially built for the Doubledays on prime coastal land with a panoramic view of Oyster Bay, was glamorous with Aubusson carpets, Louis XVI furniture and an impressive wood-panelled library. It was also a comfortable family home and the levels of luxury that Daphne, Tod and the children enjoyed there were a far cry from the chill and bareness of Menabilly. Daphne had never been a woman to pamper herself but there was something divine about warm scented baths, feather beds, delicious food brought on silver trays and civilised company (Noël Coward dropped in during her stay). 'I do adore fragrant, fragile, softness, for the simple reason, I think, that I've never had it … I could really go through life with a cake of soap and a toothbrush.'[10]

Ellen proved to be a compellingly attractive hostess and friend; the women would sit together at the end of a long day and talk. There appeared to be more confidences, however, flowing from Daphne to Ellen than in the opposite direction and when Daphne returned to England she realised how little she knew about the real woman she had embellished with her fantasies: 'I've told you everything about myself, you've told me nothing … stay well. Stay lovely.'[11]

In many ways it helped not to know too much about Ellen as Daphne's fantasy about her was so important she was disconcerted if real life intruded, at odds with the story. This meant Daphne was prescriptive about how Ellen should look – when they next met she asked her to wear her 'Mary Stuart dress', she hated her in trousers (Daphne's domain as the boy-suitor) and also told her not to perm her hair and what combs to wear.

The judge was eventually to pronounce that Daphne had no case to answer. When the trial was over, however, Daphne collapsed into bed, emotionally exhausted. In fact, she later believed she was close to a nervous breakdown. Her hostess's thoughtful ministrations triggered in her mind her lifelong hunger for a loving and sympathetic mother, and Ellen who had seemed to her both the siren Rebecca and the heroic Mary Queen of Scots, somehow fitted the bill now as her ideal mother, 'the mother I always wanted'.[12] Daphne wrote to Ellen, pointing out that she belonged to her as much as did Ellen's three children and claimed that somehow the spirit of Ellen's fourth and stillborn child had alighted on her: 'I'm your child, just the same.'[13] The idea, awkward as it might have been for Ellen, comforted Daphne. Early in their relationship Daphne described the effect on her of Muriel's antipathy to her as a child and then added, 'how distressing, if my desire to be with you at all moments of the day, is merely a sub-conscious thwarted longing to have sat on Mummy's lap at the age of two!!'[14] She recognised that the women who had obsessed her in life were psychically tied to her search for a mother-substitute. 'I have carried it [the dependence on Mother] for years, because of missing it, hence my "women" pegs,'[15] she explained to a writer friend.

Daphne was remarkably insightful about her own creative impulses and the problems they could cause in her life. She gave perhaps the best explanation to Foy Quiller-Couch, some years later, of the trans-formations she wrought on the characters of Christopher Puxley, Ellen, and later Gertrude Lawrence:

> The attributes of the living become mingled with the people we create. And then you project on to these 'pegs' attributes that are imaginary, so that the living person, when encountered, is no longer the character he or she once was, but becomes invested with the fictitious attribu-tions of the story. This can be vexing and sometimes a bit frightening![16]

This explained her adamant rejection of any sexual stereotyping of her impulses. Cornwall had always attracted artists and more than its fair share of people who felt they did not easily fit in with the main-stream of society. Daphne looked at Jeanne's and Angela's friends, some of whom were lesbian, and distanced herself from them, her obsession with particular women springing, she believed, from a completely different source:

Nobody could be more bored with all the 'L' people than I am. They either lie about in studios with dirty nails drinking brandy and painting bad pictures, or else they are incredibly hearty, wearing broad-brimmed hats, and breeding dogs. I like to think that my Jack-in-the-box was, and is, unique.[17]

Daphne resisted all her life any alignment with lesbianism, even while declaring her devotion for an idealised woman. She insisted her boy-self was something creative rather than carnal, an embodiment of freedom and adventure not of hot embraces, despite her romantic fantasies about kissing the beloved in the narratives she spun for herself. Having been an actress all her life, it was always for her about playing the boy with the sword, rather than the man/woman in the boudoir. It was more about the stimulation of her imagination and the satisfactions of power than the desires of the flesh.

In a heartfelt, headlong letter she explained to Ellen all the reasons why she had been so confounded when Ellen had first walked into her cabin. Daphne characterised her feelings as springing from her boy-self, the most creative and true part of her, suddenly finding imaginative and emotional expression after years of repression. This was something quite different, she insisted, from anything as run-of-the-mill as lesbianism. She saw herself instead as a 'half-breed': female on the outside but, in her heart, not a man but a romantic adolescent boy. It was an almost pantomime version of the Principal Boy. She longed to play the courageous protector, the heroic crusader. 'I want to ride out and fight dragons for you,' she wrote to Ellen, 'or else I want to conquer new worlds, and bring you the Holy Grail.'[18] Her imagined self was a character straight out of the historical romances she devoured as a girl. But she admitted that it was only the boy-in-the-box who was romantic, the woman in her as expressed in her erotic friendship with Christopher Puxley was 'hard and down-to-earth'.[19]

Ellen's reaction to Daphne's remarkable confession was inevitably disappointing. It was embarrassing to be the focus of a passion you could not return. It was burdensome being cast in a fantasy of heroic proportions when you were struggling to live in the present and all too aware of your failings. As a good prosaic woman, she could not appreciate the arcane nuances of what Daphne had been telling her. 'Your letter about the boy in the box didn't surprise me, dear,' Ellen wrote after nearly a month had elapsed since the confessional. She told Daphne she thought she had done exactly the right thing in suppressing her boy-self:

> a lifetime of that particular kind of love called by any name seems to me fated to frustration and deep inward unhappiness and you have been wise with your Jack-in-the-box, wise to look him in the face, control him, and not be ashamed of him. I am way out of my depth, of course, and probably not making one word of sense. Just put the whole thing down to my pre-1914 upbringing.[20]

Daphne thanked Ellen for her 'heavenly' and 'sweet' response to her revelation but was not deterred by her friend's obvious reluctance to engage. Wonderful words still flowed from her typewriter expressing a fluency of ideas, news and emotion. Far more letters winged their way across the Atlantic from Cornwall than returned in the opposite direction. But then this relationship with Ellen was always much more about Daphne and her life of the imagination than about Ellen.

In less than two weeks of intense writing in February 1948, Daphne finished her play *September Tide* (the working title was 'Mother'), inspired by this new flowering of emotion. She had been looking at a photograph Ellen had given her of a portrait of herself, and begun to fantasise about what she would have thought of the subject had she been the artist. From these seeds the play grew. Daphne set the play in Fowey, in a house much like Ferryside, where a beautiful widow, Stella, lives alone. When her daughter's artist husband falls in love with her as he paints her portrait at the house she was alarmed, then flattered and hopeful of another chance at love. Stella has to choose between fulfilling her own desires, thereby betraying her daughter, or settling for safety in a dull marriage to someone of her own genera-tion. As with her earlier play, *The Years Between*, the heroine follows the path of duty rather than of passion, although her ultimate deci-sion is left hanging in the air.

As Daphne based Stella on her idea of Ellen, both women knew that her artist son-in-law had a great deal of Daphne's manner and character. The conversation between them is quick-fire and brittle in a Cowardian way, with no real sense of love but more of an instantaneous, diverting attraction. As Daphne could not dedicate the play to Ellen by name, without people drawing comparisons and wondering about Ellen's relationship with her real son-in-law, Daphne decided on a more cryptic dedication that only the two of them would understand, but one that would also give inadvertent pleasure to Muriel. 'It is, as I say, dedicated To my Mother. And Mummy, who has never been called Mother by me in my life, will be so thrilled and happy, she has had nothing of mine dedicated to her, ever, it will delight her.'[21] It did not occur to Daphne that if people might have wondered about Ellen's relationship with her son-in-law, they would as likely wonder about Muriel's with Tommy. She also seemed unaware of Ellen's alarm that the character of Stella would be too closely associated with her.

When Ellen read it she was mightily relieved to find the likenesses between them were mostly in Daphne's imagination and that in reality there was little of herself in the character. Also rather deflatingly, she told Daphne she would never have contemplated a love affair with the artist son-in-law (whom Daphne had based on herself), who 'would have left me cold'.[22] If Daphne had been willing to listen to Ellen, this was the closest her polite and self-contained friend could come to telling her that she could not enter her romantic fantasy, and had no interest in playing along with the role Daphne had taken for herself.

In Daphne's mind, however, Stella was so psychologically important to her that when it came to cast the play she was filled with an agitated gloom at the impossibility of any actress embodying her vision. It was doubtful that even Ellen herself could have measured up to the part. But then, the real Ellen was not what interested Daphne, much more fascinating was her idea of the complete woman that Ellen conjured up in her mind. She knew she became obsessed by people who provided the spur to her imagination and recognised that it could be tedious, even alarming, for the real person on whom this artificial self was grafted. It made her question whether love was always somehow fabricated by need, 'don't think I ever had much [passion]; it was mostly imagination, clothing some unfortunate human being with my misguided fantasy'.[23]

The next person to be clothed with Daphne's fantasy was a woman much more used to make-believe than Ellen Doubleday could ever be. When Gertie Lawrence, Gerald's old flame, was eventually chosen to play the role of Stella, Daphne was at first horrified. Gertrude seemed so tawdry compared to the image she nurtured of Ellen, 'in your black and red Mary Stuart [dress] just sitting at the head of the dining-room table, completely poised, and still, radiating a sort of glow'. It made her almost physically sick to have Gertie on stage impersonating her. 'She looks, and is, or has been, a hardened dyed haired tart.'[24]

Quite quickly, however, her nostalgic du Maurier pulse started to quicken. The thrill of the theatre, the volatile expressiveness of theatre people excited her, for these were the people she had grown up with and this the atmosphere that drew her closer to her father. It was an atmosphere from which she had been exiled for so many years and which, she suddenly realised, she truly missed. Above all, Gertie reminded her of Gerald. She had always thought they were so similar, both pranksters, both insubstantial, fireflies in the stage lights, dancing as fast as they could to stop age and the glooms from overcoming them.

In fact, in a strange metamorphosis, Daphne began to behave like her father. When she went to Oxford for the play's opening night, she turned up laden with presents and flowers for every single member of the cast and a case of champagne, because that was just what he used to do. Much as Gerald would have done too, Daphne threatened to smack Gertie's bottom when she came upon her unexpectedly in her dressing room, dressed only in her underwear. She felt an overwhelming nostalgia for her childhood in which the theatre and her father loomed so large, 'like the sniff of brandy to an alcoholic. I hate it, and I love it, all in one.'[25] And Gertie's skill as an actress began to overcome Daphne's prejudices that she was not Ellen. Through the alchemy of the play, the magical atmosphere of the theatre, the imaginative pretence that characterised Daphne's life, Gertie became Ellen for that fleeting time on stage and her creator was overcome with emotion. To Ellen she wrote, 'every now and then, quite unconsciously, she gets an American inflexion in her voice, which gives me God's own nostalgia for you, so that I have to walk out of the theatre! … well, it might *be* you!'[26]

Daphne explained to Ellen that she had suddenly understood something her father had tried to explain to her for hours when she was a girl – the difference between women you marry and those with whom you have an affair and she could now see what her father had found so attractive about Gertie. She was obviously the kind of woman you did not marry, and what Daphne herself saw in Ellen, was the poised, deep, much-loved 'wife' figure. Gertie began to assume in Daphne's fertile imagination a more accessible and amusing contrast to Ellen, but somehow symbiotically attached to her through the part she played in *September Tide*. Combined with her intimate connection with Gerald, this made a strong psychic brew.

Daphne's frustrations that Ellen would not enter into her fantasy love affair began to be replaced by a make-believe game with Gertie, who was much better equipped to play. 'How much easier life would have been had you only been another sort of woman, beloved,' Daphne wrote to Ellen, 'but as you are not, and never will be, the only thing I can do is try not to think about it, but plunge into fantasy with someone who makes fantasies too. Which is cynical, and rather bloody-minded, I know, but one cant always be a hermit.'[27]

Fundamental to Gertie's character was not just her irrepressible sense of fun but also her voracious appetite for men. Even the waiter at lunch was a focus for her narcissistic ego. She was rampantly heterosexual, but was also a joker and an enthusiastic participant in any prank; perfectly happy to accommodate Daphne's kindnesses and concern, and to play along with her impersonation of Gerald. Daphne invited Gertie and her husband Richard Aldrich to spend Christmas at Menabilly, 'the sort of thing that Daddy would have done'.[28] She continued to imitate his way of dealing with leading ladies by meeting

Torosay Castle on the Isle of Mull, photographed by Angela from the famous Statue Walk when she was staying during the Second World War.

Olive Guthrie, laird of Torosay, with Impy her Pekinese, on the terrace of Torosay Castle overlooking Duart Bay, with fourteenth-century Duart Castle on the distant promontory.

Jeanne and the painter
Dod Procter.

Jeanne's lifetime partner,
the poet Noël Welch.

Jeanne with Angela's Pekinese Wendy among the sunflowers in her market garden at Pont, which she worked during the Second World War.

Jeanne (above) and Angela (right) helping to bring in the harvest during their war work in Cornwall.

Daphne studio portrait taken about 1949.

Angela with Angela Halliday's MG Midget car in which they were travelling (with Wendy the Peke) when involved in a serious car crash on their way to Scotland.

Cannon Hall in Hampstead, bought by Gerald at the height of his success as an actor-manager. It was the sisters' family home until he died in 1934.

Menabilly, the house Daphne loved and eventually leased and lived in with her family. The main inspiration for *Rebecca*'s Manderley and the storyline of *The King's General*.

Lieutenant-General Frederick 'Boy' Browning in 1944. Twelve years earlier Daphne had asked him to marry her less than ten weeks after they first met. A decorated war hero of both world wars, he was known to Daphne and his family as 'Tommy' and later nicknamed 'Moper' by her.

Daphne and Tommy with their children (from left) Kits, Tessa and Flavia Browning, in front of Menabilly in the autumn of 1944.

Ellen Doubleday, wife of Angela's and Daphne's US publisher and Daphne's creative obsession, confidante and friend.

Daphne meeting Gertrude Lawrence at Waterloo from the *Mauretania* boat train when she returned to England from New York in 1948 to star in Daphne's play *September Tide*, in the part inspired by Ellen Doubleday.

Maud 'Tod' Waddell sketching. Governess to the du Maurier sisters and later to Daphne's children, she was redoubtable, adventurous, loyal, and loved Daphne from when she first met her as a girl of eleven until Tod's own death sixty-four years later (at the age of ninety-five).

Daphne rowing across Fowey harbour to Ferryside.

Gertie for dinner and drinks at the Savoy and buying her presents from Cartier.

To Daphne's disappointment, Gertie decided at the last moment not to come to Menabilly as the weather was so cold (and perhaps she knew the house would be arctic) but Daphne's family were much relieved, especially Angela and Muriel who had complained that they did not really know her well (and Muriel may have felt she did not really want to be on too intimate terms). While Daphne's obsession with Ellen was in transition, as Gertie moved into the frame, news reached her of Nelson Doubleday's death. She was able to write some remarkable letters of comfort to Ellen, for a while forgetting her own needs. She had so wanted to practise being less selfish in her relationship with her friend and had grasped her opportunity in the summer of 1948 when Nelson was deathly ill and facing an operation.

She had decided to overcome her fear of flying and take the plane with Tommy to New York to offer her services to Ellen, promising she was there solely to support her and 'would'nt worry you with nonsense'. She had wanted just to sit silently beside her as she suffered, but couldn't resist making her own emotional demands and felt sorry afterwards and wrote to apologise. Daphne had been thinking about Ellen's suggestion that she was starved of love. On the contrary, she had insisted, she had 'all the affection in the world', from Tommy and the children and from Christopher Puxley too, but she felt she was 'taking from them all the time, and I don't want to take, I want to give'.[29]

Daphne was in fact capable of acts of great generosity and unselfishness to those within her inner circle of friends and family. In early 1949, when a big royalty cheque arrived, she gave £500 to Margaret the nanny to help her set up a business and £500 to her mother-in-law, and the same amount to a friend who was in need; all substantial amounts of money at the time. However, when in the grip of an obsession she could be blind to others and consumed by her own needs. Daphne never lost the sense that she was an actress in the play of her own life, always watching herself from the wings. She really liked the idea that she had an almost superhuman power to affect others: her beauty and wit had always drawn people into her orbit and having money to dispense to those close to her helped bolster this power.

Daphne believed, as she told Ellen, that when Nelson rallied for a while it was the force of her own will and prayers that effected the improvement. Seeing Ellen's real care for her husband, even through the trials of illness, depression and alcoholism, made Daphne think about her relationship with Tommy and admit that she could not offer him the same kind of selfless love. 'Perhaps that really is the answer,' she wrote to Ellen, 'you *are* a complete woman, and I have never been, I've only put up an act at being one, and got away with it because I was an actor's daughter.'[30]

Being an actor's daughter certainly meant the theatrical world was somewhere Daphne felt at home, and her growing fascination with Gertie and her familiar chameleon qualities was rewarded by the actress's own infinite sense of fun and capacity for make-believe. Daphne had been so long away from London theatre life, had lost touch with the energy that had suffused her childhood and animated her father, that now, reminded through Gertie and the cast of *September Tide*, she embarked on another novel to keep this rediscovered excitement alive. She decided to follow the lives and characters of three step and half siblings of a theatrical family, the Delaneys, and called her book *The Parasites*.

In this novel, the main characters were an actress Maria, a composer son Niall and an artist Celia, all aspects of her own self, she admitted, and very revealing of her feelings at the time. There were also shades of other people who mattered in her life. Gerald was strongly present in the lachrymose Pappy Delaney, Muriel in Mama (who was quickly killed off in a nasty accident), Niall was her boy-self combined with Christopher Puxley, whom Daphne had thought of as a kind of fated twin, and Gertie's histrionic energy partly inspired Maria. Even Daphne's idea of Ellen could be found in the nurturing, self-sacrificing side of Celia who gave herself up to nursing Pappy for years, as Ellen did Nelson (and indeed as did her sister Jeanne, neglecting her painting for her dutiful war work and care of their mother).

Daphne was aware how marriage, motherhood and money had protected her from the real hard labour that other women were engaged in during the war and how she, and even Angela, had been relatively free to pursue their love affairs and writing while others, like their friend Angela Halliday, risked their lives. The fighting men too: how different were their experiences from those who stayed behind. Early in the story, Maria's war-hero husband Charles, whom she finds dull, rounds on them all with contempt and exasperation. He accuses them of being like parasites feeding off the lifeblood of others:

> You always have been and you always will be. Nothing can change you. You are doubly, triply parasitic; first, because you've traded ever since childhood on that seed of talent you had the luck to inherit from your fantastic forebears; secondly, because you've none of you done a stroke of ordinary honest work in your lives, but batten upon us, the fool public who allow you to exist; and thirdly, because you prey upon each other, the three of you, living in a world of fantasy which you have created for yourselves and which bears no relation to anything in heaven or on earth.[31]

Daphne's writing hut had been delivered to Menabilly and here she could work in the garden, sealed off even from the life of the house, itself protected from the outside world by deep woods and distance. Her imaginative life and the people she created were given full rein, hardly impinged on by real people and the everyday life that surged beyond her door. She enjoyed writing *The Parasites* and indeed it had some wonderfully funny parts to it, not least when 'those dreadful Delaneys' spent a weekend with Charles Wyndham's conventional aristocratic family, with some sharply observed clashes in culture: 'To see Pappy at Coldhammer [the Wyndhams' country house] would be like wandering into the bishop's rose garden and coming suddenly upon the naked Jove.'[32] In the book Daphne explored one of her favourite themes, that of emotional incest within a family. She developed the intensity of Maria's relationship with her stepbrother Niall, who ended the book in a leaky boat without a pump, calmly contemplating death, the ocean as welcoming as a maternal lap.

Within the isolation of the hut, Daphne lived out in her imagination her unrequited passion for Ellen and her flirtation with Gertie and the dramaturgical world of her childhood. Clear-sighted and highly analytic, she reported to Ellen the flights of her fancy and the beatings of her heart. These letters were mostly light-hearted, bursting with wit and ideas, but sometimes angry and bitter with frustration at Ellen's lack of response. Yet, even at her most self-centred, even as she railed, at times with real venom, against Ellen's restraint, Daphne did not lose completely her sense of humour or her fundamentally generous spirit.

She wrote to Gertie too but, however much fun she was in person and game for anything, Gertie's letters in return did nothing to fuel the fantasy. For a start, she gave Daphne the nickname 'Dum'. Like many nicknames it brought more amusement to the giver than the receiver. Daphne was not amused and never used it in return; even though she was to Gertie always 'Darling Dum' this did not fit with the heroic boy she liked to play to Gertie's eternal girl. Gertie also had her secretary, Evie Williams, type her letters and they were mostly short, jokey, practical and completely lacking in intimacy. Daphne described them to Ellen as, 'all perfectly harmless',[33] and added that they had been burnt because she never kept letters except from her children and closest family. Daphne's letters to Gertrude were a different matter and after Gertie's death her formidable business manager Fanny Holtzmann assured Daphne, with some menace, that they 'were all under lock and key'.

In the flesh, however, Gertie was always a most flirtatious and playful creature, willing to embark on any reckless adventure. On one occasion when Daphne spent a weekend with her in Florida in November 1950, the relationship moved fleetingly into a different phase, for Daphne at least. She had visited Ellen first and had been feeling for some time the pain of being more in need of Ellen's affection than Ellen was of hers. Daphne liked to be powerful and Ellen's evident self-containment and unwillingness to enter into her games undermined her sense of control. Gertie and the sunshine of Florida beckoned and fooling about on the beach with her made Daphne feel like a girl again. It was fun to be with someone who, although older and not in the best of health, always seemed so much younger than she was, more uninhibited and at ease with her own physical self. 'We giggled like a couple of school-girls over everything and everybody,'[34] Daphne related to Gertie's secretary Evie Williams.

Sex for Gertie was always about men and an almost neurotic need for affirmation of her attractiveness and youth. However, amongst all this girlish larking about and in a moment of amused generosity it seemed that Gertrude invited Daphne into her bed and they kissed and possibly more. Then as Daphne left later that night, Gertie said rather dramatically: 'Go from me, and don't look back, like a person walking in their sleep'[35] – words Daphne gave the mysterious murderess in her short story, 'Kiss Me Again, Stranger'.

Being allowed into Gertie's arms without embarrassment or demur meant that for the first time Daphne felt truly accepted for who she was, without artifice or pretence, without judgement or categorisation. It never happened again but at the time it seemed transformative to her, mixed up as it was with her feelings for Ellen, her father, her lack of mother love, nostalgia for the theatrical way of life, but mostly her creative impulse and the imperative of work.

Always so aware of her own feelings, Daphne tried to explain to Ellen what had happened, showing remarkable insight and tenderness towards herself and the two very different women who dominated her dreams at the time:

It's all mixed up, with you. (Not your fault, darling) *But* if there had never been a *September Tide*, I would not have seen [Gertie], in fantasy, as doing what I wanted you to do, or started the gay, happy friendship ['gay' in general usage still meant carefree]. *But* for the knowledge that you really could'nt be what I wanted you to be, I would never have gone on that Florida week-end; and so become beguiled, and bewitched. (Nothing, except gay flirtation, had ever happened before that.) No regrets. It was such fun, and so happy, and so entrancing. Never sordid. I suppose, cold-bloodedly, you could say 'Two lonely people getting rid of inhibitions.' … The odd thing is, once you have loved a person physically, it makes the strangest bond. (I suppose not always, No sometimes, I think it could mean nothing, like playing tennis.) In this case, it did mean a lot. I could'nt talk to her, you know, like I can to you, or have the peace, that you give, (or the fever either!)

but there was so much warmth there and generosity of giving … there was a mutual language. Something all mixed up with theatre and writing. Knowing only that, and 'work', were what mattered most.[36]

Daphne loved Ellen but she was as emotionally inaccessible to her as was Muriel. 'How I wish there was a chink somewhere in the armour plating of the Iron Curtain,'[37] she wrote to her. Worse still, Daphne feared her demands for attention and love were sometimes tedious to Ellen. That thought was humiliating in the extreme to someone who was proud and liked always to have the upper hand. However, becoming involved with the theatre again, being reminded what it was to feel young and light-hearted with Gertie, reconnecting to her father and her du Maurier roots, had revivified Daphne. During the few years she was juggling her romances with Ellen and Gertie, her imagination was alive and her creative energies were at full throttle. She finished *The Parasites* and, although the critics were once more lukewarm, Gertie loved it and immediately wanted to play Maria in a musical or some kind of theatrical production.

This thought excited Daphne too, just as Ellen had been the prototype for Mother in *September Tide*, so Gertie, intermixed with her own actress self, was the impulse for Maria. Almost immediately Ellen was used once more as the imaginative spur for another work, but this time it would be *My Cousin Rachel*, Daphne's masterpiece written at the peak of her powers. In this, her narrator, Philip, is male, with much of Daphne in his character – as both she and Ellen admitted – and in thrall to a woman who is the irresistible centrifugal force of the book. Daphne wrote to Ellen: 'The reader never quite knows if she is loving, and warm, and human; or the most cold-blooded designing bitch ever born … I may add that Rachel will be a widow. And I *dont* want a libel case on my hands.'[38]

In a burst of creative energy in the autumn of 1950, Daphne had sketched out the whole book, making notes for each chapter, as she had done for *Rebecca*, but this time it only took her five to six days. She skipped off to America in November and, excited and liberated by her escapade with Gertie in Florida, returned fired up with the idea. After Christmas, and in the bleakest weather, she set to with a will, going daily to her hut to work with a dedication that was 'almost trappist', and wrote just under 60,000 words in less than four weeks.

Daphne was completely absorbed and enthralled by the new world she had created and wrote to Ellen that it was as exciting as falling in love, although, as with any new love affair, the thrill of writing each novel ended up being fundamentally the same. She was interested to see that she had made Rachel much nastier in her notebook, 'but in the writing of the novel [I] turned myself so completely into Philip, that I was beguiled, and she could have poisoned the entire world, I would not have minded. Besides, I dont think she did. She merely "impelled" disaster!'[39]

Atmospheric, suspenseful, brilliantly plotted, the book was a terrific success and the critics, particularly in America, hailed it as an improvement even on the mighty *Rebecca*. Everyone was intrigued by the disarming character of Rachel, and baffled as to whether she was sinned against or sinning. Film rights were quickly auctioned. Gertie Lawrence dashed off one of her characteristic notes, fizzing with energy:

> My darling Dum,
>   So very thrilled about your book and its film sale – wish I could do your kind of job in blue jeans and in privacy and make so much dough!!![40]

Twentieth Century Fox were the successful bidders and Daphne hoped that Greta Garbo might play Rachel, aware that this would upset Gertie who fancied the part for herself. Even Vivien Leigh, Daphne thought, would be better than the distinctly 'un-menacing' Olivia de Havilland, who eventually landed the role. Daphne got her way with the casting of Philip who was played to brooding effect by a young Richard Burton. The film appalled her. She thought that Olivia de Havilland looked like the Duchess of Windsor, and Flavia thought she looked like Mrs Doubleday, which gave Daphne (and Tommy, she said) pause for thought.

Daphne was surprisingly modest about the huge success, the fame and fortune her writing career brought her. She put various book and film incomes into trusts for each of her children and then barely ever looked back on her work but ploughed on to the next. The most important thing in her life after Menabilly was her creative flame and the ability to conjure up imaginary worlds in which she felt most at home. She was terrified that she might lose her remarkable capacity for building characters and castles out of air. To be prevented from inhabiting these alternative kingdoms of the mind would be worse than death.

In *My Cousin Rachel* she so closely identified Ellen with Rachel that when she killed off her fictional character, her obsession with Ellen died too, leaving just a warm friendship. Some ten years later, she looked back on it with better understanding of her creative impulse: 'When I had that (to me, rather silly, now!) "thing" about Ellen, which was pure Gondal [make-believe], it was only by making up *My Cousin Rachel*, and pegging the Rachel woman on to her, and making her die, that I was able to rid myself of it.'[41] But in the loss of obsession and the powerful fantasy element of this important relationship, Daphne lost some of her creative energy too.

The triumph of the book and the cooling of her romance over Ellen was quickly followed by Gertie's unexpected death on 6 September 1952, while performing in the huge Broadway success *The King and I*. It stunned Daphne. Gertie had represented such a powerful combination of emotions, implicating Daphne's sense of identity and her whole visionary spirit, that her death seemed for a time to have deprived her of the energy to live. Her family could not understand why she collapsed into such a trough of grief, after all, Gertie was a middle-aged actress who had been more of a friend to Gerald, it seemed, than to his daughter. What they could not know was that being with Gertie, with her appetite for life and childish sense of fun and her acceptance of whatever came her way, had liberated Daphne and filled her with inventive energy. Gertie had reconnected her to her father and her theatrical past and made her feel less alone. She was also, most powerfully, a spur to her imagination:

She was *not* a person who had filled my whole life … but a Peg, and a lovely illusion. The Peg had become so vital, and so mixed up with writing, that I felt for the time being, there was nothing left in life at all. The writing had gone too. Rock bottom.[42]

This creative dependence on people as 'pegs' for her imaginary characters, fascinated her and in a sense the loss of inspiration, the death of a muse was more devastating than the loss of any real person: 'I was quite *bouleversée* by [Gertie's] death; not because how sad a friend had died, but how bottomless – a Peg had vanished! A fabric that one had built disintegrated!'[43] Perhaps Daphne's overwhelming grief was made all the sharper as, with Gertie gone, she mourned her father in a much deeper way than she had managed to do at his death. By her own reckoning it was four years of despondency and creative dearth before she really began to be able to escape into her imagination again.

During the end of the war in Fowey, Angela had met the last love in her life, one that was to last for the next four decades. She turned forty on 1 March 1944 and had been dreading the coming decade with its sense of love lost and a life half-lived. 'Forty,' she thought, 'has an ugly sound.' But in the month of that birthday she began the love affair with Anne Treffry that would sustain them both almost to death. Life suddenly seemed full of promise again. 'Lots of strange things can happen in wartime,' she wrote cheerfully in her memoir, 'forty wasn't so dusty, as my father would have said.'[44]

Like Olive Guthrie, Anne Treffry was a remarkable woman who had been widowed young. She was the mother of four children and the matriarch of the family who owned half of Fowey, many local farms and the harbour at Par, along with Place House, their stately home in the centre of Fowey itself. Anne was thirteen years older than Angela and had great presence and elegance. Even as the family's fortunes declined in the postwar period, she was surrounded by beautiful things and lived her life with style. Her house was full of flowers, her clothes were of the finest quality and her leather gloves were sent for cleaning all the way to Scotland, to Perth, the only place that could be trusted to do the job properly.

All her life, Angela was drawn to mother figures, declaring: 'I have never thought that age should be taken into account where friendship is concerned. I have always had friends far older than myself.' She certainly felt privileged by Anne's friendship, telling a friend: 'I am in love with a very grand lady.'[45] To Marda Vanne she wrote with some exuberance: 'My new & greatest & – (pray God) – for-all-time Love … is 13 years older than me & complete & utter heaven, & it's the biggest thing that's ever been.'[46] Anne Treffry may have been grand, but she was also kind and immensely capable. The two women would set off in the car for holidays abroad, driving great distances across Europe with hardly a care. When quite elderly, they once drove to Madrid simply to visit the art galleries there.

This friendship enlivened what Angela considered her 'Aunt Jessie years'. She and Anne saw each other every day, Angela more often than not rowing herself across the river from Ferryside to Fowey, often for lunch. When they did not meet then they would telephone. Angela told Marda she was not writing novels but instead was as love-sick as a teenager, 'I wait for the telephone. And the ferry. And "all that & heaven too"'. Angela felt that instead of waiting on tenterhooks for her new friend to call she really ought to get on with writing another book, but her old health problems were troubling her: 'my inside is misbehaving v. badly [it would turn out to be fibroids]'. She decided to make a bonfire of 'every love letter I've ever had, & all the letters everyone has ever written me, but there was one person's I couldn't do away with; yours'.[47] These were the letters Marda sent to Angela once she and Gwen had gone to South Africa at the start of the war to try and set up a national theatre there.

In 1945, Anne Treffry's daughter, Pamela, probably prompted by her mother, asked Angela to be godmother to her daughter Fiona. As an unmarried woman without children of her own, Angela was godmother to a number of children and was conscientious in keeping up with them, collecting their photographs for her album, and remembering their birthdays. She told a friend, Betty Williams, that not having children herself was a lifelong regret, although as she grew older the young people she knew did not feel she was a naturally maternal type. She could be alternatively scary and stern, or full of fun, and rather like her father it was never quite clear which Angela would be to the fore.

The happy routine of Angela and Anne's relationship was rocked some nine years in by another redoubtable Cornish grandee, Lady Clara Vyvyan, the great plantswoman, explorer and travel writer. She had introduced Daphne to Frenchman's Creek, a part of the coast on her estate at Trelowarren, and had also accompanied her on a most enjoyable rambling holiday in Switzerland. Eccentric looking ('like an old gypsy' Daphne thought) and much loved, Lady Vyvyan upset Angela by staying with Anne Treffry at Place House and conceiving 'a fearful passion for her'. Angela was distraught and sought Daphne's shoulder to cry on. Anne was light-hearted and amused, 'behaving in an irritating rather laughing way', as Daphne reported to Ellen. In distress, Angela accused Anne of encouraging Lady Vyvyan, something Anne denied and casually tossed aside.

Daphne seems to have been the confidante for both sides of the jealous triangle, for not only did Angela ask her advice but Lady Vyvyan unburdened herself to her on a long walk on the cliffs. Lady Vyvyan, who was well into her sixties by then, felt she had 'treasures of riches' to offer Anne, whom she thought had 'un-plumbed depths'. Daphne was highly amused and attempted to dampen Lady Vyvyan's enthusiasm, for, as she commented to Ellen, 'if [Lady V] tries to plumb them there'll be murder from Angela'. Daphne recognised that although she took her own emotional struggles extremely seriously, she was highly entertained by the travails of others. Her sense of humour, like her father's, could be casually barbed. 'Have you got unplumbed depths, darling?' she extended the joke to express her frustrations with Ellen: 'somehow I don't think you have. I guess I know what there is in you to plumb, and that's a crumb [something small that is magnified by the recipient], if ever there was one!'[48]

Angela survived that scare and her friendship with Anne continued, with excursions to London, where theatre, concerts and ballet filled their afternoons and evenings, and trips together abroad. Angela and Muriel had decided to make their home permanently at Ferryside in Cornwall. This meant selling their London house, Providence Corner, in what was an emotional wrench as they cut physical and spiritual ties with Hampstead, their home for so long and the place that had meant so much to Gerald and his father.

Postwar London depressed Angela. She found it bomb-shattered, dirty and swarming with people who did not speak English. Distressing too was the relaxing of standards that for her made life civilised. She and Anne had booked seats in the stalls at Covent Garden to see *Sleeping Beauty* with Margot Fonteyn. The Queen was there and Angela and Anne were in full evening dress. To her dismay they were practically the only couple in expensive seats to have bothered to dress up; everyone else was in day clothes and some women even had shopping bags under their seats. The democratisation of the arts had begun and this self-confessed old-fashioned du Maurier, who remembered with nostalgia the grand occasions of her father's day, was not impressed.

Music and theatre in London flourished in the postwar years and Angela, always the most expressive and theatrical of the three sisters, was often brought to tears by the magnificent performances of family friends such as Laurence Olivier and John Gielgud. Gwen Ffrangcon-Davies, who with Marda Vanne had been away most of the war helping establish the National Theatre of South Africa, returned to the London stage as the Queen Mother of Persia in Terence Rattigan's *Adventure Story*. It was thought by the critics to be rather an over-ambitious play but it launched Paul Scofield, as a terrific Alexander the Great, and Gwen gave her usual exquisite performance. Angela was so moved that she could not stop crying in the dressing room afterwards and even burst into tears again at the Caprice Restaurant where she and Gwen went for a late drink and chat.

The end of the war was also the end of another great love, for Olive Guthrie died unexpectedly in July 1945. Angela's grief was compounded by the guilt of having abandoned her in the last year or so of her life while she pursued her affair with Anne. She had travelled up to Torosay to stay for the last time in October 1944 in order to tell her about Anne, and Olive was devastated by the news. 'I went up for a disastrous holiday in Mull 2 months ago,' she confided to Marda, '&

have never been so miserable in my life. This new [love affair] started last March. I'd *hoped* O. would take it philosophically but I had a ghastly time,'[49] as no doubt did Olive too.

Olive lived less than nine months after this painful rift with Angela. Her daughters, who had found Angela's relationship with their mother hard to accept, generously kept her up-to-date on Olive's progress and then her sudden shocking death after only two days' illness. Angela for the last time boarded the sleeper that had in the past promised so much happiness. This time she hurried north to Torosay with a stricken heart. After a full day and a night's travelling she arrived in pouring rain to hear the lament of the bagpipes keening through the sodden air. Out of the rain and mist came many hundreds of mourners, weaving their way up to the great granite cross that marked Olive's husband's grave. Crying uncontrollably, Angela watched as the ashes of 'the most remarkable woman I ever knew' were interred alongside Murray Guthrie's on Torosay's most easterly shore, 'looking forever to Loch Linnhe, Ben Nevis and the rising sun'.[50]

Olive's flamboyant nephew, the diplomat, author and supporter of Irish Home Rule, Sir Shane Leslie, wrote Angela a letter of heartfelt condolence, honouring her relationship with his much-loved aunt. Angela's reply was emotional and candid. She felt she had treated Olive badly in that last year and was filled with bitter remorse:

> I miss her terribly … I miss our more or less daily letters to each other so much. Certainly the years we gave each other were the happiest of my life, & I only pray that from 1938 to 1944 made up to her in happiness the disappointment I caused her from then until she died. I tell you this because I loved her v. much, & because I did I could not let you think me better than I was.[51]

The end of the war also brought Angela work that she enjoyed. For about three years she was employed in the Women's Land Army as a welfare worker. She said that the only reason she agreed to do it was for the coupons she would then be entitled to use for car tyres and petrol; the freedom her small car afforded her was worth any privation. Nevertheless she found the work interesting: getting to know something of the everyday lives of ordinary young women, whom she visited every month, listening to their troubles and trying to mediate between them and the farmers for whom they worked. She was confronted with how people working full time on the land really lived; sometimes it was not comfortable, but she enjoyed doing what she could to help.

Angela's fifth novel, *Lawrence Vane*, was finally published in 1946. She had so hoped that Olive might have been able to read the proofs as she had been encouraging of her writing all along and was enthusiastic about the idea, 'but then she always was where I was concerned'.[52] Angela thrived on appreciation and she did not really expect it from her own family, where Daphne was so much more successful and could be critical, and Muriel refused to read her daughters' books. Michael Joseph, her nurturing publisher, had now retired and it was a disappointment when his successor, Robert Lusty, turned down the manuscript. Luckily her cousin, Peter Davies, who had his own publishing house, generously agreed to take it on.

Again its theme was controversial for the times, and Angela had high hopes that it too could be filmed. She felt, however, that as it dealt with a white woman in an erotic relationship with a dark-skinned man (he was half-Indian) it might be hindered by prejudice, 'people were a great deal more squeamish over the subject than they are today [1966]'.[53] Her heroine, Lawrence Vane, with the oddly masculine name, is an ambitious concert pianist of world renown who has sacrificed her personal life for her art. After a car crash deprives her of sight and the use of her right hand, her life appears to be over. However, she has a persistent penpal, Paul Carron, who professes to love her and lives as the lord of all he surveys on an exotic Indian island. The book's drama turns on a rather heavy-handed exposition of racial prejudice in the English towards anyone of mixed race. Racism is also expressed by Paul Carron himself, the child of an Indian mother and a white father, towards anyone who is darker-skinned than himself.

At the time Angela was writing, English high society was perfectly happy to tolerate black entertainers, but it punished anyone, as happened with the renowned cabaret singer Leslie Hutchinson, who had the temerity to fraternise with their aristocratic women. Racial prejudice was most marked in fear of the sexual black male, as one of Angela's characters put it: 'There's something so much worse in a white woman marrying a coloured man, than a white man marrying a coloured woman'; such a relationship was 'perfectly foul'.[54]

The du Maurier sisters probably shared their class's uneasiness with mixed marriages. In a blustery note to Ellen about unorthodox love, Daphne, far from being a retrogressive conservative herself, wrote, 'People can fall in love with goats, if it makes them happy. But I think to be promiscuous is unattractive, and I draw the line at colour.'[55] It was likely that Angela felt the same way, for in her novel her heroine can overcome her initial recoil from intimacy with black people by being, literally, blind. Rather bizarrely, the only way she can continue to love her dark-skinned husband is to deliberately spoil the operation that would have restored her sight. Lawrence's willed blindness is a result of racial prejudice, for only in this way can she continue to make love to him without facing the problem of his colour. From a modern perspective, there is little sense to this central theme unless to be black-skinned is an equal disadvantage to being blind and Lawrence Vane, in seeking to save her marriage, redresses the balance of her 'superiority' of skin colour by blinding herself for the second time.

Although her device of wilful blindness allowed Angela to muffle the full impact of interracial marriage in her novel, once again she had displayed her boldness in handling a subject that was still considered generally distasteful, if not criminal. Certainly in America at the time the majority of the states had anti-miscegenation laws that criminalised marriage, even sexual activity, between whites and blacks, with the threat of imprisonment hanging over aberrant lovers. It took until 1967 before the United States Supreme Court ruled that all anti-miscegenation laws were unconstitutional. In England there was no similar law, however suspicion of mixed marriages and 'half-caste' children, as they were called, was ingrained in much of the populace. Fear and prejudice usually went unchallenged. Not even the shocking evidence at the end of the war as to the extremes that the

Nazis went in their pursuit of racial purity prevented the average man and woman in the street from recoiling at marriages between white English women and black men.

Doubleday stood by Angela and published the book in America, to lukewarm reviews. Kirkus thought it an overwritten melodrama with 'plush' prose, but it went to a second edition in England and Angela was proud enough of it and, like all her books, could imagine it brought to life on the screen, if only … It was, however, the last book of hers to find an American publisher and this added to her sense of being underappreciated. Thanks to her natural optimism, she took Daphne's past criticism seriously and started to compile a collection of short stories, that would be published in 1948 as *Birkinshaw and Other Stories*. In these Angela tried to reproduce her sister's distinctive, disenchanted view of the world and human relations, but she lacked her imaginative power, stylistic touch and feel for atmosphere, and they too often ended up leaden and uninvolving. However, 'The Nun' was written from the heart and, lacking the synthetic cynicism of the others, worked as a poignant study in love lost when two women are torn apart by a bargain made with God.

When Marda arrived back from South Africa in 1948, more than ten years had elapsed since the height of her love affair with Angela. No longer Marda's 'young lady', Angela was now a long-standing friend. When they met again one September evening on the platform at Lostwithiel station, they fell into each other's arms and realised that 'no years can destroy true friendship'.[56] Marda stayed at Ferryside and before she had left had arranged for Jeanne to spend the winter in Basutoland and South Africa's Cape Province to try and recover from the virus that had attacked her and weakened her voice during her last winter in Tenerife.

Marda also caused quite a stir in the hearts and minds of the du Maurier sisters. Jeanne was struck by her openness and the ease of conversation with her about both women's difficult emotional relationships at the time. She wrote to her with some amazement that she could confide so easily in her, but 'it does seem quite reasonable to want to write or Talk with you, after so few meetings, quite so frankly'.[57] Daphne too was affected by Marda and used her unusual name in her remarkable short story 'The Blue Lenses', about a woman who could see people as they really were – an acknowledgement perhaps of Marda's clear-eyed truth-telling that cut through the artifice of so much of English polite society.

By the middle of 1946, when Jeanne was thirty-five, she finally escaped her horticultural duties and left Ferryside to take up her artist's life with a studio in St Ives. During her years of hard labour and care of a demanding mother, she had longed for the time and energy to paint and now at last could revel in the freedom to be an artist among other artists, in one of the most exciting creative colonies in England.

She had exhibited in the St Ives Society of Artists' autumn show, an event opened by her mother. At one open day at her studio the following spring, Jeanne exhibited a self-portrait that was praised for 'its bigness of style and directness of touch'.[58] It was here that Dod Procter wandered in, liked what she saw and asked Jeanne if she would sit for her as she would like to paint her. From that point on Jeanne and Dod forged a close emotional and creative relationship.

Dod was more than twenty years older than Jeanne and, for a time, just before the war, had been the most famous woman artist in the country. She liked to paint tender sculptural portraits of young girls and women and her nudes were so real they sometimes shocked and courted controversy.

Morning, a monumental painting of hers that was hung in the Royal Academy Summer Show of 1927, so caught everyone's imagination that the *Daily Mail* decided to buy it for the nation. Suddenly, her portrait of this sturdy young goddess asleep on her rumpled bed was hailed not only as the best painting in the show but a huge popular hit with critics and public alike. *The Times* celebrated it as, 'no artificial composition reeking of the studio, but a fragment of life, nobly seen and simply stated … a creative design of compelling power and beauty for all who have eyes to see'.[59] And people clamoured to see it: every town with any pretensions to a gallery wanted to be able to display it and it toured for two years. The young daughter of a

Newlyn fisherman, Cissie Barnes, was only nineteen when she modelled for the painting and she too became almost as famous as the artist.

Dod revelled in the attention, after all she was in her late thirties when fame struck and had worked hard for decades for this kind of recognition. She loved parties and was herself a good-looking, light-boned woman, 'swift and active like a gazelle',[60] completely open about her driving ambition and confident of the excellence of her work. Dod had been widowed in 1935 when her painter husband Ernest Procter died when she was just forty-five. In 1942 she became only the second woman to be elected as an academician to the Royal Academy. She could not have been a better role model and friend for the younger more diffident Jeanne.

Dod invited Jeanne to spend their first winter travelling and working together in Tenerife. It had become for her a favourite destination of warmth and dazzling light and a refuge from the cold dark days at home. Now in the company of a virtuoso painter, Jeanne too experienced the thrill of brilliant colour and beguiling scents, the intensity of heat and the pleasures of the senses, and so embraced a more adventurous style and a high-toned palette. She now entered a bold new world where colour and light and love mattered more to her than form.

11

A Kind of Reckoning

> This is the only answer, then, to be alone. This is the ultimate reply.
> Dependent upon no soul but your own self. Dependent upon the
> sounds that flood the mind. Creator of your world, your universe.
>
> DAPHNE DU MAURIER, *The Parasites*

DAPHNE'S IMAGINATION WAS extraordinarily alive, spinning compelling narratives from a glimpse of someone's life or a moment plucked from the passing show. It was not just people whom she cloaked in make-believe, she did the same to her chosen house. Indeed the possessive love she felt for Menabilly rivalled what she felt for any living creature: she knew that Tommy not only found the house cold and uncomfortable in winter but was jealous of the place it had in her heart. 'No one realises that I have been in love, literally in love, with Menabilly for twenty years … I don't want any other house, ever … I think if I ever do go I shall burn it down behind me so that no one else shall have it,' she explained to Ellen whose love of Barberrys, the main Doubleday house, Daphne categorised as being circumstantial, made by happy memories of her family and her husband Nelson. Daphne felt her impulse was quite different:

> Mine with Menabilly is entirely possessive and personal. I wanted it
> for years, and got it, and had no associations with it whatsoever except
> those that came out of my imagination. When I consider

303

it impersonally I realise it is quite a dreary old house, lived in for centuries by quite dreary people, and possibly had no character at all, until I gave it one.[1]

She might have said the same about all the obsessions of her life – thrilling while they lasted, precious spurs to her creative imagination, and yet ultimately disappointing as daylight entered and pretence gave way to reality. Daphne thought that her heightened creative imagination was allied to sexuality, that somehow she sublimated her sexual energy into the fabrication of characters and worlds that she could inhabit for a while, ecstatic at her power of creation and control. But with the menopause came fading powers. Not only did inspiration seem to flee but Daphne even felt the grip of Menabilly loosened with the completion of *My Cousin Rachel*. Autumn and winter there depressed her, she told Ellen, and she became restless, 'such a longing for the unknown, for something – but what, God knows'.[2]

Her children were growing up and after some years being tutored by Tod had gone to boarding school, Tessa with pleasure as she was happy to have friends and be part of a wider world and Flavia with more ambivalence for, unlike Tessa, she loved the atmosphere and ghosts of Menabilly and was less well-equipped for the rough and tumble of life outside. Both girls had childhoods that were unhappy in different ways. It could not have been a more different upbringing from the one the du Maurier sisters enjoyed. The elder generation had been brought up in an elite London theatrical crowd, surrounded by people and glamorous organised activities. There had not been many children to play with but a constant stream of beautiful adults had passed through their house, and first nights, meals at the Savoy and theatrical parties were almost weekly occurrences.

Menabilly was as far away from Hampstead and the theatrical life as it was possible to be. It was Daphne's enchanted castle, fortified from the outside world where she could pursue her dreams undistracted by real life; it was a place of magic and adventure for Flavia and Kits, but to Tessa it was more like an island concealed within its deep and ancient woods, inward looking, where outsiders were not welcome. Tessa was driven to despair by the isolation and once told

Flavia that all she remembered of her childhood at Menabilly was 'the cold, the hunger and the wretched rats; and I suppose you could add loneliness'.[3] In getting away to school she discovered friends and later just how attractive she was to young men and how much fun there was to be had. Flavia was the most disregarded in the family: neither the eldest, praised for her looks, nor the son and heir. And even when she was eventually sent to boarding school it was almost on a whim of her mother's, with only a couple of days' notice, and shocking to the sensitive, unworldly girl who was bundled so unprepared onto the school train.

On the surface, Daphne was always affable, never lost her temper, was gentle and full of fun, but she was often inaccessible in a world of her own and could be extraordinarily uncomprehending of the feelings of others. Her children's passions puzzled her, if she even noticed them. Emotionally remote, she was all the more tantalising for being physically near but unreachably far. From very young, it was clear to Tessa and Flavia that they were not centrally important in their mother's life and that their longing for her unconditional love and unrivalled attention would remain unassuaged. She was so attractive with such a light-hearted manner that her elusiveness was the more painful, and her occasional dismissive comments the more wounding.

There were precious high points when they were ill, when Daphne's self-absorption was fractured by real concern for their welfare and they could bask in her almost full attention. And Christmas too was wonderful, when the house was magically transformed with decorations, installed by both their parents, and Daphne was emotionally present, playful and funny. Too soon these ecstatic interludes were over and their relationship returned to the usual maternal detachment, combined with the du Maurier critical eye. Flavia never forgot the throwaway comments on her plainness, something so far from the truth but once imbedded almost impossible to erase, and even Tessa, who was considered the sister with the looks, was compared unfavourably by her mother to Neltje Doubleday, who was the same age but much more sophisticated. Neither girl was credited with any particular talents or given much encouragement to develop those they had.

Their father was mostly away during their earliest childhood and when he returned from war was exhausted, demoralised and not entirely well. He was also not really at home at Menabilly, for it was so clearly Daphne's domain. She did not need him there and grew to resent his presence. She had her house, her imagination and her son and this was really all she wanted – and even her love for Kits did not interrupt her essential routines of work and solitude. Tommy could be the most tremendous fun when he was on form but other stresses more usually intervened and he was often irritable or morose. He came from a generation when children were seen but not heard and it would have been inconceivable to think that his children could be encouraged to voice their fears and wishes or express their unhappiness. Their Aunt Angela was neither willing nor able to step into the breach; she had a romance about the idea of children but the reality was rather more tedious to her. Like her sisters she had a good sense of humour but could be sharp and disapproving and was too often full of her own concerns. Jeanne never pretended to like or understand children but was perfectly happy to be a kind but distant aunt.

Kits had a very different childhood from his sisters. Precious from the moment he was born, adored as the golden boy, he was charming, good-looking and resolutely sunny-natured – why would he not be when treated as if he was the centre of a benign circle in which he was his mother's darling, and his sisters' pet? His important relationship with his father, however, was blighted from the start by Daphne's exclusive love of her boy (she much preferred kissing Kits to kissing anyone else – except Ellen – she told Ellen Doubleday). Tommy's concern that Daphne's indulgence of their son would undermine his ambition and ruin his character was airily dismissed: despite the importance of her own father in her life, Daphne marginalised Tommy's role in their son's childhood. In fact she liked to imagine that Kits was a reincarnation of Gerald in his charm and success with women, belonging exclusively to her, and that he had little to do with the Browning genes. Even her encouragement of Tommy's family nickname of 'Moper', coined from a chance remark of one of the children about their father moping before catching the train back to London, undermined his authority in the family.

When Kits was sent to boarding school at Winchester before he was nine years old, it was a terrible wrench for Daphne and traumatic for him. He had never been away from home on his own before, rarely played with other small boys and was more used to running wild, free to explore the gardens of Menabilly in pursuit of his own games and interests, with little interference from the adults. Treated as an equal by his mother and sisters, he was quite unprepared for the tribal cruelties of small boys in austere and unloving institutions. Although the school, West Downs, was more enlightened than most, he found the banal and arbitrary disciplines imposed on pupils hard to take at a time when spirit and individuality were seen as something to be necessarily channelled into conformity. In his first letter home, Kits managed to relay, through code, that he was miserable and friendless. Daphne was distraught. When Angela came to lunch later that day she was greeted by her younger sister, leaning out of her bedroom window with the anguished cry: 'Kits loathes his school and is dreadfully unhappy. What am I to do?'

Angela's response was unsympathetic. 'Pull yourself together for a start,' she said and then, turning to Flavia, added, 'what a fuss. I expect he is enjoying himself and just wrote that to work her up.'[4] In fact Kits was truly miserable and it took him a long time to settle in this alien and unsympathetic place. As a young girl, though much older than Kits, Angela had loathed being away from home and suffered horribly from homesickness. Her reaction showed such a remarkable lack of empathy and imagination it was possible that she too was jealous of her sister's blind devotion to her son.

Certainly Daphne felt she could not really confide in either Tommy or her sisters about just how bereft she felt and was only at ease talking about it to Ellen, whom she longed to entice to Europe so she could get away from the vacuum at home. But they were so different in their tastes. Ellen wanted luxury hotels in European cities and dressing for dinner: she loved shopping and seeing the sights, and was friendly and interested in people, attracting hangers-on in droves; Daphne told her she hated the idea of a European tour, had never been in the Ritz bar, and did not hanker after dining in expensive Parisian restaurants. She much preferred the cafés of the Rive Gauche she said (and decades later would wear Yves Saint Laurent's new scent Rive Gauche in tribute to her bohemian tastes) and aimed to travel light and unnoticed, packing only a few comfortable clothes. She did not like to share Ellen's attention with anyone, not even her children.

Ellen was not very keen on making the trip but was pressured into it by Daphne. It did not turn out well. Daphne felt Ellen at times became too 'like Mummy', not the idealised version she longed for, but the critical real life one who had so fatally undermined her childhood. She also loathed the fact that her royalties had not arrived from America and she was totally dependent on Ellen for money, a feeling of powerlessness that she had left behind long ago when she first struck out for freedom against her family.

Ellen had been unable to respond to Daphne's emotional demands and on the holiday had told Daphne she disliked her playing the gallant and carrying her parcels. She had also accused Daphne of lacking perception, of losing her sense of humour while in her presence and of being obsessed, making her into a mother substitute or a reinvention of Ferdy, her first love. All of this was pretty close to the truth and it enraged and humiliated Daphne that Ellen was emotionally detached enough to find it tedious, and tell her so. To think she might be a bore and a burden was too much to bear. Apart from her infant longing for her mother's love, Daphne had never before been the supplicating party in a love affair and she hated the sense of powerlessness this brought. Ellen had also complained of the burden of being clothed in Daphne's fantasies, expected to live up to preconceived and mistaken ideas about her character.

After the trip was over, and Ellen had left Menabilly to return to America, Daphne suddenly vented all her frustrations in a scathing letter to her, fuelled by drink. Part of her bitter response was that Ellen had become 'an endless source of profit to my literary life' and, as her fictions benefited Doubleday Inc., they were wedded to each other as 'Finance is all'.[5] She hit back at the slight that she lacked humour in Ellen's presence by declaring loftily, 'I am shaking with silent laughter most of the time, but you are possibly not aware of it … Besides, my sense of humour is rather warped.'[6]

The following day, Daphne sent a heartfelt apology for her 'stinking' letter and Ellen appeared to understand and overlook the viperish tone. But for Daphne the remorse continued. She realised with a shock that, clever and entertaining as she was, and brilliant at plotting her characters' imaginary lives, when it came to real people's feelings she lacked empathy and insight. Human relationships were such a problem for her and her lack of understanding frightened her:

> I feel I have just botched everything, and you will never really trust me again, or have any faith in me. Even if I had never written that gin and brandy letter, there would still be something at odds between us … You think you have yourself in hand, and then you suddenly realise you have nothing of the sort, and are in complete turmoil, without judgment. The realisation of this is dreadfully shaming, and baffling too; frightening almost … I am the king of advisors to other people, and quite sound too – and then when it comes to living myself, worse than a young child. I think a young child would have more common sense, more understanding.[7]

There were two 'gin and brandy' letters written to Ellen that showed a much darker, cruel underbelly to Daphne's usual witty, light-hearted self. It was not a coincidence that the short stories she was writing around this time, 'The Birds', 'The Old Man', 'Monte Verità', 'The Little Photographer' and 'Kiss Me Again, Stranger' were amongst her best, a step deeper into fear, violence and the macabre. She admitted she was struggling to come to terms with her creative masculine energy, 'the problem of Niall', so at odds with the womanly self that her husband and children needed. Her only way to try and understand the conflicts in herself was to employ her troublesome boy-self and write it out, and these remarkable stories were the result. It was a very misanthropic world that Daphne created in her imagination where people were not kind or empathic to each other, where selfishness and misunderstanding abounded and, as she so often explained, the barrier between the imagined and the real was fatally indistinct.

The shortest of the stories, 'The Old Man', about a father who kills the son who has displaced him in his wife's affections and thereby regains her love, 'no longer a third to divide them', turned out to be a swan. It was not only a reflection of Tommy's jealousy of Kits, she said, but also an allegory of most religious teaching where we have to kill the jealousy within ourselves before we can rise again. She ended it with her murderous swan, forgiven by his mate and thereby transformed into a transcendent beauty, at one with nature, '[taking off] from the water, full of power, and she followed him … I tell you it was one of the most beautiful sights I ever saw in my life: the two swans flying there, alone, in winter.'[8]

The stories were published under the title *The Apple Tree*, named after the longest story, a brilliant allegory based on the Puxley marriage, her part in its downfall, and its dogged survival. Daphne had noticed an ancient apple tree in the orchard at the Puxleys' elegant house where she and her children had been guests during the war, and been struck by its resilience. In her story, a man attempts to destroy an almost barren apple tree, seen by him as a reincarnation of his self-sacrificing wife. He longs instead for the younger more fertile tree to replace it. The old tree endures his cruel blows and continues to give of itself with shade, apples, fuel, until the man himself is destroyed in the end by its indomitable, suffocating power. Daphne's family and most reviewers were shocked by the anger and violence in much of these stories, but nothing could ever be too nasty for her old friend Hitchcock, and a decade later he would turn 'The Birds' into one of the most iconically terrifying films of his career.

On their fraught European holiday together, Ellen had urged Daphne to be a better wife and support to Tommy, especially as he was now Comptroller and Treasurer to the Household of the Princess Elizabeth and had duties that demanded his presence in London and on tour with the Princess. In honour of his own Olympic past, he was also Commandant of the British team in what became known as the Austerity Games, the Olympics of 1948, produced on a shoestring by a bankrupt Britain as host nation.

Daphne was alarmed and bored by the kind of social life that Tommy enjoyed: weekends at various royal palaces, shooting grouse and stag, sailing with Prince Philip at Cowes, dinner parties and musical shows, and most of all the ballet. She made occasional forays up to London to do her duty but could not wait to return to the embrace of Menabilly. She knew she was not giving him the love and support he so obviously needed but was struggling herself to reconcile all the various parts of a fractured personality that seethed under her surface manner of serene detachment. The drama of her own obsessions, needs and desires did not leave much energy for the outside world.

In the cold of early February 1952, Daphne was being driven up to London by Angela when they noticed that all the flags they passed were at half-mast. She was on her way to Oxford to see Tessa who was in hospital having had her appendix out. When they stopped for lunch they asked about the lowered flags and were told in hushed tones, 'the King is dead'. Angela's eyes immediately filled with tears but Daphne just felt stunned. The King was not yet fifty-seven, only a year older than Tommy himself. Tommy had just flown out to Kenya to be with Princess Elizabeth on tour but had now to fly straight back with the new Queen Elizabeth. She had been dressed in bright summer clothes when the news came through and Tommy had been the only person to think of going straight to her trunk to find the one black coat and hat for her return. When Daphne saw him that night he seemed to have aged ninety-nine years, she thought, but organisation was Tommy's forte, despite the toll on his nerves.

During their long drive from Cornwall to London the sisters were amazed to see a country transformed with mourning – shops had removed the gay spring clothes from their windows and replaced them with black, in Hammersmith the buildings were draped with purple ribbons – and Daphne felt incongruous and conspicuous in her red jacket and blue skirt. As Tommy's wife, Daphne was at the centre of all the subsequent pageantry and was moved by the overwhelming sense that here was history happening and she was included at its heart. When the coffin was brought from Sandringham to Westminster Hall, only the Queen's Household and the members of the Commons and the Lords, in their magnificent regalia, were there to greet it and the Queen Mother and new Queen walking behind it.

Daphne's age-old longing asserted itself to be not Tommy's good supportive wife but the chivalric boy, 'I did not want to be me in a veil and a silly woman, I wanted to have a sword and be wearing armour … That's the way these things take me.'[9]

Tommy's duties now changed radically too. His new position was Treasurer to Prince Philip and he moved into an office in Buckingham Palace, still with Maureen Luschwitz in attendance as his invaluable personal assistant. Her practicality and kindness extended into buying school clothes for the Browning children and caring for Tommy at weekends too. Daphne could not continue to put off joining her husband on one of his official royal engagements and in the autumn of 1953 she accompanied him to Balmoral for just under a week of stalking and shooting, 'which seemed like the longest week I have ever spent in my life'. Her letter to Ellen describing the visit was a tour de force of self-deprecating humour and fascinating detail. After dinner the 'table games' were canasta 'or that US import "scrabble" where you have to invent words, and I could only think of rude ones, and Prince P sat next to me and helped me'. Daphne found the Queen Mother extraordinarily warm and charming and even the recently widowed Princess Royal was easier to deal with than the younger generation; the Queen a 're-incarnation of Queen Victoria', and Princess Margaret 'so See Me and bounces about very pleased with herself'.[10] Prince Charles and Princess Anne, who were only toddlers at the time, were allowed in to see the visitors and Daphne thought them lively and delightful.

Jeanne meanwhile had thrown herself into her life as an artist. She had left Angela largely in charge of their mother at Ferryside while she painted at St Ives. She had rented a small studio called St Peter's Street Studio, just off St Peter's Street, on the narrow neck of the peninsula between the harbour and Porthmeor beach. It had once been a sail loft connected to a blacksmith's shop and became an artist's studio at the turn of the century. Along with Dod Procter and another of Dod's artist friends, Alethea Garstin, Jeanne became a member of the St Ives Society of Artists.

The fishing port of St Ives on the west coast of Cornwall had been attracting visiting artists from the middle of the nineteenth century.

Being so westerly it was warmer and milder than the rest of the country and being so far to the south there was more light for painting *en plein air*. The arrival of the railway and the availability of redundant sail lofts made it practical for artists to live there all the year round. Well-known painters like Whistler and Walter Sickert left London to winter there and soon a cosmopolitan band of artists had congregated in the town. The First World War interrupted the colony's organic growth but artists returned to St Ives after the Armistice.

The St Ives Society of Artists was founded in January 1927 to raise the artistic standards of the colony and exhibit work. Part of its great success in subsequent years was due to the decision to organise touring exhibitions which publicised the work of the St Ives group of painters, sculptors and ceramicists. The Second World War saw a further influx of artists and the influence of movements from Europe began to stimulate discussion and experimentation; Cubism, Futurism, Constructivism, all mixed with the tradition of English marine painting to produce a distinct style reflecting the brilliance of the light and the mastery of sea and the sky.

In 1946, Dod was elected President of the Society but was not automatically re-elected, as had been the form previously, possibly because she was too much of a modernist. The influx of younger artists after the war had begun to challenge the old orthodoxies and the traditionalists were growing increasingly irritated with what they saw as the arrogance and relaxed morality of the younger set. Nor did they appreciate their non-representational art. Stresses between the modernists and traditionalists would rumble on until a break occurred in 1949 when Barbara Hepworth and Ben Nicholson among others left to set up the Penwith Society of Arts where they could pursue their more experimental ideas. Dod Procter and then Jeanne were invited to join them. Quite soon, however, the rebel members realised that, rather than creating a new democratic union of like-minded artists, Barbara Hepworth and Ben Nicholson were largely running the show.

Jeanne and Dod set off for a working holiday of a lifetime, for it began in Oslo and, after a long and varied journey south, as suggested by Marda, encompassing Basutoland and the mysterious and magnificent Drakensburg (Afrikaans for Dragon Mountains) the highest range in Southern Africa. The lower slopes were blessed with abundant water and the landscape was vivid with wild flowers and birds. The women went on to the Cape and Jeanne was struck by the Dutch colonial farmhouses with their cool dark interiors, lovely refuges from the fierce summer sun.

While they were in Basutoland they met Noël Welch, the woman poet and writer who was to become Jeanne's partner for life. Noël remembered that at their first meeting Dod was distressed as her favourite skirt had somehow been blown from a train window. Possibly her extreme reaction caused Noël and Jeanne, newly acquainted, some amusement. Dod's distress, however, was soon forgotten as she delighted in the landscape around her. Particularly enthralling to her was the way a tree at noon stood in its own deep shadow as if it were on a pedestal. Noël would write one of her great poems, dedicated to the poet Michael Hamburger, called 'A Shadow to its Tree', admitting her own love of shadows but also perhaps remembering Dod's deeply felt response to the African tree on that distant noonday.

The meeting with Noël altered the dynamic of Dod and Jeanne's relationship, with Jeanne writing later to Marda about this time in her home country: 'Things went wrong with our lives there [in S. Africa], which I never had the chance to tell you of. Eventually there was no leisure to set them right … I don't suppose even the Kruger [National Game Park] would have redeemed things.'[11] Perhaps from this point Dod began to be replaced in Jeanne's affections by Noël. Family duties also weighed heavily on Jeanne at the time, and even travelling so far away did not allow her to escape from her responsibilities for a mother who relied on her emotionally and a sister resentful of her prolonged absence. Letters from Ferryside would arrive, sometimes three a week, from both Muriel and a desperate Angela, asking whether she had booked her passage home.

Marda Vanne was fifteen years older than Jeanne and her worldly-wise frankness both attracted and unsettled the younger woman. Having arrived back in the spring from her fateful holiday in South Africa and returned short-term to Ferryside to sort out her thoughts, Jeanne was struggling with her mother's and Angela's needs as well as the turmoil in her own personal life. 'I cannot get to sleep,' she wrote to Marda, 'Tuffet [her Pekinese] was snoring, and you are rather mercilessly sitting around in my mind, dear Marda. I should like to write you an intimate letter, but I cannot guess even how well, or little, you would care for that.'

There were obvious stresses in the household at Ferryside that she hoped would improve with time, and stresses too in her relationship with Dod:

I have been exceedingly unhappy at times lately, because finding people impossible so that you want to shake them, & apparently being bloody myself, does not, perhaps luckily seemed to have happened before with me. I have felt quite leaden with sadness & dismay, but I believe that fundamentally it cannot matter as I cannot imagine NOT wanting Dod to be the ~~most important person~~ [crossed out in the original] closest person to me. At least I can *imagine* it, because alas what a lot of love does go wrong.[12]

Although she was already hinting at the rift that had once seemed unthinkable, Jeanne was hoping to set off again with Dod for Madeira, sending a heartfelt plea to Marda to meet them there. She explained she had fallen for the island within four hours of coming ashore and decided that she would one day retire there, if she could.

Back in Ferryside and full of melancholy, Jeanne could not bear to play on the piano the *London Fantasia*, a popular piece of music recently composed by Clive Richardson as the British answer to the Warsaw Concerto, evoking the bombing of London during the Blitz. It was something she had played when Marda was at Ferryside and she wrote that it filled her with sadness over Marda and also stirred up her feelings for Catholicism. Her sense of the sacred was perhaps already well developed. When Marda had written to her about her conflicted feelings for Gwen Ffrangcon-Davies, and had suggested suicide as an alternative to the difficulties of life, Jeanne was appalled. She could not even bring herself to write the word but urged her: 'Don't for God's sake say or think about it ever again.'[13]

Daphne had been rather dismissive of both Angela and Jeanne, who had complained to her that they could not both work and look after Muriel. When Muriel came for a short visit to Menabilly to give Angela a break, Daphne was quick to point out that she had enjoyed one of her most productive periods – their complaints were 'plain silly. Or is it just that I am cleverer than they are?!'[14] In fact Jeanne had been working towards her first exhibition in London, at the Beaux Arts Gallery, a prominent exhibition space known for its promotion of avant-garde painting. Until it closed in the sixties, the gallery was run by the painter Helen Lessore and it was here that Barbara Hepworth had one of her earliest exhibitions.

It was Tommy who organised the exhibition at this prestigious gallery for Jeanne and it was probably his influence too that meant Queen Elizabeth paid a visit. Tommy was much liked by both Jeanne and Noël, but Jeanne was dismayed that Daphne did not make the effort to attend. In fact, it seemed that her family's lack of appreciation of her work became a lasting hurt. Both Angela and Daphne had been used to accepting without question their father's view of modern art and Tod, herself a talented watercolourist with conventional tastes, was naturally opinionated and continued his censure of the kind of expressionist work in which Jeanne and her colleagues were engaged. The sisters hung Dod's attractive but unchallenging paintings on their walls while eschewing their sister's.

Alongside her burgeoning career as an artist, Jeanne was struggling with her emotional life and the fact that she and Noël Welch were beginning to be drawn to each other. At some point Noël rented the next door studio to Jeanne in St Ives. A clever and beautiful young woman nearly ten years younger than Jeanne, Noël had graduated with an honours degree in English from St Hilda's College Oxford in 1943 and brought her cool fastidious intellect to everything she did.

Noël was a poet and for a time worked as reader for the talented young printer Guido Morris who had moved his Latin Press to St Ives just after the war. Good looking, creative and charming, Guido Morris had suffered a breakdown during his war service and a subsequent divorce from his wife. His passion was for print, design and typefaces and his time in St Ives was a happy and settled period in his life, printing material for the local community and embarking on the Crescendo Poetry Series. Between 1951 and the summer of 1952, he published eight pamphlets of poems by young poets, John Heath-Stubbs, himself and Noël Welch among them. Morris's print run was only in the middle hundreds and Noël's pamphlet, 'Ten Poems', published in 1952, is by far the rarest of all eight collections now. At the centre was a series of extended poems to Saint Joan, seen through her companion's piercing gaze as both armoured soldier and precocious child: 'Oh ambiguous maid/You touched most poignantly my ambiguity.' Joan of Arc had resonance in the self-image of both Daphne and Jeanne, both unconventional and ambiguous spirits in disguise.

Jeanne wrote a second confessional letter to Marda, suggesting that an answer to the complexity of her life would be to run away to live with her in South Africa, 'how exciting it would be, & what a shambles of incompatibility would be the result, to turn my back on everyone I'm caught up with, & come & live with you'. She knew it was impossible but was keen to have Marda's clarity shone on the mess she was making at home:

> to use a vulgar expression I have come to the conclusion that I have too much on my plate. I'm drawn into, and influence, too many lives. You are not on the plate at all, since you are unacquainted with any of the people … I think about you a lot. I love writing to you. I hope to God you realise there's no-one else I write to in this strain.[15]

Marda was well acquainted with Jeanne's family, so the demanding issues on Jeanne's plate at the time could only be her relationship with Dod, and the advent in her life of Noël too.

Jeanne realised, however, that work was the answer to most of her romantic problems. When she had been in South Africa the emotional strains had meant she was unable to paint, '& the more continuously I'm painting the better I feel'.[16] She was working a great deal and exhibiting regularly. Before the break with the St Ives Society of Artists she had a painting, *Spanish Vermouth*, included in a touring exhibition at the end of 1947, exhibiting in Cardiff and Swindon, amongst other towns in the west. Jeanne exhibited *Flowers in a Spanish Bowl* at the Swindon Arts Centre in the three weeks from the end of January to the middle of February in 1949; the picture's price of £50 showed just how highly she was regarded at the time.

When she had two paintings *Green Apples* and *Mimosa with Ferns* accepted for the inaugural exhibition of the Penwith Society in the summer of 1949, her prices once again were almost on a par with the already celebrated Dod Procter and Peter Lanyon. Only Ben Nicholson and Barbara Hepworth could command significantly more than the other members. Interestingly Bernard Leach was selling a large stoneware jar for half the price of Jeanne's paintings and a celadon porcelain tea set for even less. It suggests that her talent was recognised early and had she had a little more of Dod's ambition and luck, her paintings might have been much more prized and in far greater evidence than they are today.

Despite having been suffering with health problems for some time, Angela was suddenly highly productive and wrote and published three books in the first three years of the 1950s. The two novels she produced were interesting biographically as they explored the kind of life Angela felt she could have lived if she had had more encouragement and perseverance. She had reached her middle years and recognised that this was the life she had made for herself, but it did not stop her thinking of the paths she might have taken.

She had loved the theatre all her life, had tried to be an actress but given up before she had really begun, she loved music and singing and had a good voice but was put off any more training by a tough teacher in Paris. She had also been drawn to politics, both in her youth through a love affair with a committed socialist and then as a staunch Conservative in middle age. But all these careers remained just dreams. 'I never ventured further than the Never-Never-Land.'[17] She protested that she did not mind that she had led 'a full (if useless) life, who met daily people of interest, who travelled often, whose time was taken up flitting butterfly-wise an hour here, an hour there'.[18] In fact she believed she could have been a contender, if only she had had more courage and resilience.

Her novel *Reveille* was a dramatisation of her political interests. The heroine, Deborah Kilhoan, once again was like her, with an appreciation of grand estates and Pekinese dogs. She also had a touch of her sister Daphne in that Deborah only has one son and 'no wish for daughters. What should she do with a daughter?'[19] She is loved by a highly intelligent, unconventional socialist MP but, by marrying his dumb but easy-going, philandering brother, she sets up an epic hostility between the two. Political and personal arguments rage, her husband then dies in the war and the estate she loves is about to be wrested from her by the heir, her socialist brother-in-law (who intends to give it to the state). The whole struggle ends with the heir accidentally shooting himself. In a deathbed confession he admits she was the only woman he had ever loved and his 'foul' behaviour was due solely to sibling rivalry, fuelled by her choosing the wrong brother. Deborah soldiers on and triumphantly wins his parliamentary seat but this time for the Conservatives, praying to God for guidance to keep the nation steady in maintaining the status quo.

Shallow Waters on the other hand was a sparky recreation of the theatrical world of Angela's youth, with the more modern overlay of the experiences of younger actresses like Gwen Ffrangcon-Davies, Marda Vanne and Martita Hunt. The story begins in the run up to the Second World War and she made her heroine, Maureen Tempel, a young ingénue actress, much as Angela imagined she would have been if she had persevered with the profession. Maureen is considered plain as a girl who grows into 'a nice ordinary sort of person',[20] but 'there was a streak of genius somewhere in her acting'[21] that set her apart from the rest. Angela peopled the story with the real celebrities she knew and had known: her father, her great friend Betty Hicks's father Seymour Hicks, and Ivor Novello. She even provides a Svengali-like figure to promote young Maureen's career and take her into his bed. After various vicissitudes, Maureen falls in love with a rich, landed gentleman, about to become a Tory MP. In order to be the best wife and mother ('half-hearted attempts at anything are seldom successful'[22]), she decides to give up her glittering career on the stage, against all the advice of her friends and fellow professionals.

Angela wrote this conclusion with great feeling, and at some length. Her novels were either a celebration of a woman friend or a way to work out her own preoccupations. This one was dedicated to Betty

Hicks, her girlhood friend who had been widowed young and was devoted to her son.

The passion Angela invested in her heroine's apologia for giving up the stage suggested that, from the vantage point of middle age, she considered that a woman's commitment to the married state was the answer to a happy life. After all, she had not had the chance herself to be married to a devoted man, as was her heroine, but she had seen Daphne's marriage struggle. She had also known redoubtable women like Olive Guthrie and Anne Treffry and admired their roles as strong talented women who, nevertheless, put their energies into becoming supportive wives. Even Marda Vanne, the great rebel and lover of women, had wondered in later life if she might not have been happier in the end if she had remained with her husband. The heroine Maureen's paean to married love was something Angela also believed in the depths of her romantic and nostalgic soul:

> You see I know now that Jonathan [Willoughby] means more than all the parts, all the plays, all the careers in the world … I don't want to be a middle-aged wife, rushing off on a job of my own, leaving a middle-aged husband to loneliness. Or to other women! … I know you are distressed because I have said good-bye to the theatre, good-bye to audiences, and have buried Maureen Tempel. Don't be. Maureen Willoughby is so much more real a person, and so much nicer a person … there isn't a happier woman in England today than me.[23]

Perhaps she also felt, as she herself entered middle age and grew increasingly interested in the Church and its teachings, that there was something shallow about the thespian way of life, that her much-loved parents had been entertaining and charming, and wonderful actors, but had lacked that deeper purpose and identity.

Neither book caused even a ripple on publication day. Her time as a novelist had come, briefly flickered and then faded. Angela realised a tide had turned and her kind of books were considered 'old-fashioned – "square" – except to our own generation … [the critics] are sick of you, you've had your day'.[24] She protested that in an age of James Baldwin she could not change styles to suit the fashion and insert all kinds of four-letter words and obscenities. Baldwin was only ten years younger than Angela and he was writing with anger and honesty about a much tougher reality in Harlem than she could ever have imagined from the beauty and safety of Hampstead, Torosay or Cornwall. With the publication in 1953 of his semi-autobiographical first novel, *Go Tell It on the Mountain*, Baldwin took the literary world on both sides of the Atlantic by storm. Suddenly country houses and moneyed old duffers, hanging on grimly to outworn traditions, seemed completely irrelevant.

But Angela's memoir, published in 1951, was a different matter. Written much like her letters – confiding, breathless, discursive – it was a fascinating triumph of name-dropping, celebrity anecdotes, of barely veiled emotion and hinted transgressions. She offered glimpses of the glamour of the theatrical world her parents inhabited and a childhood, with her sisters, that was both privileged and deprived. In this book she wanted her readers to guess that there was much more to the middle-aged spinster author than met the eye. Only the title let it down, for it was so much more lively, confident and entertaining than the self-deprecating words implied. *It's Only the Sister* she took from an infamous incident when she was mistaken for Daphne by a gushing matron. '"I expect you think I am my sister, Daphne Browning," I explained, "I am *Angela* du Maurier." With the eyes and the voice of a Medea she turned to her husband, who was standing in the offing ready to be introduced, and cried – "It's ONLY the SISTER!" and with that she left me.'[25]

This book also attracted some admiring fans, one of whom, Betty Williams, was to become a lifelong friend. Betty was thirty years old, a dancer who had had a nervous breakdown having been treated with psychological aversion therapy to 'cure' her of an attraction towards her own sex. Angela had written in her memoir with such tolerance and understanding on the subject of homosexual love that Betty thought she would understand her own unhappy experience, and she did. Soon her newsy and reassuring letters were flying regularly to Nottingham, to where Betty had returned home to recuperate. They helped the young woman more than any drugs or therapy could do, and Betty remained eternally grateful for Angela's loyalty and care.

As Betty explained the loss of her great love after her mother's interference, Angela confided that she was in love with 'a fine lady' and when Betty was invited to Ferryside she not only met Angela's mother but Anne Treffry too. She found Lady du Maurier remote but charming, and generous with her offer to explore the house and garden. Mrs Treffry was warm and embracing and completely at ease in her own skin and her place in the world.

Angela, however, was ill at ease with hers, refusing to let Betty accompany her sea-bathing as she did not want to be seen in her swimming costume and was ambivalent about inviting her into her life. All the uncomplicated feeling and understanding she had shown in her letters became clouded and face to face Angela was a confusing mixture of affection and shame. A happy and peaceful evening rowing up the river was followed by kisses and then, '"Let's go to bed". I declined. [Angela] saw me to the gate saying, "I'm sorry I'm too selfish to keep up what you need".'[26] Betty felt Angela was full of conflict, finding it difficult to reconcile her true self, expressed in her warm and chatty letters, with her public face, the respectable middle-aged woman with a famous name, High Church principles, and the sound of her father's hysterical disapproval ringing in her ears. While Betty Williams was at Fowey, she was invited out by Angela Halliday, who was living locally and whom she found uncomplicatedly friendly and accepting, but, tentative herself and anxious not to upset her friend, she demurred.

When Betty Williams's health dramatically declined a few years later, Angela proved what a stalwart friend she could be, rushing up to see her in hospital three times during her stay there. She had been upset to find Betty's bedside was not surrounded by flowers and get-well-soon cards and so brought roses to cheer her up. Angela always believed in doing things properly. Only on her third visit did she revert to her suspicious conflicted state when, stony-faced and forbidding, she accused Betty of manipulating her into feeling responsible for her. This was soon followed by an affectionate letter, but Betty had become wary of Angela's emotional unpredictability. Only when Angela was an old lady, and both Daphne and Anne Treffry were dead, did their friendship become as well fitting as an old glove.

In the April of 1951, Angela's nagging health problems were finally diagnosed and she went into Fowey Cottage Hospital for a hysterectomy to solve the problem of fibroids. She loved this hospital, where everyone knew each other and the nursing and care was offered as if to a friend. A cheery letter to Marda captured the bawdy humour that lurked beneath the very proper, even stern, exterior:

> Darling, here I am womb-less, sex-less (?) at last. You hate things that are misshapen and unbeautiful I know, but I cannot refrain from telling you that when they cut me open they found the cause of the trouble was something matron could only describe as 'a man's genitals'!!! So now we know.

Angela obviously identified with one of her heroes, Abelard, who was castrated in revenge for his forbidden love of Héloïse, as she signed herself 'Angela Abelard'.[27] This was a strange appellation that, together with the joke about being rendered sex-less, suggested perhaps that in some deeper way she felt both mutilated and condemned.

Angela sailed through the operation but had an increased propensity, she told Daphne, to burst into tears. She clung to her friendship with Anne Treffry. 'Anne has been by me all the time, which of course was everything,' she wrote to Marda, and the only other person she wanted to see was Daphne. Angela was due to go to stay with Anne for a week to recuperate and then they hoped to be able to visit Italy for two or three weeks in May. As Jeanne was away in Spain for four months, this involved Muriel and her nurse going to stay with Daphne at Menabilly. Daphne was not happy with the arrangement and irritated that Jeanne always went off to such inaccessible places. Muriel had shingles and, although she was only just seventy years old, she was already a semi-invalid with very little interest left in life. The sisters did not have to do any physical caring for their mother, as they had installed an excellent nurse, but Muriel lived with Angela at Ferryside and thus was her main responsibility, one that she found limiting and wearisome.

Daphne's children, however, were a great delight to Angela. She thought her godchild Flavia was running true to du Maurier form:

'Heaven to look at & shy in a strange way.' Angela was gratified that she asked to be given a crucifix and a man's watch for her fourteenth birthday, '& grumbled to Daphne that one couldn't marry women … [Angela's dots] I've altered my will in her favour'.[28] This she wrote to Marda, who must have been relieved that she was no longer the beneficiary of the will – a favour that had been promised, against her wishes, when their affair ended years before.

When Jeanne returned from Spain she was, noted Daphne, 'thinner than ever',[29] and it was obvious that it had been a disappointing and trying time. Her special relationship with Dod was unravelling. An interesting legacy perhaps was Dod's peculiar voice. Michael Canney, the curator at Newlyn Art Gallery, remembered her as having 'a cracked and perhaps affected voice that suited her opinions, which could be forceful and final'.[30] Jeanne's family realised that her voice too became odd and rather cracked; Noël Welch described it as 'strange, like water breaking over stones. There are tears in it as well as laughter.'[31] If it was a mannerism like Dod's, then eventually it was shared by Noël too. However difficult her emotional life at the time, Jeanne's career was on the rise. She had had three flower pictures accepted by the Royal Academy for their Summer Exhibition and two by the Paris Salon, the prestigious French equivalent – quite a triumph indeed. Noël Welch became more important in Jeanne's life and in 1953 they moved together to a twelfth-century longhouse in a beautiful moorland village on Dartmoor. Jeanne had first seen it on a very cold spring morning and 'it was its situation rather than the cottage that made me decide to buy it'.[32]

Half Moon, its evocative name from its past life as an inn, was once three cottages, squat, thick-walled and buttressed. All the du Maurier sisters chose to live in ancient or interesting buildings. From the front, Half Moon was a charming low-built house facing the village green, but from the back it looked as if it had grown organically out of the granite and the moor, its demesne becoming progressively wilder as its borders moved from fields to wood then rocks and moorland. It was here that both the artist and the intellectual set out to create an exquisite home for themselves and a beautiful place to work. Jeanne brought various pieces of du Maurier furniture with her: George du Maurier's desk, on which he drew his iconic *Punch* illustrations, added a sense of family continuity and the rocking chair and dressing chest in her bedroom had once belonged to her father.

It was an ancient rustic house with few modern conveniences and dark wood and stone floors, softened only with rush matting. Jeanne, whose own style bordered on the austere, added Noël's elegant Hepplewhite four-poster bed, whose soaring canopy reached right to the ceiling. 'It is not a house for the timid,' she wrote almost a decade after moving in; 'all has a feeling of everlastingness that makes the shortage of cupboards, the bathroom like a rather primitive wash-house, and the fact there is nowhere to dry one's often soaked clothes, seem trivial inconveniences … the great struggle was for light but I think has been won.'[33] Throughout its atmospheric, uncluttered spaces could be heard the trill of canaries, recordings of plainsong or Jeanne's own playing of Bach, Mozart or Chopin on her piano. It was a house full of music and work that mixed painting and poetry with horse-breeding and vegetable gardening.

Over the years they carved out a meditative garden incorporating the granite outcrops, and topiarising the gorse. The whole design was conceived as being in the shape of a cross with grass and paved crosses within it, and crossing grass walks. John Donne's famous poem, 'The Crosse', pointing out the sacred in everyday things, was part of its inspiration and indeed Jeanne, from being a quietly religious girl in a non-practising family, converted to Catholicism in her adulthood. She liked to set up her easel and paint wherever a view, an angle, a collection of objects, caught her discerning eye. Jeanne would live with Noël at Half Moon for the rest of her life, with horses, dogs and a variety of other small animals, growing their own food and working at their art.

This life was under threat in the seventies through lack of funds and Daphne, always so generous with her money, came to their aid with the gift of the film rights for one of her films (possibly *Don't Look Now*, Nicholas Roeg's compelling thriller). Noël wrote to thank her effusively and pointed out they were not natural criers like Piffy

(Angela) but both had burst into tears of sheer relief and joy. She also mentioned how appreciative they were of all Daphne's years of hard work that had made such a generous gift possible.

It was taking a long time for Daphne to recover from the deadly sense that inspiration had fled with the sudden erasure of Gertie from her imaginative landscape. She was not ready for another epic creative effort but dragged herself out of depression by beginning to research her ancestress Mary Anne Clarke and her liaison with the Duke of York, with the idea of a book based on her life. Although writing *Mary Anne*, 'has put me on my feet, and toughened me up', Daphne was concerned about what she would do once she had sent the manuscript off and she feared 'another bleak six months'. She wrote to Ellen that she wished, 'I was like Noël [Coward] and could paint, and compose, and have dozens of things up my sleeve, when a book is over.'[34]

In fact she did start furtively to paint, feeling she was no good and untrained but responding to an overwhelming need 'to slap onto canvas what my mind sees, especially the deep ruddy earth!' She made a joke of it to her friend Oriel Malet, calling this new departure 'Therapy for Schizophrenics!'[35] But for a while her painting expressed the internal conflicts she was attempting to reconcile. To ally her mental state with schizophrenia, in its non-clinical manifestation, suggested she felt her two selves were at odds with each other to the detriment of the whole. Daphne also found herself drawn to writing a series of poems. She had always occasionally expressed herself in poetry, but the urge was now more insistent and she sent a couple of her efforts to Noël Welch, of whose intellect and education she was slightly in awe, and was encouraged that Noël thought them very good. Daphne confided to Oriel there was an appeal in being a poet and painter in old age, rather than someone who had to create epic fictions with her imagination at full stretch, while the real world receded in a sometimes alarming way.

But first she had a book to produce. From the details she gleaned of her great-great grandmother she created a memorable hard-nosed adventuress. Her Mary Anne Clarke dragged herself up the slippery social ladder through tireless capitalisation of her sexuality, intelligence and guile – even blackmail when it suited her interests. In the process Daphne drew a rollicking picture of the underbelly of Regency life, where people scrambled over each other for preferment, with bribery and corruption as their currency. And Mary Anne was up with the best of them.

Her reviewers commended her storytelling powers and thought Mary Anne a memorable figure. The book was 'not top drawer du Maurier, but a sure best seller',[36] and made Book of the Month in the United States. A. L. Rowse, who was a little in love with Daphne, recognised her talent for historical research, although he did not care for historical novels. He declared, however, that Daphne's own remarkable blue eyes were one of the distinguishing marks of the Hanoverian royal family, implying that he thought Mary Anne's daughter could well have been the child of the Duke of York and that Daphne and her sisters therefore had royal blood, however dubious and dilute.

The summer of 1955 was a happy one. The weather in Cornwall was consistently hot and sunny; life at Menabilly seemed all the more to be suspended in some enchantment, cut loose from time and place. Daphne went on a week's walking holiday on Dartmoor with Jeanne and thoroughly enjoyed her short stays with her younger sister and Noël on Dartmoor. She said that it was such a change it refreshed her spirit. She was called on for more onerous duties, however, when a prize mare bit Noël's face so badly she had to go for treatment from a plastic surgeon in Bristol, accompanied by Jeanne. Daphne was left in charge of their menagerie of two mares, one of them unpredictable, a foal, thirty hens, two dogs and one cat – and no help, so she had to cook for herself and care for the animals with the help of a local man Noël and Jeanne called Bump. Daphne rose magnificently to the challenge and enjoyed even the privations of cleaning out the hen house by imagining herself a lay brother in a monastery. She and Jeanne shared a love of monasteries and she had always seen the attractions of the life of a recluse.

That summer was also busy. Daphne told Ellen that both her daughters were down at Menabilly and seemed happy, Tessa married to a handsome Guards officer, Peter de Zulueta, with a 'fat and contented' baby daughter and just pregnant with her second child, and Flavia in love with the man she would marry, another Guards officer but this time from the Coldstreams, Alastair Tower. Kits was always happy when away from school and back in the embrace of Menabilly and his family. Daphne's sunny summer was topped off by a visit to France with Jeanne and Noël in search of her forebears. This bore exciting fruit and, to her immense relief, re-lit her imagination she feared had been extinguished with the death of Gertrude Lawrence and the cooling of her obsession with Ellen Doubleday.

She was buoyed by the sense of her creative spirit stirring to life once more. She could even have a laugh with Evie Williams about Gertie's husband Richard remarrying – this time his secretary – and asking that Gertie's bedroom furniture be shipped from New York to his new marital house in Spain. This Daphne thought rather insensitive and so was delighted by the cable Richard subsequently sent Evie: 'bedroom and drawing-room furniture all burnt in transit, lorry caught fire'[37] – a sign she was sure of Gertie's inextinguishable spirit still working her mischief.

Although Daphne and Angela saw each other at least once a week and Jeanne much less frequently, as she lived some seventy miles or so away, it was Jeanne with whom Daphne occasionally embarked on adventurous trips while Angela at Ferryside carried the responsibility for their ailing mother. Noël noticed that Jeanne had developed into the most ruthless of the three sisters: certainly she had announced that her art came first and she could not work while caring for Muriel. Once Jeanne had moved into St Ives and then away to Dartmoor with Noël, she maintained her separation and independence despite having been the most amenable in her youth. Angela too found that she could not write during what would be her mother's final seven years. Even after Muriel died in 1957, she felt inspiration had deserted her until 1962, when a trip to Ireland with Anne Treffry spurred her imagination once more.

Daphne, free to travel whenever she pleased, returned from France fired up not only with the stories of her ancestors, the glass-blowers, but more urgently with an idea about human greed and the problem of duality in our natures. Her love of France, her increasing identification with her own Frenchness, and the research into her ancestors' manufacture of glass, was the backdrop to a powerfully realised novel, *The Scapegoat*. Her central male narrator is a disaffected Englishman who is given his wish for another life when suddenly he is assumed by others to be a French aristocrat. But this means he steps into a life that, although apparently glamorous, is complicated by a perilous set of relationships and various onerous responsibilities as the head of an extended and failing family dynasty.

Daphne had always been intrigued by the doubleness in her own life: the tensions between the creative adventurous spirit, necessarily selfish, and the beautiful woman, expected to be nurturing and self-sacrificing. Yet all the while she was aware that the self she found most exciting, and most alive, was the energy that powered her fictions but could be destructive and egoistic in real life. Struggling with her guilt and disappointment over her emotional estrangement from Tommy, and with her own chameleon sense of identity, she posited that everyone had a double nature, that Tommy was in conflict with his good and bad sides too. She even wondered if in fact she was both Rebecca and the second Mrs de Winter in Tommy's life. She had always thought of herself as the second Mrs de Winter who could never measure up to the fantasy of the super-competent, charismatic first love. As she grew older and colder towards him, and discovered and faced up to his romances with other women, she wondered if in fact she was not more the Rebecca figure, ever-present, haunting, preventing him from being happy with another.

The Scapegoat was a powerful exploration of Daphne's own preoccupations at the time: her growing dissatisfaction with the rigidity of her and Tommy's separate lives; her pride in her own French roots; her fascination with Jung's writings on the unconscious, and her sense of a fugitive self, longing at times to escape her current restrictions and live a different more adventurous life. The story of a 'twin' being asked to impersonate another was also the main conceit in *The*

Prisoner of Zenda. This terrifically successful adventure novel was set in Ruritania and a favourite of Tommy's, surely read by Daphne too, when young. Certainly their second daughter was named after the beautiful heroine Princess Flavia, who tragically falls in love with the impostor King, yet does her duty by marrying the real one when he is restored to the Ruritanian throne. The good and evil alternate self had long exerted its power in Daphne's imagination, from her father as both Hook and Mr Darling, through the story of Jekyll and Hyde to her own creations of the de Winter wives in *Rebecca*, and the eternal mystery of Cousin Rachel's character, both devil and saint.

Daphne wrote *The Scapegoat* with great intensity. She had hopes that it might break her out of the mould of popular romantic novelist in which she felt she had been lazily confined by reviewers who patronised her and missed the point of her complex layered plots. In fact, her reviews were good and film companies vied to buy the rights. Although Cary Grant was mooted for the lead role, Daphne insisted that Alec Guinness should play the double part as he reminded her of her father. Three dull scripts were turned down before it was given to a brilliant young writer, Gore Vidal, who had become contract screenwriter for Metro Goldwyn Mayer.

Vidal was unknown at the time to Daphne, who described him to Ellen as a 'screaming pansy',[38] a categorisation he may well have resisted, writing in his memoir years later that 'there is no such thing as a homosexual or a heterosexual person. There are only homo- or heterosexual acts. Most people are a mixture of impulses if not practices.'[39] A natural American patrician, Vidal's novel, *The City and the Pillar*, written before he was twenty-three, described the coming of age of a young man with homosexual impulses. Despite its discretion, it caused such fury in America that for a while his subsequent novels were largely ignored by the critics and he turned to writing screenplays under contract to MGM to make a living. When Daphne read his script she dashed off a letter to Michael Balcon, the film's producer, 'I was frankly *appalled*. And indeed, for a time, wondered if the whole thing was a joke or leg-pull … Then I began to get angry. The whole point of the original story was gone.'[40] Vidal's script, however, was approved by the studios and the film went ahead.

The Scapegoat was eventually screened in the summer of 1959 and was not a box office success. Unfortunately, the director Robert Hamer was an alcoholic, ill and distracted, and did not inspire confidence in his cast. Bette Davis as the hero's mother and the drug-addicted, cigar-smoking matriarch of the family, seemed well cast but she and Alec Guinness did not get on. He recalled, 'she despised all the British film crew … and she obviously considered me a nonentity – with which I wouldn't quarrel greatly.' (He had won an Oscar the previous year for *Bridge on the River Kwai*.) 'But she was not the artist I expected. She entirely missed the character of the old countess … she knew her lines – and spat them forth in her usual familiar way … A strong and aggressive personality.'[41] After the film flopped, Bette Davis accused Alec Guinness of being responsible for cutting most of her part out of jealousy.

Suddenly in June 1957, completely without warning as far as Daphne was concerned, Tommy collapsed and was taken to a clinic near Harley Street. Daphne was summoned to London and was horrified to see him so thin, emotionally bereft and diminished. She had known about his excessive drinking and occasional trouble with his liver but had never really appreciated the extraordinary stresses of his life that led to this full-blown nervous breakdown. The emotional toll of two traumatic world wars had been an underlying strain throughout his adult life. The implacably high standards demanded of himself and others, the perfectionist drive to perform, all made each day an ordeal to get through.

However, unsupported by Daphne, and incapable of talking deeply to her of anything that really mattered, his heart was also in turmoil. Unbeknownst to his wife, he had been conducting two love affairs in London, one with someone whom he had met at the ballet and code-named 'Convent Garden'. This woman telephoned an already distraught Daphne to tell her she was Tommy's mistress and that his breakdown was a result of unbearable strain over his double life. Daphne's world was suddenly shattered. Her self-contained existence, pleasing herself in Menabilly, pursuing her life of the imagination, was now under threat. When Tessa suggested divorce she was surprised at her mother's emotional reaction: 'She was furious, "But I absolutely adore him," she cried, to which I replied, "You could have fooled me."' Tessa thought it the age-old response of possessiveness and jealousy when a stranger moves in on your territory.[42] Daphne was a fighter and would not relinquish her husband to another and so rose to the situation with customary courage. Once Tommy was able to leave hospital he was to come home to Cornwall. She determined to put aside her longing for solitude, nurse him back to health and rebuild their marriage.

The noblest of intentions, however, cannot hide for ever the resentments and humiliations that remain under the surface of a proud woman who has been betrayed. All her life Daphne had been the one in control: in her marriage to Tommy it had been he who needed her more, loved her more than she did him. Now this certainty was gone from her mind and, unhitched from all she had taken for granted, she started to swing wildly, grasping at theories and fantasies to explain what was happening to her world. She wrote a passionately felt letter to Tommy's much-trusted aide, Maureen Luschwitz, full of fear, anger and grief and a deep desire to understand. On Maureen's suggestion, Daphne wrote to Tommy taking her share of responsibility for the failings in their marriage. She confessed to her relationship with Christopher Puxley during the war and tried to explain how 'my obsessions – you can only call them that – for poor old Ellen D and Gertrude – were all part of a nervous breakdown going on inside myself, partly to do with my muddles troubles, and writing, and fear of facing reality'.[43]

Most of her references in her attempt to explain to Maureen the shift in power and the unravelling of her fast-held beliefs were to her own novels and short stories. In this letter to Tommy she showed her tenuous grasp on a core identity as she became in turn one character and then another. She used *Rebecca* as an extended analogy of her relationship with him and his with the other women in his life, ending with her irrational fear that she could even be at risk of being shot by Tommy, 'in a blind rage' of jealousy, because her love of writing superseded her love for him. Her short stories, 'Kiss Me Again,

Stranger', 'Monte Verita' and 'The Apple Tree' were all enlisted in her search to explain, and 'The Birds', she insisted, was the threat to those who did not recognise the evil in themselves. In her desperation to understand, she flailed from one scenario to the next. Daphne identified also with her ancestress in *Mary Anne*, thinking it might have been the story of her life if she had married Christopher Puxley. She then outlined the significance of her various psychological states with reference to *My Cousin Rachel* and *The Parasites*. Even Tommy, in the midst of his distress, was affected by the powerful evocations of Daphne's imagination and told her he feared he had become 'the bad man'[44] in *The Scapegoat*.

The confluence of fiction with reality was confusing and frightening. For a while Daphne became paranoid, barely managing to hang on to her own sanity under the strain of having to cope with this new unwelcome truth. The shock of being no longer in control of her world, 'had so shaken me from my dream-world that I began to think I was going potty, it seemed to me everyone was an enemy …'[45] A few years earlier she had been reading Adler, and was struck by how closely this related to her: 'it seems we all underline [sic] want power over our fellow-creatures, and our life-plan we settled at the age of five … mine was to be left alone, and not go down to the drawing-room. So it still holds good! But its lonely, being alone.'[46]

12

Heading for Home

Death has already orphaned us, but kept us sisters close. There is
a special 'closeness' I believe between those of the same generation,
and although one grieves bitterly when beloved parents pass on
there is an inevitability about it which we accept. Strange – maybe
wrong – as it may sound, the death of one of my sisters would be
to me much harder to bear.

ANGELA DU MAURIER, *Old Maids Remember*

THE LAST YEARS of Muriel's life were made miserable for her and
those who loved her by a form of vascular sclerosis and depressive
senility where she progressively lost interest in life. She was in her late
fifties when Gerald died and she became a widow, still pretty, still able
to exert her charm on visitors and tradesmen in town, but always
cool, detached and judgemental. She had been struck throughout her
widowhood by periods of depression, but as she grew older various
ailments meant she increasingly lost the ability to move unaided and
to take care of herself.

In her rush of confessional letters to Ellen Doubleday, Daphne
mentioned her mother more often than her father, and when she did
it was the pain of her hostility and lack of maternal love on which she
dwelt. The references to her father were few and mostly concerned
with how her son and then grandsons reminded her of him.
Occasionally she mentioned how much she missed him. She also

wrote of his style, his sense of make-believe and deliberate attempts to charm people, that she found herself imitating. Gerald did not seem to haunt her thoughts as did Muriel's antipathy and the effect it had had on her girlhood. Tod, who loved Daphne and knew her better than most, always thought that she was frightened of her mother. It may be that the main reason for Daphne's lifetime escape into fantasy, for her fundamental shyness and sense of aloneness in the world, lay more at the door of her mother and the vacuum where her love should have been, than her father's possessive and intrusive control. Certainly a large measure of the attraction she felt towards Fernande Yvon and Ellen was because they were women who seemed to embody the unconditional love and consistency of a good mother. In the letter she wrote to Maureen, as she clung to sanity in the middle of her husband's breakdown, she mentioned the 'terrific reliance and love' that she had found in both Ferdy, when she was a lost 'kid'[1] of eighteen, and then later in Ellen Doubleday.

Favouritism was celebrated in the du Maurier family with little concern for the effects on the favoured and unfavoured child. It was part of the family romance that Gerald was his mother's favourite, her little 'ewe lamb', and this convention continued with his children, where Daphne, of course, was his favourite and Jeanne Muriel's. Jeanne was referred to by Daphne in exactly the same way, as the 'ewe lamb'[2] whom Mummy wanted close. Jeanne had paid her dues to her mother during the war and was now settled in her relationship with Noël Welch in their house on the moors and unwilling to compromise further either her life or art. Both Angela and Daphne felt Jeanne could do more as Muriel became increasingly dependent. Daphne complained: 'Jeanne is not being very good. She says her painting comes first ... and says Mummy does'nt mind if she's there or not, which is not true. Jeanne is Mummy's life.'[3] Daphne was never expected to do much nurturing, although was always generous with money when it was needed. So the care of their mother largely fell to Angela, the eldest, the unattached daughter and no one's favourite, but hoping through good works to earn some special notice – as the main companion of a once lively woman, who was now chronically depressed and losing her mind.

This responsibility was dispiriting for Angela. The long years of living with Muriel at Ferryside in increasing distress took their toll on Angela's nervous system and she too lost her equilibrium. She resented being the sister relegated to the caring role, the butt once more, and had told Gwen Ffrangcon-Davies that she was having a hard time and could not share the burden with Jeanne, who in this matter 'was completely unreliable'.[4] Angela had begged a month off in the summer of 1957 and Muriel and her nurse were installed at Menabilly. This happened just as Daphne was suddenly forced to cope with Tommy's breakdown and his own immediate need of care, an unforeseen crisis that had blasted into her enchanted world, demanding action. As Angela had gone abroad with Anne Treffry, Daphne was left not only to care for a shattered husband but also for her mother, who appeared to be dying.

Instead of being a dreaded burden, Muriel in her last months was undemanding and grateful. For the first time in her life Daphne felt her mother was pleased to be in her company and during the worst of times with Tommy's rehabilitation she found herself seeking her company and finding a kind of peace. Now that her critical mind was blurred, and perhaps her mistrustfulness of Daphne long forgotten, Muriel gazed on her prodigal daughter 'as if I was the archangel Gabriel, it nearly broke my heart'.[5] And Daphne's habit of half a century's fear and resentment melted away.

At the end of November 1957, Muriel was very close to death when Daphne went to see her, for what was to be the last time. The following day she was due to catch the Riviera Express to London to be with Tommy, who was still recuperating from his nervous breakdown and could not be left alone for more than a day or so. Long retreated from the world and on the threshold of death, her mother slowly moved her head, and Daphne, bending her face towards her, was unexpectedly kissed twice on the cheek. She then left Cornwall to do her wifely duty, absolved by what she felt was 'an amazing spiritual thing' of being kissed freely, and at last, by the mother who had caused her so much grief. 'I feel all the queer strains between us right through childhood and adolescent days were somehow wiped out with that brink-of-death kiss.'[6] Along with the relief that her mother's suffering was over, Daphne also felt a pang of regret that all connections with the 'happy laughing past of theatre and youth',[7] embodied so brilliantly by her parents, and then fleetingly by Gertie, were now gone.

Daphne's relationship with her mother may have been resolved at the last but her marriage to Tommy was making its own unwelcome demands. The desperate condition to which he was reduced was having a marked impact on Daphne's own life and she felt she was slowly being asphyxiated. Living in London during the week, in what she considered to be a rat-trap of a flat, exile from her beloved house and Cornwall, all contributed to the feeling 'it is killing me'.[8] The difficulty of writing when away from Menabilly and the loss of the solitude she craved was her main grief.

Perhaps it was significant that Daphne, who confessed everything to Ellen, did not mention a word about her husband's affair with 'Convent Garden'. Ellen had been the first to be told the most important secret in her life, her struggle with the 'boy-in-the-box', and Daphne had felt no embarrassment in relating frankly how she had gone 'potty' and paranoid during the stress of Tommy's breakdown. Yet the revelation of Tommy's unfaithfulness had rocked her sense of self and belief in the stability of her marriage, and she could not expose this to Ellen. Perhaps Daphne's pride would not allow her to confide in someone who had thought her a negligent wife and had many times urged her to be less self-centred and more supportive of Tommy's career. The more conventionally minded Ellen, to Daphne the embodiment of a good woman, would have seen the challenge to her unassailable place in Tommy's life as an inevitable result of wifely neglect.

As Tommy's recuperation dragged on, Daphne's first heroic impulse to hang on to her marriage and make her husband well again, through force of will and self-sacrificing care, started to wear a little thin. She best understood real people and events through the medium of myths and stories that had some resonance for her. To Oriel Malet she wrote that she saw 'Moper' as Kay, the small boy in Hans Christian Andersen's great fairy story *The Snow Queen*, who fell under the influence of the ice queen when he got a splinter of the troll's mirror lodged in his eye, distorting his character and understanding. It helped Daphne to theorise that the Snow Queen was Tommy's lover, and she herself was perhaps Gerda, the heroine of the story. Only Gerda could release Kay from the Queen's spell through the power of simple, enduring love. This sense of temporarily disturbed vision may well have been a main impetus to her brilliantly creepy short story 'The Blue Lenses'.

As the months wore on, with Daphne doing her duty, living in London more than Cornwall, her resentment and boredom combined with despair. Menabilly was abandoned while she whiled away her time in the unprepossessing flat, cooped up and unable to work. Instead by day, Daphne turned to paint and daubed her 'out of proportion and very crude' paintings as a relief for her feelings, although she thought they had a certain kind of power, 'like paintings done by "madmen" (Perhaps I am!)'. By night she cooked Tommy's steak and asked him about his day. Tommy had returned to work for Prince Philip but he was now more silent and subdued, she felt as a result of the electric shock treatment for his breakdown. It became obvious that his unrelieved depression and general poor health meant it was too much for him to continue with his duties and, by mid-May 1959, Tommy finally retired at the age of sixty-two. Daphne was at last free to return full time to Menabilly. But this time she would no longer be alone.

Religion was an area of life where the sisters were unalike in surprising ways. Jeanne had become her own kind of Catholic, almost, Noël suggested, as an extension of her deeply embedded good manners. Daphne, more individualist, leant towards a version of animism, though she would create her own chapel when she moved to the dower house of Kilmarth and found comfort in the belief in a kind of afterlife where loved ones were united. Most conventional of all was Angela, whose romantic childhood pleasure in accompanying her aunt to High Church services (she loved the vestments, the bells and smells – another kind of theatrical experience she admitted), against the traditions of her agnostic father, had matured into a traditional belief system that did not brook much rational debate on the matter.

Writing in the mid-1960s, when Angela was just into her sixties, her irritation with the naysayers was palpable:

> I have never for one moment doubted the existence of God … I am astonished at the conceit of people who dare voice their unbelief, for not only do they argue with savants throughout the ages but against – presumably – the great teachers of all religions throughout the world, throughout the entire Universe.

She had no time for scientists who argued that the world 'had been going on for several million years', and articulated what she felt would be the killer question: 'How do they think worlds began?'[9]

There was no doubt that Angela's religion, shared with Anne Treffry, brought her a great deal of deep consolation and some affirmation of her place in the community, but it also contributed to the internal conflict between her nature and the private life she had lived and the respectable public face she so carefully maintained. It made her afraid of exposure. She had managed for a while after Gerald's death to throw off the heavy disapproving hand of her father and explore a different way of living and loving with the carefree Hampstead set that revolved around Gwen Ffrangcon-Davies and Marda Vanne. With Olive at Torosay she had learnt a devil-may-care insouciance. Yet she had never quite broken free and when middle age beckoned and small-town life in Fowey became her stage, the thundering homophobia of her father came back to haunt her in the form of the prescriptions of an Anglo-Catholic Church, where expressions of such love were a sin.

There was a real change in tone on this subject between her first autobiography, written when she was still in her forties and tolerant, even celebratory, of women's love for each other, and the defensive stance she took in *Old Maids Remember*, penned when she was into her sixties and more deeply ensconced in the Church.

There was little doubt that her relationship with Anne Treffry was of central importance in the last stage of her life, in fact in the same memoir she wrote of 'Anne without whom one's life would be incomplete, and so very much the poorer'.[10] However, given Angela's reluctance *épater les bourgeoisie* it would have been impossible for them to live together, even though they saw each other virtually every day. Their only freedom from the goldfish bowl of local life was to escape on holiday as much as possible, and these holidays, many involving touring by car, were the high points of their later lives. It was known in the family that Angela slept with a weighty railway time-table by her bed so she could consult the times of all the trains across the world, from Asia to the Americas. Her romantic enthusiasms were always as readily expressed for places as for people.

Italy had been a favourite destination since she had first visited her old friend Micky Jacob at her house at Sirmione on the southern shores of Lake Garda. Angela was known among her sisters as being the one most like Gerald in her love of luxury, much preferring suites in grand hotels and travelling in style. One of the most spectacular of hotels was on the shore of Lago di Braie in the Dolomites in the north-east corner of Italy. She and Anne drove there in Angela's trusty Mini in late June and were temporarily lost for words as they gazed on the view from their grand hotel bedroom. The mountains appeared to fall sheer into the deepest turquoise blue, lapping almost to the hotel's terrace; they spent many a happy hour on the capacious balcony just revelling in the beauty of the setting, 'we could not tear ourselves away'.[11]

Another year, the doughty pair set off to drive to Madrid to see the paintings in the Prado. While there, they decided to book into the Ritz, after Angela had read that a stay at this grandest of hotels was one of the defining moments in life. She and Anne certainly never forgot the experience, but Angela looked back with some amazement that they had managed such a long stay there and wondered how they could afford it. Jeanne and Noël Welch shared her amazement as they wandered through the same airy portals, admired the fountains in the courtyards but decided reluctantly that they could not even afford lunch of a simple paella.

A more modest trip to Ireland in 1962, again in the company of Anne, not only inspired Angela to write another novel after a creative drought of ten years but also marked her last love affair with a coun-try. The attraction of foreign places for Angela lay not in getting to know the people and their culture but in being close to her companion and sharing their own private appreciation of landscape and place. 'I much prefer to go to a hotel, and with Anne, where we're probably considered very "sidey" and stand-offish by the other guests, but which allows us to find out for ourselves the places to avoid and the views to fall in love with,'[12] she wrote in her later memoir.

Angela's ecstatic response to the countryside in counties Kerry and Connemara spurred her to write what became one of her favourite novels – a late child she called it – *The Road to Leenane*. And in fact the real road to Leenane, as she and Anne drove across the valley with not a soul in sight on their way to the beautiful Killary Harbour, filled Angela with a sense of heightened spirituality. 'Something I have never met or known before. There was a peace about that road and the stark hills which guard it that I believe one might know at death; for me it was as if one suddenly came face to face with a vision of Himself and all He has to give.'[13]

Like all Angela's novels this one was deeply felt, and tackled the large subject of faith and duty, but in a highly romantic and already dated way (it was published in 1963). She drew on all her experience in writing about the women who loved the artist Micky Renvyle, and her own emotion and religious feeling infused the story. Set in the part of Ireland she and Anne had so memorably discovered, with a powerful background of the Catholic faith that had always exerted its fascination, Angela made her hero's childhood sweetheart become a celebrity actress, partially based on Vivien Leigh. Through the character of the sensitive bespectacled Joan, who suffers in loving Micky, a married man and therefore forbidden to her, she recalls her own agony over her married love, for whom she herself was prepared to face family hostility and public ignominy. Convenient deaths of spouses and misunderstandings abound and it ends with the saintly Joan deciding to become a nun. This was the result of her, mistakenly, concluding she could never consummate her love for Micky and remain true to her faith. Thus the human heart and its desires are sacrificed to a higher purpose, and the story ends in tearing grief, then resignation. Angela's gratitude to Ireland, and to Anne, who shared the revelation with her, is clear in her dedication: 'To Anne – who showed me Killary Harbour and the road to Leenane – in love.'

The lack of reviews depressed her and Daphne wrote to Ellen asking if there was an outside chance that Doubleday might publish Angela's novel in the States. She did not rate it highly herself – 'frankly, it's a bit old-fashioned and women's magazine in the writing, but completely readable'. Both sisters, however, shared a laugh at the fact that Angela was mistaken once for Iris Murdoch, the critics' darling with her new novel *The Unicorn*, and even occasionally confused with Victoria Holt, 'who writes Cornish romances quite unlike Cornwall'.[14]

For Angela, as she grew older and the consolations of religion increased, her growing commitment was encouraged by her friendship with her parish priest Ivan Clutterbuck. Always susceptible to crushes on men and women alike, Angela found him rather dashing. An ex-Army and then naval chaplain, he was thirteen years younger than her and gratifyingly Anglo-Catholic, and therefore sympathetic to her delight in ritual and tradition. Based at the beautifully situated church of Polruan-by-Fowey, Father Clutterbuck encouraged Angela to unite her enjoyment of travel with her active love for her faith. He had been involved with a couple of pilgrimages to the Holy Land and this had caught Angela's interest, despite her loathing for mass travel and embarrassment at being part of a group of English tourists. 'You're never quite the same person after having been to Jerusalem,'[15] Ivan Clutterbuck explained to her as he showed her his photographs from previous trips.

Despite her friends' less than encouraging remarks, Angela decided in early 1966 to join the next expedition without her usual companion and see what transpired. It was not what she usually enjoyed but she felt pushed into it by an unseen presence, she wrote, and decided she would embrace it as a jaunt, an adventure, and hopefully a book, or even two, might be the result. Suddenly shy and rather snobbish, she looked askance at the 300 fellow travellers amassed at Victoria Station on a chilly April day and quickly allied herself to Ivan who strode out of the throng. The itinerary of what was billed as a three-week 'Voyage of a Lifetime' included Venice, Damascus, Jerusalem, Rhodes, Ephesus, Athens, Istanbul and Dubrovnik, at a cost of £110 and counting, depending on the quality of the accommodation (Angela's was the best she could afford).

After three weeks that might have been three centuries, so disorientated was she by the richness of all she had experienced, Angela returned to her old life at Ferryside. She found her reflections in tranquillity even more memorable and affecting. The thought of Jerusalem elicited a particularly emotional response; for days afterwards tears would fill her eyes when she talked of or even wrote the word. Angela began to write a book describing her personal view of the journey and what she had seen and felt, her customary enthusiasm, readily accessed emotions and chatty perceptions enlivening the text from start to finish. Cheerful commentary on vomit sloshing the deck on a rough ferry crossing and 'gippy tummy' (Nazareth seemed to have a particularly lethal strain) sat happily alongside her ecstatic relation of the night-time pilgrimage from Mount Zion to Gethsemane. She felt she did return a different person as Ivan Clutterbuck had promised she would.

The previous year Angela had published her second volume of reminiscences, *Old Maids Remember*, in homage to Micky Jacob and the alphabet system of subject headings that she had used so effectively in her reminiscences. This book was as well received as her first memoir had been. The critics recognised how opinionated she was, but also her touching affection and enthusiasm. *The Scotsman* encapsulated its charm: 'this is an unpretentious book by a warm-hearted woman and it holds enjoyment in every page'. This description would have done as well for her subsequent *Pilgrims by the Way*, and after the paucity of attention for her later novels, Angela must have been delighted to be reviewed by *The Sunday Times* who found the book 'an intriguing, and in the end enchanting, mixture of deep feeling and personal chatter'.

Warmth and humour percolated into all her non-fiction and her letters were full of funny and discursive chattiness, but face to face on home territory she could seem guarded and rather stern. Ellen Doubleday was delighted to find Angela so much more fun when she visited her in America than she had ever been at Ferryside, where 'those tea and cocktail visits [with Daphne] were slightly on the formal side'. Her younger sister's fame even followed Angela to the States where the customs officer on seeing her name enquired if she was the famous author, and Angela replied to the familiar question with a sweet smile, 'Oh no, I am her sister.'[16]

Buoyed on the ripple of interest in her last two books and full still of heightened emotion and religious feeling after her pilgrimage to the Holy Land, she embarked on what would be her last book, *The Frailty of Nature*. Again, Angela tackled large but now outmoded concerns, like the bitter antipathy between Low and High Church in the Anglican fold, and the struggle of a man to be both a good priest and a loving husband to a racist wife, full of disdain for his parishioners. As with all her novels, the exaggerated drama of the theatre of her youth seeped into her highly coloured plot: an unfaithful spouse dies immediately in a car crash; the most unlikely marriages are made between young women and very elderly men; a baby is born dead after a labour akin to medieval torture; and divorce is the ultimate sin. At the centre, she places a visit to the Holy Land, and her priest-hero's attempt at murdering the man who has cuckolded him, prevented only by an apparition of Jesus Christ on the road before his speeding car. Her plots were always so much more heavy-handed than Daphne's. Angela's characters, however, had a humanity that was often lacking in Daphne's best stories, and each book she wrote was suffused with feeling, if at times slightly overwrought.

Angela accepted the end of her writing career with resignation and little grief. She had admitted that her life was characterised by enthusiasms and lack of perseverance on any one thing. Friendships, love affairs, holidays; these were the central strands around which she fitted her writing, when the impulse arrived. Writing had been something she enjoyed, she would have loved to have written a bestseller or had a novel made into a film. How gratifying it would have been to be able to say, 'Yes, one of them', to that eternal question about whether she was the famous du Maurier. But writing did not define how Angela thought of herself. She consoled herself that even the critics' favourites must one day fall from grace, 'so perhaps on thinking things over, my position as "Only the Sister", and an old maid remembering, is the best road to take'.[17]

* * *

For Daphne, her imaginative life and the worlds she created, and in which she lived for the duration of a book, were her whole life. She was entirely engrossed, elated with the power of her inventive mind, and there was nothing like the thrill of pursuing her dream to its conclusion. Real life was always something she chose to escape through fantasy. She loved Menabilly for its isolation, its mystery and many-layered atmosphere, so sympathetic to her solitary imaginings. But now she was seldom alone: Tommy, fragile, unwell, depressed, had to live there too, virtually full time, relying on her for company and attention. From being a place that inspired her creative mind, it became more of a prison where, shut away from the world, she was shackled to an unhappy soul whose desperation and need of her made her guilty and resentful.

In the middle of his breakdown, Tommy had been found in the flat in London sitting with his service revolver in his hand, threatening to blow out his brains. Daphne could no longer pretend that he was just going through some kind of male menopause, as she had hopefully suggested to Evie Williams. Facing up to the seriousness of the situation was an unwelcome recall to reality. She wrote to Ellen, 'the strain is well nigh killing both of us … he gets into such near hysteria moods which are quite alarming, and here we are together, day after day, in a sort of set routine of old people, and I cant start work of course with him like this, or get a holiday.' If she was away for even a few days, with Flavia having her baby or researching her life of Branwell Brontë, Tommy's mental state deteriorated and Daphne's independent spirit rebelled at the responsibility and the invasion of her precious space. 'Coming back to my beloved Mena was like coming back to prison.'[18]

Unlike Angela with her unshakeable, unquestioning faith, and Jeanne with her own individual adherence to Catholicism, Daphne was much more intellectually curious. She was drawn to pagan myths in which spirits reside in the wind and the woods, and the ancient gods of Olympus extend their sinewy arms from the sky. At the worst times of her life she wondered if a conventional faith might not console her more, but somehow her lack of sentiment and suspicion of any group activity meant she remained resolutely apart:

I wish I had not lost that religious rather groupy feeling I once had, but looking back, I daresay that it was just a sort of emotional thing after all, and not really true. A God-damn fantasy, like everything else. What *is* real, though, that is the question. I suppose the answer is nothing, but birth, and death. They're real enough. Everything else is what one makes up in one's mind. Moonshine.[19]

The local doctor had given Tommy some anti-depressant medication that seemed at first to work almost miraculously. Within a few months he was sailing again and almost back to his old self. He was fond of a young woman in the town and flirted with her and took her out in the boat. Daphne was disconcerted and scathing about her to his face, nicknaming her 'Sixpence', a diminution of the du Maurier word 'shilling' used for anything disappointing or worthless. But her overwhelming feeling was relief that Tommy seemed to be better and she was released a little from the almost unendurable bondage of care. She felt free to get on with writing her biography of Branwell Brontë and set to with a will in the new year of 1960, intending to write nonstop until Easter.

Daphne was growing increasingly concerned about earning enough money to keep afloat the huge edifice of Menabilly, its staff and the various old aunts and retainers like Tod, for whom she felt responsible. In the good days of enormous sales and blockbuster films she had been immensely generous, sending money to friends and family in need. It was she who was the mainstay of her father's cousin Dora, supported Aunt Billy and brought her to Cornwall, installing staff to help her, when she eventually became too old to live alone in London. All of this she did with no fanfare and little complaint. Responsibility for Tod became more and more tedious, for her old governess and Tommy just did not get on, possibly as they both vied for Daphne's elusive attention and love. Daphne knew she was the love of Tod's life and realised there was no way that she could cast her off. She had sent her instead to housekeep for Kits, now living up in London, and then accommodated her at Menabilly, until she eventually paid for a flat for her up in London. Although Tessa was in Grimsby with her family, Flavia was able to keep an eye on her there.

When Muriel died, the not inconsiderable royalties from 'du Maurier cigarettes' died with her. The agreement to lend his name to an expensive tipped cigarette was made by Gerald when he was being pursued by the taxman in the late 1930s and the monies had helped ease his family's financial problems after his death. Daphne was concerned how the loss of this income might impact on her two sisters, who were partially funded from this. No doubt she stepped in to make up any shortfall in their allowances. She certainly had given Jeanne the royalties from one of her films to make it possible for her and Noël to continue to live in their much-loved house on Dartmoor. Daphne enjoyed being in complete control not only of her own destiny but the destinies of others too, but the associated responsibilities were onerous and limited her freedom and frustrated her hunger for independence. She felt that the two years of strain living with Tommy during the worst of his depression had taken its toll and feared she might appear more mute and surly, having become used to 'a kind of closed-in shell in which one has wrapped oneself'.[20]

Daphne was aware, as she worked unflaggingly on her book on Branwell, that both Victor Gollancz and Doubleday were disappointed, champing at the bit for another great work of fiction that would make them and their author even richer. While hoping for the flame of imagination to reignite, she was consoled by her love of research and history as she worked her way into the Brontë household in the bleak heart of the Yorkshire moors. Daphne had a particular sympathy for the brilliant, tragic, misunderstood boy, the adventurous leader and initiator of the fantasy worlds and secret language so influential in the genius of his sisters.

A. L. Rowse thought her biography of Branwell Brontë her most moving and remarkable book and hailed it as an important work that fulfilled her intention completely of rehabilitating 'a figure long maligned, neglected and despised'.[21] Daphne was pleased with her respectable reviews but disappointed by the sales, not much more than 10,000 in hardback in the month since publication, a very creditable number for anyone other than Daphne, who had been used to sales in the hundreds of thousands.

In the spring of 1960, Ellen Doubleday came to London and then down to Menabilly for one of her rare visits. The impetus this time was to be present at the unveiling of a blue plaque to George du Maurier on his first family house, 91 Great Russell Street in Bloomsbury. The plaque described him as an artist and writer and noted that he had lived at this address from 1863–68. Daphne had always felt a great affinity with her grandfather. From earliest memory she had absorbed from Gerald a longing for him, a sense of his genius and her likeness to him. But independent of her father, she felt she shared with George what she described as an almost agonised interest in their ancestors. Her researches with Jeanne and Noël into the glass-blowing side of her inheritance had stayed with her, exciting her interest enough to hire a researcher in France to discover more, as she planned to write a historical recreation of their lives. She wondered if the feeling she recognised as ancestor worship was not just another expression of the natural human need for idealised mother and father figures that drove people to religion. Perhaps, she thought, her writing about her ancestors was like a tribal offering of gifts in tribute to the dead. While Tommy's health held up on his largely teetotal diet of ginger beer, Daphne slogged away at her family story, periodically giving up drink and cigarettes herself for Lent.

Although she was more critical of her daughters, particularly as their marriages showed signs of strain, Daphne continued to derive enormous pleasure from Kits's company, squeezing into his uncomfortable sports cars for holidays to Italy and an enjoyable traipse round Ireland visiting the places associated with Yeats, quoting his poetry as they went. She found her son irrepressibly cheerful and funny and told Ellen she laughed herself sick at his jokes and stories when he deigned to turn up at Menabilly. For Daphne, one of the highpoints of their trip to Ireland was tracking down the atmospheric ruin of the Puxley mansion* on the Beara peninsula in western Cork.

---

* During the Irish boom years, restoration of this massive historic ruin was undertaken with the idea of creating Ireland's first six-star hotel, but by 2010 the money had run out on the €50,000,000 project and the mansion was shut up with ninety per cent of the restoration complete.

The IRA had burnt it to the ground in 1921 and this epic tragedy for the family had sparked Daphne's imaginative recreation of their story in *Hungry Hill*.

The only concern on her horizon was the news that the Queen and Prince Philip would be in Cornwall in the summer of 1962 visiting the Duchy farms and would like to drop in to Menabilly for tea. It was a gesture that honoured Tommy for his devoted service over the years and he was gratified but anxious at how Menabilly would conform to his high standards of organisation and eye for detail. The whole idea put Daphne into a panic. Tessa and Angela, both elder sisters and more Establishment-minded than she, suggested Daphne redecorate the shabby old place. Tommy said she would have to wear a hat. Daphne refused on all counts but felt her china, her catering, her pets and the lavatory facilities were lamentably not up to royal standards, and did not know where to begin.

A ferocious regime of cleaning and scrubbing was initiated by Esther Rowe, the pretty and vivacious young woman who had recently joined the staff at Menabilly as housekeeper and cheering presence. In London, Flavia was deputed to buy tablecloths and cakes from Fortnum and Mason and sent her own plates and teaspoons – as Menabilly, Daphne told Ellen, only had four. The silver cutlery was borrowed from the wild Carlyon sisters at the Tregrehan estate, famous for hybridising camellias, and Daphne was amused to see how important it looked with the Carlyon family crest proud upon each piece. Daphne herself filled twenty-seven vases of flowers and collapsed exhausted with the effort. Angela was drafted in for her social skills and the steward from the Royal Fowey Yacht Club was asked to pour the tea.

At ten minutes past four, to the precise minute, the great royal Rolls-Royce Phantom crunched up the drive, flying the Royal Standard. Despite her resistance to all the protocol and anxiety about the arrangements, Daphne felt a moment of pride as the Queen, radiant in white, with Prince Philip beside her, stepped from the enormous black limousine to enter the portals of Menabilly, the house she had raised from its decaying sleep. Still resentful of the Rashleighs' claim on the house of her imagination, she was pleased that it was

Tommy and she who brought royalty to Menabilly, she told Ellen Doubleday, and that the Rashleighs would never be able to boast such a coup. Within an hour the visit was over, the royal detectives emerged from Esther's cottage, where she had been entertaining them to tea, and as the royal party was waved off, everyone went inside to relax enough finally to have tea themselves. Hardly anything had been eaten. Daphne and Angela surveyed the serried ranks of sandwiches and cakes and the local party went home with their own private stash of food, Angela particularly pleased as she had Father Clutterbuck coming to tea the following day.

Daphne had finished her novel about her forebears and called it *The Glassblowers*. She had enjoyed living for a while in her ancestors' shoes and had been engrossed in the writing, but she feared others would find it rather dull and had little hope of glowing reviews, or the kind of stratospheric sales that had once been hers. *The Times Literary Supplement* had devoted a centre page to an analysis of her writing career and, as expected, it was equivocal, with praise for two novels, *Rebecca* and *The Scapegoat* for being significantly literary. She was lambasted, however, for the lack of authentic voice and detail in her historical novels.

Daphne had been pleased to be taken seriously in such an intellectual paper and was less concerned by the negative criticisms than was Victor Gollancz. Always touchingly modest about her extraordinary achievements, she did not even seem to realise the rare honour in 1969 of being made a DBE, Dame Commander of the Order of the British Empire, the equivalent to being knighted. Despite caring so little generally for what people thought, she did hanker after some recognition and respect from her profession. She wrote always encouragingly to her young friend, the writer Oriel Malet, who was blessed with excellent reviews for her novels, expressing her disappointment at her own treatment: 'You don't know how hurtful it is to have rotten, sneering reviews, time and time again throughout my life.'[22] She felt that all the money she made, useful as it was, never made up for the disrespect, as she saw it, shown to most of her work.

It was in Daphne's nature to be an outsider. Preferring solitude, she chose to live in a mansion hidden within deep woods on a small promontory in one of the remoter parts of the British Isles; her life was austere and focused on work. She refused to talk at any kind of literary or promotional event and held herself apart from her fellow writers and the metropolitan literary circuit. This self-imposed isolation, however, also meant that her work perhaps was more overlooked than would have been the case if she had been a literary insider, making friends and influencing people on the publishing and party circuit. She believed that her phenomenal popular success aroused a certain intellectual snobbishness towards her novels, and this also might have had some truth. There was no doubt, however, that Daphne felt generally cold-shouldered by the literary establishment.

With her new lease signed for Menabilly, and with Tommy happier than he had been for a long time, busy with plans for his expensive new boat, financed as ever by his wife's hard-pressed typewriter, Sir Frederick and Lady Browning settled into a reasonably harmonious routine together. It was surprising how much Daphne had retreated from her old carefree life of independence and adventure. She dreaded the new boat as Tommy would expect her to join him and motor far and wide. Where was the girl who loved nothing more than sailing her own boat at Fowey, who had fallen in love with a seafaring soldier and stage-managed their honeymoon to revolve around boats and boating? Now, still only in her fifties, she had lost her youthful passion for seafaring and the sea, declaring to Ellen, 'boating means damn all to me, tho' I dare not say so'.[23] Aware that the regatta was the highpoint of the town's and Tommy's year (he was commodore of the Fowey Yacht Club), Daphne wrote to her old friend Foy Quiller-Couch: 'Regatta next week. I am hoping for rain.'[24] No doubt this was in part just a joke but it carried also the truth that she had run out of energy for fun and adventure and could no longer be bothered.

Her daily routine – 'routes' – had always been important to her, perhaps to maintain some sort of control over a life that was marked by flights of fantasy and a tenuous hold on reality. But as she grew into her fifties and sixties these 'routes' became more limited and limiting, 'even travelling has lost its allure' she wrote to Ellen when she was only fifty-five and still slim, strong and fit:

> I cant see myself wanting to climb mountains or go up goat tracks in Greece any more. What is it? Age of course. There is no doubt about it, as one gets older one does get very *set*. And almost the most pleasant moment, in winter any rate, is to get into bed about 10.30, feel the electric blanket is truly on (yes, I have one now!) and read for about an hour before switching off the light.[25]

This shuttering of her external life was very marked, and seemed to follow a du Maurier pattern of withdrawal.

Daphne was very much fitter than Angela, who had had a hysterectomy and her gall bladder removed, and Jeanne, who had faced an operation to remove a cyst from her breast. She prided herself on her robust mental and physical constitution and admired her old walking companion Lady Clara Vyvyan and the protest novelist Phyllis Bottome, still living an adventurous life in her seventies and described by A. L. Rowse, who introduced them, as 'a good old war-horse, rather masculine, half-American, ready to tackle anybody'.[26] Both women were more than twenty years older than Daphne and neither recognised the concept of retreat, Clara Vyvyan still extending her invitations to Daphne to join her on another of her goat-track walks. For Daphne, it was as if the myths of the du Mauriers were stronger than her own life force. Everyone in the family was made aware of the fact du Mauriers did not live to a good old age; in keeping with the insidious ethos of Peter Pan, they were at their best when young and declined, or even died, before the less romantic reality of late middle age beckoned.

Unfortunately the equilibrium of Daphne and Tommy's life at Menabilly would be short-lived. When Tommy's health improved, his spirits recovered and he remained teetotal, and Daphne felt she could escape with Tessa for a short fortnight's holiday in Italy. They had already travelled in 1955 to Saint Paul-de-Vence, the medieval town of the south-eastern French Riviera. In these breaks she was delighted to get to know her elder daughter better and was impressed by how kind and competent she was, effortlessly managing all the driving and organising on the trip. But Daphne was disappointed how tired she felt, finding Rome and cities in general too noisy to enjoy. She was determined, however, to get to Urbino and hoped it would inspire her as the setting for a new novel. They returned in time for Daphne to attend Victor Gollancz's seventieth birthday party at the Savoy, where she was placed on his left as one of his most honoured authors. On Daphne's left sat Lord Longford, someone she knew vaguely and liked. However, these carefree days came to a juddering halt when she returned to Menabilly. Tommy had been on a drinking binge that had started five days before her return. The faithful old gardener Mr Burt and his wife, who had been left in charge of Tommy and the household, were scared witless as to what best to do as he alternated between rampage and despair, sitting once more with his loaded revolver to his head, deaf to reason.

Daphne suddenly felt overwhelmed with responsibility for her husband's welfare and the old depression returned with the thought that she could never leave him unless someone as competent as Tessa would agree to stay while she stole a few days off. How she longed for three months away from it all, she told Ellen. But Tessa was the mother of two children and busy with her own problems as her marriage to Peter de Zulueta unravelled. Daphne felt she could at least relax over Flavia, who seemed settled with Alastair Tower and was happily pursuing her painting, and Kits too, who was pursuing an Irish beauty queen he had met while working with his mother's old beau, Carol Reed, on his latest film *The Running Man*.

At Menabilly, however, things were on a downward trajectory. Tommy's state of mind improved dramatically as soon as he was weaned from alcohol once more, but he slipped again in December 1963 when he was due at a local Civil Defence meeting where, as County Group Controller, he was the man in charge. He knocked back a couple of whiskies, climbed into his Alfa Romeo, and on the way caused an accident that meant two people ended up in hospital. He was found to have been driving under the influence of drink or drugs and fined by the magistrates' court and banned for a year.

To a man of Tommy's sensibility, whose life had been circumscribed by rigorous even repressive discipline of himself and others, this public lapse of his own highest standards was humiliating in the extreme. The accident victims recovered but Tommy's mortification haunted him. It was perhaps clearly indicative of his emotional fragility, combined with a character honed by a lifetime's service, self-sacrifice and concern with the appearance of things. Not only had he always to do the right thing, but also to be seen to do the right thing. Shamed by his failure to live up to these ideals, he resigned from all his appointments and clubs. At first Daphne was sympathetic, but quite soon his misery and remorse began to irritate her. To Foy she complained that he was histrionically overreacting, behaving as if he had sinned in as flamboyant a manner as John Profumo, the scandal that had gripped the public imagination that year involving a minister of state, call-girls, frolics in a billionaire's country palace and a Russian spy. Daphne felt a drink-driving offence, reprehensible as it was, did not quite equate with this kind of public betrayal and disgrace.

In the middle of this upset, the legendary warmth of the Irish came to their aid. Kits and his Irish beauty Olive were married in Dublin in early 1964. Daphne and Tommy crossed the Irish Sea, expecting the worst, but found themselves completely swept up in the sheer enjoyment and generosity shown by all. Daphne was usually shy and retiring in social situations, but she declared she had never before had so much fun, thrilled by young Father Cleary breaking into song, while everyone joined with a spontaneous eruption of affection and exuberance of spirit. One of the best laughs was against herself when she realised that the bride's family, working class and materially so much less well off than hers, considered that their beautiful daughter Olive, celebrated as a former Miss Ireland, could have done so much better for herself than marry the gilded du Maurier heir! Even Tommy, who was not well and had been dreading the whole affair, was utterly seduced by the beauty of the bride and the infectious joy of the occasion. 'The only thing that was missing was Paddy McGinty's goat,'[27] he said to Daphne as they were driven back in the highest spirits to their hotel.

There was something ineffably sad about Tommy, Oriel Malet felt when she next visited Menabilly. Daphne was writing the book based in Urbino that she was to call *The Flight of the Falcon*, but she struggled to find the atmosphere of the place and felt constrained that she could not hide herself away in her writing hut and truly immerse herself in the plot as she liked to do, knowing Tommy was at home at a loose end. His new boat was due to be launched in the early summer and there was great excitement in the town. Anne Treffry was asked to break the bottle of champagne on its prow and Tommy could barely sleep with anxiety and anticipation.

The following month, Daphne escaped Menabilly to manage a short return to Urbino to check on places she had written about in her book. She was escorted there by Kits and Olive, prior to Kits's departure to Jamaica as the second assistant director on the film *A High Wind in Jamaica*. It was a tribute to Daphne, and to Olive and Kits too, that she could cede her premier position as the main woman in her precious son's life and be so accepting of Olive. With the du Maurier emphasis on the importance of good looks, it helped considerably that Olive was such a beauty, as well as being down-to-earth and unaffectedly friendly. Daphne's occasional trips abroad with her son and daughter-in-law were always an enjoyable interlude in her increasingly limited existence.

Tessa also managed to entice her away from Menabilly on two Swan Hellenic cruises, in 1966 and the following year, that lifted Daphne's spirits for a while. They met Sir John Wolfenden and his wife Eileen and Daphne was entertained by this academic's wide-ranging conversation and warmth of character. Sir John was obviously charmed by Daphne and both Wolfendens took Tessa under their wing. She was almost a contemporary of their brilliant only son Jeremy who had died suddenly the previous year, aged only thirty-one. Sir John was famous for being the chair of the committee that produced the groundbreaking Wolfenden Report, recommending the decriminalisation of homosexual acts between consulting adults in private, nearly a decade before. Tessa believed that Lord Wolfenden was influential in recommending her mother for the DBE.

The Flight of the Falcon was published in 1964, full of coincidences and melodrama and distinctive for the powerful nightmarish quality of its story. It would have made an exciting, atmospheric film, but this was the mid-sixties and the fashion had moved on to something more contemporary and edgy. Two Italian brothers, separated by the Second World War and both thinking the other dead, are reunited after the younger gives some money to a beggar woman, who turns out to be their old nurse, and is subsequently murdered. The colourful and complex plot deals with sibling love, power and rivalry and the thin veil that separates the present from the past. Daphne explored some of the ideas that so fascinated her about her feelings of close psychic connection with her grandfather George, and she made Aldo, the elder brother in her story, a kind of Svengali figure: 'I am a puppeteer. I pull the strings, the puppets dance. It requires great skill.'[28] This brother has much of the imaginative and charismatic power over his younger brother that Daphne had over her sisters when young, and she was intrigued by the way that the controlling figure himself became seduced into the fantasy world he conjured up. 'There has to be an explanation of why the person directing the acting … begins to make it all become real to himself, and to the students etc,'[29] she wrote to fellow writer Oriel Malet. In fiction, she had made Aldo's suggestive power as an adult extend to the university students in his care, with sinister results as they re-enacted aspects of the town's revolutionary history more than five hundred years before.

Writing the book made her think again of the influence she had had over the games of the sisters' youths. Even as Angela approached her sixtieth birthday, Daphne remembered how her sisters were roped in to enact the historical dramas that held such fascination for her then: 'I always got them to play *my* games, in which I was the leader, so I suppose it gave me Power!' Her past and the past of her ancestors were ever-present in her mind. Daphne felt that writing a book was just the same as those childhood games; pretence and dressing-up and being the grand puppet master of all your characters. Creating characters and plot in her own fiction was a way of reliving the excitement of make-believe that had coloured her girlhood and much of her life.

Daphne could no longer keep the grim reality of life from her door. Tommy's left leg was causing him excruciating pain. He had damaged it in a bobsleigh accident when a young man but now his circulation seemed to be seriously impaired and the subsequent nerve pain was almost unendurable. He was confined to bed and cared for by Esther Rowe and Daphne, who despaired of the situation. An operation to try and restore his circulation failed, and amputation of his foot to prevent gangrene was seen as the only possible solution. This was done in January 1965.

For Tommy it seemed as if his life was over. He was deathly tired. Apart from his current health concerns he had already endured more high-level stress than ten average men. Facing life with a disability, his key pleasures of boating and driving were made more difficult, now that his new companions threatened to become the wheelchair and prosthetic limb. This all demanded hard adjustments for an active, proud and dapper man. His depression returned and with it his bronchitis.

Careworn, Daphne had collapsed into bed too with jaundice that kept her from seeing her husband, but two nurses were engaged to care for him. Tommy's last letter was to his dear sister Grace, 'one sometimes wonders whether it is all worth it at my age and it really would be more dignified to fade gradually out'.[30] The evening before he died he told Daphne that he dreaded the night and could not sleep, and she had kissed him and said, 'You will, darling, you will', and left the room. She later wrote that she deeply regretted her lack of foresight and the glibness of these last words, for Tommy was found dead in his bed at Menabilly the following morning, a blood clot having stopped his heart. He was only sixty-eight.

Although she had long been concerned about her husband's health, Daphne was quite unprepared for the shock of his death. To have him suddenly no longer part of her precious 'routes' in the house was deeply disturbing. Despite everything, she had loved him and now missed him so much. Guilt for her neglect of him during the previous years assailed her. She identified with Emily Brontë, whom she believed blamed herself and her sisters for Branwell's death. 'They had neglected him. Therefore, she argued, she must be neglected likewise.

It was an unconscious form of suicide, not uncommon to the bereaved.'[31] Her children arrived at Menabilly and touched her with their tenderness and maturity. But she did not want to leave the house.

She decided on a private cremation and stated there would be no memorial service, not because the highly decorated Lieutenant General Sir Frederick Browning did not want one (he was not averse to ceremony having once said he would have liked a Viking funeral), but because she could not face one. It would have been an impressive and moving service, for her husband was much loved and highly regarded by many people from the Queen and Prince Philip outwards. The men who had served under his command and alongside him in the direst circumstances would have welcomed a chance to salute him one more time. His record in two world wars was remarkable and his honours told only a part of the story: mentioned twice in despatches, he was a Knight Grand Cross of the Royal Victorian Order; Knight Commander of the Order of the British Empire; Companion of the Order of the Bath; he was awarded a Distinguished Service Order; France awarded him the Croix de Guerre; Poland the Polonia Restituta second class and the United States had honoured him by making him a Commander of the Legion of Merit. The heartfelt letters of condolence poured into Menabilly and Daphne carefully answered every one.

Daphne's tears distressed her. She was a woman who prided herself on seldom crying; she had not even cried much as a child. This had always been in stark contrast to her elder sister Angela who was always bursting into tears and was still capable of copious crying even in old age when a piece of music or a lovely view caught her offguard. Daphne was not conventionally religious, but she had a fascination with the idea of a possible afterlife from where those one had loved 'beamed down'. In these difficult months of grief and loss, this idea consoled her.

Ellen Doubleday flew over to stay and now, with all Daphne's passion spent, the two could get on like the old friends they were. The only difficulty was that Ellen did not care to watch television in the evenings, as had become an integral part of Daphne and Tommy's routine, and Daphne found herself having to talk to her, which was entertaining but tiring. She was, however, immensely helpful with her aesthetic and practical suggestions for how Daphne could make the best of Kilmarth, Menabilly's handsome dower house that was being offered to her should the heir, Philip Rashleigh, reclaim his ancestral home.

During the last months of Tommy's life, Daphne had been full of anxiety over whether the lease for Menabilly would be renewed. All three sisters were children of the theatre; their houses were the stage on which they played out their lives. Make-believe and mutability characterised their parents, and the people who flocked to their childhood home were mostly in disguise, actors pretending to be something other than they were. This uncertain sense of self was particularly marked in Daphne, the most imaginative of them all, and she had long panicked at the thought of losing Menabilly. This was the one fixed and unchanging point in her world, the inspiration to her dreams, bulwark of her solitude and keeper of her soul. After years of bitter legal wrangling and resentment, when the dreaded news came that she would have to move, with characteristic practicality and courage Daphne accepted that this would have to be. She had three years to get the dower house ready and prepare her own mind for the next major loss. She was finally transplanted, reasonably happily, in the summer of 1969. Her transition to Kilmarth, a beautiful old house with medieval roots, was eased by the fact that its fascinating history began to stir her imagination into life.

Along with her anxiety at losing Menabilly ran the fear that she was losing her most precious gift – the power to imagine herself into other characters and live their lives in other worlds. Historical research had increasingly provided the platform from which she could launch what she dreaded was a diminishing creative force. The result of her researches into Kilmarth's past was *The House on the Strand*, a remarkable, if overlooked, novel that was biographically fascinating. Once again, Daphne identified with the male narrator Dick, an inadequate man in thrall to a more powerful mentor. On a trip to Menabilly to sort out some details of the book, her editor and friend Sheila Hodges was astounded by how clearly Daphne seemed to become Dick, as she walked the grounds and showed her the places that were significant in the novel.

In the book Daphne explored the addictive pleasures of imaginatively inhabiting an earlier world where her narrator, and alter ego, could be present, although unable to participate in the vividly realised action. Daphne imagined the time-travelling propellant to be a prototype drug, an evil cousin to the mind-expanding drug LSD that, during the mid-1960s, when the book was written, dominated debate about the merits and dangers of hallucinogens. Daphne conjured skilfully the sense she had of the thrill and satisfaction of this other world, and the drabness and complexity of the real one that Dick increasingly longed to flee. She even began to suffer some of the symptoms she gave to Dick, as a result of the over-excitation of his nervous system with the 'tripping' back to the past. 'I got so hooked on the story I actually woke up with nausea and dizziness.'[32]

To be trapped in present-day reality, never to fly to alternative realms, was worse than death for Dick, and for Daphne too. Yet the risks of this dependency on the other world were very real. There was more than a passing resemblance to Robert Louis Stevenson's seminal Dr Jekyll and Mr Hyde, with the obsession, the secrecy, the dangerous addiction to the other self and its world. *The House on the Strand* closed with Dick, almost certainly paralysed and marooned in his own time, his obsessive desire to live in the world he preferred to the present having destroyed both worlds.

Daphne wrote a poem twenty years earlier expressing this dilemma in her own life:

> Last night the other world came much too near,
> And with it fear.
> I heard their voices whisper me from sleep,
> And I could not keep
> My mind upon the dream, for still they came,
> Calling my name,
> The loathly keepers of the netherland
> I understand.

...

How fierce the flame! How beautiful and bright
The inner light
Of that great world which lives within our own,
Remote, alone.

...

But if I must
Go wandering in Time and seek the source
Of my life force,
Lend me your sable wings, that as I fall
Beyond recall,
The sober stars may tumble in my wake,
For Jesus's sake.[33]

Daphne had an enquiring mind and had long been interested in Carl Jung's writings on the collective unconscious. The idea fitted so well with her sense, since childhood, of the closeness of her ancestors, the inheritance of qualities, experiences even, passed on through the generations. She wondered if perhaps time could be 'all dimensional – yesterday, today, tomorrow running concurrently in ceaseless repetition'.[34] This suspicion that the past and future were ever-present seeped into one of her most haunting and successful short stories, 'Don't Look Now'.

She had visited Venice again, this time with Jeanne, but the story had been growing at the back of her mind for some time. Then a conversation with the philosopher and novelist Colin Wilson about his 'Great Intellectual Thoughts'[35] suddenly spurred her on. Through force of will, she determined to get the story down on paper. It dealt with the alienating aspect of grief, the fearful power of the unconscious, the menace and mystery of Venice's decaying canals and dripping back alleys, the tricks that longing plays on the mind. All those years of sitting in the darkened auditorium, as her father's melodramatic productions unfurled in front of her suggestible child's mind, paid off handsomely with her terrific sensitivity to the necessity of intricate plots and bold peripeteias. A psychic tale, the visual richness and rollercoaster action of 'Don't Look Now', with its terrible denouement, was a gift to a film-maker; Nicolas Roeg was the director with a dark enough vision himself to create the unforgettable classic movie of the seventies.

Daphne's feeling for the past and increasing recoil from the present was the prevailing mood in a book she wrote called *Vanishing Cornwall*, with atmospheric photographs taken by Kits. Elegiac about the beauty of the landscape and the vivid history of its brave, independent-minded people, its very title suggested its glories were passing. This reflected her growing disenchantment with what tourism had brought to the county she had adopted so passionately as her own. All three sisters were intolerant of the 'hoi polloi' who cluttered the beaches, clogged up the roads and paraded their ugly sun-reddened bodies in Cornwall's seaside towns. But this exclusivity was an emotional reaction that they, with their allowances and Daphne's substantial income earned outside the area, could afford to have. The doughty modern-day Cornish needed emmets' money in order to live, and their summer visitors became the main source of income for the county. There was real resentment too, however, at how little attention the London-centred government seemed to give to Cornwall and its needs for investment in manufacturing and business.

This disenchantment with the despoiling of Cornwall led Daphne to join the Cornish Nationalist party Mebyon Kernow and contributed to the atmosphere of mad anarchy in her last novel, *Rule Britannia*. This book, a satire on the invasion of Cornwall by an American force, addressed all the author's own bugbears of the tourist assault on her precious adopted land. It was not a success. However, it was for Daphne emotionally a homecoming. She claimed that the eccentric elderly woman at the centre of the action, Mad, was based on the family's great friend Gladys Cooper, and indeed she dedicated the book to her. It was, however, as much a portrait of herself as an aged Peter Pan figure, surrounded by her adopted tribe of unruly boys, the six sons she had imagined into being.

In this, her last imaginative effort, Daphne returned to her childhood world of story-telling, leading the great adventure from the front, with her elder sister Angela as the sensible Wendy in their nursery productions of *Peter Pan*. Here in *Rule Britannia*, Angela was celebrated as the delightfully literal-minded, kind-hearted Emma, one of the few truly sympathetic characters Daphne ever created. Daphne wrote to Gladys Cooper's son-in-law, actor Robert Morley, and explained how she had based Emma on Angela and the book reads like a love letter to her sister. In her recoil from the erotic fumbling of men, she made Emma like Angela. She made her much more responsible for the happiness and wellbeing of the boys than Mad could ever be, in the grip of her obsession, leading the Cornish resistance movement against the might of the United States. Daphne also captured Emma's, and her elder sister's, extreme emotionality:

> 'Old people and young children,' thought Emma, 'they don't feel things as we do. One begins to feel at eight or nine … and everything goes on hurting until one's almost fifty, when it eases off, the person goes numb.'[36]

Perhaps Daphne also appreciated how Angela, living all her life in her sister's shadow, might dream, as Emma dreamed, of standing along-side her as an equal:

> As a child [Emma] had looked up to Mad in the dream, as her protec-tress, and there was a feeling of reassurance in the echoing smile, in the squeeze of the hand, as though Mad were saying, 'It's all right, they can't hurt you, I'm here now and forever.' Then through schooldays and adolescence the protectress figure had shrunk, or rather it was that Emma grew, and now they were equal in power, she and Mad, they were identical faces on either side of a coin, and the applause was for them both …[37]

The inspiration for Mad's wild boys was not just Peter Pan's Lost Boys of make-believe, but Daphne's grandchildren too. From her surprised delight when her first grandchild, Tessa's daughter Poonie, had leapt into her arms saying '*Tay, Tay*' as her version of 'Tray' (another of her grandmother's nicknames), Daphne had embraced her role as grandmother, although love did not soften her critical eye. Her grandchildren remembered summer holidays and Christmases as times of adventure and magic. Menabilly, and then Kilmarth, became the enticing spaces in which the next generation of children acted out their own escapades and stories.

Rule Britannia was Daphne's farewell to the world of imagination that had served her so well all her life. She had managed to retreat from the dull limitations of the everyday into universes spun from her own extraordinarily creative mind. She knew the dangers of this obsession and protected herself from its addictive power by writing about these conjured worlds and the people who inhabited them, and thereby freed herself from possession. Her novels gripped the imaginations of millions of readers grateful for the exhilaration of escape. This ability to inhabit a place other than her own, thrilled and at times frightened her, but for her it was essential to happiness. With the loss of this power of invention, Daphne's life and mind began to contract.

All the sisters carried their theatricality with them throughout life and all three brought down the final curtain prematurely, when they still had years to live. They were in thrall to the myths of their ancestors and everyone knew du Mauriers were youthful spirits and did not flourish in old age. They died young, and those that did not nevertheless tended to withdraw from the full enjoyment of old age, the company of friends, the love of family, the pleasures of travel and discovery. 'I'm sixty, I've had my life,'[38] Daphne wrote to Oriel Malet.

Their houses all stood apart from the bustle of the world. Angela at Ferryside lived in an extraordinary organic building clinging to the cliff like an eagle's eyrie with a dazzling cinematic view of the harbour, Fowey estuary, and out to sea. Daphne, first at Menabilly was protected in the centre of a dark and tangled wood and then, at Kilmarth, forced more into the open but still in retreat, down a drive enfolded by shielding layers of trees, cliffs and garden. Jeanne was deeply imbedded in the mysterious heart of Dartmoor, where the scale of rock and sky and moorland diminished the mortals in its reach. Into these refuges they themselves retreated, always courteous but also impenetrable and hard to truly know.

Daphne had discussed in her own mind, and possibly with her sisters too, whether as they aged and became infirm they should come and live with her. But she realised, perhaps with relief, that each sister would not want to leave the house that had become an integral part of themselves. Jeanne anyway had her partner Noël, nearly ten years younger and more robust, who would care for her until she died. So the sisters came together at Kilmarth at Christmas and on Daphne's birthday and struggled on into old age in their own domains.

Angela had always been the most extrovert of the sisters but, after Anne Treffry's stroke when Angela was just into her seventies, the happy routines of her life, seeing Anne every day, came to an abrupt end. It was a huge shock, especially as Anne's family at first would not allow Angela to visit her. They eventually relented but from that point Anne and Angela's travelling days and the close sharing of a life was over. The Church still provided her with a purpose and solace, and the good-hearted people from the village and from Fowey who cooked and cleaned and eventually cared for her provided affection and interest. But her insistence on routine became almost as rigid as Daphne's. Two carers, who became very fond of Angela, Jayne and Kevin Giles, moved into Ferryside to look after her as she became less able to get about and care for herself. They recalled how tea had to be served in her room at four o'clock precisely. If Jayne brought it up a couple of minutes early she would be sent out to wait until the prescribed hour. But along with her pedantry over routine and the inherent sadness of her solitary state, she was funny and affectionate and for entertainment would ask for her youthful diaries and read parts of them out loud. Every morning, at nine, Daphne would ring and in their later years the conversations were almost exclusively about their bowels.

Daphne also visited Angela at Ferryside once a week without fail, but would only stay the duration of two ferry crossings and as the ferry, just below Angela's window, readied itself to return to Fowey for the third time, she would leave and board, to return to Kilmarth and her solitary routine. Although she made the best of Kilmarth, and to most visitors it was a more appealing house, smaller and elegant, filled with light and wonderful views over the sea, Daphne still mourned Menabilly. But most of all she mourned the loss of her creative powers, her escape through imagination into a world of her own making. For all three sisters a deep attachment to Barrie's play *Peter Pan* and the thrill of the drama, fantasy and the dream of child rebellion against the grown-up world, ritualistically enacted on stage and in their nursery, set the template for their lives. Daphne's last novel may have brought her creative life full circle but, unlike Angela, she could not accept her loss of power with equanimity. She longed still for the chance to write another novel, for the thrill of being once more possessed by a force larger than herself.

Once more she had to make do with historical biography, immersing herself in research into Anthony and Francis Bacon. She could still cope with the intellectual challenge of onerous research and discovered information about Anthony Bacon's fearful brush with the capital charge of sodomy (with one of his pages), an event that cowed his brother Francis, who was homosexual too, and affected some of the political decisions he made in his remarkable career. A. L. Rowse, whose speciality was the Elizabethan age, commended her warmly for this insight, but her second book on Francis showed up her lack of academic rigour in what was more of a ragbag of partial research and wishful-thinking. Desperate to work, Daphne then agreed reluctantly to cobble together a memoir from her early diaries that she chose to call *Growing Pains: the Making of a Writer*. Doubleday preferred a title with less negative connotations, and she changed it for the American market to *Myself When Young*.

Daphne immediately regretted writing the book, for reading these old diaries so engrossed her and filled her with a painful sense of how much she had lost: '[that youthful world] became more vivid than my life now ... I can see myself in the day nursery at the Regent's Park, and going for walks, far more vividly than anything in my adult life. In fact my adult life is more or less a blank. Oh, dear ...'[39] Daphne was not yet seventy when she revealed this despairing thought to Oriel Malet. The memoir was published in 1977, but from then on her writing self fell silent: the wellspring of her life had run dry. She was already suffering from the forgetfulness and anxiety that aged her so rapidly in the last ten years of her life, as she clung desperately to the straws of her 'routes'. Oriel was shocked after a visit to Kilmarth in these later years to find the brilliant, funny woman she had known and loved so diminished:

> Nothing now will make Track [Daphne] budge one iota from her 'routes', and she shuts herself off from the world behind a wall of newspapers, or turns on the radio to prevent anyone from talking to her, although I don't believe she is really reading, listening or taking anything in. She has simply given up.[40]

So the sisters' daily lives shrank back as they clung to their houses and the routines that over decades they had engraved into their day. There was a fourth element in their relationship and this was Cornwall, the duchy they had first seen as children and had loved at first sight. They had been brought up as pampered metropolitan girls in the glamorous milieu of Edwardian and then early twentieth-century theatreland, in the heyday of the actor-manager, with Gerald du Maurier at its very zenith. The family's friends who congregated on the lawns of Cannon Hall or sat around the dining table for Sunday lunch were the stars of Shaftesbury Avenue and Hollywood, from Valentino and Tallulah Bankhead to Ivor Novello, Vivien Leigh and Laurence Olivier. The sisters went dancing at the Savoy and did the Season, but never felt truly at home.

Once they had discovered Cornwall, it always beckoned, a symbol of escape and freedom, an ancient land of mysterious beauty and revelation that would offer a spiritual homecoming. With some of the most dramatic landscapes in the country and an anarchic prehistoric past still close to the surface, it was also the creative inspiration for much of their best art.

Jeanne really began to paint with colour here and found encouragement and love in the artist colonies of St Ives and Newlyn, before making her home in neighbouring Devon on its uncompromising moors. Angela wrote one of her most successful novels *Treveryan*, a gothic tale with Cornwall as its star. But it was Daphne, whose love affair with Cornwall and sensitivity to its spirit and history, who immortalised the county and its people in her finest works of fiction. Her atmospheric prose drew her readers into its powerful sense of place. She captivated them as she was captivated by its ancient menace and insinuating charm.

So these London girls one by one turned their backs on the city, Daphne leading the way while Angela, with her gregarious nature and love of music and theatre, the last to cut her ties. Jeanne's sensitivity to landscape was one of the main influences on her life and art. She cared more for places than people and her paintings rarely included a human figure, but her love for the rocky outcrops and distinctive tors of Dartmoor was to her endlessly rewarding. Angela had first fallen in love with Cornwall when the sisters were parked with a nurse in an ugly bungalow at Mullion Cove, while their parents left for the more glamorous shores of France. A lifetime later she looked back on what Cornwall meant to her as she relaxed on one of many evenings at Ferryside:

An hour or more has passed, and the lights are now glimmering in Polruan, the water has reached the grass, a small row boat has passed and a neighbour has waved; the swish of the waves behind me and the Schubert Octet are the only sounds; clouds are parting and soon the full moon will appear; maybe the light under which I'm writing will attract a bat; the three tiny gulls are slowly drifting towards me, it is time for them to go to bed. How could I live anywhere else? This is my Cornwall.[41]

Daphne had been a teenager when the family first discovered Ferryside and made it their country retreat, and she saw Cornwall as the first place she could be herself and essentially alone. She likened the young sisters' pampered existence to that of caged birds, like the ones she had set free as a child, and then again at her father's funeral. The weight of their destiny as well-brought-up girls, who had to be turned into respectable married women, weighed heavily on them:

We were all ready for adventure but the cage imprisoned us. The cage, indeed, was all we knew. Ours was the sanded floor, the seed, the water, even the rod on which to perch, the swing to make us gay. We were cherished, loved, protected. No trio of turtle-doves could wish for more … The cage was not fastened, and of the three doves I should be the first to fly.[42]

Conventional as they may have appeared, none of them lived conventional lives; at times they were not even respectable. All three sisters did fly the cage and chose to live and love in ways their parents would not have approved and, in Jeanne and Angela's cases, against the tenets of their faith. It was to their advantage that Cornwall was so far away it was out of the orbit of their father's influence and he, so restless in the country, only made infrequent and fleeting visits, leaving as withdrawal symptoms from London and the Garrick Club set in.

They had grown up in a family that felt itself distinguished and all three girls overcame the handicap of not being boys to become writers and artists on their own account. Angela wrote at least one courageous pioneering novel and a sparkling memoir of her younger days. Daphne brought to life some of the most compelling stories and fictional characters of the twentieth century, which in their turn inspired at least three unforgettable films. And Jeanne found a place amongst the best Cornish painters at the height of their powers, and continued to paint all her life. After quite different adventures, all three sisters alighted when still young in close proximity to each other in the wildest parts of the West Country. They grew old in their separate citadels but were united for ever by the bonds of family and place. Despite Daphne's marriage and her titles, for which she cared little, she, Angela and Jeanne remained until death what they had always been, children of Neverland, bold musketeers, the three sisters du Maurier.

AFTERWORD

The du Mauriers have streaks in common, even the distant branches down to the third and fourth generation who no longer bear their name. They hover between incurable optimism and profound despair ... Their hearts are large, like their purses which contain so little. And their sense of humour is apt to be warped and tinged with satire ... They die before middle age, often rather painfully, and are soon forgotten. But they leave behind them a dim fragrance of their presence, like a whisper in the air.

Letter from DAPHNE DU MAURIER *to Ellen Doubleday*

The alphabet is finished, the song is ended.

ANGELA DU MAURIER, *Old Maids Remember*

FOR THIS LAST generation of du Mauriers, death did not come stealthily nor too soon. Confounding the family romance, Angela, Daphne and Jeanne lived on into old age. However, they did withdraw prematurely from life, pulling up a metaphorical drawbridge in the process. Rheumatoid arthritis increasingly confined Angela to the top floor at Ferryside, looked after by carers from the neighbourhood, of whom she grew fond. She had been determined not to move and hoped that the last view she ever gazed upon would be the spectacular panorama from her window at Ferryside.

Daphne also was determined not to leave Kilmarth and her familiar routines. At first her children managed to tempt her away on the occasional motor trip or cruise but increasingly she grew more

371

withdrawn, forgetful, at times angry, and lost. The valiant Esther Rowe continued to care for her and, as Daphne's condition deteriorated, live-in nurses were hired to help. She had always been physically strong and fit and her decline was largely emotional and intellectual. Having lost her power to spin stories and inhabit worlds outside her own, she was now trapped in a mundane reality that no longer seemed worth living. On the day before she died, she unexpectedly telephoned Oriel Malet and asked if she was writing. When Oriel hesitated she told her urgently: 'You *must*, it's the only way!'[1]

The love of her grandchildren, children, her sisters, friends and dogs all paled in significance as Daphne struggled with this alarming loss of identity. Her last ten years seemed tragically diminished to those who loved her, finding her at times almost catatonically withdrawn and sometimes frightening. No one knew whether the drugs she had always taken rather carelessly in order to sleep were contributing to her deteriorating mental state, but any idea that she should move closer to her family she firmly resisted. Daphne's invincible will that had made her life so much to her own design was still in evidence. Just as she insisted in life on being master of her fate, so she would not relinquish control in the matter of her death. Instead she tried to will it, rather than give in at this last frontier. She attempted a drug overdose, and then alerted Esther to what she had done. She later tried to starve herself, despite Esther and the nurses' watchful care. She did not intend to wait patiently for death's call.

Daphne's last visit to Angela at Ferryside, a weekly routine that would not be allowed to lapse, however weak she had become, was memorable to those who cared for Angela. It was a cold spring day and Daphne could barely climb the stairs. When she arrived in Angela's room, and divested herself of layers of coats and scarves that were dropped to the floor, she slowly advanced to where her sister sat and painfully leant over to give her the customary kiss. Angela sat upright and, difficult as Daphne found it to reach her without falling, her elder and more robust sister did not incline towards her to meet her halfway. Angela was receiving the obeisance due to her as the eldest, 'Esau-ing' as Daphne so evocatively had called it, and Daphne concurred, even if it took her last shred of energy. She may have won all life's prizes, but at the end, in the visceral hierarchy of sisters, Angela came first, and neither of them ever forgot that.

Daphne, however, was the first of the sisters to die, at the age of eighty-one. On 19 April 1989, just before her breakfast tray arrived at her bedroom door – another of her lifelong traditions – Daphne lay back on her pillows and closed her eyes for the last time. To the end she had remained the captain of her soul.

Her sisters meanwhile lived on without her. Jeanne had the advantage of a younger partner and was cared for by Noël to the end. She too died in her own home, in the depth of the winter on 12 January 1997 when she was eighty-five. It was from there that six days later the Benedictine monks of Buckfast Abbey bore her coffin up to her favourite tor on the moors and interred her on her own land, as she had intended.

Angela outlived them all. Caring for her in Ferryside became too difficult given the house's precipitous stairs and its distance from Daphne's children, her only remaining family, and she was moved into a care home in London to be closer to Tessa. She was delighted, however, that Kits and his family would take on her beloved house and fill it with young people once more. Eventually she died on 5 February 2002, just a month before her ninety-eighth birthday. Her body was brought back to Cornwall and buried in the beautiful waterside churchyard of St Winnow that had meant so much to her in life. Jeanne and Angela had the consolations of their faith and a belief that death would reunite them at last with those they loved. Daphne was intellectually curious and naturally sceptical, and never quite so sure of anything, but she too liked the idea of the dear dead 'beaming down' and even entertained the thought that Tommy, her father and grandfather, might in some way be close to her again. But, in truth, she had always believed that life was what you dreamed into being; through imagination and force of will you could make of it what you chose. In contemplating death she wrote:

It is as though every human being born into this world burns, for a brief moment like a star, and because of it a pinpoint of light shines in the darkness, and so there is glory, so there is life. If there is nothing more than this, we have achieved our immortality.[2]

NOTES

All extracts from letters, poems and fiction and non-fiction titles by Angela du Maurier are reproduced with permission of Curtis Brown Group Ltd London on behalf of The Chichester Partnership and are the copyright of Angela du Maurier.

Poems and other papers relating to Angela du Maurier are in the du Maurier Manuscript Collections, Heritage Collections, University of Exeter, reference EUL MS 207/5.

All extracts from letters, poems and fiction and non-fiction titles by Daphne du Maurier are reproduced with permission of Curtis Brown Group Ltd London on behalf of The Chichester Partnership and are the copyright of Daphne du Maurier.

Letters to Maud Waddell ('Tod'), Lady du Maurier, copies of letters to Foy Quiller-Couch, letter to Tessa Browning, letters to Evie Williams are in the du Maurier Manuscript Collection, Heritage Collections, University of Exeter, reference EUL MS 207/2, EUL MS 307/2/1/3.

The unpublished diaries of Sir Cecil Beaton published by permission of the Masters and Fellows of St John's College, Cambridge, © The Literary Executors of the late Sir Cecil Beaton.

Abbreviations used in the Notes:

DdM – Daphne du Maurier
ED – Ellen Doubleday
CB – Unpublished diaries of Sir Cecil Beaton, Library at St John's College, Cambridge
DMM – Du Maurier Manuscript Collection, Heritage Collections, University of Exeter
GFD – Gwen Ffrangcon-Davies manuscripts, Martial Rose Library, University of Winchester

PREFACE

1 Daphne du Maurier, *The Parasites* (London, 1973), p. 21.
2 Edited Nigel Nicolson, Virginia Woolf to Vanessa Bell (London, 1982), 2 Jun 1926, *Letters Vol. III*, p. 271.
3 Angela du Maurier, *It's Only the Sister* (Truro, 2003), p. 21.
4 Ibid., p. 156.
5 Daphne du Maurier, *Growing Pains* (London, 1997), p. 95.

CHAPTER ONE: The Curtain Rises

1 Daphne du Maurier, *The Du Mauriers* (London, 2004), p. 19.
2 J. M. Barrie, *Peter Pan* (London, 1988), p. 12.
3 Daphne du Maurier, *Gerald* (London, 1970), p. 86.
4 *Only the Sister*, p. 14.
5 Ibid., p. 11.
6 Ibid., p. 13.
7 Barrie, *Peter Pan*, p. 158.
8 Angela du Maurier, *Old Maids Remember* (London, 1966), p. 23.
9 *Only the Sister*, pp. 32, 33.
10 Ibid., p. 31.
11 *Growing Pains*, pp. 24–5.
12 *Only the Sister*, p. 14.
13 *Growing Pains*, p. 22.
14 *Only the Sister*, p. 11.
15 Ibid.
16 *Growing Pains*, p. 31.
17 *Only the Sister*, p. 29.
18 *Old Maids Remember*, p. 18.
19 Ibid., p. 19.
20 Letter from DdM to ED, 13 Jan 1948. This and all subsequent letters to and from Ellen Doubleday are held in the Ellen McCarter Doubleday Papers, Manuscript Division, Department of Rare Books and Special Collections, Princeton University Library.
21 *Growing Pains*, p. 27.
22 Letter from DdM to ED, 13 Jan 1948.
23 *Old Maids Remember*, p. 9.
24 *Growing Pains*, p. 27.
25 *Only the Sister*, p. 25.
26 Daphne du Maurier, *Vanishing Cornwall* (London, 1986), p. 2.

27 *Growing Pains*, p. 34.

28 Letter from DdM to the Hon. Stephen Tennant, 26 Sep 1972, Beinecke Rare Book and Manuscript Library, Yale University.

CHAPTER TWO: Lessons in Disguise

1 *Growing Pains*, p. 64.

2 *Only the Sister*, p. 34.

3 Ibid., p. 42.

4 *Old Maids Remember*, p. 2.

5 Roger Eckersley, *The BBC and All That* (London, 1946), p. 154.

6 *The Listener*, 9 Aug 1973, p. 179.

7 *Old Maids Remember*, p. 142.

8 *The Parasites*, p. 17.

9 *Gerald*, p. 123.

10 *The Listener*, 9 Aug 1973, p. 179.

11 *Growing Pains*, p. 69.

12 *The Listener*, 9 Aug 1973, p. 180.

13 *Growing Pains*, p. 67.

14 *Gerald*, p. 120.

15 *Only the Sister*, p. 43.

16 Judith Cook, *Daphne: A Portrait of Daphne du Maurier* (London, 1991), p. 270.

17 Daphne du Maurier, *The Progress of Julius* (London, 2004), p. 247.

18 *Growing Pains*, p. 67.

19 *Only the Sister*, p. 42.

20 Ibid., p. 41.

21 *Gerald*, p. 155.

22 *Old Maids Remember*, p. 163.

23 *Only the Sister*, p. 40.

24 Letter from DdM to Tod, DMM. This and all subsequent letters from Daphne du Maurier to Maud Waddell ('Tod') are held in the du Maurier Manuscript Collection, Heritage Collections, University of Exeter, reference EUL MS 207/2.

25 *Argus*, 28 May 1926, p. 16.

26 Ibid., p. 14.

27 Email to author from Waddell family.

28 *Growing Pains*, p. 59.

29 *Only the Sister*, p. 54.

30 *Old Maids Remember*, pp. 24–5.

31 Ibid., p. 10.

32 Oriel Malet, *Letters from Menabilly* (London, 1993), p. 11.

33 *Old Maids Remember*, p. 21.

34 *Growing Pains*, p. 63.

35 Ibid., p. 119.

36 *Only the Sister*, p. 180.

37 *Old Maids Remember*, p. 113.

38 Ibid., p. 8.

39 Letter from DdM to Tod, undated, DMM.

40 Edited Denys Val Baker, *The Cornish Review*, summer 1973, p. 7.

CHAPTER THREE: The Dancing Years

1 Evelyn Waugh, *Vile Bodies* (London, 1930), p. 118.

2 *Old Maids Remember*, p. 51.

3 *Only the Sister*, p. 50.

4 Ibid., p. 51.

5 Ibid.

6 Letter from DdM to Tod, 23 Mar 1922, DMM.

7 *Only the Sister*, p. 52.

8 Letter from DdM to Tod, 23 Mar 1922, DMM.

9 *Only the Sister*, p. 54.

10 Roland Pertwee, *Master of None* (London, 1940), pp. 205–06.

11 Ibid., p. 206.

12 *Only the Sister*, p. 55.

13 Ibid.

14 Pertwee, *Master of None*, p. 206.

15 Letter from DdM to Tod, 23 Mar 1922, DMM.

16 Pertwee, *Master of None*, pp. 205–06.

17 Ibid., p. 216.

18 Letter from DdM to Tod [Apr 1922], DMM.

19 Pertwee, *Master of None*, p. 219.

20 Ibid., p. 222.

21 Letter from DdM to Tod, 11 Feb 1924, DMM.

22 *Growing Pains*, p. 65.

23 Cecil Beaton's unpublished diaries, 5 Jan 1923, CB.

24 *Old Maids Remember*, p. 157.

25 Cecil Beaton's unpublished diaries, 17 Jan 1923.

26 Undated early letter from DdM to Tod, 1920s, DMM.

27 Letter from DdM to Tod, 8 Aug 1923, DMM.

28 Ibid., 11 Feb 1924.

29 *Only the Sister*, p. 46.

30 *Old Maids Remember*, p. 43.

31 Cyril Connolly, *Enemies of Promise* (London, 1938), p. 228.

32 Letter from DdM to Tod, 4 Feb 1924, DMM.

33 Ibid., Friday 2 [Jan] 1925.

34 *Growing Pains*, p. 72.

35 James Harding, *Gerald du Maurier* (London, 1989), p. 160.

36 *Only the Sister*, p. 75.

37 Letter from DdM to Tod, Friday 2 [Jan] 1925, DMM.

38 *Only the Sister*, p. 75.

39 *Growing Pains*, p. 72.

40 *Only the Sister*, p. 79.

41 Ibid., p. 82.

42 *Only the Sister*, p. 84.

43 Ibid., p. 95.

44 Pertwee, *Master of None*, p. 230.

CHAPTER FOUR: Love and Losing

1 Letter from DdM to Tod, Friday 2 [Jan] 1925, DMM.

2 Ibid., Sunday 8 [Feb] 1925.

3 *Growing Pains*, p. 74.

4 Ibid., p. 75.

5 Letter from DdM to Tod, 22 [Feb 1925], DMM.

6 *Growing Pains*, p. 75.

7 *Only the Sister*, p. 51.

8 *Old Maids Remember*, p. 55.

9 Letter from DdM to ED, 10 Dec 1947.

10 Ibid.

11 Ibid., 9 Sep 1948.

12 *Old Maids Remember*, p. 109.

13 Angela du Maurier, *The Little Less* (New York, 1941), p. 55.

14 *Growing Pains*, p. 131.

15 *Old Maids Remember*, p. 158.

16 *Growing Pains*, p. 78.

17 Letter from DdM to ED, 10 Dec 1947.

18 *Growing Pains*, p. 108.

19 Ibid., p. 79.

20 *Only the Sister*, p. 96.

21 *Growing Pains*, p. 80.
22 Ibid., p. 84.
23 *Only the Sister*, p. 97.
24 I am grateful to Ann Willmore of Bookends of Fowey who discovered this story and suggested the possible connection with Angela's experience.
25 Naomi Jacob, *Me: A Chronicle About Other People* (Bath, 1933), p. 175.
26 Letter from DdM to Tod, 26 May 1926, DMM.
27 *Old Maids Remember*, p. 52.
28 Jacob, *Me*, p. 234.
29 Ibid., p. 175.
30 *Only the Sister*, p. 112.
31 James Agate, *Red Letter Nights* (London, 1944), p. 238.
32 Margaret Forster, *Daphne du Maurier* (London, 1993), p. 40.
33 Harding, *Gerald*, p. 138.
34 Letter from DdM to Tod, 26 May 1926, DMM.
35 Forster, *Daphne du Maurier*, p. 40.
36 *Only the Sister*, p. 121.
37 Ibid.
38 *Growing Pains*, p. 97.
39 *Julius*, p. 3.

CHAPTER FIVE: In Pursuit of Happiness

1   *Growing Pains*, p. 101.
2   *Only the Sister*, p. 85.
3   Author conversation with Betty Williams, 16 Jul 2011.
4   *Only the Sister*, p. 172.
5   *Growing Pains*, p. 108.
6   *Only the Sister*, p. 125.
7   *Growing Pains*, p. 105.
8   Ibid., p. 122.
9   Ibid., p. 106.
10 Ibid., p. 107.
11 Ibid., p. 103.
12 Ibid., p. 113.
13 Ibid., p. 114.
14 Ibid., p. 115.
15 Elizabeth Ladenson, *Dirt for Art's Sake: Books on Trial* (Ithaca, 2007), p. 114.

16 Radclyffe Hall, *The Well of Loneliness* (London, 2006), p. 284.

17 Ibid., p. 399.

18 *Only the Sister*, p. 140.

19 *Growing Pains*, p. 128.

20 *Only the Sister*, p. 141.

21 Ibid., p. 143.

22 *Growing Pains*, p. 131.

23 Camille Mauclair, *De L'Amour Physique* (Paris, 1912), p. 4.

24 Ibid., p. 78.

25 Letter from DdM to Tod, 30 Nov 1931, DMM.

26 Mauclair, *De L'Amour Physique*, p. 80.

27 Letter from DdM to Tod, 30 Nov 1931, DMM.

28 *Growing Pains*, p. 133.

29 Ibid., p. 135.

30 *Julius*, p. 271.

31 Letter from DdM to Tessa Browning, 4 Dec 1951, DMM, ref. EUL MS 207/2.

32 *Growing Pains*, pp. 135–36.

33 *Julius*, p. 237.

34 Letter from DdM to Tessa Browning, 4 Dec 1951, DMM.

35 *Only the Sister*, p. 147.

36 Ibid., p. 135.

37 *Old Maids Remember*, p. 109.

38 *Julius*, p. 271.

39 *Only the Sister*, p. 147.

40 *Old Maids Remember*, pp. 109–10.

41 Angela du Maurier, *The Perplexed Heart* (London, 1939), p. 15.

42 Ibid., p. 16.

43 Angela du Maurier, *Reveille* (London, 1950), p. 10.

44 *Gerald*, p. 225.

45 Ibid., pp. 204, 205.

46 *Growing Pains*, p. 144.

47 Ibid.

48 Malet, *Letters from Menabilly*, p. 107.

49 *Growing Pains*, p. 145.

CHAPTER SIX: Set on Adventure

1 D. J. Taylor, *Bright Young People* (London, 2007), p 225.
2 Letter from DdM to Maureen Baker-Munton, 4 Jul 1957, quoted in Forster, *Daphne du Maurier*, p. 421.
3 *Gerald*, pp. 243–44.
4 *Growing Pains*, p. 154.
5 *New Statesman*, 25 Aug 1928, quoted in Florence Tamagne, *A History of Homosexuality in Europe: Berlin, London, Paris* (New York, 2004), p. 154.
6 *The Little Less*, pp. 174–75.
7 *Only the Sister*, p. 90.
8 *Cornish Review*, summer 1973, p. 11.
9 Francis Toye, *For What We Have Received* (London, 1950), p. 216.
10 Ibid., p. 217.
11 Daphne du Maurier, *I'll Never Be Young Again* (London, 2005), p. 247.
12 Ibid., p. 250.
13 *Growing Pains*, p. 163.
14 *Only the Sister*, p. 152.
15 *The Little Less*, p. 60.
16 Ibid., p. 155.
17 *Growing Pains*, p. 166.
18 Ibid., p. 165.
19 *Old Maids Remember*, p. 182.
20 *Growing Pains*, p. 165.
21 Letter from DdM to Tod, 30 Nov 1931, DMM.
22 Ibid., 2 Jul 1931.
23 *Only the Sister*, p. 159.
24 Conversation with Tessa, Viscountess Montgomery.
25 Letter from DdM to Tod, 30 Nov 1931, DMM.
26 Letter from Mrs Ethel Keane to Margaret Forster, 16 Aug 1991, DMM, ref. EUL MS 207/2.
27 Letter from DdM to Tod, undated [but Apr/May 1932], DMM.
28 *Growing Pains*, p. 170.
29 Letter from DdM to Muriel du Maurier, 6 Jul 1932, DMM.
30 Letter from DdM to Foy Quiller Couch [Jun/Jul 1932], DMM, ref. EUL MS 207/2.
31 Letter from Tommy Browning to DdM, quoted in Forster, *Daphne du Maurier*, p. 195.
32 Letter from DdM to Foy Quiller-Couch [Jun/Jul 1932], DMM.

33 *Growing Pains*, p. 173.
34 Ibid., p. 171.
35 Daphne du Maurier, *The Rebecca Notebook and Other Memories* (London, 2007), pp. 175–76.
36 Forster, *Daphne du Maurier*, p. 81.

CHAPTER SEVEN: Stepping Out

1   Letter from DdM to Muriel du Maurier, 6 Jul 1932, DMM, ref. EUL MS 207/2.
2   Letter from Mrs Elizabeth Divine to Margaret Forster, DMM, ref. EUL MS 307.
3   *Cornish Review*, summer 1973, p. 8.
4   *Only the Sister*, p. 170.
5   Edited John Hoole, Catalogue, Museum of Modern Art, Oxford, *Bernard Meninsky, 1891–1950* (Oxford, 1981), pp. 18–22.
6   *Only the Sister*, p. 174.
7   Ibid., p. 175.
8   Letter from DdM to Tod, 2 Nov 1932, DMM.
9   *Only the Sister*, p. 166.
10 Letter from DdM to Tod, 12 Aug 1933, DMM.
11 Ibid.
12 Ibid.
13 *Only the Sister*, p. 166.
14 Ibid., p. 176.
15 *The Rebecca Notebook*, p. 122.
16 Letter from DdM to ED, 21 Jan 1948.
17 *Only the Sister*, p. 178.
18 Ibid., pp. 179–80.
19 James Agate, *Brief Chronicles: A Survey of the Plays of Shakespeare and the Elizabethans* (London, 1943), p. 179.
20 William Shakespeare, *Antony and Cleopatra* (Cambridge, 1998), p. 82.
21 *Only the Sister*, pp. 183–84.
22 *Old Maids Remember*, p. 154.
23 Caroline Ramsden, *A View from Primrose Hill* (London, 1984), p. 61.
24 Ibid., p. 68.
25 Vanne diary, 1 Aug 1935, GFD.
26 Ibid., 20 Jan 1936.
27 Virginia Woolf, *A Room of One's Own* (London, 1995), p. 35.
28 Vanne diary, 4 Apr 1935, GFD.

29 Ibid., 12 Oct 1935.

30 *Only the Sister*, pp. 184–85.

31 *Old Maids Remember*, p. 110.

32 Vanne diary, 24 Jul 1935, GFD.

33 Ibid., 31 Jul 1935.

34 *Old Maids Remember*, p. 4.

35 Vanne diary, 10 Aug 1935, GFD.

36 Letter from Angela du Maurier to Marda Vanne, 28 Dec 1944, GFD.

37 Vanne diary, 3 Jul 1935, GFD.

38 Letter from Gwen Ffrangcon-Davies to Marda Vanne, 9 Jun 1950, GFD.

39 *Only the Sister*, p. 186.

40 Forster, *Daphne du Maurier*, p. 117.

41 Letter from DdM to Tod, early 1935, DMM.

42 *Growing Pains*, p. 168.

43 Daphne du Maurier, *Jamaica Inn* (London, 2003), p. 166.

44 Letter from DdM to Tod, Jul 1937, DMM.

45 Ibid., 12 Sep 1936.

46 *Only the Sister*, p. 187.

47 Ibid.

48 Derek Patmore (ed.), *My Friends When Young: The Memoirs of Brigit Patmore* (London, 1968), p. 1.

49 Ibid.

CHAPTER EIGHT: A Transfiguring Flame

1 Letter from DdM to Tod, 7 Apr 1937, DMM.

2 *Only the Sister*, p. 196.

3 Flavia Leng, *Daphne du Maurier: A Daughter's Memoir* (Edinburgh, 1994), p. 18.

4 *Only the Sister*, p. 194.

5 Ibid., p. 191.

6 Ibid., p. 192.

7 Ibid., p. 189.

8 Valentine Ackland, *For Sylvia* (London, 1985), pp. 83–4.

9 *Cornish Review*, summer 1973, p. 8.

10 Letter from DdM to Tod, 12 Sep 1936, DMM.

11 Forster, *Daphne du Maurier*, pp. 134–35.

12 Leng, *A Daughter's Memoir*, p. 20.

13 *Old Maids Remember*, p. 89.

14 *Only the Sister*, p. 198.

15 Ibid.
16 Author conversations with Chris James, Laird of Torosay and great-grandson of Olive Guthrie, who was himself very sympathetic to his great-grandmother, pointing out how lonely she must have been in her long widowhood.
17 *Only the Sister*, pp. 248–49.
18 Ibid., p. 202.
19 Ibid.
20 Ibid., p. 205.
21 *Old Maids Remember*, p. 184.
22 See www.kirkusreviews.com/…/angela-du-maurier-2/the-perplexed-heart.
23 *Saturday Review of Literature*, Vol XX, No. 4, 20 May 1939, p. 19.
24 *The Spinning Wheel*, p. 2.
25 *Only the Sister*, p. 207.
26 Ibid.
27 Letter from DdM to ED, 4 Dec 1947.
28 Letter from DdM to Tod, 8 Oct [1940], DMM.

CHAPTER NINE: Fruits of War

1   Letter from Pam Michael (Fox) to author, 25 Nov 2010.
2   Letter from DdM to ED, 21 Nov 1954.
3   See www.kirkusreviews.com/book-revews/angela-du-maurier.
4   *Only the Sister*, p. 220.
5   Ibid., pp. 209–10.
6   Letter from DdM to ED, 21 Nov 1954.
7   Malet, *Letters from Menabilly*, p. 50.
8   Letter from DdM to ED, 10 Dec 1947.
9   Letter from DdM to Tod, 13 Jul 1940, DMM.
10 *Only the Sister*, p. 217.
11 Ibid., pp. 214–15.
12 Letter from DdM to Tod, 13 Nov 1940, DMM.
13 Leng, *A Daughter's Memoir*, p. 29.
14 Letter from DdM to Tod, 8 Jun 1941, DMM.
15 Malet, *Letters from Menabilly*, p. 134.
16 Ibid.
17 Daphne du Maurier, *Frenchman's Creek* (London, 2003), p. 106.
18 Letter from DdM to Evie Williams, 18 Nov 1948, DMM.
19 Letter from DdM to Tod, 24 Mar 1943, DMM.

20 *Milwaukee Journal*, 17 Aug 1941, p. 51.

21 *Saturday Review of Literature*, XXIV, No. 19, 30 Aug 1941, p. 15.

22 *Only the Sister*, p. 229.

23 Ibid., p. 232.

24 Ibid., p. 237.

25 Ibid., p. 223.

26 Rodney Ackland and Elspeth Grant, *The Celluloid Mistress or the Custard Pie of Dr Caligari* (London, 1954), p. 230.

27 Letter from DdM to Tod, 16 Aug [1942], DMM.

28 *Old Maids Remember*, p. 183.

29 Letter from DdM to Tod, 11 Jun 1942, DMM.

30 *Only the Sister*, p. 227.

31 Ibid., p. 235.

32 Ibid., p. 240.

33 Letter from DdM to Tod, 16 Aug [1943], DMM.

34 Ibid., 11 Jun 1942.

35 Ibid., 25 May 1943.

36 Leng, *A Daughter's Memoir*, p. 56.

37 *Milwaukee Sentinel*, 19 Sep 1948, p. 33.

38 Letter from DdM to Tod, 24 Jan [in envelope for 1943, but more likely 1944], DMM.

39 Letter from Angela du Maurier to Gertrude Lawrence, 1 Feb [1943], private collection.

40 *Only the Sister*, p. 243.

41 *Milwaukee Sentinel*, 19 Sep 1948, p. 33.

42 Letter from DdM to Frederick Kelly, 29 Mar 1967, quoted in Richard Mead, *General Boy* (Yorkshire, 2010), pp. 147–48.

CHAPTER TEN: A Mind in Flight

1 *Only the Sister*, p. 248.

2 Letter from DdM to Tod, 20 Dec 1944, DMM.

3 Letter from DdM to ED, 4 Dec 1947.

4 Letter from Tommy Browning to ED, 23 Nov 1947.

5 Letter from DdM to ED, 23 Aug 1948.

6 Ibid., 4 Dec 1947.

7 Ibid., 10 Dec 1947.

8 Malet, *Letters from Menabilly*, p. 80.

9 Letter from DdM to ED, p. 146.

10 Letter from DdM to ED, 15 Jul 1948.

11 Ibid., 4 Feb 1948.

12 Ibid., 7 Dec 1948.

13 Ibid., 6 Mar 1949.

14 Ibid., 13 Jan 1948.

15 Malet, *Letters from Menabilly*, p. 112.

16 Letter from DdM to Foy Quiller-Couch, 3 Jun 1959, DMM.

17 Letter from DdM to ED, 21 Jan 1948.

18 Ibid., 10 Dec 1947.

19 Ibid., 21 Jan 1948.

20 Letter from ED to DdM, 7 Jan 1947 [1948].

21 Letter from DdM to ED, 3 May 1949.

22 Letter from ED to DdM, 13 Apr 1948.

23 Letter from DdM to ED, 21 Nov 1954.

24 Ibid., 28 Oct 1948.

25 Ibid., 18 Nov 1948.

26 Ibid.

27 Ibid., 8 May 1951.

28 Ibid., 30 Dec 1948.

29 Ibid., 15 Jul 1948.

30 Ibid., 23 Aug [1948].

31 *The Parasites*, p. 13.

32 Ibid., p. 192.

33 Letter from DdM to ED, 23 Aug 1953.

34 Letter from DdM to Evie Williams, 22 Jan 1951, DMM, ref. EUL MS
    307/2/1/3.

35 Letter from DdM to ED, 18 Sep 1952.

36 Ibid.

37 Ibid., 9 Aug 1951.

38 Ibid., 1 Jul 1950.

39 Ibid., 9 Aug 1951.

40 Letter from Gertrude Lawrence to DdM, 13 Sep 1951, private collection.

41 Malet, *Letters from Menabilly*, p. 133.

42 Ibid., p. 111.

43 Ibid., p. 178.

44 *Old Maids Remember*, p. 4.

45 Author conversation with Betty Williams, 16 July 2011.

46 Letter from Angela du Maurier to Marda Vanne, 28 Dec [1944], GFD.

47 Ibid.

48 Letter from DdM to ED, 26 Feb 1953.

49 Letter from Angela du Maurier to Marda Vanne, 28 Dec [1944], GFD.

50 *Only the Sister*, pp. 249–50.
51 Letter from Angela du Maurier to Sir Shane Leslie, 21 Dec 1935, Sir Shane Leslie Papers at Georgetown University Library, Washington DC.
52 Ibid.
53 *Only the Sister*, p. 258.
54 Angela du Maurier, *Lawrence Vane* (London, 1946), p. 119.
55 Letter from DdM to ED, 21 Jan 1948.
56 *Only the Sister*, p. 261.
57 Letter from Jeanne du Maurier to Marda Vanne, 25 May [1949], GFD.
58 David Tovey, *Creating a Splash: St Ives Society of Artists* (Wiltshire, 2003), p. 215.
59 Alison James, *A Singular Vision: Dod Procter, 1890–1972* (Bristol, 2007), p. 78.
60 Quotation from Dame Laura Knight in Tovey, *Creating a Splash*, p. 154.

CHAPTER ELEVEN: A Kind of Reckoning

1 Letter from DdM to ED, 19 Jul 1948.
2 Ibid., 26 Feb 1953.
3 Leng, *A Daughter's Memoir*, p. 90.
4 Ibid., p. 166.
5 Letter from DdM to ED, [24] Nov 1949.
6 Ibid.
7 Ibid., 21 Dec 1949.
8 Daphne du Maurier, *The Birds and Other Stories* (London, 2004), p. 242.
9 Letter from DdM to ED [15 Feb 1952].
10 Ibid., 5 Oct 1953.
11 Letter from Jeanne du Maurier to Marda Vanne, 25 May [1949], GFD.
12 Ibid., 26 Apr [1949?].
13 Ibid.
14 Letter from DdM to ED, 21 Oct 1950.
15 Letter from Jeanne du Maurier to Marda Vanne, 25 May [1949], GFD.
16 Ibid.
17 *Old Maids Remember*, p. 184.
18 *Only the Sister*, p. 264.
19 *Reveille*, p. 161.
20 Angela du Maurier, *Shallow Waters* (London, 1952), p. 11.
21 Ibid., p. 3.
22 Ibid., p. 244.
23 Ibid., pp. 244, 247.

24 *Old Maids Remember*, pp. 185–86.

25 *Only the Sister*, p. 96.

26 Letter from Betty Williams to author, 26 Sep 2012.

27 Letter from Angela du Maurier to Marda Vanne, 18 Apr 1951, GFD.

28 Ibid.

29 Letter from DdM to ED, 8 May 1951.

30 Tovey, *Creating a Splash*, p. 154.

31 *Cornish Review*, summer 1973, p. 18.

32 *Homes & Gardens*, Oct 1961, p. 104.

33 Ibid., p. 105.

34 Letter from DdM to ED, 23 Aug 1953.

35 Malet, *Letters from Menabilly*, p. 59.

36 See www.kirkusreviews.com/book-reviews/daphne-du-maurier.

37 Letter from DdM to Evie Williams, 25 Jul 1955, DMM.

38 Letter from DdM to ED, 16 Dec 1957.

39 Gore Vidal, *Palimpsest* (London, 1995), p. 103.

40 Piers Paul Read, *Alec Guinness: The Authorised Biography* (New York, 2003), p. 308.

41 Ibid., p. 310.

42 Author conversation with Tessa, Viscountess Montgomery, 24 Aug 2012.

43 Letter from DdM to Maureen Baker-Munton, 4 Jul 1957, quoted in Forster, *Daphne du Maurier*, p. 421.

44 Letter from DdM to ED, 18 Dec 1957.

45 Ibid.

46 Ibid., 23 Jan 1953.

CHAPTER TWELVE: Heading for Home

 1 Letter from DdM to Maureen Baker-Munton, 4 Jul 1957, quoted in Forster, *Daphne du Maurier*, p. 421.

 2 Letter from DdM to Tod, 3 Jun 1945, DMM.

 3 Letter from DdM to ED, 1 Jul 1950.

 4 Letter from Gwen Ffrangcon-Davies to Marda Vanne, 9 Jun 1950, GFD.

 5 Letter from DdM to ED, 16 Dec 1957.

 6 Ibid.

 7 Letter from DdM to Evie Williams, 30 Nov 1957, DMM.

 8 Letter from DdM to ED, 16 Dec 1957.

 9 *Old Maids Remember*, p. 57.

10 Ibid., p. 54.

11 Ibid., p. 70.

12 Ibid., p. 86.
13 Ibid., p. 87.
14 Letter from DdM to ED, 24 Nov 1963.
15 Angela du Maurier, *Pilgrims by the Way* (London, 1967), p. 2.
16 Letter from ED to DdM, 18 Dec 1958.
17 *Old Maids Remember*, p. 186.
18 Letter from DdM to ED, 5 Oct 1959.
19 Ibid., 21 Dec 1949.
20 Ibid., 25 May 1960.
21 A. L. Rowse, *Friends and Contemporaries* (London, 1989), p. 278.
22 Malet, *Letters from Menabilly*, p. 164.
23 Letter from DdM to ED, 1 Mar 1963.
24 Letter from DdM to Foy Quiller-Couch, 16 Aug 1962, DMM.
25 Letter from DdM to ED, 1 Mar 1963.
26 Rowse, *Friends and Contemporaries*, p. 273.
27 Letter from DdM to Foy Quiller-Couch, 29 Jan 1964, DMM.
28 Daphne du Maurier, *The Flight of the Falcon* (London, 2005), p. 117.
29 Malet, *Letters from Menabilly*, p. 167.
30 Quoted in Mead, *General Boy*, p. 225.
31 *The Rebecca Notebook*, p. 123.
32 Forster, *Daphne du Maurier*, p. 364.
33 *The Rebecca Notebook*, pp. 178–79.
34 Daphne du Maurier, *The House on the Strand* (London, 2003), p. 42.
35 Malet, *Letters from Menabilly*, p. 243.
36 Daphne du Maurier, *Rule Britannia* (London, 2004), p. 25.
37 Ibid., p. 1.
38 Malet, *Letters from Menabilly*, p. 209.
39 Ibid., p. 284.
40 Ibid., p. 294.
41 Michael Williams (ed.), *My Cornwall* (Bodmin, 1973), pp. 35–6.
42 *Vanishing Cornwall*, pp. 5, 6.

AFTERWORD

1 Malet, *Letters from Menabilly*, p. 295.
2 *The Rebecca Notebook*, p. 127.

ILLUSTRATIONS

Other than the exceptions noted below, the photographs that appear in the plate sections have been provided by Daphne's family, for which many thanks. They are copyright of The Chichester Partnership. I am particularly pleased to be able to reproduce Kits Browning's photograph of the view from Ferryside.

Plate Section 1 (Black and White)

Page 1: Gerald du Maurier © Lebrecht Music and Arts Photo Library/Alamy.

Page 2: Gerald du Maurier at Westminster Cathedral © Topfoto.

Page 3: Jeanne, Muriel and Daphne on a stone garden seat © National Portrait Gallery, London.

Page 4: Jeanne studio portrait © National Portrait Gallery, London; Angela studio portrait © Illustrated London News Ltd/Mary Evans.

Page 7: Betty Williams, courtesy of Betty Williams.

Page 8: Carol Reed © Ronald Grant Archive.

Plate Section 2 (Colour)

Page 1: The du Mauriers © Lebrecht Music and Arts Photo Library/Alamy.

Page 3: Gerald du Maurier for *Vanity Fair* by Leslie Ward © Mary Evans Picture Library; *The Bystander* © Mary Evans Picture Library.

Page 4: Portrait of Daphne du Maurier by Jeanne du Maurier, photographed by Susanna Stables, courtesy of Ann and David Willmore.

Page 5: *The Bird Cage*, courtesy of Royal West of England Academy; *Mimosa*, photographed by Luke Mitchell, courtesy of Royal West of England Academy.

Page 6: George du Maurier and Gertrude Lawrence © Ronald Grant Archive/ ArenalPAL/TopFoto.

Page 7: Daphne with Kits, and Flavia in the background © Popperfoto/Getty Images: Daphne, Kits and Flavia picnicking © Popperfoto/Getty Images.
Page 8: The view from Ferryside © Christian Browning.

Plate Section 3 (Black and White)

Page 2: Noël Welch © Ray Bishop.
Page 6: Daphne and Tommy with their children © Getty Images.
Page 7: Daphne meeting Gertrude Lawrence at Waterloo, private collection; Maud 'Tod' Waddell sketching, courtesy of the Waddell family.

SELECT BIBLIOGRAPHY

UNPUBLISHED SOURCES

Archives

Beinecke Rare Book and Manuscript Library, Yale University, New Haven, CT: Daphne du Maurier letters to the Hon. Stephen Tennant

Du Maurier Manuscript Collection, Heritage Collections, University of Exeter, Devon: poems and other papers relating to Angela du Maurier (reference EUL MS 207/5); Daphne du Maurier letters to: Maud Waddell ('Tod'), to Lady du Maurier, copies of letters to Foy Quiller-Couch, letter to Tessa Browning, letters to Evie Williams

Ellen McCarter Doubleday Papers, Manuscripts Division, Department of Rare Books and Special Collections, Princeton University Library, Princeton, NJ: Daphne du Maurier letters to Ellen Doubleday

Gwen Ffrangcon-Davies Manuscripts Archive, Martial Rose Library, University of Winchester, Hampshire: Angela du Maurier's letters to Marda Vanne; Marda Vanne's diary and other letters

Howard Gotlieb Archival Research Centre, Boston University, MA: Naomi Jacob papers

St Ives Trust Study Centre, St Ives, Cornwall: material on the St Ives Society of Artists and on Jeanne du Maurier

Library at St John's College, Cambridge University: unpublished diaries of Sir Cecil Beaton

Seymour Hicks and Ellaline Terriss Archive, private collection, Deal, Kent: material relating to Betty Hicks

The Sir Shane Leslie Papers, Georgetown University Library, Washington DC: Angela du Maurier letters to Sir Shane Leslie

Timothy Morgan-Owen private collection: Gertrude Lawrence material

PUBLISHED SOURCES

Journals

The Cornish Review; *Kirkus Reviews* (www.kirkusreviews.com/book-reviews/
daphne-du-maurier); *The Listener* (BBC, London, 1929–91, gale.
cengage.co.uk/product-highlights/history/the-listener-historical-archive.
aspx); *Milwaukee Sentinel* (now *Milwaukee Wisconsin Journal Sentinel*,
www.jsonline.com); *New Statesman*; *Saturday Review of Literature* (now
Saturday Review, www.newyorker.com)

Books

Angela du Maurier: Fiction

The Perplexed Heart (Michael Joseph; Doubleday Doran, 1939)
The Spinning Wheel (Michael Joseph, 1940) published in the US as *Weep No
More* (Doubleday Doran, 1940)
The Little Less (Michael Joseph; Doubleday Doran, 1941)
Treveryan (Michael Joseph; Doubleday Doran, 1942)
Lawrence Vane: a Novel (Peter Davies, 1946)
Birkinshaw and other stories (Peter Davies, 1948)
Reveille (Peter Davies, 1950)
Shallow Waters (Peter Davies, 1952)
The Road to Leenane (Peter Davies; Appleton/Century, 1963)
The Frailty of Nature (Peter Davies, 1969)

Angela du Maurier: Non-Fiction

It's Only the Sister: An Autobiography (Peter Davies, 1951)
Old Maids Remember: Autobiography (Peter Davies, 1965)
Pilgrims by the Way (Peter Davies, 1967)
S is for Sin (Church Literature Association, 1979)

Daphne du Maurier: Fiction

The Loving Spirit (Heinemann, 1931)
I'll Never Be Young Again (Heinemann; Doubleday Doran, 1932)
The Progress of Julius (Heinemann; Doubleday Doran, 1933)
Jamaica Inn (Gollancz; Doubleday Doran, 1936)
Rebecca (Gollancz, 1938; stage adaptation, 1940)
Happy Christmas (Doubleday Doran, 1940) short story
Come Wind, Come Weather (Heinemann, 1940) collection of short stories

SELECT BIBLIOGRAPHY

Frenchman's Creek (Gollancz; Doubleday, 1941)

Hungry Hill (Gollancz; Doubleday, 1943)

The Years Between: A Play in Two Acts (Gollancz, 1945)

The King's General (Gollancz; Doubleday, 1946)

September Tide: A Play in Three Acts (Gollancz, 1948)

The Parasites (Gollancz; Doubleday, 1949)

My Cousin Rachel (Gollancz, 1951)

The Apple Tree: A Short Novel and Some Stories (Gollancz, 1952)

Kiss Me Again, Stranger: A Collection of Eight Stories, Long and Short
(Gollancz, 1952)

Mary Anne, A Novel (Gollancz; Doubleday, 1954)

The Scapegoat (Gollancz; Doubleday, 1957)

Early Stories (Gollancz, 1959) short story collection, written 1927–30

The Breaking Point (Gollancz, 1959) short story collection, aka *The Blue
Lenses*

Castle Dor, with Sir Arthur Quiller-Couch (J. M. Dent; Doubleday, 1961)

The Birds and Other Stories (Gollancz, 1963) republication of *The Apple Tree*

The Glass-Blowers (Gollancz, 1963)

The Flight of the Falcon (Gollancz, 1965)

The House on the Strand (Gollancz; Doubleday, 1969)

Not After Midnight, And Other Stories (Gollancz, 1971) published in the US
as *Don't Look Now* (Doubleday, 1971)

Rule Britannia (Gollancz, 1972)

The Rendezvous and Other Stories (Gollancz, 1980)

Daphne du Maurier: Non-fiction

Gerald: A Portrait (Gollancz, 1934; Doubleday Doran, 1935)

The du Mauriers (Gollancz, 1937)

The Young George du Maurier (Peter Davies, 1951)

The Infernal World of Branwell Brontë (Gollancz, 1960)

Vanishing Cornwall, with photographs by Christian Browning (Doubleday,
1967)

Golden Lads: Sir Francis Bacon, Anthony Bacon and their Friends (Gollancz,
1975)

The Winding Stair: Francis Bacon, His Rise and Fall (Doubleday, 1976)

Growing Pains – the Shaping of a Writer (Gollancz 1971) published in the US
as *Myself When Young – the Shaping of Writer* (Doubleday, 1977)

The Rebecca Notebook and Other Memories (Doubleday, 1980)

Enchanted Cornwall (M. Joseph; Viking Penguin, 1989)

Other Works Cited

Ackland, Rodney, and Elspeth Grant, *The Celluloid Mistress or the Custard Pie of Dr Caligari* (A. Wingate, 1954)

Ackland, Valentine, *For Sylvia: An Honest Account* (Chatto & Windus, 1985)

Agate, James, *Red Letter Nights* (Jonathan Cape, 1944)

Aldrich, Richard Stoddard, *Gertrude Lawrence as Mrs. A: An Intimate Biography of the Great Star* (Odhams, 1954)

Auerbach, Nina, *Daphne du Maurier: Haunted Heiress* (Penn Press, 2012)

Bailey, Paul, *Three Queer Lives* (Hamish Hamilton, 2001)

Barrie, J. M., *Peter Pan; or the boy who wouldn't grow up* (1904)

————*Peter and Wendy* (Charles Scribner & Sons; Hodder and Stoughton, 1911)

Bouvet, Vincent, and Gérard Durozoi, *Paris Between the Wars: Art, Style and Glamour in the Crazy Years* (Thames and Hudson, 2010)

Buckle, Richard, ed., *Self-Portrait with Friends: The Selected Diaries of Cecil Beaton* (Weidenfeld and Nicholson, 1979)

Clutterbuck, Ivan, *The Pelican in the Wilderness* (Gracewing, 2008)

Connolly, Cyril, *Enemies of Promise* (Routledge and Kegan Paul, 1938)

Cook, Judith, *Daphne: A Portrait of Daphne du Maurier* (Bantam Press, 1991)

Dudgeon, Piers, *Captivated: J. M. Barrie, the du Mauriers and the Dark Side of Neverland* (Chatto & Windus, 2008)

du Maurier, George, *Peter Ibbetson* (Jonathan Cape, 1891)

————*Trilby* (Harper and Brothers, 1894)

Dunn, Jane, *Virginia Woolf and Vanessa Bell: a Very Close Conspiracy* (Jonathan Cape, 1990; reissued Virago, 2000)

Eckersley, Roger, *The BBC and All That* (Sampson Low, 1946)

Forster, Margaret, *Daphne Du Maurier* (Secker and Warburg; Doubleday, 2012)

Hall, Radclyffe, *The Well of Loneliness* (J. Cape, 1928; 2006)

Harding, James, *Gerald du Maurier* (Hodder and Stoughton, 1989)

Hattersley, Roy, *The Edwardians* (Little Brown, 2004)

Hoole, John, ed., *Bernard Meninsky, 1891–1950* (Catalogue Museum of Modern Art, Oxford, 1981)

Horner, Avril, and Sue Zlosnik, *Daphne du Maurier: Writing, Identity and the Gothic Imagination* (Palgrave Macmillan, 1998)

Jacobs, Naomi, *Me: A Chronicle About Other People* (Hutchinson, 1933)

James, Alison, *A Singular Vision: Dod Procter, 1890–1972* (Sansom and Co., 2007)

Ladenson, Elizabeth, *Dirt for Art's Sake: Books on Trial* (Ithaca, 2007)

SELECT BIBLIOGRAPHY

Leng, Flavia, *A Daughter's Memoir* (Mainstream Publishing, 1999)

Malet, Oriel, ed., *Letters from Menabilly: Portrait of a Friendship* (Orion, 1994)

Mauclair, Camille, *De L'Amour Physique* (Paul Ollendorff, 1912)

Mead, Richard, *General Boy: The Life of Lieutenant General Sir Frederick Browning* (Pen and Sword, 2010)

Nichols, Beverley, *Twenty-Five* (Jonathan Cape, 1926)

Oldham, Alison, *Everyone Was Working: Writers and Artists in Post-war St Ives* (Tate Publishing, 2002)

Patmore, Derek, ed., *My Friends When Young: The Memoirs of Brigit Patmore* (Heinemann, 1968)

Pertwee, Roland, *Master of None* (Peter Davies, 1940)

Ramsden, Caroline, *A View from Primrose Hill* (Hutchinson Benham, 1984)

Read, Piers Paul, *Alec Guinness: The Authorised Biography* (Simon and Schuster, 2003)

Rose, Marshal, ed., *Forever Juliet: The Life and Letters of Gwen Frangcon-Davies, 1891–1992* (Larks Press, 2003)

Rowse, A. L., *Friends and Contemporaries* (Trafalgar Square, 1991)

Shakespeare, William, *Anthony and Cleopatra* (play)

Tamagne, Florence, *A History of Homosexuality in Europe: Berlin, London, Paris* (Algora, 2004)

Taylor, D. J., *Bright Young People* (Chatto & Windus, 2007)

Taylor, Helen, ed., *The Daphne du Maurier Companion* (Virago, 2007)

Tovey, David, *Creating a Splash: the St Ives Society of Artists, the First 25 Years, 1927–1952, Exhibition Catalogue and Dictionary of Members* (Wilson Books, 1995)

Toye, Francis, *For What We Have Received* (Alfred A. Knopf, 1950)

Vickers, Hugo, *Cecil Beaton* (Phoenix, 1985)

———ed., *The Unexpurgated Beaton Diaries* (Phoenix, 2001)

Vidal, Gore, *Palimpsest* (André Deutsch; Random House, 1995)

Waugh, Evelyn, *Vile Bodies* (Chapman and Hall, 1930)

Welch, Noël, *Ten Poems*, Crescendo Poetry Series, No. 5 (The Latin Press, 1952)

———*A Shadow to its Tree* (Moor Print, 2006)

Westland, Ella, *Reading Daphne: A Guide to the Writing of Daphne du Maurier for Readers and Book Groups* (Truran, 2007)

Williams, Michael, ed., *My Cornwall* (Bossiney Books, 1973)

ACKNOWLEDGEMENTS

In contemplating writing a biography about her American publisher Nelson Doubleday, soon after his death in 1949, Daphne du Maurier wrote to his widow:

> I like to give all truth, if I write about someone in that way … There would be so many things, in his life, like times of unhappiness, and his other marriage, and personal things, moments of elation and depression, that went to make him the man he was – this is often hard for a family to take.

In fact biographies that are neither hagiographic nor concerned mostly with an external life are often hard for a family to take. We all have our own stories of parents and forebears, burnished with the telling; and the detached and unfamiliar gaze of the biographer, working from diaries and letters and previously unknown connections can reveal a more complex story, a different kind of life. Daphne's children, Tessa Viscountess Montgomery of Alamein, Flavia Lady Leng and Christian (Kits) Browning could not have been more welcoming and generous with their time and hospitality, despite some understandable reservations about my writing about their mother and aunts. They helped enormously with their own reminiscences, pointing me towards possible leads and material and people useful in my further search for the true du Mauriers behind the charming public mask. Although surprised and not entirely happy with some aspects that emerged, to their real credit I was not put under any pressure to modify either material or interpretation in my finished work. In fact, they have continued to support the book by allowing me to quote from wonderful unpublished sources and reproduce family portraits and photos. For this generosity and large-ness of spirit, many thanks.

Kits's wife Olive (Hacker) Browning, their son Robert and Tessa's daughter Marie-Thérèse (Pooch) Johnston added more memories and insights, for which I am most grateful. Despite the disadvantages of belonging to a famous family that elicits the kind of attention that splashes everyone in their closest circle, I hope that *Daphne du Maurier and Her Sisters* in the end will encourage more people to read Daphne's and Angela's books and to seek out Jeanne's paintings, keeping evergreen the du Maurier name.

Libraries and archives were my second port of call. The du Maurier family archive is held at Heritage Collections in the Old Library at Exeter University. Here Christine Faunch, Head of Heritage Collections, and the reading room staff, Sue Inskip, Angela Mandrioli, Gemma Poulton and Mike Rickard, could not have been more help-ful: they went out of their way to accommodate all my requests. I have particularly fond memories of the pleasure of my long days there. Similarly, Don C. Skemer, Curator of Manuscripts, and AnnaLee Pauls and Charles E. Greene all in the Manuscript Division, Department of Rare Books and Special Collections at Princeton University Library were exemplary in their good humour and effi-ciency. I am also grateful to Nicholas Scheetz, Manuscript Librarian at the Special Collections Research Centre at Georgetown University Library, Washington DC for his kindness and generosity. Thanks too to Adam J. Dixon, Acquisitions Assistant, Howard Gotlieb Archival Research Centre at Boston University. The unpublished diaries of Sir Cecil Beaton are published by permission of the Masters and Fellows of St John's College, Cambridge, the Literary Executors of the late Sir Cecil Beaton. All extracts from letters, poems and fiction and non-fiction titles by Angela du Maurier and by Daphne du Maurier are reproduced by permission of Curtis Brown Group Ltd, London, on behalf of The Chichester Partnership, and are the copyright of Angela du Maurier and Daphne du Maurier respectively.

My gratitude to Kathryn McKee, Special Collection Librarian in the Library at St John's College, Cambridge, and her predecessor

ACKNOWLEDGEMENTS

Jonathan Harrison, and for the personal kindness and generosity of Hugo Vickers, executor of the literary estates of Sir Cecil Beaton and the Hon. Stephen Tennant. Owners of other private archives have been similarly generous, particularly Margaret Westwood and Ann Baldaro who shared the fascinating archive of their great aunt, Gwen Ffrangcon-Davies. I particularly want to thank Dr Helen Grime of the University of Winchester whose interest and generosity allowed me to access this archive, which is temporarily held at the Martial Rose Library at Winchester. She gave up days of her precious time to search through the uncatalogued papers and present me with the fruits of her labours. Timothy Morgan-Owen also shared with me his uniquely extensive collection of Gertrude Lawrence material. Everyone has been immensely generous in allowing me access to these treasures. Thank you.

The St Ives Trust Study Centre was a delight to visit and Diana Miller and the centre's head Janet Axten were great enthusiasts in unearthing for me nuggets of information on Jeanne du Maurier. Exhibitions and Collection Officer Louise Holt and Tristan Pollard at the Royal West of England Academy in Bristol were also helpful and super-efficient in allowing me access to Jeanne du Maurier's paintings and permission to reproduce them in the book.

So many individuals also came to my aid in various ways. Anyone who knows Fowey or loves anything du Maurier will understand my gratitude and affection for Ann and David Willmore of Bookends of Fowey. They welcomed me like an old friend and have offered endless help and interest along with the tea, cake and sympathy. Ann also helped me track down hard-to-find books and fascinating articles. I am particularly pleased to have the chance to reproduce their portrait of Daphne by Jeanne.

Professor Helen Taylor, moving spirit in the establishing of the du Maurier archive at Exeter University and the du Maurier Literary Festival at Fowey (and stalwart at Bath Literary Festival), also has been unfailingly generous, supportive and full of insight. She is a not only an excellent writer, academic and speaker but a most talented inter-viewer and chair in any discussions and tireless in her support of fellow writers and students in all their enterprises; for this heartfelt thanks.

I remember with great pleasure the 500-mile dash to Mull with my husband and two whippets in the car to see Torosay Castle and meet the fifth Laird of Torosay, Chris James and his wife Sarah. Their friendliness and honesty filled in many essential details about Angela du Maurier's wartime love affair with Chris's great-grandmother Olive Guthrie. Serendipitous meetings like these make writing biographies even more surprising and fun.

Maud ('Tod') Waddell's family are numerous and far-flung and have been enthusiastic and generous in their help, notably Susan Waddell in New Zealand, Luigi and Netanja Shaw in Canada, Eric Waddell, John Waddell and Peter Waddell.

Lucia Stuart, granddaughter of Angela's great friend from girlhood, Betty Hicks, welcomed me to her Seymour Hicks and Ellaline Terriss archive in her wonderful house in Deal. I remember with gratitude too my lunch with Father Ivan Clutterbuck at the College of St Barnabas, set in beautiful countryside in East Sussex, where he recalled his memories of Angela on their trip to the Holy Land.

Margaret Forster kindly shared her impressions of Angela and Jeanne (and Noël Welch), met while researching her great biography of Daphne when the sisters were getting elderly and frail. Irrepressible, ageless and attractive as ever, Esther Rowe, Daphne's housekeeper for thirty years, was full of tantalising memories and generous-hearted in her interest and hospitality. And Jayne and Kevin Giles, who cared for Angela at Ferryside when she was old, shared their fond memories of her distinctive and particular character.

Jo Powell was one of the first to take a serious interest in Angela and her work and I am ever grateful for our conversations and for the chance to read her thoughtful MA thesis, 'Angela: The Other du Maurier Girl'. I am also grateful to Collin Langley who, as a tireless enthusiast and researcher on Daphne du Maurier, wrote entertainingly on her poetry and humour and generously shared his findings. My thanks too to art historian and writer Alison Oldham who offered her own fascinating insights in a talk on Jeanne du Maurier and Noël Welch's poetry and has been most kind in attempting to be a go-between for me with Noël Welch, albeit unsuccessfully.

ACKNOWLEDGEMENTS

I would need a slim supplementary appendix if I thanked everyone properly, but heartfelt thanks to all for their various help and time: Jonathan Aberdeen; Barbara Atcheson; Twinkle Carter; Angus Crichton; Fiona Crichton-Berner; Stef Davies; Sam and James Fairbairn; Susan Greenhill; Georgina Hammick; Beryl Henderson; Polly Higgins; Avril Horner; Morwenna Hussey; Andrew Lycett; Dr Priscilla Martin; Annette Mercer; the late Pam Michael (née Fox); the Hon. Henry Montgomery; Wilton Morley; Peter Parker; Sarah Phillips; Rebecca Ritchie of Curtis Brown Agency; Dr Peter Shephard; Susanna Stables; Ella Westland; Sue Zlosnik.

Publishing a book takes almost as much effort as writing it. I have to thank my agent Derek Johns of AP Watt, now United Agents, who understands just how much benign neglect I need while I'm deep in the writing process. I am blessed with the best publisher in Arabella Pike, clever, canny and lion-hearted, and her in-house team of Essie Cousins and Stephen Guise, Sharmila Woollam and Joseph Zigmond, also Anne Rieley and David Atkinson. Helen Ellis's legendary enthusiasm and publicity expertise is undimmed and infectious and Kate Johnson has shown such patience and sensitivity to meaning and nuance in her editing: I can only thank them all for their cheerful efforts on behalf of the book. Sheila Murphy, dear old friend from *Vogue* days, has read everything I have ever written and always given me the benefit of her sharp and discriminating mind, but would be the first to point out that any stylistic infelicities and sloppy generalisations are entirely my own.

To my long-suffering friends and beloved family who have had to put up with me, distracted, dull, strained and unavailable for fun, all my love and thanks to you. I promise to try and pace myself better next time …

INDEX

INDEX

INDEX